⚖ NOLO   Products &

D0117130

⇨ Books & Software

Get in-depth information. Nolo publishes hundreds of great books and software programs for consumers and business owners. Order a copy—or download an ebook version instantly—at Nolo.com.

⇨ Legal Encyclopedia

Free at Nolo.com. Here are more than 1,400 free articles and answers to common questions about everyday legal issues including wills, bankruptcy, small business formation, divorce, patents, employment and much more.

⇨ Plain-English Legal Dictionary

Free at Nolo.com. Stumped by jargon? Look it up in America's most up-to-date source for definitions of legal terms.

⇨ Online Legal Documents

Create documents at your computer. Go to Nolo.com to make a will or living trust, form an LLC or corporation or obtain a trademark or provisional patent. For simpler matters, download one of our hundreds of high-quality legal forms, including bills of sale, promissory notes, nondisclosure agreements and many more.

⇨ Lawyer Directory

Find an attorney at Nolo.com. Nolo's consumer-friendly lawyer directory provides in-depth profiles of lawyers all over America. From fees and experience to legal philosophy, education and special expertise, you'll find all the information you need to pick the right lawyer. Every lawyer listed has pledged to work diligently and respectfully with clients.

⇨ Free Legal Updates

Keep up to date. Check for free updates at Nolo.com. Under "Products," find this book and click "Legal Updates." You can also sign up for our free e-newsletters at Nolo.com/newsletters.

10th edition

The Employer's Legal Handbook

Attorney Fred S. Steingold

NOLO
LAW for ALL

TENTH EDITION	MAY 2011
Editor	LISA GUERIN
Legal research	DREW WHEATON
Cover design	SUSAN PUTNEY
Proofreading	ELAINE MERRILL
Index	THÉRÈSE SHERE
Printing	DELTA PRINTING SOLUTIONS, INC.

Steingold, Fred.
The employer's legal handbook / by Fred S. Steingold. — 10th ed.
    p. cm.
Includes index.
 Summary: "The information employers need to successfully handle every aspect of the
employment relationship, from hiring to firing. The 10th edition provides updated 50-state
charts and explains the latest developments in employment law, including health care
reform."—Provided by publisher.
 ISBN-13: 978-1-4133-1390-1 (pbk.)
 ISBN-10: 1-4133-1390-6 (pbk.)
 ISBN-13: 978-1-4133-1490-8 (epub e-book)
 1. Labor laws and legislation—United States—Popular works. I. Title.
KF3455.S737 2011
344.7301—dc22
                            2010052792

Please note

We believe accurate, plain-English legal information should help you solve many
of your own legal problems. But this text is not a substitute for personalized
advice from a knowledgeable lawyer. If you want the help of a trained
professional—and we'll always point out situations in which we think that's a
good idea—consult an attorney licensed to practice in your state.

Acknowledgments

Several people generously contributed advice and information in the preparation of this book, including:

- James Bruno
- Fred Daily
- Tony Duerr
- Mark Hartley
- Joel Hearshen
- Jon Huegli
- Diane Hunter
- Nancy Keppelman
- Lonnie Loy
- Len Pytlak
- William Simmons, and
- Dave Tiedgen.

Special thanks to Barbara Kate Repa, Amy DelPo, Lisa Guerin, and Alayna Schroeder for their superb editorial guidance and to Jake Warner for his excellent additions to the manuscript.

Table of Contents

Hiring

Many state and federal laws—as well as countless court decisions—set out legal protocol for every phase of the employment relationship, including the hiring process. If you've correctly sensed that many workers today are well informed about their legal rights and are willing to fight to enforce them, you may be concerned about making costly mistakes during hiring.

Fortunately, you can steer clear of most of the legal perils of hiring employees by understanding and following these sensible guidelines:

- Avoid illegal discrimination.
- Respect each applicant's privacy rights.
- Don't promise job security—unless you mean it.
- Protect against unfair competition.
- Observe the legal rules for hiring young workers and immigrants.

The first part of this chapter discusses these key principles—some of which apply throughout the employment relationship and are discussed elsewhere in this book as well.

The rest of the chapter will explain how to keep legal risks to a minimum as you write job descriptions, advertise for workers, design job applications, interview applicants, check into their backgrounds, and offer them jobs.

RELATED TOPIC

Hiring independent contractors? Consult Chapter 12, where you'll find a detailed discussion of the legal and practical issues you'll have to consider.

Legal Guidelines for Hiring Employees

Most large companies maintain human resource departments and in-house lawyers to lead them through the intricacies of employment law—but it's a costly endeavor. And if you run a small or midsized company, this is an unaffordable luxury. In either case, the guidelines discussed here should reduce your need for outside legal help when hiring employees.

RESOURCE

Hiring your very first employee? Pick up a copy of *Hiring Your First Employee: A Step-by-Step Guide,* by Fred S. Steingold (Nolo). It can help you get started.

Avoiding Illegal Discrimination

Federal and state laws prohibit all but the smallest employers from discriminating against an employee or applicant because of race, color, gender, religious beliefs, national origin, disability, age, or genetic information. Also, many states and cities have laws prohibiting employment discrimination based on other criteria, such as marital status or sexual orientation.

These antidiscrimination laws—covered in depth in Chapters 8 and 9—apply to all stages of the employment process: preparing job descriptions, writing ads, conducting interviews, deciding whom to hire, setting salaries and job benefits, promoting employees, and disciplining and firing them.

Federal laws apply only to employers who have more than a certain number of employees, which differs for each antidiscrimination law. And many state laws apply to smaller employers who are not covered by the federal laws. To find out whether your business must comply with these laws, see Chapters 8 and 9.

A particular form of discrimination becomes illegal when Congress, a state legislature, or a city council decides that a characteristic—race, for example—bears no legitimate relationship to employment decisions. A law or ordinance is then passed prohibiting workplace discrimination based on that characteristic, making the characteristic protected. Courts get involved, too, by interpreting and applying antidiscrimination laws and ordinances. Obviously, as an employer, you need to know what types of discrimination are illegal.

At the same time, however, antidiscrimination laws don't dictate whom you must hire. You can exercise discretion based on a wide range of business considerations. You remain free, for example, to hire, promote, discipline, and fire employees and to set their salaries based on their skills, experience, performance, or reliability—or your whim. You risk violating antidiscrimination laws only when you treat a person or a group differently for reasons that are based on a protected characteristic.

Some illegal practices are obvious—such as advertising a job for people ages 20 to 30 or paying lower wages to women than men.

Other types of discrimination are more subtle, but just as illegal. Employment practices that have a disproportionate and discriminatory impact on protected groups are also barred by antidiscrimination laws. For example, if your main means of seeking job candidates is through word of mouth and your workforce consists entirely of white men, the word-of-mouth system could constitute illegal discrimination if it results in an applicant pool of mostly white men. The effect of the procedures is what counts, even if you did not specifically mean to discriminate.

To avoid violating antidiscrimination laws at the hiring stage, do all of the following:

- Advertise job openings in diverse places so they come to the attention of diverse people.
- Determine which skills, education, and other attributes are truly necessary to perform the job so that you don't impose job requirements that unnecessarily exclude capable applicants.
- Avoid application forms and screening techniques that have an unfair impact on any group of applicants.

Running afoul of antidiscrimination laws can be both time-consuming and costly. An unhappy employee or applicant may sue your business. Federal and state agencies also may take legal action against it. And publicity about a violation of antidiscrimination laws can adversely affect your business reputation, driving down revenues. If word gets out that a company has discriminated against female employees, for example, female customers may avoid dealing with the company for years—even long after the discriminatory practices have been dropped.

Respecting Applicants' Privacy Rights

As an employer, you likely believe that the more information you have about job applicants, the better your hiring decisions will be. But there's a potential problem in delving too deeply. Your desire to gather information about an applicant can conflict with the applicant's right to privacy and can sometimes violate federal and state laws.

For example, there are a number of laws that regulate how and when you can request transcripts, credit reports, and other background information. In addition, laws and court rulings restrict your right to screen applicants through aptitude tests and drug tests. We discuss those issues more fully below.

You need to be careful, too, about rejecting applicants because of their off-duty, nonwork activities. It's easy to understand why you might want to limit your payroll to people who don't smoke, drink alcohol, or use drugs—even off the job—to hold down health care costs or to keep a harmonious workforce. But the emerging law is that you can't dictate such off-the-job behavior. Where legal restrictions are in place, screening out applicants based on nonworkplace behavior can get you into trouble.

Even if you're located in a state where it's legal to reject applicants based on their lifestyle or their conduct away from work, caution is in order. To be on safe legal ground, it's best to avoid rejecting an applicant for lifestyle reasons or off-duty conduct unless you have a convincing business purpose. And, even then, be sure to apply your selection criteria evenhandedly. If, for example, you choose not to hire single parents, you must apply this standard to men and women alike or risk a discrimination lawsuit.

Because the laws vary depending on which state you are in, it's best to contact your state labor department before rejecting an applicant based on off-duty conduct or lifestyle unless it is firmly rooted in a business reason.

Avoiding False Job Security Promises

If there's no contract for a fixed term of employment, an employee works at the will of the employer and employee. The employer can fire the employee at any time—and the employee is free to quit at any time—for any reason or for no reason at all. That's the basic law, although you can't fire someone for an illegal reason—because of the color of the employee's skin, for example, or because you prefer to put a younger person in the job.

 CAUTION

The rules are different in Montana. There, an employee is only at will during the "probationary period"—the first six months of the employment relationship, unless the employer specifies a different probationary period while hiring. After the probationary period is, the employer must have "good cause" to fire the employee, defined as "reasonable job-related grounds for dismissal based on a failure to satisfactorily perform job duties, disruption of the employer's operation, or other legitimate business reason."

The at-will relationship gives you maximum freedom to fire employees, but preserving your legal right to fire at will can be tricky. Courts in many states have held that if employers are not careful about what they tell employees, what they write in employee handbooks, and what they say in documents and letters, they may lose that right. For example:

- A law firm hired Joan as a receptionist and fired her eight months later. Joan sued the law firm. She claimed that when she was hired, she was assured that she would remain employed as long as she did a good job. The court held that such assurance was sufficient to create a contract that Joan would be fired only for a legitimate business reason. (*Hetes v. Schefman & Miller Law Office*, 393 N.W.2d 577 (1986).)
- A bingo hall hired Scott as a general manager and gave him an employee handbook. Later, Scott was fired without warning or suspension. He sued, claiming that the handbook stated that the employer could fire an employee only after warnings were given and disciplinary

procedures were followed. The court ruled that the employer was required to follow the procedures set out in its own employee handbook and couldn't fire Scott at will. (*Lukoski v. Sandia Indian Management Co.*, 748 P.2d 507 (1988).)

During the hiring process, don't give assurances that you may not be able to honor and that may give an applicant a false sense of security. It can be difficult to restrain yourself when you're trying hard to entice an attractive candidate to join your workforce. You'll have a natural tendency to say positive things about your business, the candidate, and the future employment relationship. But those upbeat statements can be turned against you if your promises don't come true or if the employee is later fired.

Your best protection is to make sure your application forms, employee handbooks, and offers of employment state that the job is at will—and to have the applicant acknowledge this in writing. Then you'll have an excellent chance of terminating the employment on your own terms, without legal repercussions. Be aware, however, that some judges approach the whole idea of at-will employment with a measure of hostility or skepticism. These judges may disregard even the most carefully worded at-will language if it seems to be contradicted by other oral or written statements you've made to the applicant or new employee.

Here's an example of language you may wish to include in your job application form.

At-Will Employment. I acknowledge that if hired, I will be an at-will employee, subject to dismissal or discipline without notice or cause, at the discretion of the employer. I also understand that this means I am free to quit my employment at any time, for any reason, without notice. I understand that no representative of the company, other than the president, has authority to change the terms of the at-will relationship and that any such change can occur only in a written employment contract.

gno Initials

Another way to protect yourself is to make sure that you always have a good business-related reason for firing an employee. In legal parlance, this is called firing "for cause." If you fire for cause, the firing will be lawful, even if a court later finds that the employee was not an at-will employee after all.

Preventing Negligent Hiring Claims

The main reason to investigate an applicant's background is to make sure the person will do a good job for you and fit in with your other employees. But sometimes there's an additional, equally powerful reason to make a thorough investigation. When you hire someone for a position that may expose customers or others to danger, you must use special care in checking references and making other background checks.

Legally, you have a duty to protect your customers, clients, visitors, and members of the general public from injury caused by employees whom you know, or should know, pose a risk of harm to others. In some states, you may also have a duty to protect other employees from an employee whom you know—or should know—is dangerous. If someone gets hurt or has property stolen or damaged by an employee whose background you didn't check carefully, you can be sued for negligent hiring.

Be especially vigilant when hiring maintenance workers and delivery drivers, whose jobs give them easy access to homes and apartments.

EXAMPLE: The Village Green, a 200-unit apartment complex, hires Elton as a maintenance worker and gives him a master key. Elton enters an apartment and sexually molests a four-year-old girl while the child's parents are running an errand. Had the company checked before hiring Elton, it would have discovered that Elton had just completed a prison term for a sexual offense. The child's parents sue The Village Green for negligent hiring.

Doing a background check can be a delicate matter, because you are also legally required to respect the applicant's privacy. If you hire people for sensitive jobs, you must investigate their backgrounds as thoroughly as possible—without stepping over the line and violating their privacy rights. You can be faulted for not looking into an applicant's criminal

Truth in Hiring

Statements you make while interviewing and making job offers may later be treated as binding contracts.

In a leading case, a New York law firm recruited a lawyer who was beginning to make a name for herself in environmental law. The carrot that was dangled in front of her was that she'd head an environmental law department that the firm was starting. She bit—but wound up being assigned to general litigation work instead.

Later, when she was fired as part of a cutback, she sued the firm, claiming she'd been damaged because the firm had thwarted her career objective of continuing to specialize in environmental law. The court of appeals held that her claim was valid. (*Stewart v. Jackson & Nash*, 976 F.2d 86 (2d Cir. 1992).)

The lesson of this and similar cases is that the type of work an employee does can be important. Employees often leave one employer to join another—or turn down opportunities—because a particular job seems to offer a greater chance for career advancement. To avoid claims that you misled an applicant about the nature of the work, stick to what you know the work will consist of rather than what you think the applicant may want to hear.

Similarly, if your company is considering staff reductions in the near future—because, for example, a major account is about to move out of the state—disclose this to applicants. Otherwise, you may find yourself on the defensive end of a lawsuit, especially if the employee left a secure job elsewhere to come work for you.

Consider, for example, the case of Andrew, who held a good job in New York City—a job that paid $120,000 a year. According to Andrew, executives of a Los Angeles company strongly urged him to take a job that they said would be secure and would involve significant pay increases. The executives portrayed the company as financially strong, with a profitable future. Brushing aside Andrew's request for a written employment contract, they told him, "Our word is our bond."

That was good enough for Andrew. He quit his New York job, bought a home in California, moved there with his wife and two children, and began working for the L.A. company. Two years later, the company fired Andrew as part of a management reorganization. He sued, claiming that the company fraudulently induced him to give up his old job and move to California. He said that when the company executives induced him to change jobs, they falsely represented the company's financial condition—concealing the fact that the company's financial outlook was bleak and that the company was already planning to eliminate the job for which it was hiring him. The California Supreme Court held that Andrew could sue for both fraud and breach of contract. (*Lazar v. Superior Court (Rykoff-Sexton Inc.)*, 49 Cal.Rptr.2d 377 (1996).)

convictions—but not for failing to learn about prior arrests that didn't result in convictions, because such arrest records are often protected by privacy laws.

In doing background checks on applicants for sensitive jobs, check for felony convictions. Also, be diligent in contacting all previous employers. Keep a written record of your investigation efforts. Insist that the applicant explain any gaps in employment history. Consider turning over the prehire investigation to professionals who do this for a living. If you choose to follow this route—and can afford it—it can go a long way toward refuting later claims that you failed to use reasonable efforts to learn about the employee's history.

CAUTION

Strict rules may apply to background checks. Any time you hire a business—such as a credit bureau or investigative agency—to gather information about applicants (or employees), you must follow the strict guidelines set forth in the Fair Credit Reporting Act or FCRA. (15 U.S.C. §§ 1681 and following.) This federal law requires you to, among other things, get the applicant's consent to the investigation and give the applicant a copy of the investigative report if you decide not to hire the applicant based on its contents.

Protecting Against Unfair Competition

Whenever you hire workers, you run the risk that they'll later start a competing business or go to work for a competitor. If so, they may use information or contacts they gained at your workplace to draw away business that otherwise would be yours.

Obviously, you need not be too concerned about the employee you hire to flip hamburgers or the clerk you hire to handle dry cleaning orders. But employees who have access to inside information about product pricing or business expansion plans, for example, may pose competitive risks. The same goes for employees who serve valuable and hard-won customers—such as a salesperson who handles a $200,000 account.

You can help protect your business from unfair competition by asking new hires to sign agreements not to take or disclose trade secrets and other confidential information. You can also ask selected employees to sign covenants not to compete with your business —although such covenants must be carefully written so that a former employee has a reasonable chance to earn a living.

Trade Secrets

In hiring and working with employees, some business owners need to protect their unique assets from misuse. Some possibly protectable business assets may include, for example:

- a restaurant's recipes for a special salad dressing and a muffin that draw people from miles around
- a heating and cooling company's list of 500 customers for whom it regularly provides maintenance, or
- a computer company's unique process for speedily assembling computer boards.

If they are treated as such, the recipes, the customer list, and the assembly process are all trade secrets. Other examples are an unpatented invention, engineering techniques, cost data, a formula, or a machine. To qualify for trade secret protection, your business information must meet two requirements.

First, you must show that you've taken steps to keep the information secret—for example, by:

- keeping it in a secure place such as a locked cabinet or password-protected database
- giving employees access to it on a need-to-know basis only
- informing employees that the information is proprietary, and
- requiring employees to acknowledge in writing that the information is a trade secret.

EXAMPLE: Sue works at Speedy Copy Shop. She has daily access to the list of larger accounts that are regularly billed more than $2,000 per month. Sue quits to open her own competing shop. Before she does, she copies the list of major accounts. One of her first steps in getting her new business going is to try to get their business away from her former employer. Speedy sues Sue for infringing on its trade secret. At trial, Speedy shows that it keeps the list in a secure place and permits access only to selected employees who need the information. In light of these precautions, the judge orders Sue not to contact the customers on the list and requires her to compensate Speedy for any profits she has already earned on those accounts.

Second, the information must not be freely available from other sources. If the recipe for a restaurant's award-winning custard tart can be found in a standard American cookbook or recreated by a competent chef, it isn't a trade secret. On the other hand, if the restaurant's chef found the recipe in a medieval French cookbook in a provincial museum, translated it, and figured out how to adapt it to currently available ingredients, it probably would be considered obscure enough to receive trade secret protection.

In addition to the requirements that a trade secret must be guarded information that is somewhat obscure, judges sometimes look at how valuable the information is to you and your competitors and how much money and effort you spent in developing the trade secret.

Covenants Not to Compete

To prevent an employee from competing with you after leaving your workplace, consider having him or her sign a covenant not to compete (also called a noncompete agreement). In a typical covenant, the employee agrees not to become an owner or employee of a business that competes with yours for a specific time and in a specific location.

The best time to secure a covenant not to compete is when you hire an employee. An employee who is already on the payroll may be more reluctant to sign anything—and you'll have less leverage to negotiate the agreement.

> **CAUTION**
>
> **Not all states honor noncompete agreements.** Noncompete agreements can be difficult—or impossible—to enforce. In California, for example, courts virtually never enforce noncompete agreements, and other states enforce noncompetes only in limited circumstances. Even in the states where they are enforced, it's often hard to overcome a judge's reluctance to interfere with an employee's ability to earn a living. One way around this potential uphill battle is to ask employees to sign a nonsolicitation agreement and a nondisclosure agreement. Some courts are more willing to enforce these agreements. They can keep ex-employees from using your client or customer lists, luring employees to a competing business, or stealing your trade secrets. If you can get all of these protections, you don't lose much by forgoing a noncompete agreement.

Battles over the legality of these agreements must usually be resolved in court. Judges are reluctant to deprive people of their rights to earn a living, so the key to a legally enforceable covenant not to compete is to make its terms reasonable. In evaluating whether a covenant not to compete is reasonable, focus on three questions—each of which relates to the specific job and the specific employee.

- **Is there a legitimate business reason for restricting the future activities of the particular employee?** There probably is if you expect to spend significant time and money training a high-level employee and plan to entrust the employee with sensitive contacts on lucrative accounts. Such an employee could easily—and unfairly—hurt your business by competing with you. This would motivate a judge to find that you have a legitimate business reason for the covenant. On the other hand, if you require a new receptionist or typist to sign a similar covenant, a judge would probably find that you have no valid business purpose for restricting the employee's ability to work elsewhere.

- **Is the covenant reasonably limited in time?** A one-year limitation may be reasonable for a particular employee. A three-year limit might not be.

- **Is the covenant reasonably limited as to geographic scope?** A 50-mile limit may be reasonable for a particular employee. A limit spanning several states might not be deemed reasonable.

EXAMPLE: When Mary hires Sid to be the office manager for her profitable travel agency, she realizes that Sid will have access to major corporate accounts and daily contact with the corporate managers who make travel arrangements. Mary also knows that she'll spend considerable time training Sid and invest more than $4,000 in specialized seminars that she will require Sid to attend. She asks Sid to sign a covenant not to compete in which

Sid promises that while working for Mary and for two years afterward, he won't work for or own a travel agency within 50 miles of Mary's agency. After six months, Sid quits and starts a competing agency one mile from Mary's. The judge enforces the covenant not to compete by forbidding Sid from operating his new business and by awarding damages to Mary.

Hiring Young Workers

Federal and state laws restrict your right to hire workers who are younger than 18 years old. These laws limit the type of work for which young people may be hired and the hours they may work. (See Chapter 3 for more information.)

Hiring Immigrants

Federal law prohibits hiring workers not authorized to work in the United States. You and each new employee are required to complete Form I-9, *Employment Eligibility Verification* (discussed below).

Job Descriptions

Write a job description for each position you're seeking to fill. Listing the skills and attributes you're looking for in applicants will make the hiring process more objective. It will also give you ready standards to measure whether applicants are qualified—and which ones are most qualified. Current employees can often help you write job descriptions. They know how the business operates and the kind of skills that are needed.

In writing job descriptions, be careful not to violate the laws that prohibit discrimination in employment and that seek to assure employment opportunities for people with disabilities.

Under federal law, you can't discriminate against applicants on the basis of their race, skin color, gender, religious beliefs, national origin, disability, age (if the applicant is at least 40 years old), or genetic information. In addition, many states prohibit discrimination based on a variety of other characteristics, including marital status and sexual orientation. To learn about laws prohibiting discrimination in employment, see Chapter 8.

Necessary Elements

A well-drafted job description usually contains these components:

- **Qualifications, such as necessary skills, education, experience, and licenses.** Be careful in setting requirements for education and experience. If set at an unnecessarily high level, your requirements may have an unintended discriminatory effect on groups protected by antidiscrimination laws.
- **Essential job functions.** The federal Americans with Disabilities Act (ADA) has forced employers to take a fresh look at job descriptions—and to decide what really is the core of each job. (For more

on the ADA, see Chapter 9.) To help eliminate unfair discrimination against people with disabilities, the ADA seeks to make sure a person isn't excluded from a job simply because the individual can't perform some marginal duties listed in a job description. For example, suppose your job description for a file clerk includes answering the phone, but the basic functions of the job are to file and retrieve written materials. Other employees usually answer the phone. Someone whose hearing is impaired may have trouble handling phone calls but be perfectly able to file and retrieve papers. Phone answering isn't an essential job function and shouldn't be listed as such.

- **Nonessential job functions.** You may wish to specify functions and duties that are desirable but not required for a particular job. That's okay—as long as the job description clearly states that these additional functions and duties are not job requirements. Suppose you're seeking a receptionist. If you never or seldom require the receptionist to type, typing isn't an essential function. Listing an unnecessary or marginal skill such as typing would unfairly disqualify a person with a paralyzed hand from the receptionist job, for example. You could, however, mention typing as a desirable function if you made it clear that it's not required.

RESOURCE

Want help writing job descriptions? Check out *The Job Description Handbook,* by Margie Mader-Clark (Nolo).

Permitted Discrimination

Antidiscrimination laws recognize that in certain very limited circumstances, an employer may have a legitimate reason to seek an employee of a particular gender, religion, or ethnicity—even though such a preference would ordinarily be illegal. These are called bona fide occupational qualification (BFOQ) exceptions. Religion, sex, or national origin can be a BFOQ only if it's a reasonably necessary qualification for the normal operation of a business or enterprise—and it almost never is. Race can never be a BFOQ.

Here are some guidelines.

Religion. Religion can be a job requirement where the job involves performing religious duties. The law recognizes, for example, that being Catholic is a valid qualification for performing the duties of a Catholic priest and being Jewish is a valid qualification for performing the duties of a rabbi. But beyond that, religion rarely can be a BFOQ. A court has allowed a Jesuit university to limit teaching jobs in its philosophy department to Jesuits. (*Pime v. Loyola University of Chicago,* 585 F.Supp. 435 (N.D. Ill., 1984).) But a school established under a will that required all teachers to be Protestant couldn't enforce that restriction as a job requirement; the school wasn't teaching religion. (*EEOC v. Kamehameha Schools/Bishop Estate,* 990 F.2d 458 (9th Cir. 1993).)

National origin. National origin can sometimes, but rarely, be a BFOQ. An American subsidiary of a Japanese company involved in international trade might be allowed to make Japanese nationality a job requirement because of the need for language proficiency, cultural background, and acceptability to trading partners or customers. (*Avigliano v. Sumitomo Shoji of America, Inc.,* 638 F.2d 552 (2d Cir. 1981).) Aside from such a narrow situation, you can't use national origin as a BFOQ.

Gender. About the only time that gender can be a BFOQ is for jobs affecting personal privacy—for example, restroom attendants or security guards who are required to search employees—and acting and modeling work.

Job Advertisements

Even if you write a great job description, you can still get tripped up when summarizing the job in an advertisement, especially if you let someone who's not familiar with the legal guidelines write your ad. Nuances in an ad can be used as evidence of discrimination against applicants of a particular gender, age, or other protected characteristic.

Here are a number of semantic pitfalls to avoid when posting a job.

Don't Use	Use
Salesman	Salesperson
College student	Part-time worker
Handyman	General repair person
Gal Friday	Office manager
Married couple	Two-person job
Counter girl	Retail clerk
Waiter	Wait staff
Young	Energetic

Requiring a high school or college degree may be discriminatory in some job categories. You can avoid problems by stating that an applicant must have "a degree or equivalent experience."

The best way to write an ad that meets legal requirements is to keep it short and sweet. Stick to the skills needed and the basic responsibilities the job entails. Some examples:

- "Fifty-unit apartment complex seeks experienced manager with general maintenance skills."
- "Midsized manufacturing company has opening for accountant with tax experience to oversee interstate accounts."
- "Cook trainee position available in new vegetarian restaurant. Flexible hours."

Help wanted ads placed by federal contractors must state that all qualified applicants will receive consideration for employment without regard to race, color, religion, sex, or national origin. Ads often express this with the phrase "An Equal Opportunity Employer" or "EOE."

Some employers who are not federal contractors also use this phrase in their ads; it's a good shorthand way to let potential employees know that you'll give them a fair shake, which can help you attract a more diverse group of applicants.

Job Applications

Develop a standard application form to make it easy to compare the experience and skills of applicants. Limit the form to job-related information that will help you decide who's the best person for the job. Questions like these are fairly standard:

- What is your name, address, and phone number?
- Are you legally entitled to work in the United States?
- What position are you applying for?
- What other positions would you like to be considered for?
- If you are hired, when can you start work?
- What is your educational background—high school, college, graduate school, and other (including school names, addresses, number of years attended, degree, and major)?
- Describe your employment history—including name, address, and phone number of each employer, supervisor's name, date of employment, job title and responsibilities, and reason for leaving.
- Do you have any special training or achievements that are relevant to this position?

In designing a job application, keep two legal principles in mind:

- It's unlawful for you to seek certain information.
- You can use the application to explain employment terms and get the applicant's permission to gather background information.

Avoiding Unlawful Questions

The chart below outlines the type of information that you can ask for in applications and during job interviews. Follow the chart to comply with federal laws. The chart may also be sufficient for complying with the laws of your state, but to be sure, check with your state's fair employment office. (You can find charts listing state fair employment laws and offices in the appendix.)

In addition to the areas covered in the chart, the ADA prohibits any preemployment questions about a disability. Before you make a job offer, you may ask questions about an applicant's ability to perform specific job functions. You may not, however, inquire about the nature or severity of a disability, ask about medical history or treatment, or require any medical exam. These rules apply to application forms, job interviews, and background or reference checks. See Chapter 9 for more on the ADA.

After you make a conditional job offer and before an applicant starts work, you're free to gather more details. At that point, you can require a medical exam or ask health-related

Preemployment Inquiries

Subject	Lawful Preemployment Inquiries	Unlawful Preemployment Inquiries
Name	Applicant's full name Have you ever worked for this company under a different name? Is any additional information relative to a different name necessary to check work record? If yes, explain.	Original name of an applicant whose name has been changed by court order or otherwise Applicant's maiden name
Address or duration of residence	How long have you been a resident of this state or city?	Do you rent or own?
Birthplace	None	Birthplace of applicant Birthplace of applicant's parents, spouse, or other close relatives Requirements that applicant submit birth certificate, naturalization, or baptismal record
Age	Are you 18 years old or older? (This question may be asked only for the purpose of determining whether applicants are of legal age for employment.)	How old are you? What is your date of birth?
Religion or creed	None	Inquiry into an applicant's religious denomination, religious affiliations, church, parish, pastor, or religious holidays observed
Race or color	None	Complexion or color of skin Inquiry regarding applicant's race
Photograph	None	Any requirement for a photograph prior to hire
Height	None	Inquiry regarding applicant's height (unless you have a legitimate business reason)
Weight	None	Inquiry regarding applicant's weight (unless you have a legitimate business reason)
Marital status	Is your spouse employed by this employer?	Requirement that an applicant provide any information regarding marital status or children Are you single or married? Do you have any children? Is your spouse employed? What is your spouse's name?
Gender	None	Mr., Miss, Mrs., or an inquiry regarding gender; inquiry as to ability or plans to reproduce or advocacy of any form of birth control
Disability	These [provide applicant with list] are the essential functions of the job. How would you perform them?	Inquiries regarding an individual's physical or mental condition that are not directly related to the requirements of a specific job

Preemployment Inquiries (continued)

Subject	Lawful Preemployment Inquiries	Unlawful Preemployment Inquiries
Citizenship	Are you legally authorized to work in the United States on a full-time basis?	Questions about subjects below are unlawful, but the applicant may be required to reveal some of this information as part of the federal I-9 process: • country of citizenship • whether an applicant is naturalized or a native-born citizen; the date when the applicant acquired citizenship • requirement that an applicant produce naturalization papers or first papers • whether applicant's parents or spouse are naturalized or native-born citizens of the United States, and, if so, the date when such parent or spouse acquired citizenship
National origin	Inquiry into language applicant speaks and writes fluently	Inquiry into applicant's lineage, ancestry, national origin, descent, parentage, or nationality, unless part of the federal I-9 process in determining employment eligibility Nationality of applicant's parents or spouse Inquiry into how applicant acquired ability to read, write, or speak a foreign language
Education	Inquiry into the academic, vocational, or professional education of an applicant and public and private schools attended	
Experience	Inquiry into work experience Inquiry into countries applicant has visited	
Arrests	Have you ever been convicted of a crime? Are there any felony charges pending against you?	Inquiry regarding arrests that did not result in conviction (except for law enforcement agencies)
Relatives	Names of applicant's relatives already employed by this company	Address of any relative of applicant, other than address (within the United States) of applicant's father and mother, husband or wife, and minor dependent children
Notice in case of emergency	Name and address of person to be notified in case of accident or emergency	Name and address of nearest relative to be notified in case of accident or emergency
Organizations	Inquiry into the organizations of which an applicant is a member, excluding organizations the name or character of which indicates the race, color, religion, national origin, or ancestry of its members	List all clubs, societies, and lodges to which the applicant belongs
Personal finance	None	Inquiries about financial problems, such as garnishment or bankruptcy

questions—but only if you require this for all candidates who receive conditional offers in the same job category.

Below are some examples of questions, developed by the U.S. Equal Employment Opportunity Commission (the government agency that enforces federal workplace discrimination laws), that employers may not ask on application forms or in job interviews as prohibited by the ADA:

- Have you ever had or been treated for any of the following conditions or diseases (followed by a checklist of various conditions and diseases)?
- List any conditions or diseases for which you have been treated in the past three years.
- Have you ever been hospitalized? If so, for what condition?
- Have you ever been treated by a psychiatrist or psychologist? If so, for what condition?
- Have you ever been treated for any mental condition?
- Is there any health-related reason you may not be able to perform the job for which you are applying?
- Have you had a major illness in the last five years?
- How many days were you absent from work because of illness last year?
  (However, you may provide information on your attendance requirements and ask if the applicant will be able to meet those requirements.)

- Do you have any physical defects that preclude you from performing certain kinds of work?
- Do you have any disabilities or impairments that may affect your performance in the position you are applying for?
  (However, it's okay to ask about the applicant's ability to perform specific job functions, with or without a reasonable accommodation—a concept covered in depth in Chapter 9.)
- Are you taking any prescribed drugs?
- Are you a drug addict or an alcoholic?
- Have you ever been treated for drug addiction or alcoholism?
- Have you ever filed for workers' compensation insurance?

 RESOURCE

Want additional information on hiring and the ADA? Refer to the EEOC website, at www.eeoc.gov.

The Legal Effect of Job Applications

A well-written application form can help get the employment relationship off on a solid legal footing. Since it's filled out very early in the process, you can use the form to let the applicant know the basic terms and conditions of the job and the workplace. And, because the applicant signs the application, it can be a valuable piece of evidence if a question comes up later about what you actually promised about the job.

You can also use the job application to obtain the employee's consent to a background investigation and reference check. If the applicant consents to your investigation, the applicant will have a tough time later claiming an invasion of privacy. Indeed, if you plan to hire another person or agency to conduct a background check, you will be legally required to get the applicant's consent first.

Impress on the applicant the need to be honest and accurate in completing the form. Lying or giving incomplete information on an application can be a good legal reason to fire an employee if the correct story later surfaces. So serious is application fraud—or résumé fraud as it's sometimes called—that some courts have allowed employers to use it to justify a firing even though the employers didn't even know of the fraud when they let the employee go.

EXAMPLE: Dolores, age 42, applies for a job as a land surveyor with Progressive Engineering Consultants (PEC). On her application, Dolores states that she has a civil engineering degree from a prestigious college and is licensed by the state. The application form warns that false information will be a cause for immediate discharge. Relying on the application, PEC hires Dolores. Six months later, PEC becomes dissatisfied with Dolores's work and fires her, replacing her with a 30-year-old man. Dolores sues, claiming that the firm discriminated against her based on age and gender. PEC belatedly looks into her application statements and discovers that Dolores has neither the degree nor the license she said she had. Because of Dolores's lies, the judge dismisses the case without getting into the discrimination charges.

Including the following language in an application form can help you establish that you clearly told the applicant about the consequences of lying.

Accuracy. I verify that the statements I have made in this application are true and complete. I understand that if I am hired, any false or incomplete statements in this application will be grounds for immediate discharge.

JMO Initials

Interviews

Before you begin interviewing applicants for a job opening, write down a set of questions focusing on the job duties and the applicant's skills and experience. Some examples:

- "Tell me about your experience running a mailroom."
- "How much experience did you have making cold calls on your last job?"
- "Explain how you typically go about organizing your workday."
- "Have any of your jobs required strong leadership skills?"

By writing down the questions and sticking to the same format in all interviews for the position, you reduce the risk that a rejected applicant will later complain about unequal treatment. It's also smart to summarize the applicant's answers for your files—but don't get so involved in documenting the interview that you forget to listen closely to the applicant. And don't be so locked in to your list of questions that you don't follow up on something significant that an applicant has said or try to pin down an ambiguous or evasive response.

Interviewing Protocol

Get the interview started by giving the applicant some information about the job: the duties, hours, pay range, benefits, and career opportunities. This will give the applicant a chance to get comfortable before you start in on the questions. Questions about the applicant's work history and experience that may be relevant to the job opening are always appropriate. But don't encourage the employee to divulge the trade secrets of a present or former employer—especially a competitor. That can lead to a lawsuit. And be cautious about an employee who volunteers such information or promises to bring secrets to the new position; such an employee will probably play fast and loose with your own company's secrets, given the chance.

Keep your antennae tuned carefully to the applicant who spouts a litany of complaints against former employers. If you hire that person, your business may well become the next object of the applicant's invective. But watch your step if you learn that the applicant has sued a former employer for discrimination or filed a discrimination charge with the Equal Employment Opportunity Commission (EEOC). If you refuse to hire the applicant because of the prior proceedings, the EEOC may treat your refusal as a form of illegal retaliation, even though your business wasn't involved in the earlier problem. See Chapter 8 for more on retaliation claims.

Give applicants plenty of time to answer questions. Make sure they understand your questions; ask them to let you know if something is unclear. And ask them if they have any questions about your company or the job for which they're applying. Finally, let them know your time frame for getting back to them with a hiring decision so they won't bug you with premature phone calls.

RESOURCE

Want additional suggestions on interviewing? See *267 Hire Tough Proven Interview Questions*, by Mel Kleiman (HTG Press), and *The Manager's Book of Questions: 751 Great Interview Questions for Hiring the Best Person*, by John Kador (McGraw Hill). In addition, Nolo's *Dealing With Problem Employees*, by Amy DelPo and Lisa Guerin, devotes an entire chapter to the hiring process, including effective interviewing techniques.

Legal Restrictions on Questions

The rules of etiquette once dictated that you avoid discussing sex, religion, or politics in a social setting. While that standard has been relaxed, it still applies to job interviews—along with similar cautions to avoid focusing on an applicant's age, ethnicity, birthplace, or personal finances. In fact, such inquiries are not only bad manners; they may be illegal, plain and simple.

Review the legal restrictions on what you can and can't ask in a job application. (See "Job Applications," above.) The same guidelines and restrictions apply to interviews. As with job applications, the focus of your interviews should be to find the best person for the job based on skill, experience, education, and other qualifications needed to perform the job.

To avoid improper inquiries, stay focused on job requirements and company policies. Suppose you're concerned that an applicant with young kids may spend too much time talking with them on the phone. You can't ask: "Do you have children?" or "Who watches the kids when you're at work?" But you can say to the applicant: "We don't allow personal phone calls during work hours. Do you have a problem with that?" The applicant then knows the ground rules and can let you know if a problem exists. Just be sure you apply your phone policy to all employees.

During an interview, you can ask about the applicant's ability to perform job tasks and about any needed accommodation. You'll be walking a fine line here, so make sure to avoid potential legal problems with disability laws. Remember to focus on the applicant's ability to do the job—not on the applicant's disability.

EXAMPLE: Zack, who has only one arm, applies at ABC Industries for a job that requires driving. The interviewer avoids asking Zack if or how this disability would affect his driving. Instead, to comply with the law, the interviewer asks: "Do you have a valid driver's license?" and "Can you drive on frequent long distance trips, with or without an accommodation?" The interviewer continues: "At least 80% of the time of this sales job must be spent on the road covering a three-state territory. What is your outside selling experience? What is your accident record?" All are permissible questions.

You can describe or demonstrate the specific job tasks, then ask whether the applicant can perform these tasks with or without an accommodation. If you're interviewing an applicant for a mailroom job, you can say: "The person in this job is responsible for receiving incoming mail and packages, sorting the mail, and taking it in a cart to many offices in two buildings, one block apart. The mail clerk must also receive boxes of supplies weighing up to 50 pounds and place them on storage shelves six feet high. Can you perform these tasks with or without an accommodation?"

You can ask applicants to describe or show how they will perform specific job functions—

but only if you require this of everyone applying for a job in this category.

> **EXAMPLE:** PhoneSale, a telemarketing firm, requires all applicants to demonstrate selling ability by taking a simulated telephone sales test.

Be mindful that some applicants with disabilities will need accommodations to participate in the interview process. For example, you may need to provide an accessible location for an applicant in a wheelchair, a sign interpreter for a deaf person, or a reader for a blind person. (See Chapter 9 for an extensive discussion of the disability law requirements.)

Testing

Preemployment testing—which might include skills testing, aptitude testing, honesty testing, medical testing, and drug testing—is most common in larger businesses. But no matter what size your business is, you should know the legal limits on your ability to test applicants.

Skills Tests

Most small businesses—especially new ones—operate on a slim profit margin. This means that your employees must be up to speed from day one. If you're hiring a data input clerk, you may want to test the applicant for typing speed and accuracy. If you're hiring a person to be a clerk in your bookstore, you may want to test the applicant's knowledge of literature. If you're hiring a driver for a delivery van, a road test would be appropriate. As long as the skills you're testing are genuinely related to the job duties, a skills test is generally legal.

To avoid discriminating against applicants protected by the ADA, be sure your tests measure the actual skills and abilities needed to do a job—for example, a typing test or a sales demonstration test. (For more on the ADA, see Chapter 9.)

Aptitude and Psychological Tests

Some employers use written tests—usually multiple choice tests—to get additional insight into applicants' abilities. Others attempt to probe the psyche of their applicants.

These tests are going out of fashion, and for good reason. A multiple-choice aptitude test may discriminate illegally against minority applicants, because it really reflects test-taking ability rather than actual job skills. A personality test can be even riskier. Besides its potential for illegal discrimination, such a test may invade an applicant's privacy—by inquiring, for example, into religious beliefs or sexual practices.

If you do decide to use aptitude or personality tests, proceed cautiously. Make sure that the tests have been screened scientifically for validity and that they are correlated to job performance. Review them carefully for any questions that may intrude into the applicant's privacy.

Another concern for employers is the ADA, which lets you give a psychological test or exam to a job applicant—as long as the test or exam isn't medical. This can be tricky.

A psychological test or exam is considered medical if it provides evidence that can help identify a mental disorder or impairment. A test or exam is permissible if it measures only such things as honesty, tastes, and habits. But if it helps identify whether the applicant has excessive anxiety, depression, or a compulsive disorder, it qualifies as a medical test and is illegal if given at the wrong time.

Be aware, too, that the ADA sets special requirements when you test people who have impaired sensory, speaking, or manual skills. Sensory skills include the abilities to hear, to see, and to process information. If applicants wouldn't have to use the impaired skill on the job, you must design your tests so that they don't have to use the impaired skill to take the test.

> **EXAMPLE:** Joe is applying for a position as a food handler—a job that does not require reading. Because of dyslexia, Joe has a very difficult time reading. He should be given an oral rather than a written aptitude test. By contrast, if you were interviewing Joe for a proofreader job—which clearly requires the ability to read without help—a written test would be appropriate and legal.

RESOURCE

Want more on how to avoid legal problems when using screening tests? Go to www.eeoc.gov/policy/docs/factemployment_ procedures.html.

Honesty Tests

Lie detector or polygraph tests—rarely used by small businesses—are virtually outlawed by the federal Employee Polygraph Protection Act. With just a few exceptions, you can't require job applicants to take lie detector tests and you can't inquire about previous tests. The only private employers who can use lie detector tests to screen applicants are businesses that offer armored car, alarm, and guard services or that manufacture, distribute, or dispense pharmaceuticals—and, even in those situations, there are restrictions on which applicants can be tested and how the tests must be administered.

About the only time a typical employer can use a lie detector test is to question an employee who is reasonably suspected of being involved in a workplace theft or embezzlement.

You must post a notice of the Employee Polygraph Protection Act where employees and job applicants can readily see it. For a poster containing the required notice, contact the local office of the Wage and Hour Division of the U.S. Department of Labor. (See the appendix for contact details.)

Some employers use written honesty tests to screen job applicants. Because these tests are often inaccurate and can invade an applicant's privacy or have a discriminatory impact, the legality of the tests is doubtful in most states.

Limit honesty tests to situations in which you have a legitimate business reason to be concerned about workers' honesty—such as when hiring workers who will be handling

Testing Run Amok

One large department store used a psychology test to screen applicants for security guard jobs. The test was based on the Minnesota Multiphasic Personality Inventory, which has been used for decades and was widely accepted. Included in the test were hundreds of true-or-false questions, including:

- I feel sure there is only one true religion.
- My soul sometimes leaves my body.
- I believe in the second coming of Christ.
- I believe that there is a Devil and a Hell in the afterlife.
- My sex life is satisfactory.
- I am very strongly attracted to members of my own sex.
- I have often wished I were a girl.
- I have never indulged in any unusual sex practices.
- I like to talk about sex.

A group of applicants in California sued the store, claiming that the test violated their rights to privacy and was discriminatory. The California Court of Appeals agreed, ruling that the questions were not job related. The court held that the job applicants were entitled to a legal order prohibiting the store from using the test. (*Soroka v. Dayton Hudson Corp.*, 235 Cal. App.3d 654 (1991).)

large amounts of cash. Before using a test, ask to see scientific backup establishing the test's accuracy. And, to protect yourself against charges of illegal discrimination, test all applicants for a particular job.

 RESOURCE

Want to know more about the Polygraph Protection Act? For detailed information, including whom the law covers, what the law requires and prohibits, tips for compliance, and exceptions to the law, see *The Essential Guide to Federal Employment Laws*, by Lisa Guerin and Amy DelPo (Nolo).

Medical Tests

To avoid violating the ADA, don't ask applicants about their medical history or conduct any medical exam before you make a job offer. You can, however, offer a job conditioned on an applicant passing a medical exam. If you do require such a post-offer exam, be sure you require exams for all entering employees who will be doing the same job.

EXAMPLE: Cornerstone Corporation has openings for construction crane operators. It offers Bill a job conditioned on a medical exam showing he doesn't have a medical condition, such as uncontrolled seizures, which may be risky to other workers. Because Cornerstone requires such exams for all the crane operators it hires, and because the exam screens out only those workers who would not be able to do the job safely, the exam is legal.

If you require medical exams only for people with known disabilities or those who you believe may have a disability, you'll violate the ADA. But the scope of medical exams needn't be identical for all employees. You can give follow-up tests or exams if further information is needed. Suppose, for example, that your restaurant requires a blood test for all prospective kitchen workers. If one person's test indicates a problem that may affect job performance or is a direct threat to health and safety, you can require further tests for that person.

After making a conditional job offer, you may require a full physical exam and you may ask questions that you couldn't ask at the preemployment stage—for example, questions about previous illnesses, diseases, or medications. You can probe to find out if the person has the physical or mental qualifications needed to perform the job—or to determine if a person can perform the job without posing a direct threat to the health or safety of others.

If you withdraw a conditional job offer based on results of an exam or inquiry, you must be able to show both of the following:

- Your reasons were job related and consistent with business necessity, or the person was excluded to avoid a direct threat to health and safety.
- No reasonable accommodation could be made or such an accommodation

would cause undue hardship. (For more guidance, see Chapter 9.)

To avoid claims that you discriminated against a person with a disability, carefully document all medical inquiries and the responses to them. If you reject a prospective employee, be prepared to show how the medical facts relate to the person's ability to perform the job or reveal a direct threat to health and safety.

EXAMPLE: Kendra's medical exam reveals an impairment that will require her to frequently be away from work for lengthy medical treatment. The job requires daily availability for the next three months. The company doesn't hire Kendra. This is permissible under the ADA because Kendra isn't available to perform the essential functions of the job, and no accommodation is possible.

Drug Tests

You have a legal right to insist on a drug-free workplace. The only problem is that testing to weed out drug users may conflict with workers' rights to privacy. The laws on drug testing vary widely from state to state and are changing quickly as legislators and judges struggle to strike a balance between workers' rights and the legitimate needs of businesses. (See "State Drug and Alcohol Testing Laws," in the appendix.) Some state statutes allow you to test employees only in a narrow range of jobs, such as those concerned with safety.

TIP

Federal contractors must comply with the Drug-Free Workplace Act. The law requires federal contractors and grantees to agree to maintain a drug-free workplace. If your business has a contract with the federal government for $100,000 or more (for something other than goods you're selling to the government), you need to notify employees that they're prohibited from unlawfully making, distributing, possessing, or using controlled substances in your workplace. And you need to set up an awareness program that tells workers about the dangers of drug abuse while at work and lets them know about assistance programs that may be available.

Fortunately, even restrictive states generally allow you much more leeway in screening job applicants than in testing employees who are already on board. If your state permits testing applicants or employees and you plan to do such testing, use the application form to let applicants know of this policy. State law may also require you to give applicants a written policy statement that's separate from the application. When applicants are told up front about drug testing, it's harder for them to later claim that they expected more privacy on drug testing results.

Once an applicant becomes an employee, drug testing gets trickier. Testing is usually permitted when employees have been in an accident or you've seen them bring illegal drugs to work. Your legal right to test at random and without prior notice not as clear, in some states.

With any drug testing, treat all individuals consistently, being careful not to single out any one group. And consult with competent drug testing experts to assure that your test procedures are as accurate as possible. Because the laws of drug testing are in constant flux, talk to a lawyer before administering any tests.

RESOURCE

For help developing a drug policy, contact the Center for Substance Abuse Prevention Workplace Helpline, at 800-WORKPLACE. You can also find lots of helpful information on their website at www.prevention.samhsa.gov.

CAUTION

Recovering addicts are protected from discrimination. The ADA prohibits you from discriminating against people because of past drug or alcohol problems. This includes people who no longer use drugs illegally and those who are receiving treatment for drug addiction or who have been rehabilitated successfully.

Investigations

Because some people give false or incomplete information in their job applications, it's a good idea to do some investigating to verify application information. You might find out, for example, that an applicant doesn't have the work experience or occupational license listed in a job application—or that the applicant didn't really leave the last job voluntarily. What's more, you might learn that the applicant has a history of violent behavior or even a criminal record that would disqualify the applicant from a job that may put members of the public or other employees at risk.

Your need to investigate a job applicant is legitimate—but if you go overboard, you may violate the job applicant's legal right to privacy. The best way to reduce the risk of an invasion of privacy claim is to do both of the following:

- Seek only the background information you really need to figure out whether the applicant is suited for the job.
- Inform the applicant, in the job application, that you will be requesting information from, for example, schools, credit reporting agencies, former employers, and law enforcement agencies.

As part of the application process, ask the applicant to sign a consent form. Use a separate form rather than making the consent a part of the application. That way, you can easily photocopy the consent and send it to the people from whom you're seeking information.

 TIP

Will it tell you what you need to know? It's often a waste of time and effort to acquire and review transcripts and credit reports—although occasionally they're useful. If you're hiring a bookkeeper, for example, experience garnered on the job is much more important than the grades the applicant received in a community college bookkeeping program ten years ago. But if the applicant is fresh out

of school and has never held a bookkeeping job, then a transcript may yield some insights. Similarly, if you're hiring a software engineer, information on a credit report would be irrelevant. But if you're hiring a bar manager who will be handling large cash receipts, you might want to see a credit report to learn if the applicant is in financial trouble.

The Fair Credit Reporting Act

A federal law called the Fair Credit Reporting Act (FCRA) imposes strict rules on your ordering and use of consumer reports, which include background checks, credit reports, and other information gathered on applicants for employment. (15 U.S.C. §§ 1681 and following.)

Which Background Checks Are Covered?

The FCRA regulates your ordering and use of any report prepared by a consumer reporting agency (CRA), which is any business that assembles such reports for other businesses. If you order an applicant's credit payment record from a credit bureau, that is a consumer report covered by the FCRA. So is a report you order from a business about an applicant's driving record or criminal history (though ordering similar information from a governmental agency isn't).

You may be thinking of hiring a CRA, such as a detective agency or professional investigator, to prepare a report based on interviews the CRA conducts with an applicant's friends, neighbors, and associates. This would also constitute a consumer report—and would, therefore, be covered by the FCRA.

Checking an applicant's references may or may not come under the FCRA. If you or someone within your company does the checking, the FCRA doesn't apply—the statute doesn't cover any information you gather on your own. However, if you use an employment or reference-checking agency—or, indeed, anyone outside of your company—to do the job, you must comply with the FCRA.

Requirements for Handling Reports

Before you get a consumer report for employment purposes, you must notify the applicant or employee in writing and get that person's written permission to gather the information. And the agency you ask to prepare the report will require you to certify that you're complying with the federal law—and that you won't use the information in the report in violation of federal or state equal employment opportunity laws. These laws—discussed in Chapters 8 and 9—prohibit certain types of discrimination. Special rules apply if your business is in the trucking industry.

After you get the report, special rules apply if, based on the report, you're going to take adverse action against the applicant. In the hiring process, this is most likely to come up if you decide, based on the information on the report, not to hire the applicant.

Step 1: Before you take adverse action, you must give the applicant or employee a copy of the consumer report and a copy of *A Summary of Your Rights Under the Fair Credit Reporting Act*—a publication prepared by the Federal Trade Commission (FTC). The business that prepared the consumer report will give you the Summary, or you can get a copy from the FTC's website at www.ftc.gov.

Step 2: After you take an adverse action, you must notify the applicant or employee that you've taken the action. You can give notice orally, in writing, by email, or by fax. Your adverse action notice must:

- give the name, address, and phone number of the company (CRA) that supplied the report
- state that the CRA didn't make the decision to take adverse action and can't give specific reasons for it
- say that the applicant or employee has the right to dispute the accuracy or completeness of any information the CRA furnished, and
- say that the applicant or employee can get an additional free consumer report from the CRA upon request within 60 days.

Penalties for Violating the FCRA

You face legal trouble if you don't get an applicant's or employee's permission before requesting a consumer report or if you don't provide the required disclosures about adverse action. The applicant or employee may sue you for damages in federal court. If successful, the person may recover court costs and reasonable attorney fees. You can also be ordered to pay punitive damages—damages intended to punish you—for deliberate violations.

Also, federal and state agencies may sue you and obtain civil penalties.

RESOURCE

Want to know more about the FCRA? For detailed information about the FCRA, including whom it covers, what it requires and prohibits, and tips for compliance, see *The Essential Guide to Federal Employment Laws*, by Lisa Guerin and Amy DelPo (Nolo).

Information From Former Employers

Some job applicants exaggerate or even lie about their qualifications and experience. The best way to uncover this kind of puffery is to ask some former employers for the inside story.

Former employers are often reluctant to say anything negative for fear that if they speak frankly, they may be hit with a lawsuit for defamation. They're hesitant to do anything more than to verify that the former employee did in fact work there and to give the dates of employment. This can make it hard to get an accurate picture of an applicant's job history. As mentioned, it may be helpful to send the former employer a copy of the applicant's signed consent to a full disclosure of employment information. (See Chapter 10 for suggestions on giving references for former employees when you're the one being asked for information.)

In speaking with former employers, read between the lines. If a former employer is neutral, offers only faint praise, or overpraises a person for one aspect of a job only—"great with numbers" or "always on time"—there's a good chance some negative information is hiding in the wings. Ask former employers: "Would you hire this person back if you could?" The response may be telling. To help put the applicant in perspective, you might ask: "What are this person's greatest strengths—and greatest weaknesses?" Since no one is perfect, this may lead to a candid evaluation of the applicant.

If a reference isn't glowing and doesn't take in all aspects of the job, check several other references—and perhaps call back the applicant for a more directed interview.

TIP

Reference checks may become more informative. In response to the problem of unhelpful reference checks, many states have passed laws that allow employers to speak more frankly about their former employees. If your state has such a law, don't assume that the former employers you call for reference checks know about it. Telling them about the protection they have under your state's law may allow you to get a fuller picture of a prospective employee. To find out about your state law, contact your state labor department. (See the appendix for contact details.)

School Transcripts

Though on-the-job experience is usually more relevant to employment than an applicant's educational credentials, you may have good reasons for requiring a high school diploma or college degree for some jobs. If so, you may want to see proof that the applicant really received the diploma or degree or took the courses claimed in the job application.

If you wish to see these records, ask the applicant to sign a written release acknowledging your right to obtain them. Federal law prohibits schools that receive federal funds from turning over the records without such a release—and many schools won't deliver records to anyone except a former student. This can, of course, complicate your verification, since it creates the possibility of forgery or tampering.

Credit History

Credit information usually isn't relevant to employment, but it might come into play if you hire someone who will handle money. Applicants who can't keep their personal finances in order are probably not a good choice for a job managing your company's finances.

In most other situations, however, a credit check is an unnecessary intrusion into an applicant's private life. What's more, unless you have a good reason for doing a credit check for a particular job, you may run afoul of antidiscrimination laws. According to the EEOC, requiring an applicant to have good credit may subtly discriminate against some minority groups.

In 2010, the EEOC showed renewed interest in this issue. It held hearings on the use of credit reports in making employment decisions and filed a race discrimination lawsuit against Kaplan Higher Education Corporation, alleging that the company's policy of rejecting potential employees based on their credit history discriminated against black applicants.

In addition, several states have enacted laws barring employers from obtaining credit reports for most job applicants or employees. Typically, the only exceptions are for jobs at banks or similar positions in which credit information is substantially related to the applicant's ability to do the job. Similar laws are under consideration in many more states, and Congress is looking at a national version, called the Equal Employment for All Act.

Assuming that you have a good business reason to order a credit report on a job applicant, be sure to get the applicant's written permission first. This is required by the federal Fair Credit Reporting Act and may also be mandated by state law. And if you decide not to hire the applicant because of something you learn in a credit report, you must notify the applicant. For more information, see "The Fair Credit Reporting Act," above.

Criminal History

Asking an applicant about arrest records or making a hiring decision based on an arrest record can be a subtle form of discrimination that violates state and federal antidiscrimination laws. Many people are arrested and the charges are later dropped or found to be without merit. Asking about arrests can be particularly harmful to black applicants because blacks are arrested disproportionately to their population size. Very rarely is there a legitimate business reason to reject an applicant simply because of an arrest record.

Convictions are another matter. While it can be unlawful discrimination to automatically exclude every applicant who's ever been convicted of a crime, antidiscrimination laws generally do allow you to inquire about an applicant's conviction record and to reject an applicant because of a conviction that's job related. If you're hiring a delivery truck driver, for example, it wouldn't violate the antidiscrimination laws to reject an applicant based on a conviction for drunk driving.

State laws may specifically prohibit you from asking about arrest records—and may go even farther in restricting your inquiries into an applicant's criminal history. (See "State Laws on Employee Arrest and Conviction Records," in the appendix.) In many states, for example, you can't ask an applicant about juvenile records. In some states, you can't ask about convictions for minor offenses or misdemeanors that go back more than five years if the applicant has had a clean slate since that time.

Using the Internet to Learn About Job Applicants

The Internet can be a rich source of information about someone applying for a job, especially the information an applicant may post on social networking sites, such as Facebook, MySpace or LinkedIn. The applicant posted this information online for all to see, so you're not invading the applicant's privacy by looking at it.

But there is a potential risk: You may come upon information that you couldn't lawfully request on an application form or during a job interview—and that you can't legally consider in making job decisions. You might, for example, learn an applicant's age, religion, sexual orientation, or marital status. In some cases, you might discover that an applicant is a smoker or drinks alcohol, activities that are legal, even though some employers may not approve of them. (Employers can ban smoking in the workplace, however, and require that employees be sober while at work.)

If your business is big enough, you can arrange for a manager to review and filter the online information for others who make the hiring decisions. The person responsible for filtering would send only legally appropriate information to the decision maker, and would not play any role in hiring decisions. This type of separation of duties can help you head off potential problems from a rejected applicant who believes that you violated legal guidelines.

No matter how large or small your business, you should tell potential employees on your application form that you will be searching the Internet—including social networking sites—as part of your pre-hiring investigation.

Be aware, however, that in some states you may be required to conduct a criminal records check if a prospective employee will be dealing with vulnerable people, such as children or elderly adults (for example, if the job involves child care or home health care). If you're working in such an occupation or a similar one, check with your local police department, state attorney general's office, or state labor department to see if a criminal records check is required.

> CAUTION
>
> **Expunging the past.** Many states have laws that allow individuals to expunge, or seal, their criminal records. When a record is expunged, it is usually not available to anyone other than criminal justice agencies and the courts. If a criminal record has been expunged, an applicant is generally allowed to act as if the conviction never happened—in other words, the applicant is legally permitted to deny having a criminal record.

Driving Records

When a job requires the employee to drive, it's wise to check an applicant's driving record. You usually can obtain driving records for a modest cost from the state authority that issues drivers' licenses. You'll need the applicant's driver's license number.

Remember that if you hire a consumer reporting agency to gather this information, you must comply with the Fair Credit Reporting Act, which requires you to get the applicant's written consent. Some states may also require this consent.

Making a Job Offer

Be careful what you say orally and in writing when you make a job offer to any applicant. The positive statements you make to an applicant about long-term opportunities can come back to haunt you if you later fire the person. A judge or jury reviewing the firing may conclude that your glowing statements were actually a promise—a promise, perhaps, that the applicant's job would be secure for years or that you wouldn't fire the applicant without good cause.

To protect yourself from such misunderstandings, you can write an employment letter that includes the following key elements:

- title of the position that you're offering
- date the job begins
- starting salary
- reference to the employee handbook (if you have one)
- job benefits
- disclaimer of oral commitments
- reminder of at-will status, and
- a statement explaining (and limiting) how the at-will relationship can be altered in the future—usually, only by the signed consent of an important company official, like the president.

An example of an employment letter is shown below. Have the employee sign a copy of your letter at the bottom, as suggested in the

Sample Offer Letter

June 10, 20xx

Dear Joe Nolo,

I am pleased to offer you a full-time position with our company as a tester beginning June 25. Your starting salary will be $1,000 per week.

When you applied, I gave you a copy of our employee handbook. The handbook sets out our current employment policies and describes your job benefits, including medical coverage, paid vacation, and sick leave. It also describes your responsibilities to the company. Each time the handbook is updated, you'll receive a revised copy.

The company's commitments to you and its other employees are stated in the handbook. The company has made no oral commitments to you. No one at the company is authorized to make oral commitments regarding employment—either now or in the future.

While I hope that everything works out here, you are an at-will employee. You have the right to terminate your employment at any time, for any reason, and so does the company. No representative of the company, other than the president, has authority to change the terms of the at-will relationship and any such change can occur only in a written employment contract.

If this offer of employment is acceptable to you, please sign a copy of this letter and return it to me within ten days. I look forward to having you join our staff.

Sincerely,

Bob Bossman
Supervisor

I accept your offer of employment and acknowledge receiving a copy of your current employee handbook. I understand that my employment is at will and that either you or I can terminate my employment at any time, for any reason or for no reason. No representative of the company has made any oral commitments concerning my employment.

Signature _____*Joe Nolo*_____

Date___*June 10, 20xx*_____

Agreeing to Job Security

Most of the time, a prospective employee won't object to an at-will relationship. Occasionally, however, the best person for the job will insist on some job security. This often happens when the prospective employee is a hot commodity—like an experienced executive—or when the person will have to leave a very secure job or move from far away to take the position.

> **EXAMPLE:** Ron owns a successful wholesale business that buys, processes, and packages organic grain. When his longtime marketing manager retires, Ron advertises throughout a five-state region to find a replacement. After screening a dozen applicants, Ron decides that Natalie, who is doing similar work for another company, is easily the best candidate. The only hitch is that Natalie currently lives about 500 miles from Ron's business, and is concerned about relocating. To come and work for Ron, she'd need to sell her house and buy a new one. Her two high school kids would have to transfer, leaving behind their best friends. Her husband— an accountant—would need to find a new job. All this would be very disruptive. What if Natalie went to work for Ron and, at the end of two months, was fired? She candidly tells Ron about her worries. Ron wants to allay Natalie's fears.

He knows it's very unlikely that he'd fire her without good cause. After thinking it over, he agrees that if he fires Natalie without cause before she completes three years of work, she'll be entitled to a severance package that includes six months of her salary. This satisfies Natalie. Ron and Natalie shake hands on their deal—and then wisely put their agreement in writing.

If you're looking to hire a candidate who seems to have a legitimate need for reasonable job security, you may be willing to work out a similar agreement. Once you do, you can put these terms in your employment letter or in a more formal legal contract. Either way, you'll need to spell out what will constitute sufficient cause for you to fire the employee. Then you'll need to define what happens if you fire the employee *without* cause. Typically, this will involve your business making a significant payment to the employee to ease the pain of moving to a new job. Put another way, you'll be free to fire the employee without cause, but you'll have to pay a price.

It makes sense to have a lawyer help you craft the right wording to capture your agreement—or at least to have a lawyer review it before everyone signs it. You don't want to risk a lawsuit resulting from ambiguous language.

example. Then put that copy in the employee's file. (See Chapter 2 for more about what you should keep in an employee's personnel file.) That way, you'll have clear proof that the employee received the letter and accepted its terms.

Sample Rejection Letter

June 25, 20xx

Dear Larry Leeds,

Thank you for meeting with me last Thursday to discuss the programmer position with our company. You were among many fine people who applied. I wanted to let you know that we selected another applicant for the position.

It was a pleasure meeting you and I wish you well in your job search.

Sincerely,

Bob Bossman
Supervisor

Rejecting Applicants

It's courteous to let unsuccessful applicants know that you've hired someone else for the job. You don't, however, owe them an explanation about why they weren't hired. Keep the letter simple and upbeat. If pressed, simply tell them that the person you hired is, in your judgment, better suited to the job.

There's no ideal way to give someone the news that you've offered the job to another person. The least painful way—which also presents the fewest legal difficulties—is to send a short letter informing the rejected applicant of your decision. Send the letter as soon as you've decided whom you're going to hire or when you've narrowed the field down to a few candidates. Quickly sending your rejection letter will limit the number of postinterview calls you get from unsuccessful applicants—calls that are uncomfortable for everyone.

Some federal and state laws require you to keep a copy of employment applications for at least one year. It's a good idea to keep your rejection letters, along with the applications and other information you gathered during the screening process, for at least that long. Lawsuits by rejected applicants are rare, but you can't predict in advance which ones might take that step, and you want to have good records showing you acted fairly and legally.

Tax Compliance

Before you hire any employees, you must get an Employer Identification Number (EIN) from the IRS—unless you're a sole proprietor, in which case you can use your own Social Security number. To obtain an EIN, file Form SS-4, *Application for Employer Identification Number.* Some states have similar requirements. (See Chapter 5 for further information.)

Have new employees complete Form W-4, the *Employee's Withholding Allowance Certificate.* This lets you know how many dependents or withholding allowances the employee is claiming and the employee's filing status: single, married, or married but withholding at the higher single rate. Keep the signed form on file. If an employee doesn't complete a Form W-4, you won't know how much income tax to withhold. In that case, you must withhold tax as if the employee were a single person claiming no withholding allowances.

You needn't send the signed Form W-4 to the IRS unless either of the following is true:

- An employee claims more than ten allowances.
- The employee earns more than $200 per week and claims exemption from withholding.

You can find detailed information on your tax obligations as an employer in Chapter 5.

RESOURCE

The IRS has several free publications that may be useful in helping establish tax procedures for your business. One is IRS Circular E, *Employers Tax Guide*, containing withholding tables; it's updated periodically and is mailed automatically to every business that has an Employer Identification Number. Another is IRS Publication 334, *Tax Guide for Small Business*, which covers a wide range of tax issues. You can obtain these and other IRS publications through the agency's website at www.irs.gov.

Immigration Law Requirements

Immigration laws, enforced by the Bureau of U.S. Citizenship and Immigration

Services (USCIS), prohibit employers from hiring aliens who don't have government authorization to work in the United States. There are specific procedures you must follow to make sure prospective employees meet these requirements.

You and the new employee must complete Form I-9, *Employment Eligibility Verification*. This one-page form is intended to ensure that the employee can legally work in the United States and has proof of his or her identity.

RESOURCE

For more information, refer to the USCIS website at www.uscis.gov. On the left-hand side of the screen under "More Information," click on "For Employers."

The employee completes Section 1 of the form, attesting that he or she is a citizen or national of the United States, a lawful permanent resident alien, or an alien with work authorization. Only people in these three categories can lawfully work in the United States.

Section 2 of the form requires you to review documents—such as a passport or naturalization certificate—presented by the employee as proof of the employee's identity and employment eligibility. You must complete Section 2 within three days of the employee's start date. However, it's a good idea to get this completed right away, to clear up any eligibility problems or complications before the employee starts working. Always make sure you have the most recent version of Form I-9.

It will contain an up-to-date list of documents that an employee can use to prove eligibility. You can view and download the latest form at www.uscis.gov/files/form/i-9.pdf.

You must indicate on Form I-9 which documents you've examined. It's your responsibility to decide whether the employee's documents appear valid. The USCIS advises that you must accept documents that reasonably appear to be genuine and to relate to the person presenting them. To do otherwise could be an unfair immigration-related employment practice and therefore illegal.

You should keep photocopies of the employee's documents to prove that you reviewed these papers in case the USCIS questions your hiring practices in the future. It is okay to generate or store these copies electronically (for example, as pdf documents), but you must examine the employee's documents personally. Also, hang on to all Form I-9's for at least three years. If the employee stays with your company longer than that, keep the form for at least one year after the employee leaves. USCIS has the right to see your I-9s. You can be fined if you can't produce them.

> **CAUTION**
>
> **Are you a federal contractor or subcontractor?** If so, you must participate in a federal program called E-Verify. The program allows employers to use an Web-based system to verify an employee's eligibility to work in the United States. If you're not a federal contractor or subcontractor, participation is voluntary. For details, visit www.uscis.gov/e-verify. Arizona has a statute that requires all employers to use the E-Verify system; the U.S. Supreme Court is scheduled to decide in 2011 whether that statute is valid.

New Hire Reporting Form

Federal law requires you to report certain identifying information about new and rehired employees to a designated state agency. Under federal law, you have 20 days to provide this information, but some states require you to do it more quickly. The information becomes part of the National Directory of New Hires. It's used primarily to locate parents so that child support orders can be enforced. Government agencies also use the data to prevent improper payment of workers' compensation, unemployment benefits, or public assistance benefits.

Each state has its own form, but all require the following basic information:

- employee's name, address, Social Security number, and date of hire, and
- employer's name, address, and federal Employer Identification Number.

Some states ask for additional information, such as your state unemployment compensation number, the employee's driver's license number, and the employee's date of birth, though providing this information may be optional.

Your state department of labor can tell you how to get the forms and where to send them. (See the appendix for contact information.)

Paperwork Checklist

Here's a list of documents and forms that you should consider each time you hire someone:

- **Employment letter.** You can find an example of such a letter in "Making a Job Offer," above.
- **Employee handbook.** If you have a handbook and didn't give it to the employee during the application and interview stages, now is the time to do so. Get a written acknowledgment of receipt and keep it in the employee's file. (For more on employee handbooks, see Chapter 2.)
- **Covenant not to compete.** If legally permissible in your state, this is useful if you have employees who could harm your business if they left to work for a competitor or started a business of their own in competition with yours. (For more information, see "Protecting Against Unfair Competition," above.)
- **Confidentiality agreement.** Use such an agreement if you'll be disclosing trade secrets and other proprietary information to an employee.

- **Form I-9.** This form, required by the U.S. Bureau of Citizenship and Immigration Services, is intended to ensure that all of your employees are legally permitted to work in the United States. (See "Immigration Law Requirements," above.)
- **IRS Form W-4.** Each employee must complete this form so you can determine how much to withhold from every paycheck for taxes. (See "Tax Compliance," above, and Chapter 5 for details.)
- **New hire reporting form.** Within a short time after you hire someone—20 days or less, depending on your state's rules— you must file this form with a designated state agency.
- **Employee benefit sign-up.** If your business offers employee benefit programs such as health insurance or a 401(k) plan, you may have a sign-up procedure so employees can name their dependents and select options.
- **IRS Form SS-4** (new employers only). The IRS requires an Employer Identification Number for all employers except sole proprietorships. (See Chapter 5.)

Personnel Practices

You can avoid most legal problems in the workplace if you respect employees and treat them well. But no matter how caring you are, there will still be misunderstandings you'll be called upon to handle. Fortunately, the vast majority of job disputes can be resolved if you listen patiently to what employees have to say and are prepared to make adjustments when legitimate complaints surface.

However, even though you treat workers fairly, there's always a chance that a dispute will get out of hand and an employee will sue your business for some perceived abuse of his or her rights. Or an unhappy employee may file a complaint with a government agency, alleging that you violated a statute or an administrative regulation. If that happens, you'll have to prove to a judge, jury, arbitrator, or investigator that you met your legal obligations to the employee. That can be harder than you think. Key paperwork may have been lost—or never prepared in the first place. And witnesses may have forgotten what happened or have moved on to new jobs, where you might have trouble finding them.

To maintain a solid legal footing, you need a good paper trail. First, you need a good history of an employee's tenure with the company, which you can establish by keeping organized files. Second, you need written policies that establish the company's expectations and communicate those to your employees. Written policies can nip misunderstandings in the bud before they turn into pitched legal battles. They provide a cogent point of reference when you discuss problems with an employee, increasing the likelihood of reaching an amicable resolution. And in the worst-case scenario, these policies can help you defend yourself in a legal proceeding, showing that you treated employees consistently and fairly.

> **CAUTION**
>
> **Actions speak loudly, too.** You must start with sensible and fair policies and apply them with an even hand to all employees. A carefully developed paper trail is important, but if you've violated an employee's rights, the mere fact that you've created good paperwork won't shield you from the legal consequences.

Employee Files

Create a file for each employee, in which you keep important job-related information, including:

- job description
- job application
- offer of employment
- IRS Form W-4
- receipt for employee handbook
- periodic performance evaluations
- sign-up forms for employee benefits
- complaints from customers and coworkers
- compliments from customers and coworkers

- awards or citations for excellent performance
- warnings and disciplinary actions, and
- notes on an employee's attendance or tardiness.

Employee files can be a two-edged sword. They provide valuable documentation to support a firing, demotion, or other action that's adverse to the employee—but the employee, in turn, can point to indiscreet entries and use them against you. It would be a mistake, for example, to include unsubstantiated criticism of an employee in the file or comments about the employee that are unrelated to job performance and qualifications.

Correcting Mistakes

To err is human, but leaving an error uncorrected can turn a mistake into a problem. Knowingly keeping false information on hand increases the risk of a lawsuit for defamation. It can lead people to conclude that you're callous, unfair, or incompetent. An employee is less likely to try to resolve problems with you informally if he or she doesn't see any positive changes as a result, and a judge or jury may likewise have a poor impression of you.

EXAMPLE: Joe doesn't show up for work for a week after his paid vacation has ended. You put a note in his file documenting this. Then you learn that on the last day of his vacation he was in a serious car accident and wound up in

intensive care. Put these additional facts in Joe's file. If you don't, Joe will have good reason to be angry with you, and other people who later look at the file won't put much stock in anything else they find there.

Confidentiality

Keep employee files locked up. Make them available only to people in your company who have a legitimate business need to have access to the files—managers, for example, who must make decisions about promotions and discipline. Inform company personnel that the information in the files must remain confidential. While an employee or former employee may have a legal right to see his or her file (see "Access by Employees," below), other people don't, absent a subpoena.

It's a good idea to maintain separate confidential files for each employee's Form I-9, *Employment Eligibility Verification,* as well as the photocopies of the documents the employee gives you to comply with the form's requirements. By doing so, you reduce the chances that a supervisor will make an employment decision based on an employee's immigration status—a prohibited practice. Moreover, government agencies are allowed to inspect all your I-9 forms when they visit the workplace, and keeping the forms in a separate file protects your employees' privacy as to the rest of their personal documents.

CAUTION

Protect employees' Social Security numbers. As an employer, you'll be learning the Social Security number of each employee through a variety of sources such as Form W-4, Form I-9, the new hire reporting form, and employee benefit sign-up forms. (See the Paperwork Checklist at the end of Chapter 1.) It's well known that unscrupulous people use Social Security numbers for identity theft and other scams. To combat such misuse, you should have a privacy policy that protects the confidentiality of employees' Social Security numbers and limits who has access to those numbers. Also, don't put them on badges, parking permits, or lists that you distribute to employees. And check state law—some states, such as California, make the protection of Social Security numbers a legal requirement.

Medical Information

Special guidelines apply to medical information gathered in the workplace. The federal Americans with Disabilities Act (ADA) imposes very strict rules on how you must handle information obtained from postoffer medical examinations and inquiries, and the Family and Medical Leave Act (FMLA) and Genetic Information Nondiscrimination Act (GINA) impose the same restrictions on records relating to medical leave and genetic information. You must keep the information in medical files separate from nonmedical records, and you must store the medical files in a separate locked cabinet. To further guarantee the confidentiality of medical files, designate a specific person to have access to those files.

These laws allow very limited disclosure of medical information. Under the ADA and FMLA, for example, you may:

- inform supervisors about necessary restrictions on an employee's duties and about necessary accommodations
- inform first aid and safety workers about a disability that may require emergency treatment and about specific procedures that are needed if the workplace must be evacuated, and
- provide medical information required by government officials and by insurance companies that require a medical exam for health or life insurance.

Under GINA, there are very few circumstances in which you may disclose genetic information about an employee. If you receive a court order specifically requesting the information or your company is under investigation for GINA compliance, for example, you may disclose this information to the appropriate person. (To find out more about disclosing genetic information under GINA, go to the EEOC's website, www.eeoc. gov, and select "Genetic Information" under the "Employers" tab. Otherwise, don't disclose medical information about employees. The best policy is to treat all medical information about all employees as confidential. (For more on the ADA, see Chapter 9, and for more on the FMLA, see Chapter 6.)

Access by Employees

Many states have laws requiring employers to give employees—and former employees—access to their own personnel files. How much access varies from state to state. Typically, if your state allows employees to see their files, you can insist that you or another supervisor be present to make sure nothing is taken, added, or changed. Some state laws allow employees to obtain copies of items in their files, but not necessarily all items. A state law, for example, may limit the employee to copies of documents that the employee has signed, such as a job application. If an employee is entitled to a copy of an item in the file or if you're inclined to let the employee have a copy of any document in the file, you—rather than the employee—should make the copy.

Usually, you won't have to let the employee see sensitive items such as information assembled for a criminal investigation, reference letters, and information that might violate the privacy of other people. In a few states, employees may insert rebuttals if they disagree with information in their personnel files. And some states require employees to request to see their files in writing before employers have to grant access.

For state-by-state rules on this issue, see "State Laws on Employee Access to Personnel Records," in the appendix.

Informing Employees

Generally, the law doesn't require you to voluntarily tell employees what's in their employee files. You need only disclose information when an employee makes an appropriate request under an employee access law. About the only exception is the federal Fair Credit Reporting Act or FCRA (15 U.S.C. §§ 1681 and following), which requires you to tell employees if you're taking adverse action against them because of information in a consumer credit report. (See Chapter 1 for more information about your responsibilities under the FCRA.)

Still, it may be good practice to keep employees informed about what's going into their files. Otherwise, borderline employees may think they're doing fine and be justifiably surprised by a disciplinary action or firing. Admittedly, some employees can get demoralized if they're overwhelmed with negative information about their work, so some discretion is necessary in giving them feedback. But, basically, letting employees know where they stand prevents surprises and can lead to improved performance. And if the employee doesn't shape up and winds up being fired, anyone reviewing the facts—a judge or jury, for example—will be more likely to side with you if you've given the employee fair warning about what was wrong.

RESOURCE

Information on progressive discipline. For more information about employee discipline, including how and where to document it, see *The Progressive Discipline Handbook: Smart Strategies for Coaching Employees*, by Margie Mader-Clark and Lisa Guerin (Nolo).

Employee Handbooks

If you have more than one or two employees, consider creating an employee handbook that clearly explains your employment policies.

Advantages

An employee handbook can be of practical help in running your business. Once you give it to an employee, there can be no dispute over whether you gave the employee a list of paid days off or explained your vacation policies for new workers. It's all there in writing, and everyone is getting the same information.

Beyond the practicalities, a good handbook gives you a bonus: a measure of legal protection if you're challenged by an employee in a court or administrative proceeding. A handbook that contains clear, reasonable policies—such as one stating that sexual harassment won't be tolerated in the workplace—is the critical beginning of your paper trail if problems develop later. It's an objective piece of evidence that shows you've adopted fair and uniform policies and that you've informed your employees of where they stand.

A good handbook should tell your employees how to let you know if they feel unfairly treated or have a workplace problem. This gives you a chance to react before a small misunderstanding erupts into a full-blown legal dispute. As another benefit, a well-written handbook may reduce the anxiety that some employees feel about their jobs. Employees will know what the rules and procedures are and where they can turn if they need to discuss an issue.

Even a small business with only a handful of employees can benefit from an employee handbook. You can produce one quickly and cheaply with *Create Your Own Employee Handbook: A Legal & Practical Guide*, by Lisa Guerin and Amy DelPo (Nolo). The cut-and-paste policies in the accompanying CD-ROM make the task a breeze. If you have specific legal questions, a brief consultation with a lawyer should be sufficient to clear them up.

If yours is a very small business, keep your handbook short and sweet at the start. Then, as your business grows, the framework necessary for a more detailed version will be in place. Review your handbook and update it periodically to reflect any changes in the law or your policies.

Don't Increase Your Legal Exposure

Your handbook may be treated as a contract that can actually limit your right to fire employees. To avoid that result, state in the handbook that:

- Employees do not have employment contracts unless they are in writing and signed by the company president.
- Your company reserves the right to terminate employees for reasons not stated in the handbook or for no reason at all.

Contents

Here are topics to consider covering in an employee handbook.

Introduction. Begin the handbook by describing your company's history and business philosophy. This helps set the tone, which can be friendly and welcoming. Make it clear to employees from the start that the handbook doesn't cover every possible situation.

Hours. State the normal working hours and how overtime pay is authorized for those employees entitled to it. (See Chapter 3 for more about wages and hours.)

Pay and salaries. Be clear about how pay and salaries are set and how they're raised. In very small businesses, this may be little more than a statement that levels of pay are established and adjusted by the company president taking into consideration past performance, cost of living changes, and the ability of the business to pay. But if you do adopt a more formal procedure based on periodic performance reviews, explain how it works—and whether employees may be eligible for bonuses as well as salary increases.

Benefits. Benefits can be nearly as important as salary. Many larger businesses will have a separate publication covering this topic, but most savvy smaller businesses opt to cover it in their employee handbooks. Employee benefits typically include paid vacations, health benefits, sick pay, and unpaid leaves for extended illness, pregnancy, or family matters. (See Chapter 6 for information on family and medical leave.)

Because federal law doesn't require you to provide paid sick days or vacation days, you're free to set the terms under which such benefits are granted (provided no state laws or local ordinances require otherwise). An employee handbook is the ideal place to inform employees about the rules governing these benefits. Be clear on whether the employee can carry unused sick or vacation days into the next year and what happens to such benefits if an employee quits or gets fired. Some states require employers to compensate employees for unused paid time when they leave; others don't. Check with your state labor department to learn the rule in your state—and any others relating to vacation or sick leave. (See the appendix for contact information.)

Finally, describe any 401(k) or retirement benefits you offer. (See Chapter 4 for an extensive discussion of employee benefits.)

Grooming and Clothing Rules

If you have a reasonable business purpose for doing so, you can establish on-the-job standards for clothing and grooming as a condition of employment. There's nothing inherently illegal, for example, about requiring all employees to wear navy blue slacks during working hours.

Rules governing employees' appearance may be illegal, however, if they discriminate against a particular group of employees or potential employees. Generally speaking, you should stay away from imposing different rules on male and female employees. For example, if you have a retail store, you can't require female clerks to wear smocks while allowing male clerks to wear business attire. Courts occasionally, however, allow some latitude in imposing different rules on men and women. For example, one court ruled that a company could lawfully allow women employees to wear jewelry while prohibiting men from doing so. In another case, a casino imposed gender-specific grooming rules on its bartenders: female bartenders had to have their hair styled and wear stockings, colored nail polish, and makeup; by contrast, male bartenders had to maintain short haircuts, and couldn't wear makeup or colored nail polish. The court ruled that these requirements were legal.

Several black men have won lawsuits against companies that refused to hire men with beards or that fired men who didn't comply with no-beard rules. Many black men find that if they shave their facial hair too closely, it will cause their whiskers to become ingrown and infected. A policy of banning beards might illegally discriminate against black men.

For the sake of creating a uniform company-wide appearance, you may provide workers with some or all of the clothing that they are required to wear on the job. You may even rent suits for your employees to assure that they will be similarly dressed.

Although generally legal, such policies can violate an employee's rights if the cost of the clothing is deducted from the employee's pay in violation of the Fair Labor Standards Act (FLSA). For example, it's illegal under the FLSA to deduct the cost of work-related clothing from an employee's pay so that wages dip below the minimum wage standard. (For more on the FLSA, see Chapter 3.) And some states require employers to bear the costs of uniforms.

Drug and alcohol abuse. Most businesses have a policy prohibiting employees' use of alcohol or illegal drugs in the workplace. In addition, some businesses offer employees help in dealing with abuse of these substances—often through an employee assistance program in which the business pays for professional counseling. Spell out your policies.

Harassment. Remind employees that harassment is illegal and violates your policies. (See Chapter 8 for more on harassment.) Let them know that you won't tolerate unwelcome comments or conduct based on a protected category (such as sex or race) and that you'll assist those who speak up about it in ending any harassment in the workplace. Finally, spell out your procedures for handling sexual harassment complaints. Specify how and to whom an employee can submit a complaint. Specify what you will do to investigate any complaints that you receive. Assure employees that you will handle every complaint as confidentially as possible.

Discrimination. Employees need to know that your business obeys all laws that prohibit discrimination, including discrimination based on race, color, religion, gender, national origin, age, pregnancy, citizenship, disability, genetic information, or any other protected characteristic. State that you expect employees to conduct themselves in a nondiscriminatory manner. (See Chapter 8 for more on illegal discrimination.)

Attendance. Emphasize the importance of good attendance and showing up on time.

Tell employees the types of absences that are excused—such as illness or a family member's death—and explain any requirements for notifying you if the employee won't be coming in or will be late. Also, if you believe it's likely to be a problem, clearly explain that piling up a load of unexcused absences or coming to work late too often can be a basis for disciplinary action or even firing.

Discipline. List the kinds of conduct that can get employees in trouble—for example, theft or violence. But again, let employees know this isn't an exclusive list and that you always reserve the right to impose harsher discipline, or even terminate employment. (See "Disciplining Employees," below, for more information.)

Social media. Inform employees that they are not to use social media to disparage coworkers, customers, or vendors, or the services or products that your business offers. Also, to comply with Federal Trade Commission rules, they must disclose that they are employees of your company if they use social media to promote one of your services or products.

Electronic usage. If you provide computers, cell phones, PDAs, email accounts, or other electronic means of communication to employees, advise them not to expect privacy when using these company-issued devices or services. Clearly reserve the right to monitor employee usage. (See Chapter 11 for information on employee privacy.)

Employee safety. State that employee safety is a major concern and that employees are expected to heed the posted safety rules and to call to your attention any potentially dangerous conditions. (See Chapter 7 for more about health and safety.)

Smoking. Many states or cities prohibit or restrict workplace smoking. If such regulations exist where your business operates, make sure that your smoking policy follows them. You may have to ensure that smoking areas are segregated entirely from nonsmoking areas or that outdoor smoking areas are not next to building entrances or exits. (See Chapter 7 for more information about smoking in the workplace.)

Complaints. Let employees know what procedures they can follow to resolve complaints. Having a written complaint procedure in your handbook helps shield your business from liability if an employee sues claiming illegal harassment or discrimination.

Workplace civility. State specifically that employees at all levels of the business are expected to treat each other with respect and that the success of the business depends on cooperation and teamwork among all employees.

Documenting an Employee's Acceptance

Document that employees received the handbook by having each employee sign an acknowledgment form. This form reinforces that the handbook isn't an employment contract, doesn't guarantee continued employment, and doesn't obligate your company to continue current job benefits forever.

Include with your handbook two copies of a statement such as the one below. Then ask employees to sign both copies to acknowledge that they have received the handbook and are familiar with its terms. Keep one signed copy of the employee handbook acknowledgment in the employee's personnel file maintained by your business. The employee can keep the other copy. Have each employee sign a similar receipt each time you distribute revisions or updates of your handbook.

Employee Performance Reviews

Most large companies review and evaluate their employees periodically. This is a sound management practice and one that even small companies should consider—especially for new employees.

Benefits of Evaluations

Evaluating employees periodically gives them a chance to improve if they're not performing well. If you later find it necessary to discipline or fire an employee, it won't come as a surprise to the employee.

By putting your evaluations in writing and saving them in the employee's file, you have a credible history of documented problems you can use if an employee claims the termination was for an illegal reason. Legally, you don't have to have a good reason, or any reason, to fire an at-will employee, and you don't have to give notice in advance or afford the employee a chance to improve. However, an

Sample Employee Handbook Acknowledgment

Welcome to XYZ Company. We hope that you will have a long and productive relationship with our company. To help with this, we are providing you with your own copy of our employee handbook. Please read this handbook carefully. The information in it will acquaint you with company policies and will answer many of your questions. From time to time, these policies may be updated in writing. Copies of these updates will be provided to you.

Please keep in mind that this handbook does not contain all of the information you will need as an employee. You will receive other information through written notices as well as orally.

This handbook is not an employment contract. Unless you have a written employment contract with XYZ Company signed by the president of the company, you are an at-will employee. This means you or the company may terminate our employment relationship at any time, with or without a reason.

In the future, your status as an at-will employee can only be changed through a written contract signed by both you and the president of XYZ Company. No oral statements, promises, or contracts regarding the terms and conditions of your employment are valid.

Receipt and Acknowledgment

I have received a copy of XYZ Company's employee handbook. I have read the above information and I acknowledge that it is a correct statement of my employment status. I understand that this employee handbook is not a contract for employment and does not affect my employment status in any way.

Signature _____

Date _____

employee who is fired may claim that the firing was illegal, for example, because it was based on a prohibited characteristic, such as race or gender. You want to stand ready to rebut any possible claim that you fired an employee for an illegal reason. The best way to do this is to record, in written evaluations and other documents, the good reasons you relied on to fire the employee.

EXAMPLE: Charlotte works at the counter of Parts Plus, an auto parts retailer. Parts Plus fires Charlotte after she's been there for 18 months. She sues, claiming that Parts Plus fired her in retaliation for complaining to a state agency a month before about photos of nude women that were posted in the back room where she had to go to retrieve auto parts for customers. At trial, Parts Plus produces copies of written evaluations from Charlotte's file.

Eight months before the firing, Charlotte's supervisor had written: "You must become more familiar with our inventory of parts for imported cars. Also, you need to make fewer errors on the computer system."

Two months before the firing, the supervisor had written: "You're still having problems with imports. We will arrange for you to attend a computer training seminar at the community college at company expense, but you must improve your performance."

Company records separately show that Charlotte attended only one of the six training sessions and that, two days before the firing, she mixed up orders for three good customers. The upshot: Because of the company's thorough documentation of Charlotte's ongoing problems, the judge dismisses Charlotte's case against Parts Plus.

Evaluations have two common purposes—to help employees improve performance and to protect employers from false claims by former employees. To achieve both ends, thoroughly and objectively evaluate each employee at least twice a year. Take the evaluation process seriously, and do a careful, conscientious job. In some states, employees have successfully sued employers who used poor evaluation procedures for "negligent evaluation"—failing to review employees' work fully and honestly and to warn employees that they faced discipline or discharge if they failed to improve.

The Evaluation Process

To keep the evaluation process as consistent and objective as possible, devise an evaluation form that you can use with all employees in the same job category. (See below for a sample.) The form should focus on how well the employee has performed the various duties of the job.

Fill in the form before you meet with the employee, following these guidelines:

- Give a balanced picture of the employee's strengths and weaknesses.
- Use specific examples of where the employee has met, exceeded, or fallen short of expectations.
- Let the employee know the areas that need improvement. Set objective goals for the employee to meet.
- Where an employee's performance is substantially below par, set a date to meet again with the employee to review progress.
- If the employee's failure to improve may lead to disciplinary measures or discharge, state this clearly in the evaluation.

Leave space on the form for the employee to comment on the evaluation and to acknowledge receiving a copy of it.

Once you've completed the written evaluation, meet with the employee to go over it. If you cringe at confronting an employee with criticism, try the sandwich approach: say something positive, something negative, then something positive. Remember, too, that employees will find it easier to accept criticism—and try to improve behavior—if you focus on workplace performance and not on the employee's personality.

Whatever your approach, you must tell it like it is. Should you later have legal trouble initiated by a fired employee, a judge or jury won't look at your evaluations in a vacuum. For example, they'll sense that something is wrong if you consistently rate a worker's performance as poor or mediocre but continue to hand out generous raises or perhaps even promote the person. The logical conclusion: You didn't take seriously the criticisms in your evaluation report, so you shouldn't expect the employee to take them seriously, either.

It's just as damaging to give an employee glowing praise in report after report—perhaps to make the employee feel good—and then to fire the employee for a single infraction. That strikes most people as unfair. And unfair employers often lose court fights, especially in situations where a sympathetic employee appears to have been treated harshly.

If your system is working, employees with excellent evaluations should not need to be fired for poor performance. And employees with poor performance shouldn't be getting big raises.

 TIP

Once is not enough. Feedback should be an ongoing process. The written evaluation should be a culmination of the feedback you've given throughout the year. Your goal is to have no surprises about how an employee is doing. You should keep the employee informed of any problems and take steps to correct them through progressive discipline, discussed in the next section.

Some employers encourage employees to give their own evaluation of how they're doing—and may also ask employees to rate their supervisors. You'll benefit by making the evaluation process a two-way street. Listen carefully to what the employees say. You'll likely learn a thing or two.

RESOURCE

Want more information on perfor-mance appraisal? For an in-depth discussion of employee evaluations, including step-by-step instructions and sample forms, see *The Performance Appraisal Handbook: Legal &*

Practical Rules for Managers, by Amy DelPo (Nolo).

Sample Employee Evaluation Form

The form shown below can be adapted to meet your personal style, the setup of your workplace, and the type of work that employees perform for your business.

CONFIDENTIAL
Employee Performance Evaluation

Employee name _____

Job title _____

Reviewer _____

Review date _____

JOB PERFORMANCE
(In responding, give specific examples of strengths and weaknesses as often as possible.)

General Quality of Work
(Focus on accuracy, attention to detail, originality, timeliness, organization, degree of supervision needed to accomplish tasks.)

_____

_____

Dependability
(Focus on attendance, punctuality, attentiveness, ability to follow instructions, ability to meet deadlines.)

_____

_____

Job Knowledge
(Focus on level of knowledge and skills required to master work required, willingness to take the initiative in tackling new tasks.)

_____

_____

Personality
(Focus on cooperativeness, decision-making skills, ability to work for and with others, ability to handle confrontations.)

_____

_____

Communication Skills

(Focus on ability to use language effectively, ability to express ideas clearly and grammatically, command of oral and written language, ability to explain concepts to others.)

_____

_____

Management Ability

(Focus on ability to identify problems, ability to creatively solve problems, ability to plan, assign, and schedule workload, ability to guide an individual or group to complete a task.)

_____

_____

Other Job Requirements

(Focus on specific needs of business or needs for individual improvement: public contact, self-development, quality control, ability to stay within cost guidelines.)

PERFORMANCE SUMMARY

What are the employee's outstanding and strongest points?

_____

_____

What are the employee's shortcomings and weaknesses?

_____

_____

Specific accomplishments and changes since last performance review.

_____

_____

GOALS FOR IMPROVEMENT

What can the employee do to be more effective or make needed improvements?

_____

_____

What additional training or equipment would be helpful?

_____

In what ways could the job be changed to make better use of the employee's skills and abilities?

_____

EMPLOYEE FEEDBACK

(To be completed by the employee.)

What are your most important accomplishments on the job over the past year?

_____

What are your weakest job performance areas or those most in need of improvement?

_____

What steps could you take to improve?

_____

What can management do to support your efforts to improve?

_____

What are your supervisor's strengths and weaknesses in managing your work?

_____

Other work concerns you would like to discuss.

_____

NEXT REVIEW

Date scheduled for next review _____

Particular areas targeted for improvement:

_____

_____

Employee Signature: _____

Date: _____

Supervisor's Signature: _____

Date: _____

Disciplining Employees

Periodic evaluations can work hand in hand with another management strategy—progressive discipline—to keep employees fairly informed of how they're doing and when their jobs are at risk.

Because losing a job can obviously be painful for an employee, some employers make it a practice to fire problem employees only after the workers have gone through a series of less drastic disciplinary moves. A system of progressive discipline may not be right for all businesses—particularly smaller ones. But if you do see fit to have such a policy in place, it can go a long way toward demonstrating your fairness if you eventually have to fire an employee and the employee sues you.

Among the steps you can build into your program are coaching or counseling, verbal warnings, written warnings, and, finally, dismissal. A fired employee's potential wrongful termination claim will be weakened if you can show that the employee knew about the problems that eventually led to dismissal but failed to shape up.

If you follow this approach and generally practice a policy of progressive discipline, make it clear to employees that you reserve the right to fire employees at will—especially for serious infractions—and that your policy of progressive discipline is left to your discretion as an employer. (See below for an example of language to include in a disciplinary policy.)

Having a policy of progressive discipline can backfire if you create the impression that every employee transgression will be dealt with in that same way. A fired employee, for example, may claim the right to progressive discipline before being fired.

Obviously, there are times when you may conclude that an employee's conduct is so offensive that decisive action—including immediate discharge—is warranted. To keep an enlightened management policy from turning into a fixed employee right, make it clear that you have the option to dispense with progressive discipline when you choose to do so. (See the sample policy, below, for guidance.)

 RESOURCE

Need more infromation on progressive discipline? For an in-depth discussion, including step-by-step instructions and a sample written policy, see *The Progressive Discipline Handbook: Smart Strategies for Coaching Employees,* by Margie Mader-Clark and Lisa Guerin (Nolo).

Sample Written Progressive Discipline Policy

The following is a sample written progressive discipline policy that you can include in your handbook.

Any employee conduct that, in the opinion of XYZ Company, interferes with or adversely affects our business is sufficient grounds for disciplinary action. This action can range from oral warnings to immediate discharge. Depending on the conduct, it is our general policy to take disciplinary steps in the following order:

- verbal warnings
- written warnings, and
- termination.

To decide on the appropriate action, we may consider the seriousness of your conduct, your employment record, your ability to correct the conduct, actions we have taken for similar conduct by other employees, how your action affects customers, and other circumstances.

Some conduct may result in immediate dismissal. Here are examples:

- acting violently or threatening to do so
- theft of company property
- excessive tardiness or absenteeism
- arguing or fighting with customers or coworkers
- using or possessing alcohol or illegal drugs at work
- coming to work under the influence of alcohol or illegal drugs
- failing to carry out reasonable job assignments
- making false statements in a job application
- violating company rules and regulations, and
- unlawful discrimination or harassment.

These are only examples. You may terminate your employment at any time; the company reserves the same right.

Wages and Hours

The main federal law affecting workers' pay is the Fair Labor Standards Act or FLSA. (29 U.S.C. §§ 201 and following.) This law sets out federal requirements for the minimum wage and overtime pay. It also prohibits wage differences based on gender, requires you to pay employees for the time that you control and that benefits you, and sets out the rules regarding the employment of workers younger than 18. This chapter covers the FLSA and your obligations under it.

Although the FLSA coverage is broad, there are a few instances in which it does not apply:

- If you operate a farm, your workers aren't entitled to full FLSA coverage. For more information, go to www.dol.gov/whd/regs/compliance/whdfs12.pdf
- If you run a transportation business (such as a trucking company) that's regulated by the federal Motor Carrier Act, there's an overtime pay exemption for workers whose activities affect the safe operation of vehicles—for example, certain drivers, drivers' helpers, loaders, and mechanics. For more information on this exemption, go to www.dol.gov/whd/regs/compliance/whdfs19.pdf

Most states also have a wage and hour law. Usually the state law follows the FLSA. A handful of states, however, have more stringent requirements. If you operate your business in one of these states, you must follow the stricter rule. For example, in most instances, California's wage and hour law is more stringent than the FLSA; California employers should therefore follow the California law where it's more stringent. To learn the minimum wage requirements in your state, go to www.dol.gov/whd/minwage/america.htm. For additional information on the wage and hour rules in your state, contact your state labor department. (See the appendix for contact details.)

Overtime and Minimum Wage Requirements

The FLSA requires you to pay certain employees at least $7.25 per hour and to pay time and a half for any hours more than 40 that those employees work in a week.

Those employees who are entitled to the minimum wage and overtime pay are called "nonexempt" employees, because they are not exempt from the requirements. Those who are not entitled to minimum wage or overtime are called "exempt" employees, because they are exempt from the requirements.

In this section, we first examine who is exempt and who isn't:

- **Employees who are always nonexempt:** These employees are always entitled to overtime pay and a minimum wage.
- **Employees who are always exempt:** These employees are never entitled to overtime pay or a minimum wage.
- **Employees who are exempt if they meet certain requirements:** The bulk of workers get classified under the rules described in this section.

Wage and Hour Laws Don't Cover Independent Contractors

Wage and hour laws cover employees, not independent contractors, so it is important to understand how state and federal laws define what an independent contractor is. Here, we explain the FLSA's definition. To find out about your state law's definition, contact your state labor department. (See the appendix for contact details.)

The FLSA considers workers to be independent contractors if they're economically independent from your business. How can you tell if they are economically independent? Consider the following questions:

- Do you have the right to control how the individual performs the work, as opposed to simply accepting or rejecting a final product? The more you control the way the work is done, the more the worker looks like an employee.
- Does the worker have an opportunity for profit and loss? If the worker bears the economic risk of doing business, then that's a factor in favor of independent contractor status.
- Does the worker have any investment in equipment and facilities? The greater the investment, the more it appears that the worker is an independent contractor.
- Do the worker's services require special skills? The more specialized the skills, the more likely it is that the worker is an independent contractor.
- How permanent is the relationship between you and the worker? A long-term relationship—especially one that lasts for a year or more—is a factor in favor of employee status.
- Are the worker's services an integral part of your business? If so, it's more likely that the worker is an employee. For example, someone who works for a drugstore as a pharmacist would probably be considered to be an integral part of the business.

Independent contractors are covered in more detail in Chapter 12. You can find even more information in *Working With Independent Contractors*, by Stephen Fishman (Nolo).

- **Employees who are exempt from overtime only:** These employees are still entitled to a minimum wage.

Once you've figured out which employees are exempt and which aren't, we'll cover your duty to pay nonexempt employees a minimum wage or overtime pay.

RESOURCE

Sometimes, an employee doesn't clearly fall into one of the nonexempt or exempt categories discussed below. If you're unable to tell whether an employee or group of employees is exempt, don't risk getting it wrong. It's better to pay an employment lawyer to figure it out for you than to risk paying fines, back pay, and litigation fees. (See "The Consequences of Bending the Rules," below, for information on what happens if you misclassify an employee.) Another option is to seek confidential guidance from the U.S. Department of Labor by calling 202-693-0051.

Employees Who Are Always Nonexempt

The law sets aside a group of employees who are always nonexempt and therefore always entitled to both overtime pay and a minimum wage, regardless of whether they otherwise seem to fall into one of the exempt categories described later in this section. These employees are blue-collar employees and first responders:

- Blue-collar employees are people who perform work involving repetitive operations with their hands, physical skill,

and energy. These employees include carpenters, electricians, mechanics, plumbers, ironworkers, craftsmen, operating engineers, longshore workers, construction workers, and laborers—a term that generally refers to minimally skilled workers such as those who dig trenches or carry lumber or bricks.

- First responders are workers on the front lines of protecting safety and health. As defined by the U.S. Department of Labor, most first responders are public employees—for example, police officers and firefighters. But some first responders may work in the private sector as well. These include emergency medical technicians, ambulance personnel, and hazardous materials workers.

If you have employees who are blue-collar workers or first responders, those employees are never exempt—no matter how lofty their title or how much they earn. They're always entitled to a minimum wage and overtime pay.

Employees Who Are Always Exempt

There are a handful of employees who the law says are always exempt and therefore never entitled to overtime or a minimum wage. They are:

- employees of seasonal amusement or recreational businesses, such as a ski resort that's open only during the winter or an amusement park that's open only during the summer

- employees of local newspapers having a circulation of less than 4,000
- newspaper delivery workers
- switchboard operators employed by phone companies that have no more than 750 stations, and
- some farmworkers.

So if you run a small newspaper, for example, or operate a concession stand at a summer amusement park, you don't need to worry about the overtime and minimum wage rules described in this chapter.

Employees Who Are Exempt If They Meet Certain Requirements

The FLSA identifies several categories of employees as being exempt if they meet certain requirements. Those categories are:

- white-collar employees (that is, executive, administrative, and professional employees)
- highly paid employees
- outside sales employees
- computer workers, and
- apprentices.

In the following subsections, we look at each group in more detail.

White-Collar Employees

You do not have to pay overtime or a minimum wage to exempt white-collar employees. To fall into this category, employees must meet all of the following requirements:

- **Minimum earnings:** They must earn at least $455 per week ($23,660 per year).

- **Salary basis:** They must receive their minimum earnings on a "salary basis." We explain this requirement, below.
- **Duties:** They must perform certain duties that involve executive, administrative, or professional skill. We describe these duties in more detail, below.

Although the first requirement is easy to understand, the second two take some explaining. Let's look at them more closely.

Salary basis. To pay someone on a salary basis means that you regularly pay that person a preset amount each pay period (such as weekly or biweekly) and that you don't reduce the amount because of variations in the quality or quantity of the employee's work. If you dock an employee's salary for these variations, the employee—and every other employee with that employee's rank and duties—may no longer be exempt. Accordingly, if a salaried employee misses a few hours of work to take care of personal business, you shouldn't reduce his or her salary to make up for that time. The reasoning behind the nonreduction rule is that salaried workers often put in many hours of overtime without getting paid extra for it, so it's unfair to reduce their pay if they miss a few hours now or then. Still, there are times when it's okay to dock a salaried employee's pay without jeopardizing his or her exempt status. To find out more, see "Docking Pay Can Cost You," below.

Duties. To be exempt, the white-collar employee must perform duties that are either executive, administrative, or professional in nature. Let's look at each of these in turn.

Docking Pay Can Cost You

For an employee to fall within the executive, administrative, or professional exemption, the basic rule is that you must pay that employee a full salary for any week in which the employee performs any work, regardless of how many days or hours the employee actually works. You don't, however, have to pay the employee for any workweek in which he or she performs no work. And while docking an employee's salary will generally make an employee (and all other employees with the same rank and duties) nonexempt, in the following situations, you can dock the employee without jeopardizing exempt status:

- when the employee is absent from work for one or more full days for personal reasons other than sickness or disability
- for absences of one or more full days due to sickness or disability if you make

the deduction under a plan providing for wage replacement benefits (such as a workers' compensation plan that pays workers for time missed due to a work-related injury)

- to offset amounts the employee receives as jury or witness fees, or for military pay
- for penalties imposed in good faith for infractions of safety rules of major significance, or
- for unpaid disciplinary suspensions of one or more full days imposed for infractions of workplace conduct rules.

Also, you don't have to pay the full salary in the first or final week of employment if the employee starts or finishes work midweek or for weeks in which an exempt employee takes unpaid leave under the Family and Medical Leave Act.

Executive Employees

Typically, executive employees are people you hire to run your business or one of its departments. They perform high-level management duties such as planning budgets and monitoring legal compliance. They have a lot of autonomy in doing their jobs, and they always have people working under them.

To fit within the executive employee exemption, the employee must:

- have the primary duty of managing a business or one of its departments

- regularly direct the work of at least two or more full-time employees (or their equivalent, such as one full-time employee and two half-time employees), and
- be authorized to hire or fire employees— or make recommendations for hiring, firing, and promotions that carry special weight.

Of these requirements, the first is the most vague. After all, what does it mean to "manage"? Fortunately, the U.S. Department of Labor has issued a list of activities that qualify as management duties. An employee who performs any one of these activities will probably meet the management test, but it's better if you can point to two or more:

- interviewing, selecting, and training employees
- deciding how much to pay employees and creating their work schedules
- directing employees' work
- maintaining production or sales records for use in supervision or control
- appraising employee productivity and efficiency for use in recommending promotions or other changes in status
- handling employee complaints and grievances
- disciplining employees
- planning the work
- determining the techniques to be used
- apportioning work among employees
- determining the type of materials, supplies, machinery, equipment, or tools to be used
- determining the merchandise to be bought, stocked, and sold
- controlling the flow and distribution of materials or merchandise and supplies
- providing for the safety and security of employees or business property
- planning and controlling the budget, or
- monitoring or implementing legal compliance measures.

Let's look at a couple of examples to see these rules at work.

- **This employee fits within the exemption:** Joe works for a mail-order company, where he manages the shipping department. He receives a salary of $650 a week. He directs the work of three employees, whom he can hire or fire. Joe is an exempt executive employee.
- **This employee does not fit within the exemption:** Jerry works for a mail-order company where he is called the "shipping department manager" and receives a salary of $575 a week. Jerry packages orders and gets them ready for UPS to pick up. He also directs the work of two junior employees who are assigned to him, but he doesn't get to hire or fire those coworkers, nor does he have any say about whether they'll be promoted or receive pay increases. Jerry is not an exempt executive employee, even though his title includes the word "manager."

Administrative Employees

You may have employees who don't supervise any other workers but play important roles in making your business operate efficiently and properly. If these employees make important business decisions and have a fair amount of authority, they may qualify as exempt administrative employees.

To be an exempt administrative employee under the FLSA, a worker must:

- primarily do office or nonmanual work directly related to managing a business or its general business operations, and

• exercise discretion and independent judgment on significant business matters.

These criteria are vague and subjective—and frustratingly difficult to apply. Unfortunately, the U.S. Department of Labor provides very little practical information to guide you in real-life situations. Still, it's possible to make some sense of these standards. Let's look at each one.

Employees Who Are Also Owners

An employee who owns at least a 20% equity interest in an employing entity (corporation, limited liability company, or partnership)—and is actively engaged in managing the entity—is an exempt executive employee, regardless of whether the employee is salaried or earns a particular amount.

For example, let's say Gina owns 20% of the stock of Pizza Heaven Inc., where she is employed as a pizza maker. Because Gina isn't engaged in managing the business, she isn't an exempt executive, even though she's a part owner of the business. Unless she qualifies under another exemption, she's entitled to a minimum wage and overtime pay.

Gerald, on the other hand, owns a 40% membership interest in Nuts and Bolts LLC and is employed by the company to manage its hardware store. Because Gerald owns more than 20% of the business and is actively engaged in managing it, he's an exempt executive and isn't entitled to overtime or the minimum wage protections.

Work directly related to managing a business or its general business operations. The work must be related to running or servicing a business rather than making things or serving customers. So an employee who works on a production line, sells products in a store, or serves food in a restaurant won't meet this test. By contrast, a worker who prepares budgets or procures supplies or handles advertising and public relations typically will.

EXAMPLE: This employee does not fit this prong of the test: Helen works as a barista at a café. Her work isn't directly related to managing the business, so she doesn't meet the first test for being an exempt administrative employee.

EXAMPLE: This employee does fit this prong of the test: Harold works as an accountant for a chain of coffee houses. Because his work is directly related to managing the business, he may be an exempt administrative employee—if he also meets the second test.

The U.S. Department of Labor says that work in the following areas is related to managing a business: tax; finance; accounting; budgeting; auditing; insurance; quality control; purchasing; procurement; advertising; human resources; employee benefits; marketing; research; safety and health; personnel management; labor relations; public relations; government relations; computer network, Internet, and database administration; legal and regulatory compliance.

Discretion and independent judgment on significant business matters. This is also rather murky territory. The standards are unusually subjective—especially the term "significant business matters." Here are some factors the U.S. Department of Labor looks at in applying this regulation:

- Can the employee formulate and interpret management policies?
- Does the employee carry out major assignments affecting business operations?
- Can the employee commit your business in matters that have significant financial impact?
- Can the employee waive your established policies without prior approval?
- Does the employee provide expert advice to management?
- Does the employee handle and resolve complaints or grievances?

Here are a couple of examples to illustrate how this administrative employee exemption plays out.

- **This employee fits within the exemption:** Irma is the estimator for an electrical contracting firm. She discusses proposed new jobs with customers. She then figures out how much her firm should charge and prepares a written quote. If the customer signs the quote, Irma's company is legally bound to perform the contract at the stated price. Irma also has authority to resolve any disputes with customers. She earns a salary of $1,000 per week. Irma is an exempt administrative employee.

- **This employee does not fit within the exemption:** Irving works as a bookkeeper for an electrical contracting firm. He pays bills as they become due, prepares paychecks, and oversees the firm's bank account. He operates under written guidelines established by the firm's accountant; he can't deviate from the guidelines without prior approval from the firm's accountant or president. Irving earns a salary of $800 a week. He is not an exempt administrative employee. It's true that he does office work directly related to managing the business, but he doesn't exercise independent judgment on significant business matters.

Job Titles Aren't Everything

Job titles alone don't determine whether someone is an exempt executive, administrative, or professional employee. The actual work relationship is what counts. Mislabeling can be dangerous. Some employers try to avoid the minimum wage and overtime requirements by labeling all entry level employees "assistant managers"—and then requiring them to work well past the 40-hour workweek with no overtime compensation. The Department of Labor is well aware of such abuses. Employers who mislabel employees to circumvent the law are playing a dangerous game and may wind up paying stiff penalties. (See "The Consequences of Bending the Rules," below, for more about the dangers of violating the FLSA.)

Learned Professionals

Lawyers, accountants, doctors, dentists, engineers, teachers, scientists, architects, and pharmacists are generally exempt employees if their jobs involve using their own judgment and discretion. The same is true of certain health care professionals, such as certified medical technologists, registered nurses, dental hygienists, and physician's assistants. For anyone else who seems like a professional but who doesn't fall into one of these clear-cut cases, consult a lawyer.

Creative Professionals

A creative professional is someone who primarily performs work requiring invention, imagination, originality, or talent in a recognized artistic or creative field. Typical creative professionals include actors, musicians, composers, soloists, graphic artists, writers, cartoonists, essayists, and novelists.

Journalists may qualify if their primary work is creative—for example, contributing a unique interpretation or analysis to the news—but not if they only collect, organize, and record information that's routine or already public.

Certain Highly Paid Employees

Most employees who earn big bucks will be exempt because they qualify as executives, administrators, or professionals. Occasionally, however, a high earner can't be neatly pigeon-holed into one of these white-collar categories. Such an employee may be exempt under a special rule: You don't have to provide overtime pay to an employee who performs office or nonmanual work if he or she:

- earns a total annual compensation of $100,000 or more (which includes at least $455 per week paid on a salary or fee basis), and
- regularly performs at least one of the duties of an exempt executive, administrative, or professional employee, as summarized above.

EXAMPLE: This person fits within the exemption: Jack works for a company that makes car accessories. His job is to come up with ideas for new products that have great market potential. To do this, he keeps tabs on what competitors are doing, and he conducts market research. Each month, he presents a written report to management with his recommendations for new products and the reasons why he believes the products will sell well. Because Jack is so good at what he does and has an impressive track record, the company pays him a salary of $1,800 a week ($93,600 a year) plus a year-end bonus of $10,000. Jack is an exempt highly paid employee. He meets the earnings requirement (his total annual compensation exceeds $100,000) and performs at least one duty of an executive or administrator: performing market research and providing expert advice to management.

EXAMPLE: This person does not fit within the exemption: Joan works for a major natural food market, where she is paid $2,000 a week to inspect farms to make sure that the food the market buys meets her employer's definition of "organic." She applies her employer's standards and doesn't exercise independent judgment. Joan is not an exempt highly paid employee. Although she meets the compensation test (she earns $104,000 annually), her job doesn't require her to perform any of the duties of an executive, administrative, or professional employee.

Outside Sales Employees

Your business may employ sales people who call on current and potential customers. If so, these employees may be exempt. For an outside sales employee to be exempt, both of the following must be true:

- The employee's primary duty must be making sales or obtaining orders or contracts for services or for the use of facilities.
- The employee must regularly work away from your place of business.

Typically, an exempt sales employee makes sales or takes orders at a customer's home or business place. A driver who delivers products—and also sells them—may be exempt as an outside sales employee. The key is whether making sales is a primary duty of the employee.

Here are a couple of examples that show how to apply this exemption.

EXAMPLE: This person fits within the exemption: Jessie works for a distributor of medical devices. She regularly visits doctors and hospital administrators in a three-state region to obtain orders for the devices. Jessie is an exempt outside sales employee. Her primary duty is to obtain orders for her employer's products, and she regularly works away from her employer's place of business.

EXAMPLE: This person does not fit within the exemption: Jamie works for a distributor of medical devices. She spends most of her time in the office responding to phone and email inquiries about her employer's products. Occasionally—about once a month—she visits a customer or two to demonstrate a device, and she may take an order at that time. Jamie is not an exempt outside sales employee. Sales work is only a small part of her job. What's more, she only occasionally works away from her employer's place of business.

Employees in Certain Computer-Related Jobs

You don't have to provide a minimum wage or overtime pay to certain computer workers. To qualify for the computer employee exemption, the employee's primary duty must consist of one of the following:

- applying systems analysis techniques and procedures
- designing, developing, documenting, analyzing, creating, testing, or modifying

computer systems or programs based on design specs

- designing, developing, documenting, analyzing, creating, testing, or modifying computer programs related to machine operating systems, or
- a combination of the above duties, using the same level of skills.

This exemption applies if you pay the employee at least $455 a week on a salary basis or an hourly rate of at least $27.63.

This exemption doesn't include employees who make or repair computers and related equipment. So if your company owns a lot of computers and you hire an employee or two to keep these computers up and running, these employees won't be exempt.

The exemption also doesn't include employees who use specialized computer skills but who aren't primarily engaged in computer systems analysis or programming. Examples of such employees are engineers, drafters, and others skilled in computer-aided design software. (But watch out, because some of these employees—especially engineers—may be exempt as learned professionals.)

Apprentices

An apprentice is a worker who's at least 16 years old and who has signed an agreement with you to learn a skilled trade, such as learning to be an electrician or plumber. Be aware that your state may have a law limiting the number of hours you can hire someone to work as an apprentice. State law may also require you to pay the apprentice a certain percentage of the minimum wage. Check with your state labor department for more information. (See the appendix for contact details.)

As you may know, the next step after working as an apprentice is to become a journeyman. The FLSA requires that during the time that someone works for you as an apprentice, his or her pay must average at least 50% of what you pay journeymen.

Employees Who Are Exempt From Overtime Only

A number of employees are exempt from the overtime pay requirements only. You must still pay these employees at least the minimum wage. These employees are:

- taxicab drivers
- commissioned employees of retail or service establishments, if the employee's regular rate of pay is more than one and one-half times the minimum wage and if more than half the employee's pay comes from commissions
- employees who sell cars, trucks, trailers, farm implements, boats, or aircraft if they're working for a nonmanufacturing business that sells these items to ultimate buyers
- announcers, news editors, and chief engineers of radio and TV stations located in a town or city that has fewer than 100,000 people—or, in some cases, in a town or city that has fewer than 25,000 people

- movie theater employees
- home health care companions
- farmworkers (as noted above, workers on some farms are also exempt from the minimum wage requirements), and
- parts clerks and mechanics who service cars, trucks, or farm implements if they're working for a nonmanufacturing business that sells these items to ultimate buyers. Those who work for manufacturers or midlevel distributors aren't exempt. For example, Trisha works as a salesperson for a distributor that sells farm implements to retail dealers. Because her employer doesn't sell the implements directly to farmers (the ultimate buyers), Trisha is entitled to overtime pay.

In addition, employees of hospitals and residential care facilities get special treatment. If you operate this sort of facility, check with the Department of Labor for details.

You can require employees who lack a high school diploma or who haven't finished eighth grade to spend up to ten hours a week in reading and basic skills programs. You must pay these employees their regular wages for time spent in training, including overtime hours, but you don't have to pay them time and a half for overtime work.

Paying a Minimum Wage

You must pay all nonexempt employees (described earlier in this section) at least the minimum wage—currently $7.25 per hour. Federal law allows you to pay a training wage of $4.25 an hour to employees younger than 20 during their first 90 days on the job. You're not allowed to fire employees just so you can replace them with young workers and pay them the lower training wage.

The law in your state or even city may set a minimum wage higher than the federal rate. If so, you must pay your workers the higher rate. But if the federal rate is higher, you must pay that instead. (See "State Minimum Wage Laws for Tipped and Regular Employees" in the appendix.)

Poster Requirements

Federal law requires you to display the Federal Minimum Wage poster prominently in the workplace. It's available at the nearest office of the U.S. Department of Labor's Wage and Hour Division. You can also download this poster from the Department of Labor's website at www.dol.gov. Your state labor department may also be able to provide this poster as well as any poster that may be required by state law. (See the appendix for contact details.)

Paying Overtime

The FLSA requires you to pay nonexempt workers (described earlier in this section) at least one and one-half times their regular rate of pay for all hours worked in excess of 40 in one week. The FLSA doesn't require you to pay an employee at an overtime rate simply because the employee worked more than eight hours in one day, but some states (for example, California and Alaska) do, so be sure to double-check your state's law with your state labor department. (See the appendix for contact details.)

Generally, the FLSA mandates that you calculate and pay overtime by the week. The workweek may begin on any day of the week and any hour that you establish. In applying the minimum wage and overtime pay rules, each workweek stands alone; you can't average two or more workweeks. And you can't manipulate the start of the workweek merely to avoid paying overtime.

RESOURCE

Want to know more about overtime? For extensive information about the federal overtime rules, go to www.dol.gov. This will take you to a page with links to in-depth fact sheets, frequently asked questions, and the regulations themselves.

How you compute overtime pay for a particular employee will depend on whether you pay that employee on an hourly rate, piece rate, or salary basis. Piece rate means that you pay the worker based on the number of items produced or assembled by the worker (for example, you might pay a worker a certain amount for each desk lamp assembled).

Hourly rate. If an employee works more than 40 hours during a week, you must pay at least one and one-half times the regular hourly rate for each hour over 40. For example, let's say an employee whose regular rate is $8 an hour works 44 hours in a workweek. You must pay the employee at least $12 for each hour over 40. Pay for the week would be $320 ($8 x 40 hours) for the first 40 hours, plus $48 for the four hours of overtime—a total of $368.

Piece rate. To obtain the regular pay rate for an employee who is paid on a piecework basis, divide the total weekly earnings by the total number of hours worked that week. You must pay the employee the full piecework earnings, plus an additional one-half times this regular rate for each worked hour over 40. For example, let's say an employee who is paid on a piecework basis works 45 hours in a week and earns $405. The regular rate of pay for that week is $405 divided by 45, or $9 an hour. In addition to the straight time pay, you must pay the employee $4.50 (half the regular rate) for each hour over 40, or $22.50. Another way to pay pieceworkers for overtime is to pay one and one-half times the piece rate for each piece produced during the overtime hours. However, you and the employee must agree to this payment arrangement in advance. The piece rate you pay for the first 40 hours must always be enough to give the employee at least the minimum wage for each hour of the regular work week.

Salary. To obtain the regular rate of pay for an employee paid a salary for a regular or specified number of hours a week, divide the salary by the number of hours for which the salary is compensation. The regular rate cannot be less than the minimum wage required by the FLSA. If a salary isn't paid weekly, you must determine the weekly pay to compute the regular rate and overtime. If, for example, the salary is paid twice a month, multiply by 24 and then divide by 52 weeks to get the weekly equivalent. For example, you pay an employee a salary of $800 twice a month for working a 40-hour week. Multiply $800 by 24 and you get $19,200. Then divide by 52 and you get $369.23. That's the employee's regular rate of pay for a 40-hour week. (If you divide the weekly salary by 40, you'll find that the hourly rate is $9.23.)

You may be wondering if you can pay your employees with compensatory time rather than overtime. The answer is, probably not. The practice of granting hour-for-hour compensatory time—for example, giving a worker six hours time off at some date in the future as compensation for having worked six hours of overtime—isn't usually allowed for private sector employees covered by the FLSA. (The rules are different for public employees.)

Employers and employees are often puzzled when they learn that compensatory time isn't permitted in the private sector, because it seems like a sensible and mutually beneficial way to handle overtime in many situations. So what are the alternatives to simply paying the employee overtime? You may be able to rearrange an employee's schedule during a workweek to ensure that the employee does

not work overtime. Under federal law, as long as an employee works no more than 40 hours in a week, the employee has not worked overtime and is not entitled to overtime pay. So, for example, an employee who works four ten-hour days and then has three days off need not be paid overtime. If your state has a daily overtime standard, this may not be possible unless the law explicitly allows you and your employees to agree on an alternative workweek. A daily overtime standard means that workers are entitled to overtime if they work more than a set number of hours in a day, even if they ultimately work fewer than 40 hours in a week. California, Colorado, and Connecticut are a few states that have a daily overtime standard.

You can also adjust an employee's hours during a pay period so that the amount of the employee's paycheck remains constant. To make the math come out right, the employee must take an hour and a half off for every hour of overtime worked. For example, if an employee who generally earns $1,600 every two weeks (or $20 an hour) works an extra ten hours during the first week of the pay period, the employee is entitled to $300 in overtime pay—ten hours multiplied by one and a half times the employee's hourly rate, or $30. If the employee took 15 hours off in the second week of the pay period, however, the paycheck would remain $1,600—it would include $300 in overtime pay but would be docked $300 (15 hours x $20 an hour) for the time the employee took off.

Attitudes on Overtime Are Changing

In the recent past, most workers loved overtime work. It represented an opportunity to get ahead financially—maybe a chance to buy a boat or start a college fund for the kids.

Many workers still feel that way, but others don't feel driven to amass as much money as possible from their work. Those who aren't thrilled by overtime work may have family responsibilities or may simply place a high value on their private time.

The law allows you to schedule overtime for workers, even if they don't want it, but it may be a more sound management practice to give them some choice in the matter. Otherwise, the workers who don't relish overtime work may feel abused and will drag down morale in the workplace. If you anticipate that you'll be requiring overtime work for certain positions, put that fact in the job description so workers are aware of that likelihood right from the start. Applicants who abhor overtime work can decide to seek work elsewhere.

Some states allow employers to offer compensatory time, but the requirements can get pretty complicated. To find out about your state's rules, contact your state labor department.

CAUTION

Private deals can be risky. It's unlikely that a federal or state labor investigator will look into your compensatory time arrangements unless an employee files a complaint. Knowing this, you may be tempted to work out private deals with employees to meet your needs and theirs. This can be dangerous. You never know when a friendly, loyal employee may turn sour and look for some legal technicalities to use against you.

Equal Pay Requirements

The Equal Pay Act, which is part of the FLSA, requires you to provide equal pay and benefits to men and women who do the same or equivalent work—that is, work that requires equal skill, effort, and responsibility. Many states have a similar law mandating equal pay between men and women. Job titles aren't decisive in assessing whether two jobs are equal; the work duties are what count. It's illegal, for example, for the owner of a hotel to pay its janitors (primarily men) at a different pay rate than its housekeepers (primarily women) if both are doing essentially the same work.

The federal Equal Employment Opportunity Commission (EEOC) enforces the Equal Pay Act. (See Chapter 8 for a discussion of EEOC enforcement procedures.)

The Equal Pay Act applies to all employees who are not exempt from the minimum wage requirements. It also applies to executive, administrative, and professional employees, and outside salespeople—even though they're otherwise exempt from the FLSA requirements.

The Equal Pay Act allows pay differences based on:

- a seniority system
- a merit system
- a system that pays a worker based on the quantity or quality of what the worker produces, or
- any factor other than the worker's gender—starting salaries, for example, that are based on a worker's experience level.

EXAMPLE: The Ace Tool and Die Company was founded in 1970. The company initially hired 50 male tool and die makers. Many of those men are still working there. Since 1990, the company has expanded and hired 50 more tool and die makers, half of them male and half female. All of the tool and die makers at Ace are doing equal work, but because the company awards raises systematically based on the length of a worker's employment there, many of the older male workers earn substantially more per hour than their female coworkers who are doing equal work. The pay system at Ace Tool and Die doesn't violate the Equal Pay Act, because the pay differences between genders are based on a bona fide seniority system.

In general, two jobs are equal for the purposes of the Equal Pay Act when both require the same levels of skill, effort, and responsibility—and are performed under similar conditions. The jobs do not have to be identical to be equal. There's room for interpretation, but if there are only small differences in the jobs, they should be regarded as equal.

EXAMPLE: At a ceramics company, the major difference between the jobs performed by women and men is a weightlifting restriction—men are required to lift heavier items than women. The women and men are performing equal work because heavy lifting is only a small part of the job. (*Schultz v. Saxonburg Ceramics Inc.,* 314 F.Supp. 1139 (W.D. Pa., 1970).)

How to Pay Employees

The FLSA has rules for how you pay nonexempt employees who are entitled to the minimum wage. The law doesn't mandate any specific system of paying these employees. It does, however, require that you pay them in cash (or something, such as a check, that can be readily converted into cash) or through some other legal forms of compensation (such as food and lodging). Coupons, tokens, or scrip that can be spent only at your store do not count as wages. And, if you grant discounts to these employees, you can't count the discounts toward the minimum wage requirement.

Two common forms of compensation are tips and commissions:

- **Tips.** When an employee routinely earns at least $30 a month in tips, the federal law allows you to pay the employee as little as $2.13 an hour, as long as that amount plus the tips the employee actually earns bring the employee's hourly earnings to the current minimum wage level. If it doesn't, you must pay the employee enough so that the hourly rate plus tips equals at least the minimum wage. (Many states have their own tip credit requirements. See "State Minimum Wage Laws for Tipped and Regular Employees," in the appendix, for details.)
- **Commissions.** Commissions that you pay people for sales may take the place of wages for purposes of the FLSA. However, if the commissions divided by hours worked don't equal the minimum wage, you must make up the difference.

EXAMPLE: Julia is a salesperson at Electronics Plus. She's paid a percentage of the dollar volume of the sales she completes. During one slow week, she averaged only $4 in commissions per hour. Under the FLSA, Electronics Plus must pay Julia an additional $3.25 for each hour she worked through the first 40 hours of that week; that will bring her total pay up to the minimum wage level of $7.25 an hour.

The FLSA doesn't require you to pay employees for time off, such as vacation, holidays, or sick days. It may be standard practice for you to pay employees for such time spent away from work, but the FLSA only covers payment for time on the job.

Some state laws require paid time off for jury duty and voting, among other things. In addition, laws in some states require you to give employees time off for National Guard or other military duty and to attend a child's school conferences. Most state laws provide that you can't fire or discriminate against an employee for taking such time off. Contact your state labor department for more information about leave laws in your state. (See the appendix for contact details).

 CAUTION
Don't ignore your promises or practices. If you promise paid vacations, holidays, or sick days in an employee handbook or other written policy, or if you customarily grant such paid time off, you may be legally bound to give those benefits to all employees, regardless of whether your state law requires it.

The FLSA requires only that the pay period be one month or less. State laws often require shorter pay periods—such as every two weeks. If you have a question about pay periods, call your state's labor department. (See the appendix for contact details.)

Calculating Work Hours

Knowing you must pay employees for their work is one thing; understanding exactly which hours count as work and which ones don't can be tricky. The FLSA requires you to pay nonexempt employees for any of their time that you control and that benefits you. In general, time on the job doesn't include the time employees spend washing up or changing clothes before or after work, nor does it include meal periods when employees are free from all work duties. It's legal to round time records off to the nearest five-minute mark on the clock—but not if it results in paying workers for less time than they actually worked. In other words, you can only round up.

The rest of this section describes some common situations that confuse employers as to whether they count as paid work time.

Commuting Time

You needn't pay employees for the time they spend commuting between their homes and the normal job site; that's not considered on-the-job time.

But you do have to pay for commuting time that is actually part of the job. If you run a plumbing repair service, for example, and require workers to stop by your shop to pick up orders, tools, and supplies before going out on calls, their workday begins when they check in at your shop.

Otherwise, just about the only situation in which you must pay workers for commuting time is when they're required to go back and forth from the normal worksite at odd hours in emergency situations.

> **EXAMPLE:** Neil normally works 9 to 5 as a computer technician at Arbor City Computer and is paid hourly. One day, about two hours after Neil gets home, his supervisor calls him to say that some computer equipment is malfunctioning and preventing the late shift employees from doing their work—and asks him to go back to the office immediately to help correct the problem. It takes him half an hour to get there, two hours to fix the problem, and half an hour to drive home again. Arbor City must pay Neil for three hours—two work hours plus the extra hour of commuting time required by the company's emergency.

On-Call Time

You must count as payable time any periods when employees are not actually working but are required to stay on your premises while waiting for a work assignment.

If you require employees to be on call but you don't make them stay on your premises, then two rules generally apply:

- You don't count as payable time the on-call time that employees can control and use for their own enjoyment or benefit.
- You do count as payable time the on-call time over which employees have little or no control and which they can't use for their own enjoyment or benefit.

> **EXAMPLE 1:** Medi-Transit operates a nonemergency ambulance service that transports patients from hospitals to

nursing homes. The company hires Ryan to drive an ambulance from 8 to 5, Monday through Friday, and also requires him to carry a beeper one night a week so he can handle an occasional assignment after normal working hours. Because Ryan is free to pursue personal and social activities during nonworking hours, Medi-Transit doesn't have to pay him for his on-call time.

EXAMPLE 2: AirTec provides mechanical services for small private planes at a local airfield. Joe is an AirTec mechanic. The company requires him to be on call every fourth Saturday. When he's on call, he must stay within a five-minute drive to the airport, keep his cell phone free for calls from the company, and refrain from drinking alcohol. Because Joe isn't free to use his on-call time as he pleases, the company must pay him for the time.

Unless there's an employment contract that states otherwise, you can generally pay a different hourly rate for on-call time than you do for regular work time. But keep in mind that you must pay employees at least the minimum wage.

Sleep Time

If you require an employee to be on duty at the worksite for less than 24 hours at a time, you generally must count as payable any time during which the employee is allowed to sleep in a shift of duty. Similarly, if you require an employee to be at work for 24 hours or more, you also generally must count sleep time as payable work time. But there's a way around this: You and the employee may agree to exclude up to eight hours per day from payable time as sleep and meal periods. However, if conditions are such that the employee can't get at least five hours of sleep during the eight-hour sleep-and-eat period, or if the employee ends up working during that period, then those eight hours revert to payable time.

Lectures, Meetings, and Training Seminars

Generally, if you want a nonexempt employee to attend a lecture, meeting, or training seminar, you'll have to pay for that employee's time—including travel time if the meeting is away from the worksite.

About the only situation in which you don't have to pay for the employee's time is if all of the following are true:

- The employee attends the event outside of regular working hours.
- Attendance is voluntary.
- The instruction session isn't directly related to the employee's job.
- The employee doesn't perform any productive work during the instruction session.

Meal and Rest Breaks

You don't have to pay a covered employee for time spent on an actual meal period. But the employee must be completely relieved from work during that period so that the employee can enjoy a regularly scheduled meal. If, for example, you require employees to remain at their desks during the meal period or to keep an eye on machinery, you must pay for the meal time.

Similarly, you don't have to pay for rest periods or coffee breaks if the employee is truly free from job duties. If an employee must listen for the phone or watch for merchandise deliveries during the break, it's not free time and you must pay for it.

Many states have laws requiring employers to provide meal and rest breaks and specifying minimum times that must be allowed. (See "State Meal and Rest Break Laws" in the appendix.) In some states, these breaks must be paid. If your state requires more than the FLSA, then you must follow the stricter state law requirement.

As of 2010, federal law requires employers to make life easier for employees who are new mothers. You must provide a nursing mother with reasonable break time and a place to express her breast milk. The place must be shielded from view and free from intrusion by coworkers and the public; a restroom doesn't qualify. You don't have to compensate the employee for this break time, however. Smaller businesses—those with fewer than 50 employees—don't have to comply with these new requirements if doing so would impose an undue hardship, defined as significant expense or difficulty, considering the employer's size, structure, and resources.

An increasing number of states have similar laws, some of which provide even greater protection for nursing mothers. You can find information on your state's requirements in "State Meal and Rest Break Laws," in the appendix.

 TIP

It's better not to quibble. Most employees today expect to get one or two paid breaks during an eight-hour shift. Such breaks may help employees work more efficiently, because they'll return to the job refreshed. It can put a damper on employee morale if you try to avoid paying for that time.

Record-Keeping Requirements

The FLSA requires you to keep records of wages and hours for all employees. For nonexempt employees, your records must include:

- the employee's name, address, social security number, occupation, and gender
- the employee's birth date if the employee is younger than 19 years old
- the hour and day when each workweek began
- the total hours worked each workday and each workweek
- total daily or weekly earnings
- regular hourly pay rate for any week when overtime was worked
- total overtime pay for the workweek
- deductions from or additions to wages

Nonagricultural Occupations That Are Hazardous to Young Workers

Under rules of the U.S. Department of Labor, workers younger than 18 cannot perform the following types of jobs:

- manufacturing or storing explosives
- driving a motor vehicle or being an outside helper on a motor vehicle*
- coal or other mining
- logging and saw milling
- anything involving power-driven wood-working machines**
- anything involving exposure to radioactive substances and to ionizing radiations
- anything involving power-driven hoisting equipment
- anything involving power-driven metal-forming, punching, and shearing machines**
- meatpacking or processing (including anything involving power-driven meat slicing machines)
- anything involving power-driven bakery machines
- anything involving power-driven paper-product machines**
- manufacturing brick, tile, and related products
- anything involving power-driven circular saws, band saws, and guillotine shears**
- wrecking, demolition, and ship-breaking operations
- roofing operations,** and
- excavation operations.**

* A 17-year-old worker who has a driver's license and no record of any moving violations can drive a car or small truck during daylight hours if the driver has completed an approved driver education course, the car or truck has seat belts, and the driving is only occasional—no more than one-third of the worker's work time any day and no more than 20% of work time in a work week. Among other rules, the young driver can't tow vehicles, drive a delivery route, or drive beyond a 30-mile radius from your business place.

** There are limited exceptions in these types of jobs for apprentices and students.

For a complete list of nonagricultural occupations deemed hazardous for young workers, and for the special rules that apply to workers who are 14 and 15 years old, go to www.dol.gov/whd/regs/compliance/childlabor101_text.htm.

- total wages paid each pay period, and
- date of payment and pay period covered.

A bit less information is required for employees who are exempt from the minimum wage or overtime pay requirements. Also, you must keep special information for employees to whom you extend lodging or other facilities. You must retain most records for all current employees and for at least three years after an employee stops working for your company.

Your state may impose different or additional requirements. Contact your state labor department for details. (See the appendix for contact information.)

 RESOURCE

Want more information on your record- keeping duties? You can view a U.S. Department of Labor fact sheet at www.dol.gov/whd/regs/compliance/whdfs21.pdf.

Child Labor Rules

The FLSA has special rules for younger workers. Those rules are designed to discourage young people from dropping out of school too soon and to protect them from dangerous work such as mining, demolition and wrecking, logging, and roofing. State laws may impose additional restrictions on hiring young workers, so if you intend to employ workers younger than 18, you should contact your labor department to find out what your state rules are. (See the appendix for contact details.)

The rules are different for youngsters in agricultural and nonagricultural jobs. We discuss each below.

Agricultural Jobs

In agricultural work, the following rules apply to younger workers:

- You may hire a worker who is 16 years or older for any work, hazardous or not, for unlimited hours. (See "Agricultural Occupations Hazardous to Young Workers," below.)
- You may hire a worker who is 14 or 15 years old for any nonhazardous agricultural work outside of school hours.
- You may hire a worker who is 12 or 13 years old for any nonhazardous agricultural work outside of school hours if the child's parents work on the same farm or if you have their written consent.
- You may hire a worker who is younger than 12 years old for nonhazardous work on a farm outside of school hours if the farm isn't covered by minimum wage requirements—but you need the written consent of the child's parents.
- You may hire a worker who is ten or 11 years old if you've been granted a waiver by the U.S. Department of Labor to employ the youngster as a hand harvest laborer for no more than eight weeks in any calendar year.
- If you own or operate a farm, you can hire your own children to do any kind of work on the farm, regardless of their ages.

Agricultural work is essentially any work that would be performed on a farm, specifically the following:

- cultivating and tilling the soil
- dairying
- producing, cultivating, growing, and harvesting any agricultural or horticultural commodities
- raising livestock, bees, fur-bearing animals, or poultry, or
- any practices performed by a farmer on a farm as part of farming—for example, forestry, lumbering, and preparing items for market.

Agricultural Occupations Hazardous to Young Workers

The U.S. Department of Labor has identified several agricultural occupations that are deemed hazardous for children age 15 and younger, including:

- operating a tractor that has more than 20 horsepower
- working in a yard, pen, or stall occupied by a bull, a stud horse maintained for breeding purposes, or a sow with suckling pigs
- felling timber with a diameter of more than six inches
- working from a ladder or scaffold at a height of more than 20 feet, and
- handling or using blast agents.

For a complete list, go to www.dol.gov/whd/regs/compliance/childlabor101_text.htm.

Nonagricultural Jobs

The FLSA sets out a number of restrictions on young workers hired to do nonagricultural jobs:

- You may hire a worker who is 18 years or older for any job, hazardous or not, for unlimited hours.
- You may hire a worker who is 16 or 17 years old for any nonhazardous job for unlimited hours.
- You may hire a worker who is 14 or 15 years old outside school hours in various nonmanufacturing, nonmining, nonhazardous jobs, but some restrictions apply. The employee can't work more than three hours on a school day, 18 hours in a school week, eight hours on a nonschool day, or 40 hours in a nonschool week. Also, work can't begin before 7 a.m. or end after 7 p.m., except from June 1 through Labor Day, when evening hours are extended to 9 p.m.

Fourteen years old is the minimum age for most work, but there are a few jobs that workers younger than 14 can perform, including:

- delivering newspapers
- performing in radio, TV, movie, or theatrical productions
- working in a nonfarm business solely owned by the parents—if it's not a manufacturing or hazardous job
- gathering evergreens, and
- making evergreen wreaths.

In addition, there are special rules for young people who cook as part of their jobs. A worker who is 14 or 15 years old can only:

- cook on an electric or gas grill (no open flames)
- warm food in a microwave oven, or
- use a deep-fat fryer that automatically lowers food into the hot oil.

These youngsters can also dispense food from food warmers and steam tables.

Payroll Withholding

Federal law requires you to withhold income taxes and Social Security and Medicare contributions from employees' paychecks. States and municipalities that have income taxes also require withholding—usually under a system that parallels the federal procedures. (See Chapter 5 for more about federal payroll taxes.)

Under federal law, you may also deduct the cost of meals, housing, transportation, loans, debts owed to you, child support and alimony, payroll savings, and insurance premiums. There are exceptions to these rules and limits on how much you can withhold or deduct.

> CAUTION
>
> **State rules may differ.** Your state may prohibit some deductions that the federal law allows. In this situation, you must follow your state's law. Before you take any deductions, contact your state labor department to learn your state's rules. (See the appendix for contact information.)

Meals, Housing, and Transportation

Under federal law, you may legally deduct from an employee's paycheck the reasonable cost or fair value of meals, housing, fuel, and transportation to and from work even if these deductions reduce the worker's pay to less than minimum wage. But you must show that you customarily paid these expenses and that all of the following are true:

- They were for the employee's benefit.
- You told the employee in advance about the deductions.
- The employee voluntarily accepted the meals and other accommodations.

Debts Owed to an Employer

If you lend money or extend credit to an employee, federal law allows you to withhold money from the employee's pay to satisfy that debt. However, it's illegal to make such a deduction if it would drop a nonexempt employee's pay below the minimum wage.

> **EXAMPLE:** Roadmaster Auto Parts Store hires Bruce at $8 an hour to make deliveries. One morning, the battery in Bruce's car dies. Roadmaster allows him to replace the battery with a new one from the store's stock—and Bruce agrees that Roadmaster can deduct the price, $80, from his paycheck. Under the FLSA,

Roadmaster can legally deduct no more than $30 per week (40 hours x $.75) from Bruce's gross pay to cover the battery. To deduct more would drop Bruce's pay rate of $8 per hour to below the required minimum of $7.25.

Debts and Wage Garnishments

You may be sent an order from a judge requiring your business to withhold money from an employee's paycheck to satisfy a debt the employee owes to someone else. This order is part of a legal process called wage attachment or wage garnishment. Usually, a judge will issue such an order only after a judgment has been signed stating that the employee actually owes the money—but such a judgment may not be necessary for garnishments based on an employee's failure to pay student loans, child support, alimony, or taxes.

If you receive a garnishment order, read it carefully—it will specify deadlines you must meet for processing the order. You may have to pay a penalty if you don't comply with the terms and timetables of the garnishment. Procedures vary from state to state, but most likely you'll be required to file a form with the court disclosing how much you owe to the employee for wages. Then you'll be required to send a portion of those wages to the court or, perhaps, to the creditor or creditor's lawyer.

A federal law, the Consumer Credit Protection Act (15 U.S.C. § 1673), prohibits a judgment creditor from taking more than 25% of an employee's net earnings through a wage garnishment. A few states offer greater protection to the employee. In Delaware, for example, a judgment creditor can't take more than 15% of an employee's wages. Usually the papers you receive as part of the garnishment order will explain how much of the employee's earnings you should deduct and where to send the money.

The Consumer Credit Protection Act also prohibits you from firing an employee because of a garnishment order to satisfy a single debt. But if two judgment creditors garnish an employee's wages or one judgment creditor garnishes an employee's wages to pay two different judgments, you're free to fire that employee. Again, some state laws place stricter limits on your right to fire an employee because of garnishments. In Washington, for example, you can't fire workers for judgments owed unless their wages are garnished by three different creditors or to satisfy three different garnishments within a year. In Connecticut, you can't fire a worker unless you've had to deal with more than seven creditors or judgments in a single year.

Although statutes limit your right to fire employees because of garnishments, you can still fire such employees for a legitimate business reason—or for any reason that isn't illegal, if the employee works at will—as long as you can establish that the firing wasn't based on the garnishments.

Child Support

The federal Family Support Act of 1988 (102 U.S.C. § 2343) requires that new or modified child support orders include an automatic wage withholding order. If you receive a copy of such an order, you must withhold a portion of the employee's pay and send it on to the parent to whom it is owed.

You can't discipline, fire, or refuse to hire people just because their pay is subject to a child support wage withholding order.

Back Taxes

If an employee owes taxes to the federal government and doesn't pay, the IRS can grab most—but not all—of the employee's wages. The amount the employee gets to keep is determined by the number of dependents and the size of the standard deduction to which the employee is entitled.

If you receive a wage levy notice from the IRS, don't ignore it. If you go ahead and pay the employee in full, you'll be liable to the IRS for whatever amount you wrongly pay.

Most state and some municipal taxing authorities have similar power to seize a portion of an employee's wages.

The Consequences of Bending the Rules

The Wage and Hour Division of the U.S. Department of Labor enforces the FLSA regulations described in this chapter. Almost always, it is tipped off to investigate a business by an unhappy employee who has complained. Be aware that it's illegal to fire or discriminate against an employee for filing a complaint or participating in a legal proceeding under the FLSA. And many states have similar laws prohibiting such retaliation.

The department can fine you up to $10,000 for violating the FLSA—and send you to jail for a second offense if you acted willfully. But fines and jail time are used in only the most blatant cases. More typically, you'll be required to pay the employee all unpaid wages, including overtime pay. The real cost comes in the time and expense of being involved in enforcement proceedings—not to mention the damage to employee morale and the animosity that can be created in the workplace, particularly if several employees claim their rights were violated.

Beyond the chance of being pursued by the government, there looms the possibility of a private lawsuit. And—especially if yours is a larger company—the private lawsuit may be a class action, with potentially disastrous results for your business. An employer's exposure to huge verdicts in such lawsuits is so great that many businesses wind up settling. Here are some publicized cases in which it was alleged that the employer incorrectly classified employees as exempt:

- A rental car company settled a class action for close to $8 million.
- A coffee house chain settled a class action for $28 million.

- A phone company settled one class action for $35 million and another for $27 million.
- An insurance company settled a class action for $130 million.
- A drug store chain settled a class action for $11 million.
- An auto club settled a class action for $19.5 million.

Many of these settlement sums included large amounts earmarked for lawyers' fees and litigation costs.

Of course, class actions against small-scale employers are relatively rare—and the verdicts and settlements won't be in the stratospheric range. But even a $100,000 judgment against a small company could be devastating. So before you conclude that certain employees are exempt and, for that reason, are not entitled to overtime pay, make sure you're on solid legal ground. If in doubt, the legally safe course is to consult an attorney who specializes in these matters.

Employee Benefits

Employee benefits are such a common part of the workplace terrain today that many assume these benefits are required by law. But, generally, the decision about whether or not to provide such benefits is up to you. (Of course, health care reform will bring changes here, including penalties for larger employers that don't offer health insurance.)

Even though providing benefits is largely optional, enlightened employers frequently do offer some type of benefit package. Offering benefits can reflect your commitment to keeping a satisfied workforce and help you remain competitive in attracting competent workers.

Federal tax laws allow an employer to deduct the cost of many employee benefits as a business expense, which greatly reduces the financial burden of providing these benefits. Benefits that qualify for favorable tax treatment include health and dental coverage, term life insurance, disability insurance, approved pension plans, educational assistance programs, and dependent care assistance. But if a benefit plan is rigged to favor the owners of a business or employees who receive the highest compensation, the plan may not qualify for a tax deduction.

If you provide health care coverage or pension plans, federal and state laws impose requirements on these plans.

RESOURCE

Want details on how the federal tax laws apply to many of the benefits discussed in this chapter? See IRS Publication 15-B,

Employer's Tax Guide to Fringe Benefits, available at www.irs.gov.

Employees Can Help You Plan

In putting together a benefit program, consider taking a survey of employees or setting up an employee committee to recommend the benefits they'd most like to have. Then, after exploring the options and deciding on the benefits you'll offer, communicate that decision—and your reasons for the choice—to the employees.

Perhaps some employee suggestions will be too expensive or even impossible to adopt. You may want to reconsider others in the future. Whatever the situation, when employees go to the trouble of making suggestions, make sure to let them know that you gave their ideas serious consideration.

Health Care Coverage

Health care coverage is the benefit most employees covet. Medical treatment is expensive today, and it's difficult for an individual to find affordable coverage. Of course, employees enjoy the greatest benefits if the employer foots the entire bill. But even if an employer doesn't pay the cost of coverage— or pays just a part of it—the employee benefits by being able to participate at relatively low group rates.

Beginning in 2014, the health care picture will change significantly for employers—especially larger ones—because of the 2010 Patient Protection and Affordable Care Act (the official name of the health care reform law). In 2014, the "pay or play" mandate kicks in, which will penalize larger employers that don't provide benefits. Even before 2014, this legislation will affect your business. The key provisions are summarized later in this chapter.

Types of Coverage

Traditionally, employers who provide health care coverage do so through an indemnity or reimbursement plan that pays the doctor or hospital directly or reimburses the employee for medical expenses already paid.

While traditional coverage allowing employees to seek out their preferred medical provider is still widely used, a growing number of employers today provide coverage through the alternatives of a health maintenance organization (HMO) or a preferred provider organization (PPO).

An HMO is a group of hospitals and doctors who provide specified medical services to employees for a fixed monthly fee. Within the HMO service area, covered employees must use the HMO hospitals and doctors unless it's an emergency or they receive permission to go elsewhere.

A PPO is a network of hospitals and doctors who agree to provide medical care for specified fees. Often the network is put together by an insurance company that also administers the program. Employees usually can choose between using the network's hospitals and doctors or going elsewhere (although an employee may have to pay a higher fee to use doctors or facilities outside of the plan).

Making the Best Choice

If you provide health insurance coverage to employees, explore all the alternatives: group health insurance policies, HMOs, and PPOs. Until you compare, you won't know which arrangement will be least costly to your business and your employees.

Under some plans, employees pay for a portion of their medical expenses—usually called copayments. The theory is that employees will seek only essential treatment if they're paying some of the cost.

Your business must decide who will pay the monthly, quarterly, or semiannual premium for health care coverage. There are several choices for who pays the tab:

- Your business can pick up the full amount.
- You can split the cost of premiums with the employees—perhaps paying 80% and having employees pick up the other 20% through a paycheck deduction.
- You can pay for coverage in full but require employees to pay the extra cost of covering their dependents.
- You can require employees to pay the entire charge. Although employees won't perceive that as much of a benefit, the group plan will undoubtedly be cheaper than individual coverage.

Another way to shift some costs to your employees is through a deductible plan, which requires employees to pay a specified amount of medical bills each year—$500, for example—before the plan's coverage kicks in.

TIP

Consider flexible coverage arrangements. Depending on where your business is located and how many employees you have, you may be able to offer your employees several different choices of coverage. For example, some employers opt to pay 100% of coverage under an HMO. If the HMO doesn't require all employees to join, some employers allow employees who opt out to buy their own coverage. Then the employers reimburse them at the HMO rate. Depending on the required copayments, deductibles, and other plan features, employees who select a different plan may pay a bit more or less than the HMO rate.

You should decide, too, whether to cover employees who work part time. You might, for example, provide full benefits for those who work 30 hours or more per week and prorated benefits for those who work at least 20 hours but fewer than 30. Such an approach may help you qualify for cheaper group rates.

CAUTION

Children may have rights, too. If you have a group health care plan, a child of a divorced employee may have a right to coverage—even if the child doesn't live with the employee or isn't a financial dependent of the employee. An employee's child will be covered if a domestic relations settlement agreement or a court order requires such health care coverage. If you receive a copy of such a settlement agreement or court order and are unsure about what to do, check with the plan administrator or an employee benefits lawyer.

Coverage Limitations

The federal Americans with Disabilities Act (ADA) is designed to eliminate workplace discrimination against people with disabilities. (See Chapter 9 for a complete discussion of the ADA.) The ADA doesn't require you to offer health care benefits to employees, but it does require you to give people with disabilities the same health care benefits you offer to others. If your business is covered by the ADA, you may not deny insurance coverage or limit benefits based on a worker's disability.

Your plan probably violates the ADA if it excludes specific disabilities such as deafness, AIDS, or schizophrenia. Similarly, it's illegal to exclude groups of disabilities—for example, cancers, muscular dystrophy, and kidney diseases—or to exclude all conditions that substantially limit a major life activity.

The Mental Health Parity and Addiction Equity Act applies to health care plans that include more than 50 employees. If the plan covers mental health or substance-abuse conditions, the coverage for those conditions can't be more limited than the coverage for physical illnesses.

Under the Genetic Information Nondiscrimination Act (GINA), it is illegal of an employer or health plan to discriminate based on an employee's genetic information. Insurers cannot adjust premiums or contribution amounts based on genetic information, or require that employees or their family members undergo genetic testing, except in very limited circumstances.

Many states also have laws prohibiting discrimination in health care benefits. These laws may apply to your business even if the ADA does not (for example, because your business is too small).

Preexisting Conditions

There are legal limits on your ability to offer a health care plan that doesn't cover preexisting conditions. A health care plan will violate the ADA if it excludes specific preexisting conditions, such as blood disorders.

The federal Health Insurance Portability and Accountability Act further limits your right to exclude preexisting conditions in any health care plan that you provide to employees. That law provides that any exclusion for a preexisting condition:

- must relate to a condition for which the employee received medical advice or treatment during the six months before the employee's enrollment date

- cannot last for more than 12 months—18 months for late enrollees—after the employee's enrollment date, and
- cannot include pregnancy.

State laws may also regulate your ability to offer a plan with preexisting condition exclusions.

The health care reform law enacted in 2010 bars insurance companies from excluding children under the age of 19 who have a preexisting condition. Beginning in 2014, insurance companies will be unable to exclude anyone—of any age—because of a preexisting condition.

RESOURCE

Want to learn more about the complexities of the health care portability law? Consult the online guide, *Compliance Assistance for Group Health Plans: HIPAA and Other Recent Health Care Laws,* at www.dol.gov/ebsa/publications/caghp.html.

Treatment Restrictions

A plan that doesn't cover experimental drugs or treatment or that excludes elective surgery doesn't violate the ADA. Similarly, it's not a violation to put a monetary cap on certain types of treatment—for example, to limit payments for X-rays or blood transfusions—even though such a cap may adversely affect people with certain disabilities.

Discrimination in Group Health Plans

Under federal law, a group health plan can't discriminate in eligibility for coverage or premiums based on an employee's:
- health status
- medical condition
- claims experience
- medical history
- genetic information
- evidence of insurability, or
- disability.

This list applies to the employee's dependents as well.

But the law doesn't require a group plan to cover any given procedure—and a group plan may limit the level of benefits it provides, as long as the plan doesn't discriminate among similarly situated employees.

Continuing Coverage for Former Employees

A federal law called the Consolidated Omnibus Budget Reconciliation Act, or COBRA (29 U.S.C. § 1162), applies to your business if you have 20 or more employees and you offer a group health care plan. If your business is too small to be covered by COBRA, you may still have to comply with a similar state law. (See "State Health Insurance Continuation Laws" in the appendix.) If COBRA applies to your business, you must offer employees and former employees the option of continuing health care coverage if their coverage is lost or reduced because:
- their employment has been terminated for any reason—except gross misconduct
- their hours have been reduced, or
- they've become eligible for Medicare.

Members of the employee's family must also be given the opportunity to continue their coverage. "COBRA's Continuing Coverage for Former Employees," below, depicts the circumstances—called qualifying events—that trigger an employer's obligation to allow continuing health care coverage under a group plan. COBRA gives rights to different people, depending on the qualifying event. How long the benefits must be continued is determined by the qualifying event and by whether the covered employee is disabled. Special rules define a qualifying event if your business is covered by the Family and Medical Leave Act (FMLA) and an employee fails to return to work at the end of an FMLA leave.

Usually, the employee must pay the cost of continuing coverage under COBRA, including both your share and the employee's share of the premiums. You can charge 102% of the premium cost—using the extra 2% to cover administrative costs. The cost to the employee or the employee's family for continuing coverage must be similar to the cost of covering people still on your payroll.

COBRA covers HMO and PPO plans in addition to traditional group insurance plans. COBRA also covers all other types of medical benefits, including dental and vision care and plans under which an employer reimburses employees for medical expenses.

If your business is covered by COBRA and has a group health care plan, the plan administrator—the person who handles the plan's paperwork—must give employees and their spouses a written explanation of their COBRA rights when they first become eligible to participate in the plan. A single notice can be sent to an employee and spouse if they live at the same address. Otherwise, the spouse is entitled to a separate notice.

SEE AN EXPERT

Help is available. Small businesses usually find it convenient to let the insurance company serve as the plan administrator and coordinate COBRA notices. The insurance company can provide even more help and information, including a clear explanation of how the plan meets the requirements of COBRA and similar state laws. Any reputable company should be able to provide clear, concise explanatory materials that you can hand out to your employees and, if asked, may send representatives to conduct training seminars and answer employee questions.

COBRA's Continuing Coverage for Former Employees		
Qualifying Event	**People Entitled to Continue Coverage**	**How Long**
The employee quits	Employee, spouse, dependents	18 months; 29 months for disabled worker
You fire or lay off the employee for reasons other than gross misconduct	Employee, spouse, dependents	18 months; 29 months for disabled worker
You reduce the employee's hours, causing the employee to lose coverage	Employee, spouse, dependents	18 months; 29 months for disabled worker
The employee dies	Surviving spouse, dependents	36 months
The employee divorces or becomes legally separated	Former spouse, dependents	36 months
The employee goes on Medicare	Spouse, dependents	36 months
The dependent loses coverage through marriage or age	Dependent	36 months

When a qualifying event occurs that gives an employee or family member the right to continue coverage, you must send them a notice listing their rights under COBRA. These beneficiaries have 60 days following the notice to let you know if they want to continue their coverage (unless the exception above applies). If so, the employee or eligible family member sends you the premium each month, and you send it on to the insurance company. If the beneficiaries don't send the payment when due—or within the grace period—you can cut off coverage.

A number of states also have laws giving former employees the right to continue group health care insurance coverage after leaving a job. Depending on the state where you do business, state law may give employees more rights, provide for longer continued coverage, or apply to smaller employers. (See "State Health Insurance Continuation Laws" in the appendix.)

Reducing Costs

Small businesses often feel overwhelmed by the spiraling costs of providing health care benefits to employees. But there are some steps you can take that may help hold down costs, mostly by eliminating unnecessary medical expenses.

Look for a health care plan that practices managed care—requiring participants to get a second opinion before they have surgery or requiring preapproval by the insurance company for expensive diagnostic procedures.

Requiring employees to pay a part of the monthly coverage fee as well as a portion of each medical bill may encourage employees to be judicious in seeking treatment.

Look into offering coverage through a health maintenance organization (HMO) or preferred provider organization (PPO) instead of traditional insurance or reimbursement coverage. But be sure to shop around to make sure that the overall cost of a PPO or HMO plan really is lower than traditional coverage.

Look Into Wellness Grants

The Department of Health and Human Services (HHS) has grants available to help small businesses create wellness programs for employees. Your business may qualify for a grant if you have no more than 100 employees who work at least 25 hours a week. Qualifying wellness programs include those that promote:

- smoking cessation
- weight management
- stress management
- physical fitness
- nutrition
- heart disease prevention
- healthy lifestyle support, and
- diabetes prevention.

The grants will be available through 2015.

Money put into preventive care is well spent. You can, for example, call in experts to teach employees the benefits of a healthy diet, exercise, and preventive care. Beyond that, you can set a good example by making low-fat food available in your lunchroom and installing exercise equipment in an unused area of the workplace. Consider paying for seminars to help employees quit smoking. And encourage periodic physical checkups—perhaps by offering to pay part of the usual deductible payment. For more ideas, read *Healthy Employees, Healthy Business: Easy, Affordable Ways to Promote Workplace Wellness*, by Ilona Bray (Nolo).

Health Savings Accounts

One way for employers to save money on health coverage for their employees is to provide a plan that has a high deductible. To help employees deal with the high deductibles, consider participating in an employee's health savings account (HSA). An HSA is like an IRA, except that the money is for health care costs, not retirement.

Here's how it works. Let's say that you provide a high-deductible health insurance plan for employees. (In 2011, this means a plan with an annual deductible of at least $1,200 for an individual or at least $2,400 for a family. Also, the annual out-of-pocket expenses—deductibles, co-payments, and amounts other than premiums—can't exceed $5,950 for individual coverage or $11,900 for family coverage. These figures will be adjusted for inflation each year.) You or the employee can open an HSA, to which you or the employee or both can contribute money.

These funds are tax free to the employee if used to pay for:

- medical expenses
- COBRA insurance, or
- Medicare and retiree health insurance premiums (but not Medicare supplement premiums).

If an employee younger than 65 withdraws funds for other purposes, the withdrawn funds are taxable and subject to a 10% penalty. After age 65, such withdrawals are still taxable, but there's no penalty.

In 2011, you and your employees can contribute a total of up to $3,050 for an individual or $6,150 for a family. (Contribution limits will change each year.) For an employee who is 55 years or older, or who turns 55 by the end of the year, you or the employee can make an additional catch-up contribution of $1,000. Workers decide how to invest the money.

Money left in an HSA can be rolled over from year to year.

 TIP

Also look into health reimbursement accounts (HRAs). When paired with high-deductible insurance, HRAs may better meet the needs of chronically ill employees—such as those with diabetes—who are likely to exhaust their HSAs each year. Unlike HSAs, however, workers can't put their own money into HRAs or decide how the funds should be invested. The unspent money is rolled over from year to year, but workers stand to lose the money if they switch jobs.

Coverage for Pregnant Women and Older Workers

Federal law imposes some special insurance requirements for pregnant women and older workers.

Women. You must treat women affected by pregnancy and related conditions the same as other employees based on their ability or inability to work. For example, if a woman can't work because she's pregnant, you must provide her with the same health care coverage as you generally provide to employees who become ill or have a disability. (See Chapter 8 for more on the Pregnancy Discrimination Act.) The Family and Medical Leave Act allows workers to take up to 12 weeks a year of unpaid leave connected with childbirth, adoption, and foster placement. (See Chapter 6 for more about family and medical leave.)

Older workers. You must offer workers age 40 and older the same health care coverage you offer to younger workers— and, if your plan requires that all your workers be covered, you can't make older workers pay more to join. But if the insurance isn't mandatory, older workers can be charged more, so long as actuarial charts show their health care costs are higher.

Health Care Reform Law

The provisions of the 2010 Patient Protection and Affordable Care Act are being phased in

gradually. Here are the main changes that may affect your business:

- **Health care tax credit.** If your business is a "qualified small employer," you can now receive a tax credit of up to 35% of your employee health care coverage expenses. You qualify for this credit if you have no more than 25 employees, and their average annual wages don't exceed $50,000. In 2014, this tax credit will increase to up to 50% of health care expenses. Note that the law is worded in terms of "full-time equivalent (FTE) employees." This means that if your business uses part-time employees, it may qualify even if you have more than 25 employees.

- **Form W-2 reporting.** The Form W-2 for 2012 (that you'll mail to employees in January 2013), and for future years, will need to state the value of any health care coverage you've provided that's not part of the employee's gross income.

- **Health insurance requirements.** If your group health plan includes dependent coverage, that coverage must now be available for unmarried children younger than age 26. Also, the plan can't place lifetime limits on benefits or discriminate in favor of highly paid employees. Beginning in 2014, you'll face additional requirements. If you have more than 200 employees, for example, you'll have to automatically enroll employees in any health insurance coverage that you offer (though employees may opt out). And, starting in 2014, the federal government will mandate minimum standards for all health insurance that an employer provides.

- **Health insurance exchanges.** By 2014, states should have health insurance exchanges in place. These exchanges are intended to help reduce insurance costs.
- **Play-or-pay mandate.** Beginning in 2014, if you have 50 or more full-time employees and you don't offer health coverage, you may be subject to a penalty called a "shared responsibility payment." Even if you do offer health coverage, you may have to pay a penalty if you have one or more employees enrolled in state exchange plan.

The health care reform law is immensely complex. It will take time for all of us to sort through the details and to know exactly how employers—large and small—will be affected. Government agencies will need to write regulations, courts will need to weigh in, and Congress may even take further action. So stay tuned.

Retirement Plans

Retirement plans provide income to older people when they're no longer part of the workforce. If the plans you offer meet certain IRS guidelines, your contribution to the benefits qualifies as a business expense and is deductible from your company's gross income.

We look at a few of your options below. Large businesses may want to look into a defined benefit plan or defined contribution plan, as described below. Small businesses will probably be better off considering a 401(k) plan or IRA plan; these plans typically cost less and require minimal paperwork. If you are interested in providing retirement benefits to your employees, talk to a benefits specialist to find a plan that will work for you.

Defined Benefit Plans

In a defined benefit plan, you promise to pay an employee a fixed amount of money, usually in monthly increments, after the employee retires. You may base the payments on a formula that combines the number of years the employee has worked and the amount of earnings. You may also choose some other method of setting the timing and amount, such as a fixed monthly sum not tied to length of service or earnings.

To fund a defined benefit plan, employers typically invest money in stocks, bonds, and mutual funds that are expected to grow over the years. You must contribute enough to the plan to pay the promised benefit. Otherwise, you'll have to make up the difference if the plan's investments go bad.

To help protect employees if a business lacks the funds to pay that difference, employers who offer defined benefit plans must generally contribute to the Pension Benefit Guaranty Corporation. For details, visit the agency's website at www.pbgc.gov.

Defined Contribution Plans

In a defined contribution plan, you set up an account for the employee and contribute to it. At retirement, the employee gets whatever is in the account. You don't promise that the employee will receive a specific amount of income after retirement.

You may structure the defined contribution plan as a money purchase pension plan, in which case you'll promise to contribute a specific amount per employee each year, such as five cents for each hour worked. Or you may structure it as a profit sharing plan in which you have the discretion to decide each year how much to contribute, with your contributions allocated to the employees' accounts in a specified way—usually in proportion to their pay. In either case, the size of the pension check an employee receives each month after retirement will vary according to the interest rate paid on the employee's pension account and other economic factors.

401(k) Plans

A 401(k) plan is a type of profit sharing plan. It consists of a retirement account for each employee who participates. An employer can choose whether or not to make contributions and how extensive those contributions will be. You might, for example, choose to contribute only if company profits reach a certain level or to match contributions of only the lower-paid employees. In 2011, the total amount you and an employee can contribute to all of an employee's defined contribution plans—including a 401(k)—is $49,000 or an amount equal to the employee's annual compensation, whichever is less.

Even if you don't contribute to the 401(k) plan, it still constitutes a valuable benefit to employees, because it helps them save for retirement with tax-deferred dollars. If you set up an employee-funded 401(k) plan, employees can defer the income tax on the money they stash away, which allows their investments to grow faster.

A typical plan, administered by a major mutual fund company, calls for regular payroll deductions from an employee's earnings, in an amount specified by the employee. In 2011, the IRS limits the employee's contribution to $16,500. Employees who are 50 years or older can also make an additional "catch-up" contribution of $5,500 in 2011.

The employee gets to allocate the account among several different mutual funds—and to change the mix from time to time. The funds on the menu run the gamut from conservative to aggressive, so the employee can choose the level of risk. Be aware, however, that it may cost you a few thousand dollars to set up a 401(k) plan for your business—and there may be ongoing expenses for plan administration. (See "Administration Requirements," below.)

 TIP

Check out the Roth 401(k). It looks like a mix of the familiar Roth IRA and the traditional 401l(k). Like with the Roth IRA, contributions are taxable when put into the plan, but when the employee withdraws funds at age 59½ or later, the withdrawals are tax free. The contribution limits are the same as those of the traditional 401(k).

TIP

Special protection for older employees. The Older Workers Benefits Protection Act, an amendment to the Federal Age Discrimination in Employment Act (29 U.S.C. § 621), generally prohibits you from providing reduced benefits to older people in your retirement plan. But the act does allow for some lesser coverage for certain benefits, such as health and disability insurance, if you can show there's a rational cost reason for doing it. For more information, see *The Essential Guide to Federal Employment Laws*, by Lisa Guerin and Amy DelPo (Nolo)—it includes a chapter explaining the requirements of the Older Workers Benefits Protection Act.

Retirement Benefit Options for Small Businesses

If your business is small, you may want to look into three additional arrangements that may allow you to offer retirement savings options to your employees with limited costs to the business.

- **Payroll deduction IRA.** Your business doesn't contribute cash, but you make it easy for employees to contribute periodically to an Individual Retirement account (IRA) through payroll deductions. In 2011, an employee can deduct up to $5,000 for the year.
- **SEP IRA.** Under such a plan, your business can make generous, tax-deductible contributions to the IRAs of company employees (including your own, if you're the business owner). In 2011, for example, your business can make tax-deductible contributions of up to 25% of an employee's compensation—but no more than $49,000. Employer contributions are discretionary, and the money is not taxed until the employee starts making withdrawals.
- **SIMPLE IRA.** This option is only available to employers with 100 or fewer employees who each made $5,000 or more in the preceding calendar year. It is funded mainly by employee contributions, though an employer must contribute a matching or nonelective amount. Employer contributions are tax deductible; employee contributions can be made tax free. In 2011, an employee can contribute up to $11,500. An employee age 50 or over can contribute an additional $2,500.

These IRA plans are flexible, require minimal paperwork, and often have lower administrative costs than traditional plans. See your tax adviser for details.

Meeting IRS and ERISA Requirements

When maintaining a retirement plan for your employees, you must comply with two sets of federal laws: the Internal Revenue Code, which sets out the tax law requirements for your plan, and the Employee Retirement Income Security Act (ERISA), which sets out the administrative requirements for your plan. (29 U.S.C. §§ 1001 and following.)

Tax Law Requirements

While you don't have to include all workers in your retirement plan, there are complicated laws that govern whom you can include, whom you can exclude, and for what reasons. In addition, you can't structure the plan to benefit only the top executives or to otherwise discriminate against lower-paid workers.

A retirement plan that passes muster with the IRS is called a qualified plan—meaning your contribution qualifies as a tax-deductible business expense. Your contributions won't be taxed as income to employees until they actually receive the benefit.

RESOURCE

Get help from the IRS. For a helpful introduction to these requirements, see IRS Publication 535, *Business Expenses,* available at the IRS website at www.irs.gov.

Administration Requirements

Under ERISA, you'll need to appoint a plan administrator—someone who is responsible for following through on the law's paperwork requirements. This can be a person in your business or an outsider who's associated with the retirement plan. If you have a relatively small business, it may be simpler and cheaper to have an outsider—such as a worker at a bank or mutual fund company—act as plan administrator. It's difficult to develop enough expertise within your business to meet all the legal requirements that affect retirement plans.

The ERISA requirements are heavy on paperwork. There are a number of documents your plan administrator must give to participating employees.

Summary plan description. This is a booklet that describes how your plan operates. Your plan administrator must give employees the summary plan description within 90 days after they begin participating in the plan. Employees are also entitled to plan updates. The description must include the formula for determining an employee's benefits or the contributions that you'll make to the plan. It must also explain any formula for vesting— the point at which the employee's right to retirement benefits becomes locked in and can't be taken away.

Summary annual report. This is a yearly accounting of the plan's financial condition and operations.

Survivor coverage data. This is a statement of how much the plan will pay to the surviving spouse of an employee if the employee dies.

In addition, each year the plan administrator must give participants a detailed, individual statement of the benefits they've earned. And you must annually file with the IRS a Form 5500, which includes a census of employees and participants and is accompanied by summary financial reports.

SEE AN EXPERT

Get help if you can. ERISA is an extremely complicated law that can trip up even the most well-intentioned and savvy employer. Unless you have a large company with an experienced benefits administrator, you'd be wise to hire a professional to help you meet the law's requirements. Often, whatever company administers your plan for you will also take care of ERISA. Talk to your plan administrator to be sure.

Plan Termination Requirements

If you decide to terminate a defined benefit plan—one that promises specific benefits— you must notify covered employees of the approaching termination at least 60 days before the plan ends.

If you decide to reduce the rate of benefit accruals or terminate either a defined benefit plan or a money purchase plan, you must notify covered employees within a reasonable period of time before the amendment takes effect.

CAUTION

Former spouses' retirement benefit rights. In many divorces, an employee's retirement benefits are divided as part of the property settlement. The spouse of an employee may acquire rights under what ERISA calls a qualified domestic relations order (QDRO). When that happens, your company has ERISA obligations to the employee's spouse similar to your obligations to the employee. These include reviewing the court order to see if it meets the requirements for a QDRO, paying out money to the spouse as required by the order, and giving the spouse plan information if benefits aren't paid to the spouse immediately.

Who's In—And Who's Out

You don't have a completely free hand in deciding whom to include in a retirement plan. In general, ERISA requires you to include everyone who:

- is 21 years old or older, and
- has worked for your business for at least a year—1,000 or more hours in the last 12 months.

In an exception to this general rule, you can require employees to be with your company for two years before they will be eligible to participate in the plan. But if you do, you must also provide that an employee's rights become fully vested as soon as the employee begins participating in the plan.

Other Employee Benefits

Here's a rundown of several other benefit programs that the IRS recognizes as tax-deductible business expenses.

Life Insurance

One of the least expensive benefits you can offer to employees is group term life insurance. This is life insurance that pays off only if the employee dies during the policy term—usually five, ten, or 20 years. You can deduct the premiums you pay for up to $50,000 of group term life insurance for each employee. And employees don't pay tax on the premiums you pay.

If your business doesn't have at least ten full-time employees, you'll need to meet some special requirements to qualify for this tax treatment. For example, you'll have to provide life insurance for all full-time employees, and you can't require physical exams for the coverage. However many employees you have, you can't weight your group term plan in favor of highly paid employees.

Some employers pay for the first $10,000 or so of term life coverage, giving the employee the option of buying additional coverage under the same group plan. This allows employers to offer a growing benefit without having to put out a growing outlay of cash.

In selecting a group insurance policy, look for one that allows terminated employees to switch to an individual policy without having to prove that they are still insurable. Of course,

after such a conversion, the former employee becomes responsible for paying the premiums.

Disability Insurance

Consider offering disability insurance to help employees offset income lost if they suffer a serious injury or illness. You can probably find a group policy under which you pay part of the premium and the employee pays part. Some plans give employees the option of continuing their coverage after they leave your business. They then become responsible for the entire premium.

Your business can take a tax deduction for the premiums it pays, but if an employee receives payments under the insurance policy, the employee will owe income tax on those payments. If the employer and employee each pay part of the premium, the employee will owe income tax on part of the payments received.

Educational Assistance Programs

You may want to pay all or part of the cost of schooling that employees pursue outside working hours. You can set up a written plan with guidelines for the type of continuing education your business will finance, how much you're willing to spend, and the point at which you'll reimburse an employee for tuition.

Under such a plan, you can deduct as a business expense up to $5,250 per year for the educational costs you pay for an employee—

and these costs are not included in the employee's taxable income.

A few restrictions apply:

- The education assistance program can't favor highly paid employees or their spouses or dependents.
- No more than 5% of the program's payments during a year can be used to benefit a business's shareholders or owners—or their spouses or dependents.
- You can't offer employees a choice between receiving the educational assistance or other payment that's includable in the employees' gross income.
- Assistance can't be used for courses involving sports, games, or hobbies.

Dependent Care Assistance

The tax law lets your business deduct expenses you pay for assistance to employees who must care for their dependents—a major concern today as more workers have to take care of young children, aging parents, or both.

Your payments qualify for the tax deduction if they enable an employee to care for:

- dependents age 12 or younger for whom the employee can claim a personal exemption
- dependents who are physically or mentally incapable of taking care of themselves, or
- the employee's spouse, if the spouse can't take care of himself or herself.

The amounts you deduct can be for bills you pay or money you reimburse to an employee for:

- at-home child care
- in-home care for elderly or disabled adults who live with the employee
- care at a licensed nursery school or kindergarten, or
- care at a dependent care center that provides day care for more than six people.

You can also provide dependent care assistance at your own on-site facility.

Dependent care payments up to $3,000 for one dependent—or $6,000 for two or more dependents—are tax free to the employee; as noted, your business can deduct these payments as a business expense. For employees with lower household incomes, there's a dependent care tax credit that will be more valuable to them than any dependent care assistance provided by an employer, even though the care the employer provides won't be included in the employee's income for tax purposes. If you offer a dependent care plan, let employees know about tax credit alternatives so they can choose the best option.

Adoption Assistance Programs

You can assist employees with adoption expenses. The cap on how much you can pay changes annually; the limit in 2011 is $13,360 for the adoption of an eligible child. You'll need to write up an adoption assistance plan and make sure it meets requirements similar to the ones that apply to educational assistance programs. (See "Educational Assistance Programs," above, for information about this type of plan.)

With such a plan in place, you can deduct your payments for adoption expenses as a business expense. If the employee's tax return shows an adjusted gross income of less than $185,210, the employee can exclude your entire assistance payment up to the $13,360 limit. For an employee who reports income of more than $185,210 the exclusion amount starts to phase out.

These numbers will increase from time to time for cost-of-living adjustments.

Benefits That Cost Little or Nothing

In addition to benefits such as health care or retirement savings contributions that cost money, there are other, less tangible benefits that can help you attract and keep good employees. Free or low-cost benefits may include:

- **Good working conditions.** Workers are likely to appreciate a well-lit and ventilated office or shop with a view, and access to a kitchen for preparing lunch.
- **Flexible hours.** This makes it easier for employees to juggle competing time demands, such as caring for children or older parents, or attending classes.
- **Free parking.** Parking on the premises or nearby can save your employees from the daily hassle of finding space on the street, having coins on hand to feed the meter, or paying for space in a public garage.

- **Opportunity to learn new skills and advance.** This can be a powerful incentive for an employee who looks ahead to more lucrative employment. It can help you attract ambitious, motivated employees.
- **Ability to work from home.** Telecommuting has never been easier. It won't work for all businesses, but many office-based businesses can easily arrange for an employee to work at home, at least part of the time.
- **Supplying beverages and snacks.** This can help make your employees feel comfortable and experience less stress on the job.
- **Membership in a trade or professional organization, or a subscription to a work-related publication.** This will appeal to employees who want to get ahead in the business or professional world.

Cafeteria Plans

Under a cafeteria plan, an employee gets to choose from a menu of benefits such as:

- health insurance
- dental coverage
- vision care
- disability insurance
- group term life insurance
- group legal services
- additional contribution to a 401(k) plan
- additional paid vacation days, and
- cash.

Typically, the employer provides a monthly allowance to be allocated by the employee. If an employee selects benefits that exceed the allowance, the employee pays the additional amount through payroll deductions. If an employee doesn't use the full allowance, the leftover amount is added to the employee's paycheck.

These plans are attractive because they allow employees to tailor their benefits to their particular needs, while giving the employer some control over benefit costs.

Benefits for Domestic Partners

Traditionally, employers who have provided benefits to employees have extended many of those benefits—especially health insurance coverage—to the spouses of married employees. Today, more and more employers are also including the domestic partners of unmarried employees, though often only those involved in same-sex relationships.

The Legal Context

In many places, including domestic partners in an employee benefits program isn't legally mandated. No federal law requires an employer to give domestic partners the same benefits that married couples enjoy. And while laws in an increasing number of states do recognize same-sex domestic partnerships, these laws typically don't address employee benefits. Hawaii law, however, does. Its statute requires private employers to give same-sex partnerships (called "reciprocal beneficiaries") the same health insurance coverage as is given to married couples. A few cities, such as San Francisco, have ordinances that require employers to give equal benefits to same-sex and opposite-sex couples. (These laws change rapidly, so check with your state and local governments.)

For the most part, however, employers who extend benefits to domestic partners (whether same-sex or opposite-sex) do so voluntarily in a spirit of fairness. It's true that some employers fear that offering benefits to domestic partners may offend customers, suppliers, or employees on moral grounds. But many major companies have examined this risk and have concluded that, on balance, offering these benefits is the right thing to do.

Issues to Consider

If you're inclined to extend benefits to domestic partners, you'll need to grapple with and resolve several issues, including:

- How will you define a domestic partnership?
- Will you include both same-sex and opposite-sex partnerships?
- What proof of domestic partnership will you require?
- Which benefits will you cover?

Common benefits you might consider include health and dental plans, pension and retirement plans, bereavement leave, and family leave.

 SEE AN EXPERT

The tax implications of domestic partner benefits are complex. You and the affected employees need to understand the full tax picture. Please consult a tax adviser for help.

Taxes

As an employer, one of your roles is that of tax collector. The government treats you as an unpaid revenue agent whose job it is to withhold income taxes and Social Security and Medicare taxes from employees' paychecks and pay over those amounts to the IRS. In addition, Uncle Sam requires you to match employees' Social Security and Medicare taxes and to pay a federal unemployment tax based on your payroll. And Uncle's nieces and nephews in state government also look to you to help rake in their dough. You must also account to every employee for the taxes you've withheld and the amounts being sent to the government.

Whether you personally handle employee tax matters or turn them over to someone else—a bookkeeper or an accountant—you must understand at least the fundamentals of the system. If you handle taxes incorrectly, you can be hit with interest and penalties. And you may even be held personally liable if your business fails to transmit employee withholdings to the government. The IRS doggedly pursues its targets, so you don't want to get caught in its clutches.

This chapter will help you acquire a good working knowledge of how the tax laws affect you as an employer and how the pieces of the tax system fit together.

Handling Employee Taxes

Determine how involved you want to be in handling employee taxes and whether there are tasks you want to delegate to others.

If you want to do it yourself, the IRS puts out some excellent publications to guide you through the process. Relevant IRS publications are noted throughout this chapter. You can get them at the agency's website at www.irs.gov.

A part-time bookkeeper can help compile organized, detailed business records without demanding too much of your time. An accountant can help you set up a plan for your bookkeeper to follow and periodically monitor it to ensure that you meet all tax obligations.

A word of caution about one other possible source of assistance: IRS employees. Most of them are hardworking and well-meaning, but their training and supervision are often inadequate. Unfortunately, it's common to receive bad advice in answer to your questions. And if the advice proves to be so inaccurate that it causes you to be assessed interest and penalties, the fact that you got it from an IRS employee won't get you off the hook. In short, it's often cheaper to rely on the advice of an experienced small business accountant than to rely on a free oral opinion from the IRS.

⚠ CAUTION

Beware of the state. This chapter focuses on federal tax law. In addition to being scrupulously mindful of federal payroll taxes, find out whether your state and municipality impose payroll taxes. For example, if your state or city has an income tax, you may be required to withhold taxes from employees' pay much like the federal system—but some states and cities follow different procedures. Contact your state and city treasurers for detailed information.

Employer Identification Numbers

If your business has employees, get an Employer Identification Number (EIN) from the IRS, regardless of whether the business is a sole proprietorship, a partnership, a C corporation, an S corporation, or a limited liability company. Technically, if your business is a sole proprietorship, you can use your personal Social Security number instead of an EIN, but it's still a good business practice to get an EIN to differentiate between personal and business finances.

How to Apply

To get an EIN, file Form SS-4, *Application for Employer Identification Number*. You'll need your EIN before you file a tax return or make a tax deposit. In some cases, a bank will require you to have an EIN before you open a business account.

There are two recommended methods for applying for an EIN. The first is to apply online by going to www.irs.gov/business. Click on "Starting a Business," and then click on the link to EINs. From there go to "Apply for an EIN Online." You'll answer a series of questions and get your EIN immediately. You can then download, save, and print your confirmation notice.

The second speedy method is to complete a hard copy version of IRS Form SS-4. Then call the IRS at 800-829-4933 between 7 a.m. and 10 p.m. You can read the information to the IRS representative, who will give you your EIN. Write the number on the upper right-hand corner of the form. Sign and date the form, and keep it for your records. You'll receive confirmation of your EIN by mail. While on the phone, the IRS representative may ask you to fax or mail a copy of the form to the IRS office.

You can also apply by completing Form SS-4 and mailing it or faxing it to the IRS, but the online and phone methods are far more efficient.

The instructions tell you how to submit the completed form. A completed sample form is shown below.

The form isn't difficult to fill out if you follow the IRS instructions. Here are a few pointers.

Space 1. Insert your official corporate name if you're a corporation. If you're a partnership, use the partnership name shown in your partnership agreement. If you're a sole proprietor, insert your full name.

Space 12. Here you're asked to state the closing month of your business accounting

Form **SS-4**	**Application for Employer Identification Number**	OMB No. 1545-0003
(Rev. January 2010) Department of the Treasury Internal Revenue Service	(For use by employers, corporations, partnerships, trusts, estates, churches, government agencies, Indian tribal entities, certain individuals, and others.) ▶ See separate instructions for each line. ▶ Keep a copy for your records.	EIN

1	Legal name of entity (or individual) for whom the EIN is being requested **Ted Anderson**	
2	Trade name of business (if different from name on line 1) **The Poster Warehouse**	3 Executor, administrator, trustee, "care of" name
4a	Mailing address (room, apt., suite no. and street, or P.O. box) **555 Main Street**	5a Street address (if different) (Do not enter a P.O. box.)
4b	City, state, and ZIP code (if foreign, see instructions) **Ann Arbor, MI 48104**	5b City, state, and ZIP code (if foreign, see instructions)
6	County and state where principal business is located **Washtenaw County, Michigan**	

7a	Name of responsible party **Ted Anderson**	7b	SSN, ITIN, or EIN **555-55-5555**

8a	Is this application for a limited liability company (LLC) (or a foreign equivalent)? . . . . ☐ Yes ☐ No	8b	If 8a is "Yes," enter the number of LLC members . . . . ▶

8c If 8a is "Yes," was the LLC organized in the United States? . . . . ☐ Yes ☐ No

9a **Type of entity** (check only one box). **Caution.** If 8a is "Yes," see the instructions for the correct box to check.

- ☑ Sole proprietor (SSN) **555 : 55 : 5555**
- ☐ Partnership
- ☐ Corporation (enter form number to be filed) ▶
- ☐ Personal service corporation
- ☐ Church or church-controlled organization
- ☐ Other nonprofit organization (specify) ▶
- ☐ Other (specify) ▶
- ☐ Estate (SSN of decedent)
- ☐ Plan administrator (TIN)
- ☐ Trust (TIN of grantor)
- ☐ National Guard ☐ State/local government
- ☐ Farmers' cooperative ☐ Federal government/military
- ☐ REMIC ☐ Indian tribal governments/enterprises
- Group Exemption Number (GEN) if any ▶

9b	If a corporation, name the state or foreign country (if applicable) where incorporated	State	Foreign country

10 **Reason for applying** (check only one box)

- ☑ Started new business (specify type) ▶ **sales**
- ☐ Hired employees (Check the box and see line 13.)
- ☐ Compliance with IRS withholding regulations
- ☐ Other (specify) ▶
- ☐ Banking purpose (specify purpose) ▶
- ☐ Changed type of organization (specify new type) ▶
- ☐ Purchased going business
- ☐ Created a trust (specify type) ▶
- ☐ Created a pension plan (specify type) ▶

11	Date business started or acquired (month, day, year). See instructions. **August 1, 20xx**	12	Closing month of accounting year **December**

13 Highest number of employees expected in the next 12 months (enter -0- if none).

If no employees expected, skip line 14.

Agricultural	Household	Other
0	0	1

14 If you expect your employment tax liability to be $1,000 or less in a full calendar year **and** want to file Form 944 annually instead of Forms 941 quarterly, check here. (Your employment tax liability generally will be $1,000 or less if you expect to pay $4,000 or less in total wages.) If you do not check this box, you must file Form 941 for every quarter. ☐

15 First date wages or annuities were paid (month, day, year). **Note.** If applicant is a withholding agent, enter date income will first be paid to nonresident alien (month, day, year) . . . . ▶ **September 1, 20xx**

16 Check **one** box that best describes the principal activity of your business.
- ☐ Construction ☐ Rental & leasing ☐ Transportation & warehouse ☐ Accommodation & food service ☐ Wholesale-other ☐ Retail
- ☐ Real estate ☐ Manufacturing ☐ Finance & insurance ☐ Other (specify)
- ☐ Health care & social assistance ☐ Wholesale-agent/broker

17 Indicate principal line of merchandise sold, specific construction work done, products produced, or services provided.
sale of posters

18 Has the applicant entity shown on line 1 ever applied for and received an EIN? ☐ Yes ☐ No
If "Yes," write previous EIN here ▶

	Complete this section **only** if you want to authorize the named individual to receive the entity's EIN and answer questions about the completion of this form.	
Third Party Designee	Designee's name	Designee's telephone number (include area code) ( )
	Address and ZIP code	Designee's fax number (include area code) ( )

Under penalties of perjury, I declare that I have examined this application, and to the best of my knowledge and belief, it is true, correct, and complete.

Name and title (type or print clearly) ▶ **Ted Anderson, Owner**

Applicant's telephone number (include area code) **(555) 555-5555**

Signature ▶ *Ted Anderson*   Date ▶ **7/14/xx**

Applicant's fax number (include area code) **(555) 555-5555**

For Privacy Act and Paperwork Reduction Act Notice, see separate instructions.   Cat. No. 16055N   Form **SS-4** (Rev. 1-2010) year. Your answer, however, isn't binding. You make your binding election of a fiscal year end on the first federal income tax return that you file for the business.

Sole proprietors, partnerships, S corporations, and personal service corporations are generally required to use a calendar year—that is, a year ending December 31—for tax purposes. Personal service corporations have two basic characteristics:

- The professional employees of the corporation own the stock.
- The corporation performs its services in the fields of health, law, engineering, architecture, accounting, actuarial science, performing arts, or consulting.

To use a tax year other than a calendar year, an S corporation must demonstrate to the IRS that it has a substantial business reason to do so, such as the seasonal nature of the business. Basically, the IRS wants to make sure that permitting you to claim a tax year other than the calendar year won't substantially distort your income.

A regular corporation that's not a personal service corporation has more freedom in choosing a fiscal year. Most small businesses find that, even where there's a choice, the calendar year is the most convenient way to proceed. Sometimes, however, there are tax planning reasons for a business owner to choose a different tax year for the business. See IRS Publication 538, *Accounting Periods and Methods*, for details.

SEE AN EXPERT

An accountant or other experienced tax adviser can help you decide whether you and your corporation can realize a tax advantage by using a fiscal year instead of a calendar year.

Space 13. These numbers can be estimated.

Space 18. This question refers to the business, not the owner. Normally, a partnership or corporation has only one Employer Identification Number (EIN). A sole proprietor may have several businesses, each with a separate number.

Use your EIN on all business tax returns, checks, and other documents you send to the IRS. Your state tax authority may also require your EIN on state tax forms.

When to Get a New Number

If your S corporation chooses to change to a regular corporation—or your regular corporation chooses to change to an S corporation—it doesn't need a new EIN; the one you already have is still sufficient. However, you'll need to get a new EIN if any of these changes occur in your business:

- You incorporate your sole proprietorship or partnership.
- Your sole proprietorship takes in partners and begins operating as a partnership.
- Your partnership is taken over by one of the partners and begins operating as a sole proprietorship.
- Your corporation changes to a partnership or to a sole proprietorship.

- You purchase or inherit an existing business that you'll operate as a sole proprietorship.
- You represent an estate that operates a business after the owner's death.
- You terminate an old partnership and begin a new one.

Federal Employment Taxes

There are several types of employment-related taxes the federal government exacts from businesses.

RESOURCE

These taxes are all explained clearly and in great detail in Circular E, *Employer's Tax Guide*, published by the IRS. Updated whenever the tax rates change, Circular E is available at all IRS offices and is mailed automatically to all businesses with an EIN.

Federal Income Tax Withholding (FIT)

You must withhold income taxes from employees' paychecks based on:

- the employee's filing status (single, married, or married but withholding at the higher single rate)
- the number of dependents (withholding allowances) declared by the employee, and
- the size of the employee's salary.

Each employee should give you a signed Form W-4 stating the withholding allowance. Save these forms in case the IRS wants to see them.

Use the tables in Circular E to figure out how much income tax to withhold.

RESOURCE

Need tax help? IRS Publication 334, *Tax Guide for Small Business*, and, if you're just getting started, IRS Publication 583, *Starting a Business and Keeping Records*, are well worth reading. You can download these publications at the IRS website, www.irs.gov.

Working for Yourself: Law & Taxes for Independent Contractors, Freelancers & Consultants, by Stephen Fishman (Nolo), is a comprehensive guide for those starting their own businesses. It includes detailed information on taxes.

Small-Time Business Operator, by Bernard Kamoroff (Bell Springs Publishing), is a modestly priced and clearly written book that covers not only taxes but also many other practical aspects of doing business, including bookkeeping.

U.S. Master Tax Guide (Commerce Clearing House) is updated annually and available in law libraries, business school libraries, and the reference departments of major public libraries. It features in-depth explanations of tax complexities.

The Kiplinger Tax Letter, published by the Kiplinger Washington Editors, is a biweekly newsletter. It's pricey but does keep you up to date on what's happening in the tax field. To subscribe, go to www.kiplinger.com/orders/ktl2.

Social Security Taxes (FICA)

You must withhold the employee's share of the Social Security tax and Medicare tax from the employee's pay. And you must also pay the employer's share.

The amounts to be withheld are listed in the most current edition of Circular E. In 2011, for example, the employee is required to pay 5.65% on the first $106,800 of his or her annual wages; 5.65% is the sum of the 4.2% Social Security tax and the 1.45% Medicare tax. The employer is required to pay 7.65% on the first $106,800 of the employee's annual wages; 7.65% is the sum of the 6.2% Social Security tax and the 1.45% Medicare tax. There is no Social Security tax on the portion of the employee's annual wages that exceed $106,800—only Medicare tax; the employer and employee each pay the 1.45% Medicare tax on the excess amount. The rates and the cut-off point for the Social Security tax change annually.

Federal Unemployment Taxes (FUTA)

You must report and pay the federal unemployment tax (FUTA); it's not withheld from the employee's pay. In recent years, the FUTA rate has been 6.2% of the first $7,000 of the employee's wages for the year. Employers receive a credit for participating in state unemployment programs. The credit has reduced the FUTA rate to 0.8% for most employers, which translates into $56 for an employee earning $7,000 or more per year. Because many states owe money to the federal government for loans taken from the federal unemployment fund, however, the credit in those states will now be less than in the past—and the FUTA rate will be higher. For example, in 2011, the FUTA rate for Michigan employers will be 1.4% rather than 0.8%; an employer in that state will need to pay $98 per employee rather than $56.

Use Form 940 to report federal unemployment tax. Sole proprietorships and partnerships don't pay the FUTA on the owners' compensation.

Withholding From an Owner's Paycheck

If you own most or all of the stock of a regular corporation, chances are you probably pay yourself a salary—which means that you're an employee as well as an owner. Similarly, if you're an owner and officer of an S corporation and perform substantial services for the company, you're considered an employee for tax purposes.

With either type of corporation, if you receive compensation for your services, you must complete and submit a Form W-4 to the corporation just like any other employee, and the corporation must withhold income, Social Security, and Medicare taxes from your paychecks.

Periodic Payments

You must periodically remit to the IRS the income tax you withhold from employee paychecks and the employer's and employee's shares of Social Security and Medicare taxes. The IRS requires you to do this electronically through its Electronic Federal Tax Payment System. For detailed information on using the system, go to www.eftps.gov. How often you must pay is based on the size of your payroll and amounts due. A typical small business makes monthly payments.

In January of each year, you must give each employee a completed Form W-2, Wage and Tax Statement, listing the employee's total earnings for the prior year and the amount of employment taxes that you have withheld. The Form W-2 for 2012 (that you'll mail to employees in January 2013), and for future years, will also need to state the value of any health care coverage you've provided that's not included in the employee's gross income.

 CAUTION

Deposit taxes on time. Be sure to withhold taxes as required by the tax laws— and to deposit those taxes on time. There are substantial penalties if you don't. And if you're an owner of a small business and personally involved in its management, you can be held personally liable for these taxes and the additional penalties, even if the business has the funds to pay them. The IRS has discretion to go after whomever it chooses. If your business suddenly runs into financial trouble, put the withheld taxes at the top of the list for payment. If that means not paying suppliers and others, so be it. The debts of the other creditors can be wiped out in bankruptcy if the business continues to go downhill. Not so with the withheld taxes. You can remain personally liable for these amounts even if the business goes through bankruptcy.

RESOURCE

Get a copy of IRS Publication 509, *Tax Calendars,* to see when to file returns and make tax payments. It's available from your local IRS office. You can also obtain it at the IRS website at www.irs.gov. The publication is updated annually.

Federal Self-Employment Taxes

The self-employment tax applies to income you receive from actively working in your business—but not as an employee of that business. Technically, it's not an employment tax, but a first cousin to that tax—so closely related that you should be aware of it to fully understand employment taxes.

If you're a sole proprietor or a partner, you must pay the federal self-employment tax in addition to regular income tax. The self-employment tax is equal to the employer's and employee's portion of the Social Security and Medicare taxes that you and your employer would pay on your compensation if you received it as an employee.

Payroll Taxes Made Easy

If you're overwhelmed by the requirements for calculating payroll taxes and the fine points of when and where to pay them, you can pay a bank or payroll service to do the work for you. A reputable payroll tax outfit that offers a tax notification service will calculate the correct amount due, produce your employees' paychecks and the checks to pay your taxes, and notify you when the taxes are due.

One big advantage of a payroll service over a bank is that it could give you more control over your money. A bank will withhold the amount of the tax from your account when the payroll is done, even though the tax isn't due yet. That means the bank, not you, gets the use of the money in the interim. A payroll service that offers tax notification will prepare the checks and tell you when they must be deposited. Depending on how often you must

make payments, that can give you the use of the money for an extra month or more.

At the end of each quarter, the payroll service will produce your quarterly payroll tax returns and tell you how to file them. At the end of the year, the service will also prepare W-2 forms and federal and state transmittal forms.

Payroll services can be cost effective for even very small businesses. But when you look for one, it pays to shop around. Avoid services that charge setup fees—basically, a fee for putting your information into the computer—or extra fees to prepare W-2 forms or quarterly and annual tax returns.

For added convenience, some payroll services—such as PayCycle (www.paycycle.com) and Paychex (www.paychex.com)—let you use the Internet to enter employee information into a system that crunches the numbers for you.

Compute this tax each year on Schedule SE, then attach it to your personal Form 1040. Add the self-employment tax to the income tax that you owe. In 2011, for example, the self-employment tax is set at 13.3% on earnings up to $106,800 and 2.9% on earnings over $106,800.

If you have income from another job that's subject to withholding—common for people just getting started in business—the income from your other job will reduce the tax base for your self-employment tax.

Federal Tax Deductions for Salaries and Other Expenses

A number of employee-related expenses can be deducted from your business income in computing your federal income tax.

Salaries

You can deduct from your gross income the salaries, wages, and other forms of compensation that you pay to employees for their services, as long as the payments are reasonable. Fortunately, you have broad discretion to decide what's reasonable. Short of a scam—such as paying a huge salary to a spouse or relative who does little or no work—the IRS will almost always accept your notion of what pay is reasonable.

If your business uses the cash method of accounting, you deduct the payments that were actually made during the tax year. For employers using an accrual method of accounting, the rule is different and more complicated. The salaries are deductible for the tax year in which you established your obligation to make the payments, even if you deferred payment to a later time.

Vacation Pay

You can also deduct vacation pay from business income in determining the base for your federal income tax. If you're on a cash basis accounting method, you deduct vacation pay as wages when you pay the employee. If you use an accrual method, you can deduct vacation pay in the year it's earned only if you pay it by the close of your tax year or within two and a half months after the close. If you pay later than this, you deduct it in the year you actually pay it.

Bonuses and Gifts

Many businesses give bonuses to employees to reward them for a job well done or because the company has had a profitable year. You

Computing Your Estimated Taxes

Many taxpayers receive income from sources other than paychecks—for example, from investments and royalties. These taxpayers often owe surprising amounts in income taxes on April 15. Sometimes, that's because they had no employer to withhold income tax during the year. Other times, it's because even though there was an employer, the amounts withheld were insufficient to cover the taxpayer's nonemployment income.

As you may know, the IRS doesn't want you to wait until April 15 to pay. Instead, the IRS requires you to pay your taxes in advance in quarterly installments if not enough is being withheld from your salary. These installments are known as estimated taxes. If you don't pay sufficient taxes in advance, you face the burden of paying interest and penalties.

In figuring out what your tax bill will be and whether you need to pay any quarterly installments of estimated taxes, don't overlook the self-employment tax that is added to your regular income tax on your Form 1040 as part of your tax obligation. Make sure your quarterly installments are large enough to cover your self-employment tax as well as your usual income tax.

For more on this subject, see IRS Publication 505, *Tax Withholding and Estimated Tax*, available at the IRS website at www.irs.gov.

can take a tax deduction for bonuses you pay to employees if they're intended as additional payment for services and not as gifts; most bonuses qualify for deduction. The bonuses are subject to payroll tax withholding.

If your business distributes cash or gift certificates that can be converted to cash, the value of these gifts is considered additional wages or salary regardless of the amount—and is subject to employment taxes and withholding rules.

Noncash gifts are also generally treated as income to the employee, but not those that are clearly of an advertising nature, such as pens embossed with your company name. Other noncash gifts to employees may also be excluded from the employee's income if they are of nominal value.

> **EXAMPLE:** To promote employee goodwill, Pebblestone Partnership distributes turkeys, hams, and other merchandise of nominal value at holidays. The partnership also gives each employee a check for $200. The value of the turkeys, hams, and other merchandise isn't salaries or wages, but the partnership can deduct the cost of these items as a business expense. The checks can also be deducted but must be treated as income to the employees subject to withholding.

Meals and Lodging

You can deduct at least some of the cost of meals and lodging you provide to employees if these expenses are a reasonable part of doing business. In some cases, the value of the meals or lodging you furnish must be reported as part of the employees' income for tax purposes.

Meals

Normally, you can deduct as a business expense only 50% of the cost of providing meals to employees. You can, however, deduct the full cost if any of the following is true:

- You operate a restaurant or catering service and furnish the meals to employees at the worksite.
- You furnish the meals as part of a recreational or social activity, such as a company picnic.
- The value of the meals is included in employees' income. Meals must be included in an employee's income unless the meals are furnished on your premises and for your convenience or consist of food that qualifies as a minimal fringe benefit—coffee, doughnuts, or soft drinks, for example, or the occasional meal you provide to enable an employee to work overtime.

EXAMPLE 1: Carol is a waitress at Sunshine Cafe. The restaurant provides two meals at no charge during her 7 a.m. to 4 p.m. workday. Sunshine Cafe encourages—but doesn't require—Carol to eat breakfast there before starting work. She must eat lunch there. Since Carol works during the normal breakfast and lunch periods, the value of her breakfast and lunch are not treated as income to her. If Sunshine Cafe allows Carol to have free meals there on her days off, the value of those meals would be included as income to Carol.

EXAMPLE 2: Frank is a clerk at Omni Department Store, working 9 a.m. to 5 p.m. Omni gives Frank his lunch without charge at a lunch buffet it maintains at the store. This helps Omni limit Frank's lunch break to 30 minutes—a benefit to Omni since its busiest time is during the normal lunch period. If Frank left the store to have lunch, he'd be away much longer than 30 minutes. The value of these meals is not income to Frank.

In addition to the above situations, you can deduct the full cost of the meals you serve on your premises to all employees—as long as more than one-half of them receive this benefit as a convenience to your business. In the example above, suppose that Omni Department Store were to provide the lunch buffet to 30 of the store's 50 employees as a convenience to the store. Omni could deduct the cost of providing the food to the other 20 employees as well.

Lodging

You can deduct as a business expense the cost of furnishing lodging to employees if it's a reasonable part of doing business. Generally, you must include the value of lodging as part of the employees' income. The value can be excluded, however, if you furnish the lodging on your business premises for your convenience and require the employee to live there to perform the job.

EXAMPLE: Felice is a swimming pool attendant at The Highlands, a resort complex that's 15 miles from town. The Highlands gives Felice the choice of living at the resort free of charge. If Felice chooses to live at The Highlands, the resort must include the value of the lodging in her income. It is not necessary for Felice to live at the resort to properly perform her job duties. It's merely a matter of convenience.

Fringe Benefits

Your business may be able to deduct as a business expense a number of employee fringe benefits, including:

- health and dental insurance
- medical reimbursement plans for items not covered by health insurance
- group term life insurance—limits apply, based on the policy value
- educational assistance programs
- adoption assistance programs
- moving expenses
- qualified employee benefit plans, including profit sharing plans, stock bonus plans, and money purchase pension plans, and
- cafeteria plans that allow employees to choose among two or more benefits consisting of cash and qualified benefits.

(See Chapter 4 for a detailed discussion of employee benefits.)

Be aware that there are restrictions—some of them complex—on deducting these benefits and that deductions may be available to some forms of business and not others. Not only are employee benefits tax-deductible by your business, but they also are not taxed to the employee.

But while these benefits sound attractive, there are two serious drawbacks. First, many small businesses—particularly those just starting out—won't have the funds to finance them. Second, the IRS has stringent rules to discourage top-heavy plans—those designed to benefit primarily the owners and highly paid employees of a business. If your plan doesn't meet these guidelines, your business won't be able to deduct the cost.

Independent Contractors

Some people you hire will be independent contractors rather than employees. (The differences between these two categories of workers are explained in detail in Chapter 11.) If you do hire someone who meets the IRS tests for an independent contractor, you don't have to withhold income taxes or Social Security taxes from that person's pay, nor are you required to make an employer's contribution to the worker's Social Security fund.

If, however, you pay an independent contractor $600 or more during a calendar year, you must report this to the IRS on Form 1099-MISC.

Ask all independent contractors you hire to complete Form W-9, giving their Social Security numbers or their Employer Identification Numbers. You'll need this information when you report the payments you made. Because some independent contractors have tried to foil the IRS's attempts to track income, the government has enacted regulations to protect the integrity of the system. If an independent contractor doesn't give you an identification number—Social Security or Employer Identification Number—or if the IRS says you were given a wrong number, you may have to withhold 31% of the independent contractor's pay to assure that taxes aren't evaded.

> **CAUTION**
>
> **Be sure workers are properly classified.** The IRS believes it has lost large amounts of tax revenues because many employers and workers have improperly agreed to classify the workers as independent contractors rather than employees. In many of these cases, the employer hasn't withheld taxes—and the worker has neglected to report the income and pay tax on it. Given that background, the IRS enforces strict tests for determining who is and who isn't an independent contractor—and if you misclassify someone who should have been called an employee, you may be heavily penalized. (To avoid costly problems, see Chapter 12 for a fuller explanation of the IRS criteria.)

Statutory Employees

Statutory employees are a kind of legal hybrid. They tend to be people you might ordinarily think of as independent contractors rather than employees, but they are employees because the law says they are. For statutory employees, your responsibilities for withholding taxes are less extensive than your responsibilities for other employees. You don't withhold income taxes from their pay, but you must withhold Social Security and Medicare taxes and you must make the matching employer's contribution.

The following are statutory employees.

Delivery people. A driver who either distributes meat products, vegetable or fruit products, bakery products, or beverages other than milk, or who picks up or delivers laundry or dry cleaning, if the driver is your agent or is paid on commission.

Insurance salespeople. A full-time life insurance salesperson.

Home workers. A person who works at home on materials that you supply and that must be returned to you or someone you name, if you also furnish specifications for how the work is to be done.

Traveling salespeople. A full-time traveling salesperson, who's not an agent or commission driver, who works on your behalf and turns in orders to you from wholesalers, retailers, contractors, hotels, restaurants, or other similar businesses. The goods sold must be merchandise for resale or supplies used in the buyer's business operation.

There's another twist in the statutory employee story: Not every person who falls into one of the above four categories is treated as a statutory employee. A statutory employee must meet three additional conditions:

- There must be a service contract stating or implying that the person must personally perform the services.
- Someone other than the worker must have invested substantially in the facilities used to perform the services—except for a car or truck.
- The worker must perform the services on a continuing basis.

If these conditions all apply, then you become responsible for withholding the worker's share of Social Security and Medicare taxes and paying the employer's share.

One more wrinkle: You need only pay federal unemployment tax (FUTA) on statutory employees who are delivery people or traveling salespeople.

 RESOURCE

Get IRS help on statutory employees. For more information on statutory employees, see IRS Publication 15-A, *Employer's Supplemental Tax Guide,* available at www.irs.gov.

Family and Medical Leave

t's often been difficult for working people to deal with family obligations such as caring for a seriously ill child or parent or attending to the special needs of a newborn infant or newly adopted child. And, some employees who have taken time off work to recover from their own serious illnesses have worried about being demoted or fired.

To help employees balance the demands of the workplace with personal and family needs, Congress enacted the Family and Medical Leave Act, or FMLA. (29 U.S.C. §§ 2601 and following.) Under the FMLA, if your business has 50 or more employees, you may be required to give an employee up to 12 weeks of unpaid leave for certain family and medical reasons. And the law requires you to return the employee to the same or a similar position when the leave is over—except when it would be prohibitively expensive for you to take back a highly paid employee.

In 2008, the FMLA was amended to allow certain employees with family members in the military to take leave. As part of their 12-week entitlement, employees may take FMLA leave to handle practical concerns relating to a family member's call to active duty. The amendments also create a 26-week leave entitlement for employees who need time off to care for a family member who is suffering from a serious illness or injury related to his or her military service. These provisions are covered in "Leave for Military Families," below.

This chapter discusses the federal law. Your state might have its own family leave law. To find out more about state law requirements, see "Related Laws," below.

RESOURCE

The FMLA is a complicated law with complicated requirements. To get detailed information about whether it applies to your company, how to administer leave, how the FMLA interacts with other laws, and more, see *The Essential Guide to Family & Medical Leave*, by Lisa Guerin and Deborah C. England (Nolo).

Informing Employees

If your business is subject to the FMLA, you must display a poster in the workplace titled "Employees' Rights and Responsibilities Under the Family and Medical Leave Act." It's available at the nearest office of the U.S. Department of Labor's Wage and Hour Division. Your state labor department may also be able to provide this poster, as well as posters describing workplace rights and responsibilities under state law.

You must also inform employees about their rights to FMLA leave, in your employee handbook, if you have one. Otherwise, you must give employees written guidance when they request FMLA leave. The easiest way to do this is to print out the Employment Law Guide, posted at www.dol.gov/whd/regs/compliance/posters/fmlaen.pdf, and give employees a copy.

Who Is Covered

The FMLA covers your business if it has had 50 or more employees for 20 or more weeks in the current or preceding year. The count, for FMLA purposes, includes all employees on your payroll—part time, full time, and those already on leave.

An employee in a covered business is eligible for FMLA leave only if the employee works within a 75-mile radius of 50 or more employees and has worked for you:

- for at least 12 months (these months do not have to be consecutive), and
- for at least 1,250 hours during the 12 months before the leave.

Reasons for Taking a Leave

If your business is covered, you must grant unpaid leave to an eligible employee to care for a seriously ill parent, child, or spouse, to recover from a serious illness, to bond with a new child, or to handle issues relating to a family member's military service. Generally, the employee is entitled to a total of 12 work-weeks of leave during any 12-month period. Some employees may be eligible for up to 26 weeks off; see "Leave for Military Families," below.

> CAUTION
>
> **Don't retaliate against employees for exercising leave rights.** The FMLA prohibits you from retaliating against an employee who has asked for or taken leave. Retaliation can take many forms. It can be blatant (such as transferring the employee to a job that pays less or carries less status) or more subtle (such as assigning the employee less desirable tasks).

Family Health Problems

An eligible employee may take FMLA leave to care for a spouse, son, daughter, or parent who has a serious health condition.

Defining Serious Health Condition

The FMLA rules for determining who has a serious health condition are complicated. Generally, however, an injury or illness may qualify as a serious health condition if it involves inpatient care—an overnight stay in a hospital or other medical care facility. The person who has been hospitalized is considered to have a serious health condition for as long as the individual can't work, attend school, or perform other normal life activities.

In addition, an injury or illness may qualify as a serious health condition if the patient requires continuing treatment (two or more treatments by a health care provider—or one treatment and an ongoing regimen of care—in a 30-day period) and cannot perform normal activities for more than three consecutive days. A person who needs continuing treatment for pregnancy or prenatal care, a chronic health condition, or a long-term or permanent health condition may also have a serious health condition.

Defining Family

An employee is only eligible to take FMLA leave to care for certain family members: the employee's spouse, parent, or child. A spouse is an employee's husband or wife as recognized under state law, which may include common-law spouses in the minority of states that recognize common-law marriage. However, same-sex partners or spouses don't qualify under the law.

An employee's parent can be a biological parent or a person who took the place of a parent when the employee was a child— someone, for example, who took care of and financially supported the child. In-laws aren't considered parents under the FMLA.

An employee's son or daughter can be a biological, adopted, or foster child; a stepchild; or a legal ward. A child whom the employee cares for or financially supports also counts. Children must be younger than 18—or, if age 18 or older, they must be incapable of caring for themselves because of a mental or physical disability.

 TIP

State laws may define "family" differently. Many states have family and medical leave laws similar to the FMLA. (See "Related Laws," below, for more information.) These laws may define "family" to include in-laws, domestic partners, and more. So even if the FMLA doesn't apply when an employee asks for time off to care for a family member, make sure to check your state's law, too.

Employee's Health Problems

An eligible employee may take FMLA leave for a serious health condition that makes the employee unable to perform the job.

Birth, Adoption, or Foster Care

An eligible employee may take FMLA leave because of the birth of a child or because a child has been placed with the employee for adoption or foster care. Under the FMLA, foster care is defined as 24-hour care for a child away from parents or guardians—and it must be based on a court order or an agreement approved by a state agency.

The period for taking leave based on birth, adoption, or foster care expires one year after the child is born or placed. Men as well as women are eligible for this leave. An expectant mother may begin FMLA leave before the birth of the child for prenatal care or if her condition makes her unable to work. You can require medical documentation of the need for prenatal care or inability to work before you grant a prebirth leave because this is a leave for the employee's serious health condition, not for bonding. Likewise, an employee with a pregnant wife may be eligible for FMLA leave to care for his pregnant spouse before the baby is born, if she needs such care.

Similarly, FMLA leave can begin before actual placement or adoption of a child if an absence from work is necessary. Such an absence may be necessary, for example, if an employee must attend counseling sessions, appear in court, consult with a lawyer or doctor representing the birth parent, or submit to a physical exam.

If a husband and wife both work for your company, you can limit the total number of workweeks taken by both spouses to care for a child to 12 during any 12-month period. However, if the child's parents are not married to one another, each parent is entitled to the full allotment of 12 workweeks of leave. On the other hand, an unmarried man isn't eligible for FMLA leave to care for his pregnant partner during pregnancy, because he doesn't meet the definition of "family member" under the FMLA.

Leave for Military Families

The FMLA also provides leaves to the families of military service people in two cases: when a serviceperson is injured during military service, and when the serviceperson is deployed to active duty. These provisions cover adult children.

Injury or Illness

Recognizing the strain placed on the families of military servicepeople, the FMLA provides time off for the spouse, son, daughter, parent or next of kin of a member of the armed forces who suffers a serious injury or illness incurred in the line of active duty. This includes a service member with a pre-existing injury or illness that was aggravated in the line of duty. It also extends to veterans who were in the military within the past five years and are being treated for a duty-related injury or illness.

The covered family member can take up to 26 weeks of leave during a single 12-month period to care for the service member. (The 26-week cap combines all types of FMLA leave.)

"Qualifying Exigency"

The FMLA provides that if an employee's spouse, son, daughter, or parent is called to active duty in the military, the employee can take up to 12 weeks of FMLA leave during a 12-month period for a "qualifying exigency." Such events include:

- **Short-notice deployment.** This applies when the service member receives notice of a call-up within seven days of the deployment. The FMLA leave for this purpose is limited to seven calendar days from when the service member receives the notice.
- **Military events.** This allows the family member to attend official ceremonies, programs, or events related to the service member's active duty or call-up.
- **Childcare and school activities.** This includes arranging alternative child care, caring for children on an immediate, urgent basis, and attending school meetings.
- **Financial and legal arrangements.** This gives the family member the time to make or update financial or legal plans to address the service member's absence. For example, this can include making a will or trust, or preparing a power of attorney.

- **Counseling.** The employee can take time off to receive counseling.
- **Rest and recuperation.** The employee can take FMLA leave to spend time with the service member who is on short-term R&R during a period of deployment. These leaves are limited to five days for each instance of R&R.
- **Post-deployment activities.** This includes arrival ceremonies, reintegration briefings, and other official programs within 90 days after the deployment ends. It also includes leave to address issues relating the service member's death.
- **Additional activities.** The employee can take FMLA leave for other events related to the service member's deployment—but only if the employer and the employee agree to the timing and length of the leave.

Scheduling Leave

Many times, an employee may request large blocks of time off—days or weeks—under the FMLA. Other times, however, the employee may wish to take off only an hour or two—to attend a follow-up appointment after a surgery, for example—or on an "as needed" basis. You and an employee can agree to flexible work scheduling for the leave time to which employees are entitled under the FMLA. If the employee is taking the leave for his or her own serious health condition, to care for a family member who has a serious health condition, or for qualifying exigency leave, the FMLA may require your company to provide this intermittent leave. However, the company isn't required to provide intermittent leave to employees taking leave to bond with a new child—it can require the employee to take the leave all at once. But it can provide this option, if it wants to.

> **EXAMPLE:** Bill, an employee of Rendex Corporation, normally works Monday through Friday. Bill's wife has given birth to a son. Rendex and Bill agree that he'll use his leave rights in two-day segments by working Monday through Wednesday and staying home on Thursday and Friday.

Alternatively, the leave may be taken by reducing the employee's weekly work hours. Again, you are not required to allow employees on bonding leave to reduce their work schedules, but you must allow employees on leave for a serious medical condition to do so, if a health care provider says a reduced schedule is medically necessary.

> **EXAMPLE 1:** Tim works for Enterprise Associates. His father has a serious health condition requiring radiation treatments each week at a university medical center 100 miles away. Tim needs to drive his dad to treatment every Friday. Enterprise Associates must allow Tim to use unpaid leave time on Fridays.

EXAMPLE 2: Carla, an employee of Cormark Company, adopts a daughter. Cormark and Carla agree that she'll exercise her leave rights by temporarily working from 1 p.m. to 5 p.m. rather than her normal 8 a.m. to 5 p.m. schedule.

Temporary Transfer to Another Job

If it is disruptive to your business to allow a particular employee to have a flexible or reduced work schedule, check to see whether there's another job open that will accommodate the employee's request with less disruption. If so, you can transfer the employee temporarily to the other job. The alternative job must have equivalent pay and benefits. The duties, however, needn't be equivalent as long as it isn't obviously a demotion—which raises the appearance that your company is retaliating against an employee for taking FMLA leave, and could create legal problems.

EXAMPLE: Hilda works for Project Systems Inc. as a manager of ten employees. She is suffering from a major depressive episode which will require psychotherapy three times a week for six months. Project Systems must grant Hilda's request for a reduced leave schedule to permit her to get the necessary treatment. The company also transfers Hilda temporarily to a research position in which her absences will be less disruptive to the company.

Workplace Politics: A Delicate Business

When you temporarily transfer an employee, other employees—especially those who have been eyeing the open job—may feel resentful. This is a delicate situation, and you may be inclined to reduce tensions by informing the other employees about the medical reasons behind the transfer. Restrain yourself. You must respect that person's privacy, and could get into legal trouble for disclosing confidential medical information.

Substituting Paid Leave

You're not required to pay for FMLA leave, but if you offer paid time off—vacation, personal, family, or sick leave—as a job benefit, you can require, or the employee can voluntarily substitute, paid leave for unpaid FMLA leave in most situations.

You or the employee may substitute paid time off for unpaid FMLA leave as long as the reason for leave is covered by your paid leave policy and the employee meets the other requirements of your paid leave program. For example, if your company allows employees to use their sick leave to care for family members who are ill, they may substitute paid sick leave for FMLA leave used to care for a family member with a serious health condition. However, you don't have to allow employees to use sick leave for purposes that aren't covered by your program, such as bonding with a new child.

You may also require employees to follow your usual procedures for paid leave, but you may not deny them unpaid FMLA leave if they don't follow those procedures. An employee's failure to follow company policies for paid leave affects only their right to paid leave, not their rights under the FMLA.

EXAMPLE: Lou works for Star Baking Company. Star's paid time off policies require employees to give at least one week of advance notice before taking vacation time. Lou's mother has emergency surgery, and Lou immediately calls his supervisor and arranges to take three weeks of FMLA leave to care for her. He isn't entitled to use vacation time to get paid for the first week of FMLA leave, because he didn't give notice one week in advance. However, he may use vacation time for the second and third weeks of his leave, after the one-week notice requirement is met.

⊘ CAUTION

How much time off is owed. If an employee uses paid leave under circumstances that don't qualify as FMLA leave, the leave won't count against the 12 weeks of FMLA leave to which the employee is entitled. For example, if an employee uses paid sick leave for a condition which isn't a serious health condition as defined in the FMLA, the time off doesn't count against

the 12 weeks of unpaid FMLA leave to which the employee may later be entitled.

Creative Solutions for Hard Problems

Family and medical leave laws address only a small part of the issues facing employers and employees in balancing the competing demands of the family and the workplace. To ensure a happy and productive workforce, you may need to work with employees to come up with creative solutions. Consider this list of possibilities from Renee Magid, founder and president of the consulting firm Initiatives Inc.:

- flexible career paths
- flexible worktimes for full-time employees
- permanent part-time employment, with benefits
- job sharing
- work-at-home options
- cafeteria-style benefit plans
- education and support programs
- financial assistance with child care, and
- direct child care.

Advance Notice of Leave

Often, an employee can foresee the need for medical or bonding leave. For example, most employees know approximately when a baby will be born or can schedule a nonemergency surgery well in advance. You can require, in these situations, that an employee notify you at least 30 days before the unpaid leave is to begin.

But such advance notice isn't always possible—and the FMLA takes this into account. For example, if a child is born prematurely or an adoption or placement goes through unexpectedly, the employee can give you a shorter notice; the test is what is practical. If an employee doesn't give you 30 days' notice, you are allowed to ask the employee to explain why providing such notice wasn't practicable.

Similarly, where there's a medical emergency involving the employee or a member of the employee's family, it usually won't be practical for the employee to give you any advance notice of the need for leave. In such cases, advance notice isn't required. Where the need for FMLA leave isn't foreseeable, the employee or a family member can notify you either in person or by phone, fax, or email of the circumstances requiring the leave.

If an employee's leave is based on a serious health condition that requires planned medical treatment, you can require the employee to make a reasonable effort to schedule the treatment so that it won't unduly disrupt your business.

Certification

Theoretically, an employee could abuse the system by falsely claiming that the employee or a family member has a serious health condition. The FMLA recognizes this and allows you to require proof—a certificate from the patient's health care provider stating:

- the date the serious health condition started
- the length of time the condition is likely to last
- diagnosis of the condition
- treatment prescribed, and
- whether inpatient treatment is required.

You're free to decide when to ask for a certificate and when not to—but it's best to follow a uniform policy, rather than a selective one. Otherwise, someone who's required to provide a certificate may claim you're discriminating, and you may have trouble justifying why a particular employee was singled out.

The certification requirements for a qualifying exigency caused by an active serviceperson's deployment are a little different. An employer may require the employee to provide a copy of the covered military member's active duty order for each separate call to active duty. The employee may also be required to submit a certification that includes:

- a signed description of the facts supporting the leave request, with supporting available documentation
- the approximate date of the qualifying exigency
- if the request is for a specific time period, the beginning and end dates of that period; or if it is intermittent or a reduced schedule, that schedule, and

- if the exigency involves meeting with a third party, the contact information for that third party and a description of the purpose of the meeting.

There's also a separate certification form for family members who take leave to care for a seriously ill or injured service member.

The Department of Labor has developed an optional certification form for each type of FMLA leave. You can find them at www.dol.gov/whd/fmla/finalrule.htm.

Employee's Own Condition

If the employee seeks leave because of the employee's own serious health condition, you can require that the certificate state either that the employee can't perform work of any kind or that the employee can't perform the essential functions of the job. Give the employee or the doctor a list of the job's essential functions.

Family Member's Condition

If the employee seeks leave to care for a family member, you can require that the certificate state that the patient needs help meeting basic medical, hygiene, nutritional, safety, or transportation needs—or that the employee is needed to provide care. The employee must indicate on the certificate what care the employee will provide and how long that care is likely to be required.

Intermittent Leave or Reduced Leave Schedule

If the employee seeks to take intermittent leave or asks for a shortened work schedule, you can require that the certificate state the medical need for or desirability of such leave and how long the situation requiring leave is expected to last.

Unclear or Incomplete Certifications

If you receive a certification that's incomplete or insufficient (that is, some of the spaces on the form are left blank, it isn't signed, or the information provided is vague or doesn't provide the information the form requires), you must tell the employee in writing and explain what information is necessary to make the certification complete and sufficient. You must give the employee at least seven calendar days to hand in a complete certification.

Even if the certification you receive is complete, you may need to seek clarification or authentication from the employee's health care provider. For example, you might ask for clarification if you can't read the doctor's handwriting or you don't understand a response on the form. You might ask for authentication if you want the health care provider to verify that the information and signature on the form are accurate. To clarify or authenticate a certification, you must first notify the employee and give him or her seven days to fix it, as you would for an incomplete certification. If the employee is unable to resolve the problem, someone from your company may contact the health care provider directly. Because the law protects the confidentiality of health care information, however, you must follow these rules:

- You may seek only authentication or clarification, as defined above; you may not seek more information than the form requires.
- Only a health care provider, human resources professional, leave administrator, or management official may contact the health care provider. The employee's direct supervisor may not contact the health care provider.
- You must follow the requirements of the Health Insurance Portability and Accountability Act (HIPAA), which, among other things, may require the employee to consent in writing to the conversation.

Second and Third Opinions

If, after receiving a certification, you are not fully convinced the request entitles the employee to FMLA leave, you can require the employee to get an opinion from a second health care provider. This can be someone you designate or approve—but it can't be someone you regularly employ, such as a company doctor. And you, rather than the employee, must pay for the second opinion.

CAUTION

Weigh the odds of asking for more. Just because the FMLA allows you to get a second opinion doesn't mean it's a smart thing

to do. Often it's not. Think long and hard before getting adversarial with employees over health determinations. If you make an employee jump through hoops to qualify for an unpaid absence, you'll probably wind up with a resentful employee who will never again give you full effort and loyalty. And the fallout from being unnecessarily suspicious about one employee can easily infect the entire workplace.

If you wind up with conflicting opinions, you can require a third opinion from another health care provider—one approved by both you and the employee. This third opinion is binding on both of you.

You may not request second or third opinions for either type of military family leave.

Health Care Providers: What's in a Name?

Generally, a doctor of medicine or osteopathy will sign the employee's medical certificate or render the second or third opinion. But technically, under the FMLA and its regulations, such certificates can be signed by a health care provider—a term that includes not only MDs and DOs but others, such as podiatrists, dentists, clinical psychologists, optometrists, physician assistants, nurse practitioners, nurse midwives, clinical social workers, and, for some conditions, chiropractors.

Recertification

You can ask an employee to give you a recertification of a medical condition to support a leave request. You can require recertifications every six months, or every 30 days, for short-term conditions. You can request recertification more often if any of the following is true:

- The employee requests an extension of leave.
- Circumstances have changed significantly—for example, the duration or nature of the illness becomes different from what was anticipated.
- You receive information casting doubt on the continuing validity of the certification.

Health Benefits

If you have a group health plan for employees, you must maintain coverage for employees who are on FMLA leave. You must keep the coverage at the same level the employees would have if they worked continuously.

In some cases, however, you can require an employee to repay the premiums you paid for this continuing coverage. Generally, you can demand reimbursement if the employee doesn't come back to work after the leave period expires. But you can't demand reimbursement if the employee doesn't return to work in either of the following situations:

- The employee or a family member has suffered continuation, recurrence, or

onset of a serious health condition—the kind of thing that would have justified taking the unpaid leave in the first place.
- There are other circumstances beyond the control of the employee. Examples of this include: An employee's spouse is unexpectedly transferred to a job location more than 75 miles from the employee's worksite, a person other than an immediate family member has a serious health condition and the employee is needed to provide care, or the employee is laid off while on leave.

Returning to Work

The FMLA normally gives employees the right to return to their jobs when their leave has been completed.

Job Protection

When an eligible employee returns from taking a leave, your company must restore the employee to the job that the employee held when the leave began or to a similar job—one with equivalent pay, benefits, and other terms of employment. However, an employee has no greater right to reinstatement or other benefits than if the employee had been continuously employed during the FMLA leave period.

> **EXAMPLE:** Anton takes ten weeks of unpaid family leave from his job as a production worker at Smokestack Industries, Inc. While he's away,

Smokestack eliminates the night shift on which Anton was working and lays off all employees working on that shift. Smokestack would have laid off Anton had he been working instead of taking leave. Smokestack doesn't have to reemploy Anton.

Exemption for Highly Paid Employees

Recognizing that it's difficult for many businesses to carry on in the absence of the customary executives and decision makers, the FMLA lets you decline to take back some highly paid employees after their leave. The exemption applies only if both of the following are true:

- The employee is among the highest paid 10% of the salaried people you employ within 75 miles of the place where the employee works.
- Taking back the employee will cause what the statute calls "substantial and grievous economic injury" to your business.

Unfortunately, the FMLA regulations don't precisely set the level of economic hardship or injury that excuses you from taking back an employee. It's clear that minor inconveniences and costs are not enough to justify cutting off a key employee who's taken a leave. On the other hand, you don't have to show that taking back the employee would threaten the existence of your business.

One test is whether it's feasible to temporarily replace or do without the employee on FMLA leave—or whether you must hire a permanent replacement. If the employee on leave is your company's $125,000-a-year sales manager, you may find that no competent people are willing to take over the job on a short-term basis. And, since you need a sales manager, you have no real choice but to hire a permanent replacement. Reinstating the employee on leave to an equivalent job may be much too costly for your business—particularly if you must create a new job to do this. In such a situation, you'd likely be excused from taking back the employee after the leave.

As soon as you determine that substantial economic harm will result if you take back a key employee who has sought a leave under the FMLA, notify the employee in writing. In a letter, explain that your decision is based on your wish to prevent major injury to the business. If the employee then starts or continues the leave, you'll be protected by the FMLA.

Note that if an employee doesn't return to work after you give notice that you intend not to hire the employee back, you must still maintain the employee's health benefits for the full leave period, and you can't recover the cost of health insurance premiums.

Fitness to Work

If an employee has taken leave because of a serious health condition, the FMLA lets you require a medical certification that the employee is able to resume work. You can only impose this requirement if it's part of a policy you uniformly apply to all employees returning from medical leave.

There may be a state law, local ordinance, or union contract that governs the terms under which employees who have taken medical leave can return to work. The FMLA doesn't supersede these other legal controls. You must also comply with the Americans with Disabilities Act (ADA) rule that any physical exam required of an employee returning to work must be job related. (For more on the ADA, see Chapter 9 and "Related Laws," below.)

Related Laws

You must comply with other laws that affect an employee's right to take a leave.

State Family and Medical Leave Laws

Some states have laws guaranteeing some form of family or medical leave. (See "State Family and Medical Leave Laws" in the appendix.) The FMLA doesn't cancel out state law provisions that provide greater family or medical leave rights or that apply to smaller employers than the FMLA does. Leaves granted under a state leave law and the FMLA run simultaneously and are not added together if the leave is covered by both laws.

EXAMPLE: State law where Tess works entitles her to 16 weeks of family and medical leave over two years. Tess takes her 16 weeks of state-permitted leave in one year. This also exhausts her 12 weeks of FMLA leave for that year—she can't take 16 weeks plus 12 weeks.

Under most state laws, the leave is unpaid. In California, New Jersey, and Washington, however, employees are entitled to receive payments from a state fund while on certain types of leave. If you do business in one of these states, contact your labor department for more information.

Americans with Disabilities Act

An employee with a disability has rights under the Americans with Disabilities Act (ADA) as well as the FMLA. (See Chapter 9 for a comprehensive discussion of the ADA.) It requires special attention to coordinate your responsibilities under these two laws.

The FMLA entitles an employee to 12 weeks of leave for a serious health condition, with health benefits maintained during this period. At the end of the FMLA leave, you must reinstate the employee to the same or an equivalent position.

If the employee can't perform the equivalent job because of a disability and the employee has exhausted FMLA leave, the ADA may permit or require you to place the employee in a part-time job, with only the benefits provided to part-time employees. In some cases, you may have to let an employee take·unpaid leave beyond the 12 weeks allowed by the FMLA. Under the ADA, such additional leave may be required as a reasonable accommodation to a disabled employee if the additional leave wouldn't impose an undue hardship on your business.

Here are two other variations:

- The ADA may require you to offer an employee a job with a reasonable accommodation. If the FMLA entitles an employee to unpaid leave, you can't avoid granting the leave by requiring the employee to take an accommodation instead.

- If you require certification that an employee is fit to return to work as permitted by the FMLA under a uniform policy imposed by your business, you must also comply with the ADA requirement that the certification be related to the job.

 RESOURCE

Other state and federal laws can also overlap with the FMLA. These include laws prohibiting discrimination, requiring time off in certain situations, or requiring disability

---

Small Necessities Laws May Be the Next Big Thing

In what may be the start of a trend, a number of states have enacted so-called small necessities laws to help employees balance their work, personal, and family responsibilities. These laws recognize that employees sometimes need to be away for short periods during a workday. Employees, for example, may need to take off briefly to attend a parent-teacher conference or other important school activity, or they may need to take a child or elderly parent to a doctor's appointment.

Details of these laws vary from state to state, though school-related matters are most often recognized as a valid reason to take some hours of leave time. The California law, for example, applies if you employ 25 or more people at one location. If so, you can't fire or discriminate against an employee for taking up to eight hours of leave time a month (maximum of 40 hours a year) to participate in activities at a child's or grandchild's school or day care facility. The employee must give you reasonable notice and can use existing vacation, personal leave, or comp time for this purpose—and, in some cases, unpaid leave may be available.

You can find information about your state's law in "State Family and Medical Leave Laws" in the appendix—contact your state labor department to find out more about your obligations. If your business is covered by both the FMLA and state law, you'll need to comply with both. Typically, there's not much overlap between the FMLA and the state small necessities law, so the time off allowed for small necessities will be in addition to time off under the FMLA.

If your state doesn't have a small necessities law, consider including a policy in your employee handbook for dealing with such leave.

or workers' compensation leaves or payments. To learn how these different laws relate to the FMLA, take a look at *The Essential Guide to Family & Medical Leave,* by Lisa Guerin and Deborah C. England (Nolo). You can also check out the Equal Employment Opportunity Commission (EEOC) fact sheet, *The Family and Medical Leave Act, the Americans with Disabilities Act, and Title VII of the Civil Rights Act of 1964,* available online at www. eeoc.gov/policy/docs/fmlaada.html.

Enforcement

An employee who believes his or her rights have been violated may file a complaint against your business with the U.S. Department of Labor or your state labor department, or the employee may file a private lawsuit. If the employee proves your company violated the FMLA, you may have to pay the employee wages, employment benefits, or other compensation, depending on the nature of the violation. You may also have to reimburse the employee for the cost of providing care for a child or ill family member, up to a sum equal to 12 weeks of wages. And you may be ordered to reinstate or promote the employee, pay penalties and interest, and pay reasonable fees for the employee's lawyer and expert witnesses.

RESOURCE

The U.S. Department of Labor provides online guidance on the legal require- ments for family and medical leave. You'll find lots of information and answers to key FMLA questions at www.dol.gov/whd/regs/compliance/ whdfs28.pdf

Health and Safety

As an employer, there are many good reasons—in addition to your humane instincts—for creating a safe and healthy workplace. Obviously, healthy workers will be happier and more productive. There will be fewer disruptions to work schedules due to absenteeism. And, health insurance costs may be reduced. Then there are the legal reasons: Federal and state laws and an increasing number of local ordinances require you to take steps to make the workplace safe and healthy.

Workers today are well informed about the link between workplace conditions and health problems. Most know, for example, that secondhand smoke can cause or aggravate respiratory and heart problems and that repetitive motions can lead to carpal tunnel syndrome. And an increasing number of workers will not hesitate to press legal claims against employers who fail to rectify unsafe or unhealthy conditions.

In addition to health and safety statutes, state law requires your business to provide workers' compensation coverage to pay for medical bills and partial wage loss when an employee is injured in the workplace. By reducing on-the-job injuries and eliminating the workplace causes of disease, you can lower the cost of workers' compensation coverage.

TIP

Get employees involved. In meeting your legal responsibilities for keeping the workplace safe and healthy, don't overlook an obvious resource: your employees. Involve them in identifying safety and health problems and suggesting ways to solve such problems. Organizing a safety committee made up of equal numbers of rank-and-file employees and managers is a good starting point. Consider holding company safety seminars at which you encourage employee suggestions. If employees can voice their safety concerns to you and to other employees who are able to initiate changes, there's less chance that they'll jump the gun and go straight to government authorities to report a complaint. Having such a safety committee can also earn you a break on workers' compensation insurance premiums.

The Occupational Safety and Health Act

In 1970, Congress passed the Occupational Safety and Health Act (the OSH Act), a comprehensive law designed to reduce workplace hazards and improve health and safety programs for workers. (29 U.S.C. §§ 651 to 678.) It broadly requires employers to provide a workplace free of physical dangers and to meet specific health and safety standards. Employers must also provide safety training to employees, inform them about hazardous chemicals, notify government administrators about serious workplace accidents, and keep detailed safety records.

Although there can be heavy penalties for not complying with the OSH Act, such penalties are usually reserved for extreme cases in which workplace conditions are highly dangerous and the employer has ignored warnings about them. If your workplace is inspected—an unlikely event for a typical small business, unless there is an accident—the government will work with you to eliminate hazards.

> **CAUTION**
>
> **Don't forget state law!** In addition to federal law, you must comply with state law. To learn more about state health and safety laws, see "State OSHA Laws," below.

Covered Employers

Virtually all businesses must comply with the OSH Act, with a few exceptions. The OSH Act won't apply to your workplace if any of the following are true:

- You're self-employed and have no employees.
- Your business is a farm that employs only your immediate family members.
- You're in a business such as mining, which is already regulated by other federal safety laws.

Safety Standards

The OSH Act sets a general standard for all covered businesses. As an employer, you must provide a place of employment that's free from recognized hazards that are causing or are likely to cause death or serious physical harm to employees. Recognized hazards are not clearly defined, which can make it difficult for you to know how to comply with the law. The broad language covers an almost impossibly large range of potential harm—from sharp objects that might cause cuts to radiation exposure.

But there's more. In the OSH Act, Congress created the Occupational Safety and Health Administration—called OSHA—as a unit of the U.S. Department of Labor. And, Congress authorized this agency to set additional workplace standards, which it has done in great profusion. The specific standards cover a wide range of workplace concerns, including:

- exposure to hazardous chemicals
- first aid and medical treatment
- noise levels
- protective gear—such as goggles, respirators, gloves, work shoes, and ear protectors
- fire protection
- worker training, and
- workplace temperatures and ventilation.

Posting, Reporting, and Record Keeping

You must post a notice called "Job Safety and Health Protection," which is available from the nearest OSHA office. If your business is located in a state that has its own approved OSHA program, you may have to post a state form instead of the national version. Check with your state OSHA office to find out. (See "State OSHA Laws," below, for contact details.)

You must notify OSHA within eight hours after learning that an employee has died from a job-related accident or that three or more employees have been hospitalized because of a workplace accident. Call or visit an OSHA office to report the location and time of the incident, the number of fatalities or hospitalized employees, the name and phone number of a contact person, and a brief description of the incident. Expect a follow-up investigation.

Unless your business is exempt from OSHA record-keeping requirements (see "Exemption From Record Keeping," below), you must maintain several types of records.

- **Injury and illness log.** You must keep a log (OSHA Form 300) of all workplace injuries and illnesses, except minor injuries requiring only first aid. Throughout February, you must post the log for the previous year.
- **Medical records.** You must keep up-to-date medical records and records of employee exposure to hazardous substances or harmful physical agents.
- **Training records.** You must keep records of your safety training sessions and make them available for review by employees.
- **Retention.** You must maintain required records for specified periods of time—sometimes as long as 30 years.

RESOURCE

For more information on the OSH Act's provisions, requirements, and enforcement procedures, see *The Essential Guide to Federal Employment Laws*, by Lisa Guerin and Amy DelPo (Nolo).

Exemption From Record Keeping

The OSHA requirements for record keeping apply only to businesses with ten or more employees—although state OSHA regulations may impose record-keeping requirements on smaller businesses. In addition, the following businesses are exempt from record keeping:

- retail trade—except for businesses selling general merchandise, building materials, and garden supplies
- real estate, insurance, and financial businesses, and
- service businesses—except for hotels and other lodging places, repair facilities, amusement and recreation facilities, and health services.

Training

OSHA considers safety training part of your general duty to provide a safe workplace, but individual OSHA rules also impose more specific training requirements, depending on what your business does and what hazards might be present in your workplace. These rules are too extensive to summarize here, but following some commonsense guidelines will help you get started. For example, make sure that all employees know about the materials and equipment with which they'll be working, the known hazards in your business, and how you're controlling those hazards. Pay special attention to the use of chemicals, making sure to train employees in:

- methods of detecting the release of a hazardous chemical in the work area—for example, monitoring devices or recognizing appearance or odor of released chemicals
- physical and health hazards of the chemicals
- measures employees can take to protect themselves from the hazards—safe work practices, emergency procedures, and protective equipment, and
- details of your labeling system and worksite locations where employees can find chemical safety data. (See "Hazardous Chemicals," below, for more information.)

Don't let employees start a job until they have received instructions in how to do it safely. The exact training you offer will, of course, vary according to the nature of the business. It may be helpful to call in an OSHA consultant to recommend specific training for your workplace.

Don't overlook the need to train existing employees who are moving into new jobs or are starting to use new equipment. And all employees need refresher instruction from time to time, since it's human nature to become complacent and forget the safety rules.

You must maintain records of your safety training efforts and be prepared to show these records to OSHA inspectors.

Inspections

OSHA inspectors can inspect your workplace at any time without advance notice or authorization by a court. Based on what they find there, they can issue citations and impose penalties. However, inspectors are unlikely to make random inspections unless you're in a particularly hazardous business, such as construction. There aren't enough inspectors to go around; OSHA must use its resources prudently.

If you have a workplace with ten or fewer employees and you're in an industry that has a low injury rate, you're exempt from random inspections by federal OSHA officials. State safety and health laws, however, may empower local inspectors to randomly inspect smaller businesses. But if yours is a small insurance agency, retail store, computer repair shop, or similar low-injury business, your chances of receiving a random inspection are remote.

Most small businesses are inspected only if one of the following occurs:

- An employee has complained to OSHA.
- A worker has died from a job-related injury.
- Three or more employees have been hospitalized because of a workplace condition.

As explained above, you're required to report such fatalities and hospitalizations to OSHA.

Even though you may be at low risk of inspection, you're not free to ignore safety and health concerns. You're legally required to take the initiative in identifying and eliminating safety and health problems that can affect employees.

Special Rules for Home Workers

If you allow an employee to do office work at home, OSHA won't inspect the home office, and won't hold you liable for conditions there. Office work at a home-based worksite typically consists of such tasks as filing, keyboarding, computer research, reading, and writing. The employee will probably be using office equipment such as a telephone, fax machine, scanner, or copier.

The rules are different for other types of work an employee performs at home. OSHA has found that some types of work in a home setting can be hazardous, such as assembly of electronics, casting lead head jigs for fishing lures, use of unguarded crimping machines, and handling adhesives without protective gloves. If OSHA gets a complaint about non-office work at an employee's home involving a danger to health or safety, OSHA may inspect the home worksite. As an employer, you can be responsible for at-home hazards caused by materials, equipment, or processes that you provide or require the employee to use.

A typical inspection follows a set pattern.

The opening conference. The inspector meets with you and a representative selected by your employees. All of you discuss procedures for the inspection. The inspector reviews your records on health and safety problems as well as any steps you've taken to monitor workplace conditions such as noise, ventilation, and hazardous chemicals.

The walkaround. The inspector observes the working conditions, looking for signs of health and safety hazards. Are all required signs and notices posted? Are there strong odors in the air? Eye irritants? Dust or fumes? How about noise and temperature levels? Are there signs of spilled or leaking chemicals? These and other problems are noted. The inspector may make measurements of noise levels and take samples of dust and air to be analyzed.

Review of safety and health programs. The inspector checks to make sure that you have qualified people and the right equipment to monitor levels of hazardous materials—and also looks at whether your employees are taking part in training programs on workplace hazards and emergency procedures.

The closing conference. The inspector discusses the safety hazards that have been found and ways to correct the problems. You're given a specific deadline by which you must make the corrections. The inspector documents all violations of OSHA standards and, if a violation is more than a minor one, issues a citation. If you receive an OSHA citation, you must post it near where the violations occurred. This allows employees to get involved in any further enforcement actions by OSHA.

CAUTION

Inspectors can obtain search warrants. OSHA officials can't inspect your place without your consent. If you refuse an inspector entry, the inspector must obtain a search warrant from a judge before coming into your workplace. But, by insisting on a search warrant, you practically assure that the inspector will go through your place with a fine-tooth comb. Cooperation rather than resistance is usually the wiser course of action. However, if you're nervous about what an inspection may disclose, ask the inspector for an extension of time and seek advice immediately from a lawyer.

Penalties for Violations

Penalties ordered by OSHA depend on the seriousness of the violation. For willful or repeated violations, your company may have to pay thousands of dollars in penalties. And, if a worker has died because you violated OSHA standards, you could even be sent to prison. For less serious violations—problems that are unlikely to cause serious harm or death—the penalty may be up to $1,000.

In assessing penalties, OSHA looks at several factors, including:

- the seriousness of the hazard
- your history of violations
- whether you've made a good faith effort to comply with OSHA standards, and
- the size of your business.

You can challenge an OSHA citation through an appeal process. If the citation is issued by the federal OSHA, you have 15 days to file a notice of contest with the agency. If a state OSHA issues citations in your state, check with that agency to confirm the filing deadline. It makes sense to consult a lawyer before embarking on an appeal.

After you file the notice of contest, an administrative law judge will conduct a hearing, giving you and others concerned a chance to present evidence. If you disagree with the decision of the administrative law judge, there's an additional appeal process within OSHA. Ultimately, you can appeal to a court if you can't reach an acceptable resolution within OSHA. Fortunately, most OSHA disputes are resolved through voluntary settlements.

Workers' Rights

Although workers have many rights under the OSH Act, we discuss only the two most basic ones in this chapter.

First, workers have a right to complain to OSHA about safety or health conditions without being penalized for doing so. Retaliating against employees who have made such complaints is a violation of OSH Act provisions.

Second, in some situations, workers have a right to refuse to work if they think the workplace is unsafe. The legal test is this: Does the worker have a reasonable and good faith belief that there's an immediate risk of serious injury or death? If so, the worker can walk off the job and refuse to work until you've corrected the problem or you've determined, after an investigation, that there's no imminent danger. While you investigate or correct the problem, you can place the worker temporarily in another job at equal pay. It's usually unwise to react by demoting or firing the complaining employee—that can be another violation of the OSH Act if the complaint is determined to be well-founded.

> **EXAMPLE:** Mildred runs a local delivery service. One afternoon, Arlene, one of the drivers, hears that the brakes locked that morning on one of the business vans. She refuses to drive that van until the brakes are checked out by a qualified mechanic. Mildred, believing that the brake problem was caused by careless driving, orders Arlene to use the van. When Arlene says no, Mildred fires her. Arlene sues. Even though the brakes are later found to be adequate, Arlene wins because the court determines that, based on the information she had, Arlene had a reasonable and good faith belief that she'd be exposed to an immediate risk of serious injury or death if she used the truck. Mildred is ordered to reinstate Arlene and to pay her for the time she's missed since being fired.

Getting Help

Your eyes will probably glaze over at the thought of poring over pages of federal regulations on health and safety in the workplace. Fortunately, there are easier ways to learn what you must

do to comply with OSHA requirements—and doing your homework will cost you little or nothing.

Worksite Consultations

Each state has an agency (funded mostly by the federal office of OSHA) that offers free, on-site consultations. For information about the agency in your state, go to www.osha.gov/dcsp/smallbusiness/consult.html.

As in a formal OSHA inspection, you and the consultant will tour the workplace together. The consultant will point out safety and health risks and then, at a closing conference, give you practical advice on how to eliminate hazards. The consultant won't issue citations or propose penalties, however. Nor will the consultant provide information about your workplace to the OSHA inspection staff, except in extreme circumstances.

Although OSHA encourages employees to participate in the consultant's walk-through, you're free to exclude employees from the consultation process—unless a union contract gives employee representatives the right to take part.

 CAUTION

Opening the door to enforcement action. If the consultant finds a serious condition—one from which it's reasonably predictable that death or serious harm could result—the consultant will work with you to control or eliminate the hazard within a time period that you jointly determine. If the consultant isn't satisfied with your progress, the consultant may report you to an OSHA official. According to OSHA, however, consultants rarely find conditions that require them to report a business.

Safety Codes

Written safety codes are a good way to let employees know that you take safety seriously. Because each workplace is different, you'll have to make sure that your safety code is tailored to the specific needs of your business.

OSHA has suggested a safety code that you may find useful as a starting point—but you'll undoubtedly need to make changes to make it fit. See "Safety Code of ABC, Inc.," below, for an example of how we modified OSHA's code. You can find OSHA's version in the agency's *Handbook for Small Business.* (See "Additional Help From OSHA," below.)

State OSHA Laws

If a state has a health and safety law that meets or exceeds federal OSHA standards, the state can take over enforcement of the standards from federal administrators. This means that all inspections and enforcement actions will be handled by your state OSHA rather than its federal counterpart.

So far, 21 states have been approved for such enforcement regarding private employers. They are Alaska, Arizona, California, Hawaii,

---

Additional Help From OSHA

For additional help with OSHA rules and regulations, see the *OSHA Small Business Handbook*—OSHA Publication 2209-02R—available at www.osha.gov/Publications/smallbusiness/small-business.html. It contains self-inspection checklists covering such topics as fire protection, personal protective equipment and clothing, walkways, floor and wall openings, stairs and stairways, elevated surfaces, exit doors, hand tools, and equipment. These checklists can help you and employees identify potential problems.

You can also find lots of helpful materials on OSHA's website at www.osha.gov. If you want to order the full text of the OSHA regulations, these materials are available from the U.S. Government Printing Office at a small cost or can be found in the Code of Federal Regulations at most law libraries. There are four separate sets of standards:

- General Industry—29 CFR § 1910
- Construction—29 CFR § 1926
- Maritime Employment—29 CFR §§ 1915–1919, and
- Agriculture—29 CFR § 1928.

Indiana, Iowa, Kentucky, Maryland, Michigan, Minnesota, Nevada, New Mexico, North Carolina, Oregon, South Carolina, Tennessee, Utah, Vermont, Virginia, Washington, and Wyoming. Connecticut, New Jersey, and New York also have OSHA-type laws, but they

Safety Code of ABC, Inc.

1. All employees of this company must follow these safe practice rules and report all unsafe conditions or practices to a supervisor.

2. Supervisors will require employees to comply with all safety rules.

3. All employees periodically will be given instruction on workplace safety and health.

4. Anyone under the influence of alcohol or drugs will not be allowed on the job while in that condition.

5. No one will be permitted or required to work while his or her ability or alertness is impaired by fatigue or illness.

6. Employees must make sure that all guards and other protective devices are in place and must wear protective equipment and clothing in specified work areas.

7. Horseplay, scuffling, and other acts that may endanger employees are prohibited.

8. Work should be planned to prevent injuries when working with equipment and handling heavy materials. Back injuries are the most frequent and often the most persistent and painful type of workplace injury.

9. Workers must not handle or tamper with electrical equipment, machinery, or air or water lines unless they have received instructions from their supervisors.

10. Report injuries promptly to a supervisor. A first aid kit is located at _____

_____ .

Emergency phone numbers are located at _____

_____ .

Adapted from: *OSHA Small Business Handbook*

only apply to government employees. You can find an up-to-date list, along with contact information, at www.osha.gov/dcsp/osp/index.html.

If your business is located in a state that has an OSHA law, contact your state agency for a copy of the safety and health standards that are relevant to your business. State standards may be more strict than federal standards, and the requirements for posting notices may be different.

Hazardous Chemicals

The federal OSHA rules include a section called the Hazard Communication Standard. (29 CFR § 1910.1200.) Many people call this the right-to-know law. Basically, the standard requires you to give information to your employees about the hazardous chemicals they handle.

Many states also have right-to-know laws, including those shown in "Right-to-Know Laws (Hazardous Chemicals)" in the appendix. If your state is not listed, it has no laws or regulations governing private employers. However, you must comply with the federal standards.

These informational requirements vary somewhat from state to state. If your business handles any chemicals, be sure to get a copy of your state's rules. Because most of the state laws are similar to the federal right-to-know rules, this discussion will focus on the federal law. If your state has standards that are more

stringent than the federal ones, there are still some unresolved questions about whether you need only comply with the federal standards. Until this legal issue is clearly resolved, it's wisest to follow the stricter standards.

To understand the right-to-know laws—state or federal—you must first become familiar with the Material Safety Data Sheets (MSDSs) supplied by manufacturers of all hazardous chemicals. They contain a wealth of information, including:

- the physical hazards of the chemical, such as flammability and explosiveness
- health hazards—the symptoms of exposure and the medical conditions that can be made worse by exposure
- how the chemical enters the body and the limits of safe exposure
- whether the chemical is known to cause cancer
- how to safely handle the chemical
- recommended protection methods, including protective clothing and equipment, and
- first aid and emergency procedures should a chemical be mishandled.

Obviously, if an employee is working with hazardous chemicals, this is essential information. That's why the law requires you to keep the MSDS for each hazardous chemical and make it accessible to employees. You must also keep a list of all the hazardous chemicals used in your business and label all containers. And, you're required to train employees in the safe use of hazardous chemicals.

EXAMPLE: Ace Water Treatment Corporation sells water treatment systems to rural homeowners whose water comes from underground wells. Ace issues demonstration kits to its sales staff so they can demonstrate to potential customers the extent of impurities in the homeowner's water supply. In one test, the salesperson adds a few drops of potassium hydroxide to a sample of the customer's water so that certain impurities will collect at the bottom of the test tube. Potassium hydroxide is a hazardous chemical sometimes known as lye.

The chemical comes from the manufacturer with an MSDS explaining its dangers and how it should be handled—for example, goggles should be used to protect the user's eyes. To comply with the right-to-know law, Ace keeps the MSDS and makes it available to employees. Ace makes sure that all containers are properly labeled and that all employees are thoroughly trained in how to use and handle the chemical. To further protect its employees, Ace issues protective goggles to those who perform water tests using the chemical.

Workers' Compensation

The workers' compensation system provides replacement income and medical expenses to employees who suffer work-related injuries or illnesses. Benefits may also extend to the survivors of workers who are killed on the job.

Workers' compensation is a no-fault system. The employee is entitled to receive stated benefits whether or not the employer provided a safe workplace and whether or not the worker's own carelessness contributed to the injury or illness. But the employer, too, receives some protection, because the employee is limited to fixed types of compensation—basically, partial wage replacement and payment of medical bills. The employee can't get paid for pain and suffering or mental anguish. Except in cases of intentional conduct, the employee cannot file a private lawsuit. (See "You're Still Liable for Intentional Injuries," below.)

To cover the cost of workers' compensation benefits for employees, you'll usually need to pay for insurance—through either a state fund or a private insurance company. While self-insurance is a possibility in some states, the technical requirements usually make this an impractical alternative for a small business.

Coverage Requirements

Although each state has its own workers' compensation statute, one thing is clear: If you have employees, you probably need to obtain workers' compensation coverage. (A few states require coverage only if you have three or more employees.) Your state workers' compensation bureau can tell you about any legal requirements for informing employees of their rights—generally, you do this by displaying a poster.

State laws vary as to whether sole proprietors, partners, and executive officers can or must be covered by workers' compensation. In some states, these individuals get to choose. If you're in one of these states and you want this coverage—which will give you the same benefits as other workers who are injured—mention this when you apply for coverage.

Similarly, in some states, sole proprietors, partners, and executive officers are automatically covered, but you have the option of excluding them. Ask a representative of the state fund or private insurance carrier how to do this when you apply for coverage.

CAUTION

Rejecting coverage can be a mistake. In two states—New Jersey and Texas—workers' compensation coverage isn't mandatory for an employer. In Wyoming, it's mandatory only for employers engaged in extra-hazardous occupations. So, in those states, you can generally choose whether you want to secure workers' compensation insurance for your workplace. But if you opt not to, you can be sued by an employee who claims to have been injured on the job by your negligence; if you had workers' comp coverage, these types of lawsuits would be barred. Therefore, most wise employers obtain workers' compensation, no matter where their businesses are located.

Arranging for Coverage

Some states allow an employer to self-insure—a process that typically requires the business to maintain a hefty cash reserve earmarked for workers' compensation claims. Usually, this isn't practical for small businesses. Most small businesses buy insurance through a state fund or from a private insurance carrier. If private insurance is an option in your state, discuss it with the insurance agent or broker who handles the basic insurance policy for your business. Often, you can save money on premiums by coordinating workers' compensation coverage with property damage and public liability insurance. A good agent or broker may also be able to explain the mechanics of a state fund where that's an available option or is required.

In most states that have a state-run workers' compensation fund, you have a choice of buying coverage from the state or from a private insurer. In the following states, however, you must purchase from the state fund: North Dakota, Ohio, Washington, and West Virginia. In Wyoming, you must purchase coverage from the state fund if you are engaged in an especially hazardous industry.

TIP

Make sure telecommuters are covered. In most situations, an employee who works at home is entitled to the same workers' compensation benefits as any other employee. Make sure your workers' compensation provider knows about any telecommuters on your payroll.

You're Still Liable for Intentional Injuries

Although workers' compensation is the employee's exclusive remedy for most work-related injuries or illnesses, there's a major exception: injuries or illnesses caused by the intentional actions of the employer. An employee who can prove that your intentional actions caused an injury or illness can take you to court and seek a full range of damages—including, for example, damages for pain and suffering as well as economic losses.

Obviously, if you or a supervisor were to physically assault an employee, that would qualify as an intentional action. But courts sometimes treat other workplace events as intentional, too. Suppose, for example, that, to speed up production, you remove the safety devices from a dangerous machine. An employee is injured using the machine, but you continue to require workers to use the machine in its unsafe condition. You've probably set yourself up for an intentional injury claim, because you can be pretty certain that additional workers will be injured by that machine.

In that situation, injured employees would not be limited to their remedies under your state's workers' compensation law. They would be able to sue you and your business under traditional tort (personal injury) theories. And they could ultimately get more money than they would have under the worker's compensation system.

Controlling Costs

Premiums are based on two factors: industry classification and payroll. If your premium is above a certain amount—$5,000 in many states—your actual experience with workers' compensation claims will affect your premiums. Your rate can go up or down, depending on how your claims compare with other businesses in your industry. The number of claims filed by your employees affects your premium more than the dollar value of the claims. If you have a lot of accidents, it's assumed that you have an unsafe workplace and that the insurance company eventually will have to pay out some large claims.

Here are some steps you can take to try to keep your workers' compensation costs down.

Preventing Accidents

Emphasize safety in the workplace. Provide proper equipment, safety devices, and protective clothing. Train and retrain your employees in safe procedures and how to deal with emergencies. Set up a safety committee made up of both managers and workers. Promote employee health by offering wellness and fitness programs.

Buying Coverage Wisely

Seek out a participating plan in which the insurance company pays dividends to its insured employers. It helps to find a solid company with a long history of paying dividends—but dividends are never guaranteed.

Consider being put on a retrospective rating plan (unfortunately, this isn't usually available to many small businesses). In such plans, the insurance company agrees to adjust your premium at the end of the year based on your actual claims experience. If you have a strong safety program, this program can be better for you than a dividend-type program—which generally looks at the insurance company's claims experience, not just the history of your business.

Make sure your business and your employees are properly classified. Don't let the insurance company mistakenly place your business in a class that pays a higher premium because of job hazards. And, since workers are also classified based on the nature of their work, check to see that the insurance company has classified them correctly.

Following Up

Use light-duty or modified work assignments to help workers who have been injured on the job but are allowed back to work on a trial basis.

Monitor claims. If you learn that an employee seems to have recovered but is still accepting workers' compensation benefits, ask for an explanation. If something still seems amiss, notify the insurance company or state fund.

Injuries and Illnesses Covered

As an employer, you needn't dig very deeply into the fine points of workers' compensation law. The state fund or private insurance company that covers your workplace will have its own lawyers resolve legal questions about whether a worker is entitled to compensation for a particular disability and, if so, how much the worker is entitled to receive. When a worker seeks to receive benefits that are questionable, these lawyers will challenge the employee on your behalf.

Still, as a well-informed employer, you may want to learn a bit more about how the system works. While workers' compensation law varies somewhat from state to state, there's enough similarity among the states to justify some general statements.

To be covered by workers' compensation, an employee's injury needn't be caused by a sudden accident such as a fall. Basically, any injury that occurs in connection with work is covered. Many workers, for example, receive compensation for repetitive motion injuries, such as carpal tunnel syndrome, which primarily afflicts the wrists, hands, and forearms. (See "Repetitive Stress Disorder," below, for more about this type of injury.)

In theory, if a worker's injury was intentionally self-inflicted or was caused by substance abuse or by some other nonwork cause (such as a hobby), the injury won't be covered. But, in a disputed case, the worker is still likely to get the benefits by showing that the worker's behavior wasn't the only thing that caused the injury.

Workers may also be compensated for some illnesses and diseases. An illness is likely to be covered by workers' compensation when the nature of the job increases the workers' chances of suffering from that disease. Illnesses that are the gradual result of work conditions—for example, emotional illness, heart conditions, lung disease, and stress-related digestive problems—increasingly are being covered by workers' compensation.

Finally, there are death benefits. Dependents of workers killed on the job can usually collect workers' compensation benefits.

> ! **CAUTION**
>
> **Don't penalize workers who file claims.** In most states, it's a violation of the workers' compensation statute or public policy to discriminate against an employee for filing a workers' compensation claim. This means you can't fire, demote, or take any other negative action against a worker for filing a claim.

Benefits Paid

Workers' compensation covers the employee's medical and rehabilitation expenses. It also provides income to the employee to offset a big part of lost wages. Typically, workers receive two-thirds of their average wage, up to a fixed ceiling. But, since these payments are tax free, a worker who receives average wages fares reasonably well.

In most states, workers become eligible for wage loss replacement benefits as soon as they've lost a few days of work because of an injury covered by workers' compensation. The number of days required to qualify varies by state. Some states allow the payments to be made retroactively to the first day of wage loss if the injury keeps the employee out of work for an extended period.

Workers may receive lump sum benefits if they have a total disability or a permanent partial disability. In some states, there are specific amounts provided for permanent partial disability such as the loss of an eye or a foot.

Independent Contractors

Workers' compensation insurance is required only for employees—not for independent contractors who work for you. (Independent contractors are covered in greater detail in Chapter 12.) Small businesses sometimes buy services from independent contractors to save money on workers' compensation insurance, as well as taxes and other expenses normally associated with employees. That's fine, as long as you correctly label people as independent contractors rather than employees. But if you make a mistake and a person improperly labeled as an independent contractor is injured while doing work for your business, you may have to pay large sums to cover medical bills and lost wages that should have been covered by workers' compensation insurance.

In addition, you can sometimes have a problem with a properly classified independent contractor who hires employees to perform some work for you. If the independent contractor doesn't carry workers' compensation insurance and doesn't have the money to compensate an employee who's injured on the job, the injured worker—in a search for deeper pockets—may sue your business for failing to keep a safe workplace.

Employees With HIV or AIDS

Under the federal Americans with Disabilities Act (ADA) and similar state laws, a person who is HIV positive or has AIDS is considered to have a disability. You can't discriminate against that person. You may also need to provide a reasonable accommodation so that the person can perform the work required. Normally, your duty to reasonably accommodate a person with a disability—including AIDS—is triggered by that person requesting an accommodation. In the case of someone who has AIDS, the accommodation may consist of a flexible work schedule, reduced hours, work at home arrangements, or a reduction in travel.

You don't have to permit an HIV-infected person to continue in a position if the infection poses a health threat to others. This generally comes up only in the health care field.

The ADA also prohibits discrimination against people who associate with those who have AIDS. So it's unlawful, for example, to reject a job applicant for living with someone who has AIDS.

If you learn that an employee has AIDS or is HIV positive, keep the information confidential. Use it only to accommodate the person in performing the job.

TIP

Require proof of insurance. When hiring an independent contractor, ask to see an insurance certificate establishing that the independent contractor's employees are covered by workers' compensation insurance. For good measure, make sure that the independent contractor also has general liability insurance.

RESOURCE

Need more information on contractors? To learn more about hiring independent contractors, including the tests for distinguishing independent contractors from employees and information on taxes and workers' compensation insurance premiums, see *Working With Independent Contractors*, by Stephen Fishman (Nolo).

Disease Prevention

Under the OSH Act, your business may need to take precautions to protect employees from infection in the workplace. The OSHA rules apply to employees who may be exposed to blood or other potentially infectious material—and so primarily affect employees who work in hospitals, clinics, medical offices, and nursing homes.

If it's reasonably likely that your employees will come into contact with blood and other infectious materials, check with OSHA to learn the requirements for protective practices and equipment.

Tobacco Smoke

A state law or municipal ordinance may limit or prohibit smoking on your business premises. Some laws and ordinances are designed primarily to protect nonsmoking employees from secondhand tobacco smoke. Others seek to protect nonsmoking customers and other visitors as well.

Here are a few examples of state laws:

- In Alaska, if your business has a designated smoking area, you must ventilate it to ensure that nonsmokers aren't subjected to tobacco smoke.
- In California, you can't permit smoking in an enclosed place of employment. There are some exceptions, such as employee break rooms; if you do allow smoking in permitted areas, you must separately ventilate these areas.
- Florida does not permit smoking in enclosed, indoor workplaces, but it does allow smoking in certain standalone bars and outdoor eating areas.
- In Vermont, you must adopt a smoking policy that either prohibits smoking throughout the workplace or restricts it to enclosed designated areas—although in certain circumstances, with employee approval, you can allow smoking in designated areas even if they are not enclosed.

For up-to-date information on your responsibilities and options concerning smoking in the workplace, check with your state and local health departments.

In addition to meeting the requirements of laws and ordinances that limit or prohibit smoking in the workplace, be aware that you may be liable to nonsmoking employees if you don't take appropriate action on their complaints. For example, an employee who develops bronchial asthma from exposure to tobacco smoke may be entitled to workers' compensation benefits. And an employee who has a severe respiratory ailment that's aggravated by tobacco smoke may be entitled under the ADA to a smoke-free workplace.

Although you can prohibit smoking on the job, avoid a policy that prohibits an employee from smoking off the job as well. Such a broad prohibition can invade a worker's privacy and is specifically barred by some state laws.

TIP

Smokers can use some help. Recognize that giving up smoking can be difficult. Some experts equate nicotine addiction with a cocaine or heroin habit. To demonstrate your concern, you might offer to pay the cost of an employee's tuition in a stop-smoking program if the smoker successfully kicks the habit.

Drug and Alcohol Abuse

There is no law that prevents you from combating the use of illegal drugs and alcohol in the workplace. There are, however, some limits on your ability to test employees for drug usage.

Legally, you're free to:

- prohibit the use of illegal drugs and alcohol in the workplace
- require that employees not come to work or return from meals or breaks under the influence of alcohol or drugs, and
- require that employees who use alcohol or illegally use drugs meet the same performance standards you impose on other employees.

You needn't tolerate absenteeism, tardiness, poor job performance, or accidents caused by alcohol or illegal drug use.

Most states deny unemployment benefits to workers who are fired for misconduct involving drugs or alcohol. Similarly, most states bar workers' compensation benefits for workers injured in an on-the-job accident caused by a worker's use of drugs or alcohol.

TIP

Helping those in need. One enlightened approach—especially if an employee with a drug or alcohol problem has valuable skills—is to offer an assistance program to help the employee deal with the problem. Or you might consider a modified work schedule to permit the person to attend a self-help program.

CAUTION

You can only combat illegal drug use. Please note that this discussion pertains to your right to address illegal drug use in your workplace. Illegal drug use encompasses both the use of illegal drugs and the improper use of legal, prescription drugs. If an employee is using a prescription drug legally, you are faced with a different set of rules from the ones discussed here. The employee's legal drug use may fall under the protection of the federal Americans with Disabilities Act or the state law equivalent. See Chapter 9 for more information.

Illegal Drug Use

There's nothing wrong with firing an employee or rejecting an applicant who uses, possesses, or distributes drugs illegally. This includes the use of illegal drugs and the illegal use of prescription drugs that are deemed controlled substances under federal drug laws.

> **EXAMPLE:** Starbright Corporation fires Lucy after determining that she takes amphetamines without a doctor's prescription. Amphetamines can be legally prescribed but are classified as controlled substances because of their potential for abuse. If a doctor didn't prescribe amphetamines for Lucy, Starbright would be justified in firing her for illegal use of drugs.

The most reliable way to establish that an employee is using drugs illegally is through a drug test. Testing is left to your discretion. If you choose to test, however, you must observe legal guidelines.

Federal Laws

There are a few situations in which a private employer is required to test employees for drug use. The U.S. Department of Transportation, for example, requires drug testing of airline pilots and other transportation employees who hold jobs in which drug abuse can affect public safety. And the U.S. Department of Defense requires similar testing by companies that contract with it.

The Drug-Free Workplace Act of 1988 (41 U.S.C. § 701) requires all contractors with the federal government to certify that they will provide a drug-free workplace. To comply, you must:

- inform workers that illegal drug use is prohibited in the workplace
- create and maintain a drug awareness program
- require employees to notify you of any conviction for drug usage in the workplace—in which case you must notify the government, and
- impose remedial measures on employees convicted for using drugs in the workplace.

However, the Drug-Free Workplace Act doesn't require you to test employees.

Discretionary Testing

Preemployment testing is the safest type of testing from a legal standpoint. (Drug testing of job applicants is covered in Chapter 1.) After an employee is hired, testing is controlled by federal and state laws, as well as court decisions. Because these laws are rapidly changing, be sure to double-check your state law at a nearby library or on the Internet. (See "Legal Research," in Chapter 14, for guidance.)

If you do decide to test, your primary motive should be to ensure the safety of workers, customers, and members of the general public. You're most likely to withstand a legal challenge if you limit testing of employees to these three situations:

Safety and security. You can likely require periodic testing of employees whose jobs carry a high risk of injury to people and property—for example, heavy equipment operators and workers who handle explosives. Similarly, periodic testing is generally permitted for security workers—for example, those who transport large sums of cash or guards who carry guns. And you can periodically test employees who routinely work with vulnerable people such as children, the developmentally disabled, or the elderly.

Accidents. You can likely require testing of an employee who's been involved in an accident—for example, a food server who's dumped a carafe of scalding coffee on a customer or a maintenance worker who's drilled through a water pipe.

Retesting. You can likely require periodic retesting of an employee who is currently in or has completed a drug rehabilitation program or an employee whom you've given a second chance—for example, one who tested positive for drugs after a personal injury accident but was kept on the job anyway.

Even though you may have a right in these situations to require a drug test as a condition of continued employment, you can't force employees to submit to a test against their will. In most cases, however, you can fire an employee who refuses to be tested. Also, you must follow any state-mandated procedures or requirements for testing.

Avoid a policy of testing all employees—not all of them will be in a position to cause harm through drug usage. Similarly, avoid a program of random drug testing. If you test all employees, test them randomly, or test without a good reason, you may get sued for invasion of privacy or infliction of emotional harm.

To keep your drug testing program on a solid legal footing, follow all of these guidelines:

- Use a test lab that's certified by the U.S. Department of Health and Human Services or accredited by the College of American Pathologists.
- Keep the results of drug tests confidential.
- Be consistent in dealing with those who test positive.

CAUTION

Documentation is essential. Because drug testing is always subject to a legal challenge, it's important to keep good records documenting why and how tests are administered. Request a receipt from employees acknowledging that they have been given a copy of your drug and alcohol policy—or include the policy in your employee handbook and get a receipt for the handbook. Don't give a drug test without having the employee sign a consent form. Keep a record of what tests were performed, what drugs were found, and in what amounts. Finally, document the chain of custody of the tested sample (that is, who had possession of it) so you can show who handled it at all pertinent times.

Alcoholism

The law treats alcoholism differently from drug abuse. A person disabled by alcoholism is entitled to the same protection from job discrimination as any other person with a disability.

On the other hand, you're not required to overlook the effects that this disability can have on job performance. Under the Americans with Disabilities Act (ADA), you can discipline, discharge, or deny employment to an alcoholic if the person's job performance or conduct is so badly affected by alcohol usage that the worker isn't qualified to do the job.

> **EXAMPLE:** Don, an alcoholic, often is late for work and sometimes is unable to perform his job. His employer disciplines him because of his tardiness and poor performance. The company holds Don to the same standards as its other employees—and disciplines him accordingly. This doesn't violate the ADA.

Neither the ADA nor its regulations define alcoholic or alcoholism. The lack of definitions may have little practical effect, however, since the ADA allows you to judge the employees by their ability to do the job. People who have an alcohol problem aren't legally entitled to any special consideration. (For more on the ADA, see Chapter 9.)

Repetitive Stress Disorder

The number of workers suffering from repetitive stress disorder (RSD) is rapidly growing—due in large part to the increased use of computers in workplaces. A familiar form of RSD is carpal tunnel syndrome, which causes swelling inside the tunnel created by bone and ligament in the wrist. This swelling can put pressure on nerves passing through the tunnel—leading, in turn, to pain, tingling, and numbness. Other types of RSD include:

- tendinitis—tears in tissue connecting bones to muscles
- myofascial damage—tenderness and swelling from overworking muscles
- tenosynovitis—irritation of the boundary between the tendon and surrounding sheath, and
- cervical radiculopathy—compression of disks in the neck.

The last disorder often develops in workers who hold a phone on their shoulders while using computers. All of these disorders are painful and can be disabling.

It isn't clear what role OSHA will eventually play in establishing and enforcing ergonomic standards to help stem the rising tide of RSD cases. Currently, OSHA provides voluntary guidelines for specific industries such as grocery stores, nursing homes, and poultry processing plants. In addition, the agency occasionally issues ergonomics-related citations. These citations are issued under general provisions of the OSHA law requiring employers to maintain safe workplaces.

But even though addressing ergonomic issues is largely voluntary, as an enlightened employer you may want to take steps to protect employees from carpal tunnel syndrome and other repetitive stress disorders. You may, for example, change the equipment employees use, train them in improving work techniques, and modify the layout of work stations. Larger employers might consider hiring an ergonomics consultant to help them figure out what changes to make.

What the Future May Bring

Several states are considering regulations for businesses that use video display terminals—better known as computer workstations. Rules adopted in New Mexico for state employees who use computers can serve as a model for your business.

- Maintain room lighting at a level that reduces eyestrain and glare.
- Control glare by indirect lighting and nonreflecting furnishings.
- Use acoustic pads to control noise levels.
- Locate workstations at a reasonable distance from heating and cooling vents.
- Provide chairs that are flexible and easily adjusted.
- Allow frequent work breaks.

Illegal Discrimination

To give workers a fair opportunity to get and keep jobs, Congress and state legislatures have passed laws prohibiting discrimination in the workplace. The main federal law prohibiting discrimination in the workplace is Title VII of the federal Civil Rights Act of 1964. It outlaws discrimination based on race, color, religion, gender, and national origin. Harassment in the workplace is also prohibited as a type of illegal discrimination. Depending on the state you are in, it might also be illegal to discriminate against workers based on other factors, such as testing positive for HIV; being single, married, or divorced; obesity; sexual orientation; or gender identity.

Federal laws also bar several other kinds of workplace discrimination:

- **Age.** The Age Discrimination in Employment Act prohibits discrimination against older workers. The Older Workers Benefit Protection Act outlaws discrimination in employee benefit programs based on an employee's age. The protections in both laws apply only to workers who are at least 40 years old. Your state's anti-age-discrimination law might protect people of other ages from discrimination. For example, Minnesota protects people who are 18 years of age or older from age discrimination. To find out about your state's law, see "State Laws Prohibiting Discrimination in Employment" in the appendix.

- **Pregnancy.** The Pregnancy Discrimination Act makes it illegal to discriminate against a woman in any aspect of employment because of pregnancy, childbirth, or related medical conditions.

- **Citizenship.** The Immigration Reform and Control Act prohibits discrimination based on whether a person is a U.S. citizen.

- **Genetic information.** Federal law prohibits discrimination based on a person's genetic information—for example, a genetic predisposition to a certain disease.

- **Pay.** The Equal Pay Act outlaws discrimination in wages on the basis of gender. (See Chapter 3.)

- **Disability.** The Americans with Disabilities Act makes it illegal to discriminate against people because of a disability. (See Chapter 9.)

- **Union membership.** The National Labor Relations Act prohibits discriminating against workers because they do or do not belong to a labor union. (See Chapter 13.)

 RESOURCE

Want help understanding discrimination laws? You can find lots of helpful information by visiting the website of the Equal Employment Opportunity Commission (EEOC), the federal government agency that administers and enforces antidiscrimination laws, at www.eeoc.gov. The website offers numerous fact sheets, frequently asked questions, guidance on how the EEOC interprets and enforces these laws, and much more.

Jobs That Require Discrimination

Under Title VII and other antidiscrimination laws, you have a very limited right to hire on the basis of gender, religion, or national origin if a job has special requirements that make such discrimination necessary. Such a special circumstance is called a bona fide occupational qualification (BFOQ).

EXAMPLE: A religious organization employs counselors who answer telephone inquiries from those interested in becoming members of that religion. The organization can require that the counselors it hires believe in that religion. Being a member of that denomination is a BFOQ.

(For more on BFOQs, see "Permitted Discrimination" in Chapter 1.)

Title VII of the Civil Rights Act

Title VII (42 U.S.C. §§ 2000 and following), enforced by the U.S. Equal Employment Opportunity Commission (EEOC), is a federal law that addresses many types of workplace discrimination.

Businesses Covered

Title VII applies to your business if you employ 15 or more people, either full time or part time. Most state laws impose similar prohibitions against discrimination and many cover employers with fewer employees.

Discrimination Prohibited

Under Title VII, you can't use race, color, religion, gender, or national origin as the basis for decisions on hirings, promotions, dismissals, pay raises, benefits, work assignments, leaves of absence—or any other aspect of the employment relationship. Title VII applies to everything from help wanted ads to working conditions, performance reviews, and postemployment references.

Obviously, a business that flatly refused to hire female, black, or Hispanic applicants would be ripe for legal action under Title VII or its state equivalents. Of course, few businesses today would attempt such a flagrant violation of the law. But the mere absence of a discriminatory policy isn't enough to avoid enforcement action.

A business violates Title VII if it treats people differently because of the characteristics protected by law (race, religion, and so on). If a company with 50 employees always passes over its African American employees for managerial positions, there's a good chance the company is discriminating—even though the company hasn't explicitly stated a policy of no African Americans in management. Call it corporate culture. Call it coincidence. But if the end result is that African Americans don't get management jobs, it looks like discrimination in the workplace.

If challenged by an employee or the EEOC, the business should be prepared to show that its promotion decisions have been based on objective criteria and that the more qualified applicant has always gotten the promotion. Without a convincing business reason for the failure to promote any African American managers, the company may be found to have violated Title VII.

Title VII also prohibits employer practices that seem neutral but have a disproportionate impact on a group of people. Such a policy is legal only if there's a valid business reason for its existence. For example, refusing to hire people who don't meet a minimum height and weight is permissible if it's clearly related to the physical demands of the particular job—felling and hauling huge trees, for instance. But applying such a requirement to exclude applicants for a job as a cook or receptionist wouldn't pass legal muster. The height and weight standard seems neutral on its face but would have a disproportionate impact on women and people of Asian descent, for example. There is no legitimate business reason to require a cook or receptionist to meet this requirement, so it would violate Title VII if it ruled out disproportionate numbers of applicants of a particular race or gender. (For more about indirect discrimination, see "Avoiding Illegal Discrimination" in Chapter 1.)

TIP

Stay alert for indirect discrimination. To head off allegations of indirect discrimination, review your employment practices at least once a year to make sure you have a solid business reason for everything you do. And don't brush aside complaints you get about practices that seem neutral to you but may unfairly affect some employees. Take such complaints seriously. The workers who complain may be doing you a big favor by alerting you to a potential discrimination problem.

EEOC Enforcement of Title VII

If an employee files a complaint with the EEOC, the EEOC may choose to investigate the claim. If this happens, a staff lawyer or investigator may interview the employee. The interviewer will probably then interview you and possibly some other employees.

The EEOC will likely try to work out a settlement of the complaint through conciliation—an informal process that resolves any legal violation for the employee who filed the complaint (and any employees who are in a similar situation). Terms of the agreement will be set out in a written statement. The agreement will require the complaining employee to give up the right to sue your business, in exchange for your agreement to take the steps outlined in the document.

If the agreement requires you to take some action, such as restoring a demoted employee to an earlier job or holding training sessions to make managers more sensitive to subtle discrimination in the workplace, the EEOC will follow up periodically to make sure you're complying.

Consider Arbitrating Discrimination Claims

The Civil Rights Act of 1991 encourages employers to resolve job discrimination disputes through settlement negotiations, mediation, and arbitration. In mediation, a neutral expert—the mediator—helps the employer and employee reach a voluntary resolution of the dispute. In arbitration, a neutral expert—the arbitrator—makes a binding decision that can be enforced in court.

Arbitration is often an excellent way to bring a dispute to a swift conclusion. It's quicker and cheaper than judicial proceedings—and arbitration hearings are conducted in private.

But in an employment discrimination case, an arbitration agreement isn't always binding on the employee. If the employee has a change of heart and decides to pursue a discrimination claim in court, a judge will have to decide whether the arbitration agreement must be honored. Although these agreements are generally enforced, judges have been more willing to reject or limit contracts that force employees to arbitrate discrimination disputes, since such contracts may allow employers to avoid the full impact of civil rights laws.

Judges are especially reluctant to enforce arbitration agreements that:

- the employee didn't enter into voluntarily
- limit the damages an employee can collect if the arbitrator finds that the employer violated the law
- limit the employee's right to obtain

information (in legal jargon, prearbitration discovery)

- shorten the period for filing a claim
- make the employee pay the costs of arbitration, or
- allow the employer to choose the arbitrator.

If a judge finds that one or more provisions in an arbitration clause are unfair, the judge may refuse to enforce those provisions or may rule that the entire arbitration agreement is invalid.

And even a valid arbitration agreement won't prevent a governmental agency from suing an employer to enforce an antidiscrimination law. For example, in a 2002 case (*EEOC v. Waffle House Inc.*, 534 U.S. 279), the U.S. Supreme Court said that even though Eric Baker—a Waffle House employee—had signed a valid arbitration agreement and was therefore unable to sue his former employer in court, the EEOC could sue on his behalf for an alleged violation of his rights under the Americans with Disabilities Act.

For help drafting arbitration provisions that are likely to be legally enforceable, look at *Resolving Employment Disputes: A Practical Guide*, published by the American Arbitration Association and available online at www.adr.org/sp.asp?id=29177. Check out the "Due Process Protocol" near the end of the document.

The Lilly Ledbetter Fair Pay Act

After working for Goodyear Tire & Rubber Co. for many years, Lilly Ledbetter learned that she was being paid a lot less than male employees doing the same work. She sued under Title VII of the Civil Rights Act, claiming she had been discriminated against based on her gender. Her case made its way to the U.S. Supreme Court, where she lost. The Court said that Ledbetter hadn't filed her claim in time, because the discriminatory decisions that resulted in lower pay had taken place many years ago. Ledbetter had argued that each paycheck constituted a "continuing violation" and that she didn't have any way of knowing about the discriminatory act at the time, but the Court didn't agree. (*Ledbetter v. Goodyear Tire and Rubber Co.*, 550 U.S. 618 (2007).)

After the court made its ruling, Congress passed legislation allowing employees in Ledbetter's situation to file a lawsuit. If an employee doesn't know about a discriminatory decision but it continues to affect his or her salary or other benefits, the law today permits the employee to proceed with a suit within 180 days of receiving a paycheck that reflects the disparity.

If you and the employee who filed the complaint can't reach an agreement, the EEOC will likely give the employee a right-to-sue letter, allowing the employee to sue your business in federal court for violating Title VII. Because it has limited resources, in many cases, the EEOC issues this letter without conducting an investigation, so you may not go through this conciliation process first. The letter doesn't mean the EEOC believes the employee's allegations are true. In rare cases that it finds especially egregious or groundbreaking, the EEOC may file a lawsuit against your business on behalf of the employee.

If an employee files a complaint with a state fair employment agency for violation of state antidiscrimination laws, the investigation procedure will be much the same. Likewise, the state agency might issue a letter authorizing the employee to sue, without first conducting an investigation or going through the conciliation process.

TIP

Consider settlement. Never pass up the chance to resolve a complaint through conciliation. You have everything to gain and nothing to lose. A key advantage of conciliation is its confidentiality. Information in EEOC files concerning settlement attempts generally isn't available to the public. Neither the EEOC nor the complaining employee is allowed to make public anything that occurs during conciliation, and they can't use information disclosed there as evidence in a later proceeding without your consent. This is not true of a court case, which is public.

SEE AN EXPERT

Because the stakes can be high in a confrontation over alleged job discrimination, it may be prudent to consult a lawyer. (See Chapter 14 for guidance on finding an attorney.) If you choose to attend the conciliation conference without legal counsel, you should at least ask a lawyer to review any written agreement before signing it. And, because the antidiscrimination laws are somewhat technical, you'll undoubtedly need assistance from a lawyer in defending a lawsuit in which your business has been accused of employment discrimination.

There are a number of remedies that a court can order if it finds workplace discrimination. You may be ordered to:

- rehire, promote, or reassign the employee to whatever job was lost because of the discrimination
- compensate the employee for salary and benefits lost because of the discrimination (including wages, pension contributions, medical benefits, overtime pay, bonuses, vacation pay, and participation in your profit sharing plan)
- pay damages to compensate the employee for emotional suffering, inconvenience, and mental anguish—and punitive damages to punish your business if you've acted maliciously or recklessly
- change your policies so that similar discrimination won't take place in the future, or
- pay the employee's legal fees.

CAUTION

An employee may have additional recourse. If the EEOC doesn't issue a right-to-sue letter or file a lawsuit on the employee's behalf, the employee may take other legal action against your business, such as suing in state court for breach of contract or wrongful discharge. The employee may also be able to sue you for violating state antidiscrimination laws.

Affirmative Action Plans May Correct Past Abuses

An affirmative action plan is one means of trying to undo the effects of past illegal discrimination. Under such a plan, an employer makes employment decisions based on race or sex—factors that ordinarily can't be considered—to restore equal opportunity for groups that have faced discrimination.

When a court finds that a business has discriminated and there are no other effective means to remedy the discrimination, the court may require the business to take affirmative action. For example, a court may order a company to hire one black employee for every two new white employees hired until the company's workforce resembles the racial mix of the community.

A business may also have to set up an affirmative action plan as part of voluntarily settling a court case or EEOC proceeding. Any voluntary program must meet the EEOC's Guidelines on Affirmative Action Plans.

Retaliation

It's illegal for you to retaliate against an employee for opposing illegal discrimination, for filing a complaint under Title VII, or for cooperating in the investigation of such a complaint. Clearly, you can't retaliate by suspending or firing the employee, but many other responses are also prohibited. You mustn't take any action that would tend to dissuade a reasonable worker from making or supporting a claim of discrimination. For example, if a forklift operator made a discrimination claim, reassigning him or her to duties as a railroad track laborer would be improper because the new duties would be harder and dirtier. This would be so even if the track duties fall within the employee's original job description.

An adverse action is retaliation only if it is done because the employee complained. You are free to take adverse actions against an employee for other reasons, even if that employee has complained about discrimination or some other unlawful workplace situation. For example:

- If the employee performs poorly on the job, you can give the employee a negative performance evaluation.
- If the employee is habitually late for work, you can discipline the employee for tardiness.
- If the employee brings a gun to work, you can fire the employee.

The problem for employers is that some employees will claim that these adverse actions are retaliation even if they have nothing to do with the employee's complaint.

If you must take an adverse action against an employee who has complained, be prepared to defend that action and to show that you had valid reasons that were unrelated to the complaint. Those reasons should be supported, if possible, by prior warnings to the employee that you have documented and preserved in your files.

> **EXAMPLE:** George works for Cool Sweats —a company that sells sportswear by mail order. He files a complaint with the EEOC, complaining that he was passed over for a supervisor's position because he is black. A month later, Cool Sweats suspends George without pay for three days for a violation of company rules. George asserts that the suspension was in retaliation for filing the Title VII complaint.
>
> Cool Sweats is able to refute this allegation by showing that George violated the company rules against charging personal expenses on the company's credit card and using the company van for personal business—rules stated in Cool Sweats's employee handbook. Cool Sweats is also able to show that six weeks earlier it warned George about similar infractions and that a three-day suspension is consistent with the discipline meted out to other employees for such rule violations.

A New Defense in Discrimination Cases

Some employers are fighting back in cases of alleged discrimination by arguing that the employee shouldn't have been hired in the first place. If an employer wins this argument, the employee's lawsuit may be thrown out or the damages the employee could win may be severely limited.

> **EXAMPLE:** Local Transit, Inc., hires Lorna to drive a delivery van. In the first few months, Local Transit cites Lorna for infractions for which male drivers were not cited. Then the firm fires Lorna. She sues, claiming sex discrimination. In defending the lawsuit, Local Transit argues that Lorna lied on her job application by claiming she had a perfect driving record, when, in fact, she had two drunk driving convictions. Local Transit claims that had Lorna disclosed the truth about her driving record, the company never would have hired her. Since she

isn't entitled to the job, says the company, she can't complain about discrimination. The court rules that Local Transit had a valid reason to fire Lorna.

But employers don't always win based on this defense. One skeptical judge wrote: "A false statement on an employment application is not an insurance policy covering bigotry."

To help lay the groundwork for this type of defense in a discrimination or wrongful discharge case, consider adding the following language to your job application forms in prominent type above the applicant's signature:

"I acknowledge that any misrepresentations or omissions in this application will be grounds for termination."

And make sure to enforce this policy evenhandedly against everyone—not just those employees who have complained or filed lawsuits against you.

Harassment

Title VII doesn't specifically mention illegal harassment. But under federal law, harassment is a form of discrimination.

Sexual Harassment

In 1980, the U.S. Equal Employment Opportunity Commission (EEOC) issued guidelines stating that harassment in the workplace is a form of sex discrimination prohibited by Title VII. In 1986, the U.S. Supreme Court agreed that harassment on the job is, indeed, a form of sex discrimination—and is therefore illegal. (*Meritor Savings Bank v. Vinson*, 477 U.S. 57.) The Court held that illegal harassment occurs when unwelcome sexual advances, requests for sexual favors, and other verbal or physical conduct of a sexual nature creates a hostile or abusive work environment. In 1993, the Supreme Court made it clear that a harassed employee is entitled to legal relief even without proof that the offending behavior has injured the employee psychologically. (*Harris v. Forklift Systems Inc.*, 114 S.Ct. 367.)

Most states have additional laws prohibiting sexual discrimination in the workplace. Although the specifics may differ from federal law, these state laws are generally interpreted to include harassment as a type of prohibited discrimination.

If an employer or manager makes unwelcome sexual advances or demands sexual favors in return for job benefits, promotions, or continued employment, that's harassment. But harassment in the workplace can consist of a wide variety of other behaviors, including:

- posting sexually explicit photos that offend employees
- telling sex-related jokes or jokes that demean people because of their gender
- commenting inappropriately on an employee's appearance
- requiring employees to dress in scanty attire
- repeatedly requesting dates from a person who clearly isn't interested
- having strippers perform at a company gathering, or
- stating that people of one gender are inferior to people of the other gender or can't perform their jobs as well.

In short, any hostile or offensive behavior in the workplace that has a sexual component can constitute harassment—and violate the law.

Civility Is Desirable—But Not Legally Required

The laws prohibiting discrimination, harassment, and retaliation don't require you to maintain a courteous workplace, although that is a worthy goal. Some rude—but not lewd—conduct can occur without putting your business in legal jeopardy. The laws don't protect workers from petty slights, minor annoyances, simple teasing, or other behavior that Miss Manners may not approve of. Nonetheless, you are free to regulate conduct like this through company policy, and should make clear that harassment isn't acceptable and *does* violate the law.

Although harassment is most often behavior committed by men against women, that's not always the case. There are instances in which women sexually harass men and where people harass others of their own gender. Laws prohibiting harassment offer protection in all of these situations.

Harassment Based on Other Characteristics

Employers and employees alike tend to focus on sexual harassment because it is the type of harassment that is the most notorious. You should know, however, that harassing an individual because of any characteristic protected by state or federal law—for example, race, color, religion, national origin, disability, genetic information, or age—is also considered a form of discrimination and is therefore illegal.

Here are some examples of activities that are not sexual in nature, but can amount to illegal harassment:

- using racially derogatory words or epithets
- making gestures or displaying pictures that would offend a particular racial or ethnic group
- commenting on a person's skin color or other racial or ethnic characteristics
- making disparaging remarks about a person's gender that are not sexual
- commenting negatively about a person's religious beliefs—or lack of such beliefs
- expressing negative stereotypes about an employee's birthplace or ancestry
- making negative comments about a person's age when referring to employees who are 40 years old or older, or
- making derogatory or intimidating remarks about an employee's mental or physical impairment.

Complying With the Law

Your business can be held responsible for harassment if executives or supervisors knew, or should have known, that it was being committed. You're also under a legal duty to take all necessary steps to prevent harassment. Your first step in meeting these obligations is to promptly investigate every complaint. If you determine that there's merit to a complaint,

discipline any employee who harassed another on the job. Where the harassment is especially serious, the only reasonable solution may be to fire the offending employee.

If you learn of workplace conditions that might create an uncomfortable work environment for some workers—such as the presence of pornographic magazines—take decisive steps to eliminate the offending conditions. An employee may challenge you by asking: "Who's offended by this?" The simple answer: "Me."

You're also required to take corrective action if an employee is being harassed by other people who come into the workplace—clients, patients, customers, suppliers—who are not employees of your business.

EXAMPLE: Stella waits on tables at the lounge at Take Ten Bowling Lanes. One night after winning the league championship, a boisterous team of male bowlers comes into the lounge and begins to harass Stella. The lounge manager quickly sizes up the situation, switches Stella to another table, and compensates her for the tip she missed from the boisterous bowlers. The manager also threatens to expel the rowdies if they continue their behavior. Through this prompt action, Take Ten meets its legal duty to Stella.

By adopting an anti-harassment policy and a sound procedure for investigating and dealing with complaints, your business may be able to fend off a costly verdict if an employee sues. In a pair of cases known as *Faragher/Ellerth,* the U.S. Supreme Court ruled that an employee who suffers harassment in the workplace should let the employer know so steps can be taken to stop it. If the employer has a policy in place and handles complaints in good faith, the employee has to take advantage by making an internal complaint; an employee who doesn't do so may lose the right to sue the company for damages.

> **TIP**
> **Look beyond legal liability.** Avoiding legal liability is just one reason for a business to crack down on harassment. Harassment has a negative impact on employees, causing anxiety and unhappiness. You can't expect high morale and productivity in a workplace in which harassment is tolerated.

Preventing Harassment

Your attitude toward harassment—and the steps you take to prevent it—can help assure that you won't become the object of a formal complaint. Most potential charges can be handled effectively within the workplace.

Start by adopting a formal policy stating clearly that harassment won't be tolerated. Let employees know who within your business they can complain to if they've been harassed. And provide a backup person to handle the complaint just in case the main person handling complaints is the accused harasser. Distribute a copy of the policy to each

employee or put the policy statement in your company's employee handbook.

The sample harassment policy shown below can be modified to fit the needs of most workplaces.

Age

As the baby boomers age, there are increasing numbers of older people in the workforce. And there are laws protecting them from discrimination on the job.

The Age Discrimination in Employment Act

The federal Age Discrimination in Employment Act (ADEA) prohibits discrimination against those 40 years old or older. It applies to private businesses with 20 or more employees as well as the federal government. Although the ADEA also protects state government workers, these workers cannot file a lawsuit against the state for age discrimination—only the EEOC can take action to protect state employees from age discrimination. As is true of Title VII, the ADEA prohibits discrimination in all aspects of employment: hiring, firing, compensation, and all other terms of employment.

The ADEA prohibits you from discriminating against older workers in favor of those younger than 40. But also, in dealing with workers who are 40 years old or older, you can't give favorable treatment to younger members of that group.

Anti-Harassment Policy

Our company is committed to providing a work environment where all employees can work together comfortably and productively, free from harassment, which is illegal under both state and federal law—and will not be tolerated here.

This policy applies to all phases of employment—including but not limited to recruiting, testing, hiring, upgrading, promotion or demotion, transfer, layoff, termination, rates of pay, benefits, and selection for training, travel, or company social events.

This policy applies to the conduct of owners, supervisors, managers, coworkers, and customers.

Prohibited Behavior

Prohibited harassment includes any offensive or unwelcome conduct—verbal or physical—that is based on a membership in a protected class. It also includes discrimination or discriminatory comments based on a person's race, color, religion, gender, national origin, age, disability, genetic information, or any other characteristic protected by state or federal law.

Prohibited harassment also includes unsolicited and unwelcome contact that has sexual overtones. This includes, but is not limited to:

- written contact, such as sexually suggestive or obscene letters, notes, invitations
- verbal contact, such as sexually suggestive or obscene comments, threats, slurs, epithets, jokes about gender-specific traits, sexual propositions
- physical contact, such as intentional touching, pinching, brushing against another's body, impeding or blocking movement, assault, coercing sexual intercourse or contact, and
- visual contact, such as leering or staring at another's body, gesturing, displaying sexually suggestive objects or pictures, cartoons, posters, or magazines.

Harassment also includes continuing to express sexual or social interest after being informed directly that the interest is unwelcome—and using sexual behavior to control, influence, or affect the career, salary, or work environment of another employee.

It is impermissible to suggest, threaten, or imply that failure to accept a request for a date or sexual intimacy will affect an employee's job prospects. For example, it is forbidden either to imply or actually withhold support for an appointment, promotion, or change of assignment, or suggest that a poor performance report will be given, because an employee has declined a personal proposition.

Also, offering benefits, such as promotions, favorable performance evaluations, favorable assigned duties or shifts, recommendations, or reclassifications in exchange for sexual favors is forbidden.

Harassment by Nonemployees

In addition, Company will take all reasonable steps to prevent or eliminate harassment by nonemployees—such as customers, clients, and suppliers—who are likely to have workplace contact with our employees.

Monitoring

Company shall take all reasonable steps to see that this policy prohibiting harassment is followed by all employees, supervisors, and others who have contact with our employees. This prevention plan will include training sessions, ongoing monitoring of the worksite, and a confidential employee survey to be conducted and evaluated periodically.

Discipline

Any employee found to have violated this policy shall be subject to appropriate disciplinary action, including warnings, reprimand, or discharge, according to the findings of the complaint investigation.

If an investigation reveals that harassment has occurred, the harasser may also be held legally liable for his or her actions under state or federal antidiscrimination laws or in separate legal actions.

Retaliation

Any employee bringing a harassment complaint or assisting in investigating such a complaint will not be adversely affected in terms and conditions of employment or discriminated against or discharged because of the complaint. Complaints of such retaliation will be promptly investigated.

Complaint Procedure and Investigation

Joe Smith is designated as the harassment counselor. All complaints of harassment and retaliation for reporting or participating in an investigation shall be directed to the harassment counselor or to a supervisor of your choice, either in writing or by requesting an individual interview. All complaints shall be handled as confidentially as possible. The harassment counselor will promptly investigate and resolve complaints involving violations of this policy and recommend appropriate action to management.

Training

Company will establish periodic training sessions for all employees concerning their rights to be free from harassment and the legal options available if they are harassed. In addition, training sessions will be held for supervisors and managers, educating them on how to keep the workplace free from harassment and how to handle harassment complaints.

A copy of the policy will be distributed to all employees and posted in areas where all employees will have the opportunity to freely review it. Company welcomes your suggestions for improvements to this policy.

EXAMPLE: Mary is 53 years old and Wilbur is 43 years old. Both apply for the same job. The employer can't choose Wilbur simply because he's younger, even though both applicants are protected by the ADEA. But the employer is on safe ground if Wilbur is chosen because of his superior skills.

The reverse isn't true, however. Within the group of workers who are 40 years old or older, you are permitted to treat older workers more favorably. You can agree, for example, that, upon retirement, current employees who are at least 50 years old will continue to receive health care coverage. You needn't promise similar future benefits to current employees who are younger than 50.

Some employers believe that it costs more to hire older workers than younger workers. They overlook the possibility that younger workers may be less competent and need more training, making them more expensive. At any rate, a desire to save costs isn't a legitimate reason to discriminate against older workers.

Older Workers Benefit Protection Act

The federal Older Workers Benefit Protection Act (29 U.S.C. §§ 623 and following) makes it illegal for your business to use an employee's age as the basis for discrimination in benefits. Like the ADEA, this act covers employees who are at least 40 years old. Under this law,

you cannot, for example, reduce health or life insurance benefits for older employees, nor can you stop their pensions from accruing if they work past their normal retirement ages. The Act also discourages your business from targeting older workers when you cut staff. Most of the provisions of this law are very difficult for anyone but an experienced benefits administrator to understand. You'll probably have to consult with such an expert if you plan to take action involving a cutback of older workers' benefits.

One relatively clear provision of the law regulates the legal waivers that some employers ask employees to sign in connection with early retirement programs. You might, for example, offer a handsome retirement package to induce an older employee to leave your company voluntarily. As part of the process, you'd ask the employee to sign a waiver—often called a release or covenant not to sue—in which the employee would agree not to take any legal action against your business.

The law sets limits on your use of such waivers as they relate to age discrimination claims under the ADEA:

- You must write the waiver in plain English.
- The waiver can't cover rights or claims that may arise after the worker signs the waiver.
- The waiver must specifically state that the worker is waiving any rights or claims the

worker may have under the federal Age Discrimination in Employment Act.

- You must offer the worker something of value—something over and above what you already owe to the worker—in exchange for the waiver.
- You must advise the worker, in writing, to consult with a lawyer before signing the waiver. (Of course, you can't require the worker to hire a lawyer.)
- You must give the employee a fixed period of time in which to decide whether to sign the waiver. That period must be at least 21 days if the waiver has been presented to the employee alone. If you've presented the waiver to a group or class of employees, you must give each worker at least 45 days to decide whether or not to sign. In either case, a worker has seven days after agreeing to such a waiver to revoke the decision.

In addition, if you're making the offer to a group or class of employees as part of an incentive program to encourage early retirement, you must tell each employee in writing and in plain English what class or group of employees is covered by the program, the eligibility requirements for the program, any time limits for accepting the offer, the job titles and ages of all the individuals to whom the offer is being made, and the ages of all the employees in the same job classification or unit who are not eligible for the program.

Because the statute doesn't specify how many employees it takes to constitute a class or group, the most prudent course of action is to provide the information any time you seek a waiver from an employee who's at least 40 years old if you're also offering a retirement incentive package to one or more other employees.

Avoiding Age Discrimination Claims

A few sensible precautions can help you avoid discrimination claims by older workers.

Be aware of remarks that betray a subtle—or not-so-subtle—age bias. A thoughtless comment such as "You can't teach an old dog new tricks" may be used against you if an older employee sues your company. Emphasize to supervisors that your business won't tolerate such unfair comments.

Apply your performance standards even-handedly to all employees, regardless of their age. Because older people are disproportionately represented on many juries, you want to be able to show that your business deals equally with all employees.

Offer equal training opportunities for employees of all ages. If you're inclined to put more money into training younger workers on the assumption that they'll be with your company longer, forget it. That kind of strategy is a great way to invite an age discrimination lawsuit.

Pregnancy

The federal Pregnancy Discrimination Act (PDA) is an amendment to Title VII. (92 U.S.C. § 2076.) Under the PDA, it's a form of gender discrimination to treat an employee differently because of pregnancy, childbirth, or related medical conditions. If a woman is affected by such a condition, you must treat her the same way that you treat other people in the workforce who are either able or unable to work. You violate the PDA, for example, if you fire a woman whose pregnancy keeps her from working, but you don't fire other workers who are temporarily unable to do the job because of other physical problems. Similarly, if a pregnant worker is able to do the job, you can't lay her off or put her on leave because you think it's in her best interests to stay home.

On the other hand, you don't violate the PDA if you apply medically based job restrictions to a pregnant woman—as long as you apply those same policies to employees who are not pregnant but who are under medical restrictions.

Note also that the Family and Medical Leave Act allows unpaid leave for childbirth, adoptions, and foster care placements—and for an employee's serious health condition, which can include some complications or conditions relating to pregnancy and childbirth. (See Chapter 6 for a discussion of family and medical leave.)

Don't Make Assumptions About Employees With Caregiving Responsibilities

Today, many workers have the responsibility of caring for children or elderly family members. In many cases, primary caregivers are female.

The EEOC recognize that employers sometimes make discriminatory assumptions or decisions about female applicants or employees with caregiving responsibilities. Such gender-based stereotyping is unlawful.

EXAMPLE: Patricia, a recent business school graduate, interviews for a marketing assistant job at a public relations firm. Bob, the interviewer, sees her wedding ring and asks, "How many kids do you have?" Patricia says she has none now, but that she plans to in the future. Bob explains that the job is very demanding, and asks Patricia how she will balance her work with childcare responsibilities. She says that she will share those responsibilities with her husband. However, Bob doesn't believe men are reliable caregivers, and decides not to hire Patricia for this reason, explaining to her that being a mother is not compatible with a fast-paced business environment. This decision is unlawful.

For more on this topic, see "Enforcement Guidance: Unlawful Disparate Treatment of Workers with Caregiving Responsibilities," at www.eeoc.gov/policy/docs/caregiving.html.

Citizenship

The Immigration Reform and Control Act of 1986 (IRCA), which applies to businesses with four or more employees, makes it illegal to discriminate against workers who are not U.S. citizens or nationals. The law forbids you from discriminating against aliens who have been lawfully admitted to the United States for permanent or temporary residence—and aliens who have applied for temporary residence status.

This can be tricky because, as an employer, you must meet specific legal requirements to avoid hiring illegal aliens, including asking new employees to show you documents verifying their citizenship and their legal ability to be employed in the United States. (See "Legal Guidelines for Hiring Employees," in Chapter 1, for these hiring rules.) In meeting these verification duties, you can't ask to see more or different documents from those required for completion of Form I-9—and it's illegal to refuse to honor documents offered by the employee, as long as they appear to be genuine.

Genetic Information

As an employer, you may come into possession of information about an applicant's or employee's genetic make-up. The person may have a genetic predisposition or family history of a disease such as diabetes, heart disease, cancer, or Alzheimer's. This doesn't always mean that someone will develop the disease—just that the risk of getting the disease may be greater than average. Genetic tests that reveal these differences are often useful in finding individualized ways to detect, treat, and prevent disease.

However, the Genetic Information Nondiscrimination Act prohibits employers from discriminating on the basis of this genetic information. The law is intended to help ease concerns about discrimination that might keep people from getting genetic testing that could benefit their health. Many states also have laws that prohibit discrimination on the basis of genetic information. (To find the rule in your state, look at "State Laws Prohibiting Discrimination in Employment," in the appendix.)

The nondiscrimination law applies to health care insurers as well, but not to providers of life insurance, disability insurance, or long-term care insurance. For more information on how these laws affect health care insurers, see Chapter 4.

Religion

An increasing number of employees are claiming religious discrimination. In the past, the typical complaint would have been that a person was fired or disciplined or denied a promotion because of practicing a certain faith. But today, claims of religious discrimination tend to be much more subtle—and challenging. An employee might claim,

English-Only Rules

The law remains unclear on whether and when you can require employees to speak only English on the job. The EEOC views English-only rules as a form of national origin discrimination—and takes a very dim view of such rules. The EEOC says you can require that workers speak only in English at certain times, but only if you can show there's a business necessity for the rule.

The courts may take a more lenient position toward employers than the EEOC does. In a leading case, Spun Steak Company received complaints that two employees were making racist comments in Spanish about two coworkers—one of whom was African American and the other Chinese American. For this and other reasons, Spun Steak adopted this rule:

"It is hereafter the policy of this Company that only English will be spoken in connection with work. During lunch, breaks, and employees' own time, they are obviously free to speak Spanish if they wish. However, we urge all of you not to use your fluency in Spanish in a fashion which may lead other workers to suffer humiliation."

Spanish-speaking workers sued. The court of appeals held that to show that the English-only rule was discriminatory, the workers would have to show that the rule had a significant, adverse impact on them. Nearly all of the workers were bilingual; as to those workers, the court held that the rule didn't have a significant, adverse impact and, therefore, wasn't discriminatory. As to workers who weren't bilingual, the court sent the case back to the trial judge to determine whether there was an adverse impact. (*Garcia v. Spun Steak Co.*, 998 F.2d 1480 (1993).)

Even though that employer won, if you're thinking of implementing an English-only rule, it's best to proceed cautiously and to be quite sure you can show there's a business necessity for the rule. If language is a problem in your workplace, one alternative is to offer instruction in English as a second language so that workers can become more proficient in its use and not feel under attack because they're more comfortable speaking another language.

The EEOC offers the following examples of situations in which business necessity would justify an English-only rule:

- for communications with customers, coworkers, or supervisors who speak only English
- in emergencies or at other times when workers must speak a common language to promote safety
- for cooperative work assignments in which the English-only rule is needed to promote efficiency, or
- to enable a supervisor who speaks only English to monitor the performance of an employee whose job duties require communication with coworkers or customers.

For more on the EEOC's position on English-only rules, go to www.eeoc.gov/policy/docs/national-origin.html#V.

for example, that a supervisor is seeking to impose his or her own religious beliefs on the employee by pressuring the employee to attend prayer sessions or Bible study meetings at work. Or an employee may claim being unfairly deprived of the right to pray at work or to use a company meeting room to discuss the Koran with other employees. Still another employee may claim that wearing a "Stop Abortion" badge with a color photo of a fetus is an exercise of religious rights—while other employees may find the badge disturbing, offensive, and a violation of their own rights. Complicating matters is the fact that religion, unlike other protected characteristics, is not inherent—it is based on a belief system, which can change or grow over time, and which varies from person to person.

Unfortunately, the law in this delicate area is unclear. As always, tolerance and common sense are your best guides. If employees complain to you that a coworker is badgering them with religious hectoring, you have a right—if not a duty—to intervene, although you must, of course, use the utmost tact and sensitivity.

The law protects your right to discuss your own religious beliefs with an employee, if you're so inclined, but you can't persist to the point that the employee feels you're being hostile, intimidating, or offensive. So, if an employee objects to your discussion of religious subjects or you even get an inkling that your religious advances are unwelcome, back off. Otherwise, you may find yourself embroiled in a lawsuit or administrative proceeding.

While you may feel that the best way to resolve these knotty problems is to simply banish religion from the workplace, that's generally not a viable alternative. You're legally required to make a reasonable accommodation to the religious needs of employees. You don't, however, need to do anything that would cost more than a minimum amount or that would cause more than minimal inconvenience. Allowing workers to use an empty office for voluntary group prayer at lunchtime might be a reasonable accommodation. Letting workers take a limited amount of time off work to attend religious observances might also be a reasonable accommodation—although it might be better to simply give all employees a few days of personal leave time each year so that religious workers aren't viewed as receiving special privileges.

Recognizing that the issue of religious discrimination is a complicated one for employers, the Equal Employment Opportunity Commission recently released an updated compliance manual that explains how legal protections should be interpreted and applied in cases involving religion. For more information, visit the EEOC's website at www.eeoc.gov/policy/docs/religion.html.

Sexual Orientation

Although there is no federal law that specifically prohibits private employers from discriminating on the basis of sexual orientation, such discrimination is illegal in many states and the District of Columbia. (See "State Laws Prohibiting Discrimination," in the appendix, to learn your state's rules.)

If your state does not have a law that prohibits workplace discrimination on the basis of sexual orientation, your city or county might. There are hundreds of cities and counties throughout the country that prohibit sexual orientation discrimination in public or private employment—or both—from Albany, New York, to Ypsilanti, Michigan.

If you are a private employer and you operate your business in a state, county, or city that has a law or ordinance prohibiting sexual orientation discrimination, you must follow that law, despite the fact that there is no federal law in place.

Furthermore, even if there is no law in your state, city, or county prohibiting sexual orientation discrimination, you must still tread lightly in this area. If you have an employee who feels unfairly treated and/or is injured because of the employee's sexual orientation, that employee can still sue you under a number of legal theories that apply to everyone, including gays and lesbians. Those theories include:

- intentional or negligent infliction of emotional distress
- harassment
- assault
- battery
- invasion of privacy
- defamation
- interference with an employment contract, and
- wrongful termination.

 TIP

To find out whether your city, county, and/or state prohibits sexual orientation discrimination in the workplace, visit the Lambda Legal Defense and Education Fund website at www.lambdalegal.org, where Lambda maintains an updated list of state and local antidiscrimination laws.

State and Local Laws

Nearly all state and local laws prohibiting discrimination in employment are echoes of federal antidiscrimination law in that they outlaw discrimination based on race, color, religion, gender, age, and national origin. But state and local laws also tend to go into more detail and may protect employees from discrimination on other bases as well—such as based on marital status or sexual orientation—that aren't covered by federal law. These laws often apply to smaller employers than do the federal laws.

"State Laws Prohibiting Discrimination in Employment," in the appendix, is a state-by-state synopsis of factors that private employers may not use as the basis for any employment decisions. In legal parlance, people who have these characteristics fall into what are called "protected classes."

Keep in mind that this is only a synopsis. Each state has its own way of interpreting who is or is not a member of a protected class. For example, states may differ in how they determine who has a disability. In addition, many of the laws in this chart apply only to employers with a minimum number of employees, often five or more.

For details about your state laws, contact the agency listed in the appendix. Where no special agency has been designated to enforce antidiscrimination laws, your state's labor department or the closest office of the federal Equal Employment Opportunity Commission should direct you to the agency or person who can give you information about fair employment laws in your state.

You can also learn details about your state laws by reading the laws themselves. To do so, use the citations listed in the chart. You can find the statutes at your local law library or by using Nolo's online research center at www. nolo.com/legal-research.

The chart describes only state laws. Your city or county may have its own set of fair employment ordinances. To learn more about those, contact someone within your local government, such as your county clerk's office. Also, local offices of the Small Business Administration or the Chamber of Commerce can be good sources for information about local laws.

Workers With Disabilities

Some employers are reluctant to hire people who have disabilities. They assume that an applicant with a disability won't be able to handle a particular job. This assumption may be correct for some applicants and some jobs but way off the mark for many others. Not only is it bad business sense to prejudge people with disabilities—it's illegal. The federal government and many state governments have laws prohibiting discrimination based on disability. In this chapter, we take a close look at the main federal law. To find out if your state has a disability discrimination law, refer to "State Laws Prohibiting Discrimination in Employment" in the appendix.

The Americans with Disabilities Act

To help eliminate discrimination against people with disabilities, Congress passed the Americans with Disabilities Act, or ADA. (42 U.S.C. §§ 1201 and following.) The ADA was significantly amended in 2008 by the ADA Amendments Act (ADAAA). We'll explain those changes throughout this chapter too.

One part of the ADA sets out rules for how businesses must deal with job applicants and employees. That part of the law, known as Title I, is explained in this chapter.

The idea behind the employment provisions of the ADA is that it's unfair to write off every applicant who has a disability. Many people who have a disability are able to perform many kinds of work. Some may need an accommodation—special equipment, perhaps, or a simple adjustment in their working conditions—to help them get the job done.

Basically, the ADA states that, in making hiring and employment decisions, it's illegal to discriminate against anyone because of a disability. If a person is qualified to do the work, or to do it once a reasonable accommodation is made, you must treat that person the same as all other applicants and employees. Although the concept is simple, the ADA requirements can get fairly complicated.

RESOURCE

The U.S. Equal Employment Opportunity Commission (EEOC) maintains a website at www.eeoc.gov. There you'll find extensive information about your responsibilities under the ADA and a list of helpful publications you can order. Especially valuable is *The Americans with Disabilities Act: A Primer for Small Business*, which you can download or read online.

Businesses That Are Covered

You're covered by the ADA if you have 15 or more employees working for you for 20 or more weeks during the current calendar year—or if you had that many for 20 or more weeks last year. Part-time employees are counted.

Numbers Tell the Story

- Only 32% of people with disabilities who are aged 18 to 64 work full time or part time, compared to 81% of the nondisabled population, a gap of 49%.
- Fully 57% of people with disabilities aged 18 to 64 feel that they are capable of working despite their disability or health condition. More than half of those people (56% of that group) do work—shrinking the gap between them and people without disabilities who work to 25%.
- More than three out of ten people (36%) with disabilities who are employed say they've run into some form of discrimination due to their disabilities— typically, not being offered a job for which they're qualified.
- Of those people who have disabilities and do not work, two out of three (67%) would prefer to be working.

Source: Poll by Louis Harris and Associates, commissioned by the National Organization on Disability, 2000

Who Is Protected

To be protected from job discrimination, a person must not only have a disability, but must also be qualified for a particular job.

People With Disabilities

To have a disability under the ADA, a person must:

- have a physical or mental impairment that substantially limits one or more major life activities
- have a record of being substantially limited, or
- be regarded as having a disability.

Because this definition can take on unexpected twists, it's useful to look at each part of it.

Impairments Limiting a Life Activity

When deciding whether an applicant or employee is protected by the ADA, you must first determine whether that person has a disability.

To qualify as an employee with a disability, the employee must have a physical or mental impairment that substantially limits a major life activity. Over the years, court cases interpreting the ADA very strictly limited who qualified for protection by narrowly defining what "substantially limits" and "major life activity" mean. It was difficult for an employee to prove a qualifying condition.

However, the ADA Amendments Act (ADAAA), passed in 2008, expanded the definition by more broadly construing what constitutes a "major life activity." According to the ADAAA, major life activities include:

- taking care of oneself
- performing manual tasks
- seeing
- hearing
- eating
- sleeping

- walking
- standing
- lifting
- bending
- speaking
- breathing
- learning
- reading
- concentrating
- thinking
- communicating, or
- working.

Additionally, the ADAAA makes clear that impairments of bodily functions that might limit major life activities also count as disabilities. These include functions of the immune system, normal cell growth, digestion, bowel and bladder functions, or neurological, brain, respiratory, circulatory, endocrine, or reproductive functions.

What constitutes a "substantial limitation" is also being revisited. In the past, courts have interpreted "substantial limitation" to mean that an employee must be very

ADA Coverage Is Broad

Under the ADA, you can't discriminate against a person with a disability in any aspect of employment, including:

- applications
- interviews
- testing
- hiring
- job assignments
- evaluations
- disciplinary actions
- training
- promotion
- medical exams
- layoffs
- firing
- compensation
- leave, or
- benefits.

In addition, you can't deny a job to someone or discriminate against an employee because that person is related to or associates with a person who has a disability. For example, you can't:

- refuse to hire someone because that person's spouse, child, or other dependent has a disability
- refuse to hire someone because that person's spouse, child, or other dependent has a disability that's not covered by your current health insurance plan or that may cause increased health care costs, or
- fire an employee because that employee has a roommate or close friend who has AIDS, or because the employee does volunteer work for people who have AIDS.

significantly restricted by a disabling condition. If a mitigating measure like a medication or medical device helped the employee do his or her job, the employee was not considered "substantially limited" in a major life activity and thus not disabled.

Now, an employer cannot take mitigating measures into account. So even if a person's disability can be overcome by medications or medical devices, the person may nonetheless be considered a person with a disability. For example, a person whose diabetes is controlled by insulin, or a person whose hearing loss is corrected by a hearing aid, is still entitled to ADA protections. The ADAAA makes an exception for individuals with vision that is corrected by contact lenses or glasses.

> **EXAMPLE:** Chuck is nearsighted. Without glasses, his vision is 20/200, but with glasses, he has normal 20/20 vision. Chuck's nearsightedness does not qualify him as a person with a disability protected by the ADA.

Also, the ADAAA interprets the phrase "substantially limited" more broadly than courts have interpreted it in the past. The ADAAA considers a condition that "materially restricts" an individual to be substantially limiting. Through the ADAAA, Congress directed the Equal Employment Opportunity Commission—which regulates this area of the law—to write a new definition of "substantially limits" to take this broader approach into account.

RESOURCE

Check in for updates. To see how the EEOC responds to the ADAAA, check out www.eeoc.gov. Also check www.nolo.com—we'll notify you of any updates.

Record of Impairment

The ADA also protects people with a history of a disability—cancer or heart disease, for example—whose illnesses are either cured, controlled, or in remission. And it protects people with a history of mental illness.

If a person has a record of disability and you rely on that record to reject that person for a job, that's a violation of the ADA if the person is currently qualified to do the work.

> **EXAMPLE:** Beatrice, who has a learning disability, applies for a job as a secretary-receptionist. Records from a previous employer state that she is developmentally delayed. Still, her résumé shows that she meets all requirements for the secretary-receptionist job. The new employer doesn't interview her because he doesn't want to hire a person who is developmentally delayed. Relying on the records from the prior employer violates the ADA.
>
> In this situation, it's best to determine the applicant's ability through practical tests that measure the skills needed for the job—for example, handling phone calls, taking messages, greeting customers, sorting mail, and doing light typing.

Regarded as Impaired

Some job applicants do not have a disability—yet, employers perceive them this way. And, acting on these false perceptions, employers discriminate against these people.

> **EXAMPLE:** Jill is fired because of a false rumor that she has HIV. She has no impairment but is being treated by her employer as if she does. Therefore, her firing falls within the ADA.

In considering whether to hire an applicant or to demote or fire an employee who has a disability, you may be concerned about productivity, safety, insurance, liability, or attendance. Or you may worry that your business will have to spend money to accommodate a disability or that coworkers and customers won't accept the applicant or employee. The best way to avoid problems under the ADA is to get the facts before you act; you must base all employment decisions on legitimate, nondiscriminatory reasons.

People Who Are Qualified for the Job

To be protected by the ADA, a person must not only have a disability; the person must also be qualified to do a particular job. This emphasizes a key point about the ADA: You don't have to hire or retain anyone who can't do the work. However, you may have to offer an accommodation that will allow the employee to get the job done.

To figure out if a disabled person is qualified for a job in your business, go through these two steps.

Step 1: Define the essential job functions. Make sure you know what skills and abilities the job requires. Employers often create job descriptions for this purpose—to identify exactly what's required to get the job done.

Step 2: Determine whether the person is qualified for the job. Look at the person's education, work experience, training, skills, licenses, certificates, and other job-related requirements—good judgment, for example, or the ability to work with other people.

> **EXAMPLE:** Trudy, a bookkeeper who has cerebral palsy, applies for a job as a bookkeeping manager. If the company's policy is that all managers must have at least three years of experience working with the company and Trudy has worked there only two years, she's not qualified for a management position. Therefore, she's not protected by the ADA.

Requirements used to screen out candidates must be job related and based on business needs.

Step 3: Determine if the person can perform the essential functions of the job. When making this determination, consider whether the employee can do the job—with or without a reasonable accommodation from you. (To learn what constitutes a reasonable accommodation, see "Providing Reasonable Accommodations," below.)

The ADA puts a lot of weight on two words: essential functions. The reason is that historically, many people with disabilities who were able to perform the basic tasks necessary for a job were denied employment because they couldn't meet requirements that were marginal at best.

> **EXAMPLE:** The job description for a file clerk at Stony Creek Corporation states that the job includes answering the phone. In fact, most time on the job is spent filing and retrieving written materials; other employees usually answer the phone. A hearing-impaired person may have trouble handling phone calls but may be perfectly qualified to file and retrieve papers. Under the ADA, Stony Creek shouldn't disqualify a hearing-impaired applicant for the file clerk job, because answering the phone isn't an essential job function.

If you can write an accurate job description that identifies the essential functions of a job, you'll have an easier time deciding whether a person with a disability is qualified for the job. This emphasizes the importance of periodically reviewing your job descriptions to make sure they are current.

Exceptions to Coverage

Certain people and conditions aren't protected by the ADA.

Illegal Drug Users

People can't claim they're disabled and entitled to ADA protection because they illegally use drugs. This includes people who use prescription drugs illegally as well as those who use illegal drugs. Applying this part of the ADA becomes tricky, since the law may protect people who have been rehabilitated after drug use or who are in a drug or alcohol rehab program.

Gay and Lesbian Workers

Homosexuality and bisexuality are not considered disabilities under the ADA, although many state laws prohibit discrimination based on sexual orientation. (See Chapter 8 for a discussion of these laws.)

Sexual Identity and Behavior

The term disability doesn't include the following sexual identity and behavior:
- transvestism, transsexualism, pedophilia, exhibitionism, voyeurism, gender identity disorders not resulting from physical impairments, or other sexual behavior disorders
- compulsive gambling, kleptomania, or pyromania, or
- psychoactive substance use disorders resulting from current illegal use of drugs.

Physical and Psychological Characteristics

Under the ADA, simple physical characteristics —eye or hair color, left-handedness, or height or weight within a normal range—are not treated as disabilities. Nor are personality traits such as poor judgment or quick temper. Also, environmental, cultural, or economic disadvantages—such as lack of education or a prison record—are not disabilities.

EXAMPLE: Rita can't read because she has dyslexia, a learning disability; Rita has an impairment under the ADA. Sonny can't read because he dropped out of school; his lack of education isn't a legal disability.

You don't have to hire or retain an employee who would pose a direct threat to his or her health or safety—or that of other employees. But be careful. You can't deny employment to a person with a disability because of a slightly increased risk. If you turn down an applicant or fire someone you've already employed, you must be prepared to show there is or would be a significant risk and a high probability of substantial harm if that person remained part of the workforce.

EXAMPLE: Carlita has Parkinson's disease, which restricts her manual dexterity. An employer can't assume that Carlita can't work in a lab because she'd pose a risk of breaking bottles that contain dangerous chemicals. The employer must evaluate Carlita's specific abilities and limitations.

Sometimes, you can get rid of or reduce the health or safety risk through a reasonable accommodation—a legal concept discussed

---

Be Alert for Harassment of Workers With Disabilities

Just as you need to spot and crack down on sexual harassment and racial harassment in the workplace, you need to nip in the bud any harassment of disabled workers, whether by supervisors or coworkers. Otherwise, you may get sued for tolerating the bad behavior. Cases against employers have been brought by:

- a hair salon manager with AIDS who claimed that his coworkers had threatened a walkout
- a saleswoman with multiple sclerosis who claimed that her supervisor mimicked and ridiculed her speech and gait, and
- a store manager with a back injury who claimed that his supervisor told him he had to work every minute of his shift and threatened to "ride him until he quit."

Of course, it's out of line to make light of someone else's disability. But, as an employer, you can't depend on employees always exercising good judgment and good manners. You need to make sure that employees know they'll be disciplined or even discharged if they engage in this type of behavior. Make a clear statement to that effect in your employee handbook—and be prepared to take prompt disciplinary action if this objectionable behavior surfaces.

at greater length below. If an employee were to contract tuberculosis, for example, a reasonable accommodation might be to grant the employee a two-week leave of absence. With proper medication, the employee would no longer be contagious at the end of the two-week period.

Psychological behavior is more difficult to evaluate. However, if an employee is violent, aggressive, or destructive—or makes threats—the worker may pose a direct threat to the safety of others. Still, before you make an employment decision based on such behavior, you may want to protect your legal position by asking a psychologist or other mental health professional to evaluate the behavior and the potential for harm.

Providing Reasonable Accommodations

The ADA requires you to accommodate the physical or mental limitations of a qualified applicant or employee who has a disability. However, you're excused from this requirement if making an accommodation would place an undue hardship on your business. (For more on what constitutes undue hardship, see below.)

The idea of a reasonable accommodation is quite simple: You may have to make some changes to help a person with a disability do a job. This can take a number of forms, such as changing the job, the work environment, or an employment practice. But you need not be psychic. Generally, the person with the disability needs to ask you for a reasonable accommodation or at least do something to let you know such an accommodation is needed, as we'll discuss below.

When Accommodations Are Required

You may have to make a reasonable accommodation for any part of the employment process—from completing the application, to changing workplace conditions.

Job applications. Someone using a wheelchair may need an accommodation if the hiring office or interview site isn't wheelchair accessible; you may need to move the interview to a place that the applicant can access. A person with bad eyesight may need help filling out an application; you may need to provide the needed assistance at company expense.

Job performance. Someone with poor hearing may need a special telephone that amplifies voices to perform a job. You may need to provide such a telephone at company expense. (See "Improving Accessibility," below.)

Access to benefits. Employees with disabilities must have unrestricted access to lunchrooms, lounges, rest rooms, meeting rooms, and other services such as health programs, transportation, and social events. You may need to modify existing facilities or schedules.

Undue Hardship

The ADA doesn't require you to accommodate a disabled applicant or employee if it would place an undue hardship on the business—that is, if it would require significant difficulty or expense. Many legal battles have been waged over this imprecise language.

Whether something is an undue hardship is decided on a case-by-case basis. What's easily managed by a large company may be very difficult for a small or midsized business. The law takes this into account by focusing on your business, not businesses in general. Under EEOC guidelines, several factors are considered in determining whether an accommodation would place an undue hardship on your business.

The net cost of the accommodation. The cost of accommodating an employee may be less than it first appears. You may qualify for a tax credit or deduction, and there are sources of funding to help pay for some accommodations. (See "Financial Assistance," below.)

The size of the business and its financial resources. Obviously, larger and wealthier businesses are better able to put money into accommodations.

The structure of the business. A small facility that's part of a larger company may have access to funds from the home office. If so, the company's total resources become part of the equation.

The impact of the accommodation on business operations. Even an affordable accommodation might be an undue hardship if it changes the nature of your business.

EXAMPLE: Flo, who has an eyesight problem, applies for a waitress job at Rendezvous Night Club. The club keeps its lights dim to create an intimate setting. Flo requests bright lighting so that she can see to take orders. Rendezvous doesn't have to accommodate her; to do so would seriously affect the nature of the business. If Flo were applying for a bookkeeping position at the same nightclub, and would work in a poorly lit office away from customer areas, the employer could be required to provide brighter lighting as a reasonable accommodation.

Similarly, you wouldn't be required to raise the workplace temperature to accommodate a disabled employee if doing so would make it uncomfortably hot for other employees or customers. That solution would be unduly disruptive—but you could be required to provide a small space heater.

Sometimes, the right of one employee to a reasonable accommodation can conflict with the seniority rights of another employee. The U.S. Supreme Court, in *US Airways v. Barnett* (535 U.S. 391 (2002)), ruled that the ADA doesn't usually require you to accommodate a disabled employee by offering a job that normally would go to a more senior employee. However, the Court did leave the door open for a disabled employee to show some "special circumstance" that might require you to override your seniority rules. For example, if you make frequent exceptions to the seniority system for other reasons, a disabled employee can reasonably argue that you should make a similar exception as a reasonable accommodation.

Deciding What Accommodations Are Needed

Figuring out viable accommodations usually requires cooperation between the employer and the applicant or employee with a disability. In fact, you are legally required to engage in an interactive dialogue with the employee. If a person with a disability asks for an accommodation, chances are excellent that the individual will be able to explain the functional limitations to you. But, if the person isn't articulate or is medically unsophisticated, it may take a letter from a doctor or psychologist to clarify the nature of the problem.

You may have your own creative ideas about an appropriate accommodation, but don't overlook the person with a disability as a good source of ideas. In fact, the EEOC recommends that you consult with the employee or applicant to identify potential accommodations and assess how effective each would be in enabling the person to do the job. Such consultation gets the relationship started on a positive note, as you and the individual are working together to solve a problem. Moreover, this cooperative approach can yield dollars-and-cents benefits to your business; a person with a disability is often able to suggest a cost-effective accommodation that you wouldn't have considered.

EXAMPLE: Tandex Company, a small manufacturer, believes that hiring Chester, a prospective employee who uses a wheelchair, will require it to install a special lower drinking fountain. Chester, however, points out that he can use the existing fountain if Tandex simply provides paper cups next to the fountain.

Sometimes, there are several accommodations that would enable a person with a disability to handle a job. The EEOC recommends that you consider the preference of the disabled person. Still, under the ADA, you're free to make the final choice—for example, selecting an accommodation that's cheaper or easier to provide.

Refusing an accommodation can be costly. So, think twice before you decide to save a few dollars by denying a reasonable accommodation to a worker with a disability.

EXAMPLE: Carol, a computer operator with multiple sclerosis, asked her employer for a covered parking space. Carol's doctor confirmed to the employer that the heat of an uncovered space would worsen her condition. Nevertheless, the employer refused, claiming it had already made a number of accommodations for Carol's illness. When Carol's condition worsened and she became bedridden, she sued. She was awarded $225,000—considerably more than what it would have cost the employer to grant the request for a covered space.

SEE AN EXPERT

Get help identifying reasonable accommodations. The Job Accommodation

Solutions That Don't Cost a Bundle

As noted earlier, the Job Accommodation Network (JAN) is a free service funded by the federal government. Its consultants can offer practical suggestions for accommodating disabled workers. You can reach JAN by calling 800-526-7234 or logging on to its website at www.askjan.org.

Many examples from JAN and other sources for accommodating people with disabilities are contained in A Technical Assistance Manual on the Employment Provisions (Title I) of the Americans with Disabilities Act.

Here are some examples of low-cost accommodations:

- A timer with an indicator light allowed a medical technician who was deaf to perform laboratory tests.
  Cost: $27
- A clerk with limited use of her hands was provided a rotating file holder that enabled her to reach all materials needed for her job.
  Cost: $85
- A groundskeeper who had limited use of one arm was provided a detachable extension arm for a rake. This enabled him to grasp the handle on the extension with his impaired hand and control the rake with his functional arm.
  Cost: $20
- A desk layout was changed from the right to the left side to enable a data entry operator who is visually impaired to perform her job.
  Cost: $0
- A telephone amplifier designed to work with a hearing aid allowed a plant worker to retain his job and avoid being transferred to a lower-paying job.
  Cost: $24

Network (JAN) is a federally funded service that provides free information and advice on making reasonable accommodations for employees with disabilities. For a telephone consultation, call 800-526-7234. Visit the agency's website at www.askjan.org for more information.

You can also seek assistance from the U.S. Equal Employment Opportunity Commission, from state or local vocational rehabilitation agencies, or from state or local organizations representing or providing services to individuals with disabilities.

Improving Accessibility

As an employer, you must make it possible for an individual to apply for a job, which may include moving the interview site. You must also provide access to the job for an employee with a disability. This includes access to a building, to a worksite, to needed equipment, and to all facilities used by the employee. You must provide such access unless it would cause an undue hardship.

The ADA doesn't require you to change existing facilities unless and until a particular applicant or employee with a particular disability needs an accommodation. Then the modifications should meet that individual's work needs. You don't have to make changes to provide access in places or facilities that won't be used by that person.

Here are some workplace alterations you might consider:

- Install a ramp at the entrance to your building.
- Remove raised thresholds.
- Reserve wide parking spaces close to the worksite for people in wheelchairs.
- Provide accessible toilet stalls, sinks, soap, and towels in rest rooms.
- Rearrange office furniture and equipment.
- Make drinking fountains accessible.
- Provide clear paths to copying machines, meeting and training rooms, lunchrooms, and lounges.
- Remove potential hazards from the path of blind people.
- Add flashing lights to alarm bells to alert hearing-impaired people in an emergency.

Other Types of Accommodation

Not all accommodations involve physical changes to the workplace. There are other things you can do to help qualified people with disabilities work effectively. You might, for example, restructure a job by transferring marginal or nonessential functions to another employee. Or you might modify work schedules. You could permit a worker with a mental disability to take off time for twice-a-week visits to a psychiatrist. Or you could assign a fixed shift to a diabetic employee who needs to eat on a regular schedule and take insulin at set times each day—departing from your usual practice of requiring employees to rotate their shifts.

Similarly, a reasonable accommodation might consist of having a flexible leave policy. You don't have to give additional paid leave, but consider allowing employees to use accrued leave or leave without pay to get needed rest or medical treatment. Or, you may decide that it's better to reassign an employee to a different job. But be careful in choosing this option. To avoid discriminating against other employees on the job, it's best to reassign the worker to a position that is vacant and for which the worker is qualified.

Often you can buy equipment—or modify existing equipment—to accommodate an employee. Some examples of equipment and devices that may be used include:

- TDDs (Telecommunication Devices for the Deaf) that enable people with hearing or speech impairments to communicate over the phone
- telephone amplifiers, useful for people with hearing impairments
- software to enlarge print or convert print documents to spoken words for people with vision or reading disabilities
- telephone headsets and adaptive lights for people with cerebral palsy or other manual difficulties, and

- speakerphones, effective for people who are amputees or have other mobility impairments.

For many types of jobs, you might consider allowing the employee to work at home. Thanks to computers and the Internet, this type of accommodation is often a possibility.

Workers With Emotional or Mental Impairments

According to the EEOC, about 13% of ADA cases involve workers claiming emotional or psychiatric impairment. This includes workers with anxiety disorders, depression, bipolar disorder (manic depression), and schizophrenia.

The EEOC has issued guidelines to help you meet your responsibilities to workers and job applicants with these and other mental difficulties.

Covered Disorders

The ADA protects workers who have a mental impairment that limits a major life activity or have a record of such an impairment. The impairment must be more than just a short-term problem. The EEOC offers these examples:

- Jane has had major depression for almost a year. She has been intensely sad and withdrawn and has had problems sleeping and difficulty concentrating. The depth and duration of her problems qualify her for ADA protection.

- Joe, on the other hand, was distressed by his breakup with his girlfriend and, for about a month, sometimes became agitated at work. He sought counseling and his mood improved. He doesn't have a disability under the ADA.

Handling Psychiatric Information

Your job application form must not ask about mental or emotional illness or psychiatric disability, treatment, or hospitalization. In addition, don't ask disability-related questions before you offer someone a job—although you can inquire further if an applicant asks for a reasonable accommodation for the hiring process itself.

For example, suppose an applicant for a secretarial job asks to take a typing test in a quiet location instead of a busy reception area "because of a medical condition." You can ask for additional information to verify that the applicant needs a quiet location for the test.

After you offer someone a job, you can require a medical or psychiatric exam—as long as you do the same for all entering employees in that job category.

Be sure to keep medical information confidential. This includes psychiatric information. You can only share this information with supervisors on a need-to-know basis and with first aid and safety workers who may need to deal with emergencies.

Probably the knottiest confidentiality problem is what to tell other employees when you provide time off or other accommodations to a worker with psychiatric problems. In response to coworkers' questions, you can say, for example, that you're "acting for legitimate business reasons" or "acting in compliance with applicable laws," but not much more.

Reasonable Accommodations

Reasonable accommodations vary from case to case. Examples of some accommodations that may reasonably be required for a person with a mental disability include:

- giving the employee time off from work or a modified work schedule
- installing room dividers, partitions, or other soundproofing or visual barriers between workspaces for an employee who has trouble concentrating
- moving an employee away from noisy machinery or lowering the volume or pitch of telephones
- providing a job coach
- modifying a workplace policy, and
- adjusting supervisory methods.

The last two points—workplace policies and supervision—provide the most common glitches for employers. A couple of illustrations may help.

EXAMPLE 1: Workplace policies: A store doesn't let its cashiers drink beverages at checkout stations. Cashiers are limited to two 15-minute breaks during an eight-hour shift, in addition to a meal break. Lillian, a cashier, needs to drink water every hour to combat dry mouth, a side effect of psychiatric medicine she takes. To accommodate Lillian, the store should consider changing its policy against drinking beverages at checkout stations or changing its policy limiting cashiers to two 15-minute breaks.

EXAMPLE 2: Supervision: Ted asks for more guidance and feedback because of limitations associated with his psychiatric disability. It's reasonable for Ted's employer to consult with him, his doctor, and his supervisor to work out a plan for adding structure to his job, such as weekly meetings with the supervisor to review long-term projects.

On a related point, you're not expected to make sure that an employee takes medication as prescribed.

Unacceptable Conduct

You remain free to discipline an employee for violating standards of conduct—even if the misconduct resulted from a mental disability. Nothing in the ADA prevents you from maintaining a workplace free of violence or threats of violence or from disciplining a worker who steals or destroys property, for example.

In some cases, strict enforcement of an employer's dress code and courtesy rules can violate the ADA rules—especially if the enforcement isn't necessary from a business standpoint.

EXAMPLE: Arthur, an employee with a psychiatric disability, works in a warehouse loading boxes onto pallets. He has no customer contact and doesn't come into regular contact with other workers. Lately, Arthur has come to work appearing disheveled. His clothes don't fit right and are torn. When coworkers try to engage him in small talk, he turns his back and walks away. When he must talk to a coworker, he's abrupt and rude. The employer's handbook requires employees to have a neat appearance and to be courteous to one another. Arthur claims that his appearance and behavior are the result of a psychiatric disability and that the rules shouldn't be strictly applied to him. The EEOC agrees, based on its conclusion that these rules of conduct are not job related for Arthur's warehouse job. Because Arthur has no customer contact and doesn't come into regular contact with other employees, the standards aren't a business necessity. Therefore, the EEOC reasons, if the employer discharges or disciplines Arthur for not complying the rules, the employer is violating the ADA.

Here are examples of some other situations in which an employer may have to yield to or provide an accommodation for an employee's disruptive conduct if the conduct results from a psychiatric condition:

- A reference librarian with Tourette Syndrome frequently loses her temper, disrupting the library atmosphere by shouting at patrons and coworkers. Her employer may discipline her for violating a rule prohibiting disruptive conduct, because the rule is job related and consistent with business necessity. But the employer should grant a request for a leave of absence to seek treatment for her condition, as long as it won't cause an undue hardship.

- An employee with depression is often late because his medicine makes him groggy in the morning. He can be disciplined for his tardiness, but the employer should consider adjusting the work schedule, perhaps allowing the employee to work from 10 to 6:30 instead of the normal 9 to 5:30 workday.

Financial Assistance

There may be financial help available to assist you in complying with the ADA.

Tax Credit for Small Businesses

If your business has gross receipts of $1 million or less for the tax year, or if you have 30 or fewer full-time employees, you can take a tax credit of up to $5,000 a year for accommodations you make to comply with the ADA. You can take this credit for one-half the cost of certain access expenses, including removing physical barriers and providing interpreters or readers. The credit applies to expenses only to the extent that they exceed $250, up to $10,250.

EXAMPLE: ABC Company spends $10,250 to widen doorways to accommodate employees in wheelchairs. The company gets a tax credit of $5,000 (($10,250 – $250) ÷ 2).

To be eligible, you must meet the ADA Accessibility Guidelines. These are available for viewing and downloading at www.access-board.gov, the website maintained by the Architectural and Transportation Barriers Compliance Board. The guidelines deal with technical details, such as how wide aisles must be to accommodate the needs of people using wheelchairs.

Tax Deduction for Removing Barriers

Any business can deduct up to $15,000 a year for the cost of removing specified architectural and transportation barriers—including steps, narrow doors and inadequate parking spaces, toilet facilities, and vehicles. If your business meets the size and income requirements for the tax credit described above, it can take both the tax credit and the tax deduction. The allowable deduction is equal to the difference between the total expenditures and the amount of the credit claimed. Contact a local IRS office for more details.

EXAMPLE: CompuWay Corporation, a company with gross receipts of $950,000, spends $20,000 to widen its parking spaces and to add wide bathroom stalls that are accessible to workers with disabilities. CompuWay can take the $5,000 tax credit

and can deduct the remaining $15,000 of expenditures from its taxable income.

Work Opportunity Tax Credit

Your business may also be eligible for a tax credit if you hire specific people with disabilities who were referred to you by a qualifying governmental agency, such as a state or local vocational rehabilitation agency, state commission on the blind, or the U.S. Department of Veteran Affairs. These workers must be certified by a state employment service.

If you hire such an employee, you can take a tax credit of up to 40% of the first $6,000 of the first-year salary. Congress authorizes this program on a year-to-year basis. For more information, or to check the current status of this credit, check with the office in your state that helps place employees.

 RESOURCE

Want to know more about tax credits? For more information on these credits, visit the IRS website at www.irs.gov and search for "Tax Benefits for Businesses Who Have Employees With Disabilities."

Health and Safety Standards

The ADA doesn't stop you from establishing standards to ensure that your workplace is safe and that your workers are qualified and competent. You're free to set minimum

Ten Tips on Communicating With People Who Have Disabilities

1. When talking with a person who has a disability, speak directly to that person rather than through a companion or sign language interpreter who may be present.

2. When introduced to a person with a disability, it is appropriate to offer to shake hands. People with limited hand use or who wear an artificial limb can usually shake hands. It's perfectly acceptable to greet people by shaking hands with the left hand.

3. When meeting a person who is blind or has partial sight, always identify yourself and others who may be with you. When conversing in a group, remember to identify the person to whom you are speaking.

4. If you offer assistance, wait until the offer is accepted. Then listen to or ask for instructions.

5. Treat adults as adults. Address people who have disabilities by their first names only when extending that same familiarity to all others present. Never patronize people who use wheelchairs by patting them on the head or shoulder.

6. Leaning or hanging on a person's wheelchair is similar to leaning or hanging on a person and is generally considered annoying. The chair is part of the personal body space of the person who uses it.

7. Listen attentively when you're talking with a person who has difficulty speaking. Be patient and wait for the person to finish, rather than correcting or speaking for the person. If necessary, ask short questions that require short answers, a nod, or a shake of the head. Never pretend to understand if you are having difficulty doing so. Instead, repeat what you have understood and allow the person to respond. The response will clue you in and guide your understanding.

8. When speaking with a person who uses a wheelchair or crutches, position yourself at eye level in front of the person.

9. To get the attention of a person who is deaf or hard of hearing, tap the person on the shoulder or wave your hand. Look directly at the person and speak clearly, slowly, and expressively to establish if the person can read your lips. Not all people with a hearing impairment can lip-read. For those who do lip-read, be sensitive to their needs by facing the light source and keeping hands, cigarettes, and food away from your mouth when speaking.

10. Relax. Don't be embarrassed if you happen to use accepted, common expressions, such as "See you later" or "Did you hear about this," that seem to relate to the person's disability.

Source: Adapted by Karen Meyer for United Cerebral Palsy Associations, Inc.

requirements based on education, skills, and work experience—and to specify physical and mental standards needed for job performance, health, and safety. And, you're able to hire the best qualified person for a job. However, the ADA requires that your standards and selection criteria for workers be job related and consistent with real business needs.

CAUTION

Don't forget the reasonable accommodation rule. If your job standards are job related and consistent with your business needs, you must also consider whether a person with a disability could meet the standards through a reasonable accommodation—such as a modified workstation or special equipment.

You can require, as a job standard, that a person not pose a direct threat to the person's own health and safety or to the health and safety of others in the workplace.

EXAMPLE: Alex applies for a position at Truck Parts Unlimited. The job requires employees to use a forklift truck to move heavy loads through a parts storage facility. Alex is disabled by narcolepsy; he frequently and unexpectedly loses consciousness. The job poses a risk to Alex and other employees working in the building, since they could be seriously injured if Alex were to lose consciousness while operating the forklift truck. Because

the risk to others can't be reduced by reasonable accommodation, Truck Parts Unlimited may refuse to hire Alex without violating the ADA.

Employers Can Refuse to Let Employees Endanger Themselves

In *Chevron v. Echazabal* (536 U.S. 73 (2002)), the U.S. Supreme Court confirmed that employers can refuse to hire applicants for positions that would pose a direct threat to their own health or safety. In this case, Chevron refused to hire Mario Eschazabal, who had hepatitis C, to work in an oil refinery because Chevron's doctors found his condition could be aggravated by exposure to toxins at the refinery.

Before this case was decided, there was dispute over whether the ADA allowed an employer to refuse to hire workers who posed a direct threat only to themselves. Although the language of the ADA itself mentions only direct threats to others, the EEOC's regulations interpreting the ADA say that an employer can refuse to hire someone if doing the job in question would pose a direct threat to the applicant's own health or safety. In the *Chevron* case, the Supreme Court resolved this issue: Employers may legally refuse to hire an applicant for a position that would create a direct threat to the applicant's safety or health.

Special Rules for Food Handlers

The ADA recognizes that people with certain infectious or communicable diseases may be a direct threat to the health or safety of others if they're handling food. Each year, the U.S. Department of Health and Human Services and its Centers for Disease Control and Prevention update a list of contagious diseases that may be transmitted through food handling—diseases such as hepatitis and salmonella poisoning. The list also describes the methods by which these diseases are transmitted.

The list is short—and, in conformance with medical opinion, doesn't include AIDS or the HIV virus.

The list emphasizes that the greatest danger of food-transmitted disease comes from infected animals and contamination in food processing. If someone with a listed disease applies for a food handling job, the usual rules apply: Consider whether there's a reasonable accommodation that would eliminate risks to the health of others. In the case of an employee who becomes infected with one of the diseases on the list, see if you can reassign the person to a job that doesn't require food handling. Be sure that the person is qualified, the job is vacant, and the reassignment wouldn't pose an undue hardship.

The ADA requirements for exempting job candidates on health or safety grounds are intentionally tough—designed to prevent employers from acting on a stereotype or patronizing assumptions about people with disabilities. If you plan to exclude someone from consideration for a particular job on health or safety grounds, be sure you have specific evidence that the employee would create a risk.

Medical Exams

The strict ADA rules that govern medical inquiries and exams during the hiring process are described in Chapter 1. After you hire someone, the rules are even tougher. Any medical exam or medical inquiry about the employee must be job related and justified by business necessity. You may order an exam if you learn of a problem related to job performance or safety, but, again, the exam must be related to job performance. In the case of a physically demanding job, you may order an exam to find out if employees continue to be fit to perform the work.

> **EXAMPLE:** Nelson is a warehouse laborer. He has a back impairment that affects his ability to lift objects. Nelson's employer can require that he be examined by an orthopedic surgeon—but can't require Nelson to submit to an HIV test. Such a test isn't related to either the job or to Nelson's impairment.

You can, however, order a medical exam or make medical inquiries if any of the following is true:

- An employee is having difficulty performing the job effectively.
- An employee becomes disabled.
- The exam is needed for you to make a reasonable accommodation to an employee's disability.
- Exams, screening, or monitoring are required by other laws.

You can also conduct medical exams and tests as part of wellness and health screening programs—but only if they are voluntary.

Enforcement

As explained previously, the EEOC enforces the employment provisions of the ADA. The EEOC sometimes investigates charges of discrimination and attempts to resolve any discrimination it finds. If those attempts don't succeed, the EEOC may sue on its own or—more likely—may issue a right-to-sue letter to the person who filed the charge.

The EEOC has acknowledged that disputes about ADA requirements are often the result of misunderstandings between employers and people with disabilities. It emphasizes that those who have a conflict should try to resolve these disputes through informal negotiation or mediation if possible.

If an ADA case goes through the formal enforcement procedures and your business

is found to have discriminated, you may be ordered to take a number of steps, including hiring, reinstating, or promoting the individual; giving back pay or front pay; making reasonable accommodation; or taking other actions. Your company may also have to pay lawyers' fees, expert witness fees, and court costs. What's more, if you're found to have discriminated intentionally, your company may have to pay compensatory and punitive damages.

RESOURCE

The following sources can provide additional information about the ADA.

Information About Employment Provisions:

Equal Employment Opportunity Commission
131 M Street, NE
Washington, DC 20507
202-663-4900
800-669-4000
www.eeoc.gov

Information About Public Accommodation Provisions:

Office on the ADA
U.S. Department of Justice
Civil Rights Division Disability Rights
  Section—NYA
950 Pennsylvania Avenue, NW
Washington, DC 20530
800-514-0301
www.justice.gov/crt/about/drs

Architectural and Transportation Barriers
 Compliance Board (the "Access Board")
1331 F Street, NW
Suite 1000
Washington, DC 20004-1111
800-872-2253
www.access-board.gov

Termination

Most employees don't have job security: absent a written contract, employment is "at will. " For the most part, that means you're free to fire the employee for any reason—or for no reason at all. On the flip side, the employee can quit at any time.

There are some limits, however, on your right to freely fire an at-will employee. As explained below, some of the limits are based on statutes prohibiting things like racial or gender discrimination; other limits are founded on "public policy." In addition, courts sometimes find that an employee has attained job security based on the employer's oral promises or statements in an employee handbook.

And even if it looks like you're on safe legal ground when it becomes necessary to fire an employee, it pays to proceed cautiously. Lawsuits by fired workers are on the increase. After all, if an employee is fired for no reason or is given a reason that looks like a flimsy excuse, the employee is bound to be suspicious that you're covering something up—maybe even an illegal motive. And juries, composed of people who are mostly employees themselves, are often sympathetic to fired workers. The guidelines in this chapter are designed to help keep you out of court when it's time to let an employee go.

RESOURCE

Want more information on firing employees legally? For a more in-depth discussion of how to fire employees without running afoul of the law or harming your business, see *Dealing With Problem Employees: A Legal Guide*, by Amy DelPo and Lisa Guerin (Nolo).

Wrongful Discharge Cases

Cases in which a former employee claims that employment was terminated for an improper reason or that an employer bungled the process are known as wrongful discharge cases—and they're based on a number of legal theories. You can better avoid being sued for wrongful discharge if you grasp these legal principles.

Because the laws and court decisions of each state vary, not all of the legal theories for wrongful discharge will be available to all former employees. Also, because the law can change—and many recent changes favor workers, not employers—you need to keep up to date on the specific rules in your state.

Statutes

If you discriminate illegally in firing an employee, a statute may give that employee the right to sue you for wrongful discharge on that basis. Other statutes prohibit firing an employee for specified reasons, unrelated to discrimination. The main statutes that employees rely upon in asserting wrongful discharge claims are briefly described here, and more fully described in earlier chapters.

- **Race, color, and national origin discrimination.** Under federal law and the laws of many states, it's illegal to discriminate against workers based on race, color, or national origin. (To find out what characteristics your state antidiscrimination laws protect, see the chart in the appendix.) These same statutes make it illegal to retaliate against a worker who complains about discrimination or who otherwise asserts rights under the statute.

- **Gender and pregnancy.** Federal law and the laws of many states prohibit discrimination based on gender, including pregnancy.

- **Age discrimination.** Under the Age Discrimination in Employment Act (ADEA), it is illegal to discriminate against an employee who is 40 years or older on the basis of age.

- **Sexual orientation or gender identity.** Federal law does not expressly prohibit discrimination on the basis of sexual orientation or gender identity, but the laws of many states do. And under federal law, acting on sex-based stereotypes—for example, that a male is too effeminate—is a form of sex-based discrimination.

- **Religion.** It is illegal under federal law and many state laws to discriminate against employees based on their sincerely held religious beliefs.

- **Genetic information.** Under the Genetic Information Nondiscrimination Act (GINA), it is illegal for an employer to discriminate based on an employee's genetic history.

- **Harassment.** Harassment is a form of illegal discrimination based on membership in a protected class. It is considered a form of discrimination. If you fire a worker for complaining about sexual harassment, for example, or decide to resolve a harassment problem by getting rid of the harassed employee rather than taking action against the harasser, you will run afoul of these laws.

- **Disability discrimination.** Federal law and the laws of many states bar discrimination against people with physical or mental disabilities. They also bar retaliation against people who complain about discrimination or who otherwise assert rights under these statutes.

- **Refusal to submit to lie detector test.** A federal law, the Employee Polygraph Protection Act, makes it illegal to fire an employee for refusing to take a lie detector test. Many state laws also set out strong prohibitions against using lie detector tests in employment decisions.

- **Alien status.** The federal Immigration Reform and Control Act prohibits you from using alien status as a reason to fire a worker who is legally eligible to work here.

- **Complaining about safety or health conditions.** Under the Occupational Safety and Health Act and many state health and safety laws, you can't fire (or otherwise retaliate against) someone for complaining that working conditions don't comply with state or federal safety and health rules.

Court Decisions

Wrongful discharge lawsuits are not always based on statutes. Many courts have awarded wrongful discharge damages to former employees for nonstatutory or common law reasons—that is, legal theories that courts have developed when deciding individual cases. The main ones are discussed here.

Breach of Contract

Employers sometimes make promises to job applicants to entice them to become employees. And some employers may also dangle inducements in front of current employees to discourage them from leaving. A number of judges have ruled that, if a person relies on such promises, an enforceable contract of employment can be created. An employer may be held liable for wrongful discharge if the employee is fired in violation of that contract.

> **EXAMPLE:** Betty, a diligent worker at AutoTec, is offered a job by a rival employer. She declines the job after AutoTec's president tells her she'll have a job for life at AutoTec if she continues to effectively manage her workload. Three years later, AutoTec fires Betty, even though she has kept up with her work. Betty sues for wrongful discharge, claiming AutoTec violated its employment contract with her by firing her.

Specific promises of job security—either written or oral—are not always necessary for a judge to rule that an employee can't be fired arbitrarily. Some judges have allowed fired employees to collect damages or be reinstated to jobs because the employer created a legitimate expectation that employees wouldn't be fired without good cause. The typical focus in these cases is on implications of job security made by the employer in a written document such as an employee handbook. It, too, may be enforced as a contract. As explained in Chapter 2, that makes it important to include language in your employee handbook that reminds employees that employment is at will, and that the at-will relationship can be modified by written contract signed only by a high level employee (like the president of the company).

> **EXAMPLE:** After six months on the job, Tom is fired from Syspro, a small software house. He sues for wrongful discharge, claiming that Syspro's employee handbook led him to believe that he'd only be fired for good cause—and that, in fact, Syspro fired him without a good reason. The judge agrees that it was reasonable for Tom to conclude, after reading the employee handbook, that his job was secure. The court rules that the employer's wording of the handbook constituted an implied contract.

Breach of Good Faith and Fair Dealing

Some wrongful discharge cases are based on the premise that every employment relationship includes an automatic commitment by the employer to deal fairly and in good faith with the employee. Applying this doctrine, judges have held that a discharge was wrongful when an employer has dealt arbitrarily with an employee. Many of these cases have involved longtime employees who were fired as they neared retirement age.

> **EXAMPLE:** Rita has worked for Jones Enterprises for nearly 25 years. The company fires her just three months before her retirement benefits are to become permanent. In a wrongful discharge case against Jones, the judge finds that the company fired Rita to save itself the expense of paying her the full benefit of her retirement program. The judge rules in Rita's favor because the firing breached the implied covenant of good faith and fair dealing.

Violation of Public Policy

Judges sometimes rule that a firing was wrongful because it was against the best interests of the public. Most courts do not allow an employer to fire an employee who was trying to correct an illegal or dangerous business practice, for example.

> **EXAMPLE:** Clinical Lab Center, a small company that processes blood tests for doctors, fires Joe, a medical technician, because he has twice complained to management that the inadequate testing of blood samples by other technicians has led to many inaccurate test results. A judge rules that Joe's firing was wrongful because it violated public policy. Workers, the judge notes, should be free to speak up about sloppy practices they find on the job—especially those affecting public health or safety.

Courts have held that it's against public policy to fire a worker for refusing to file phony reports with a state environmental agency, bribe public officials, commit perjury, or engage in industrial espionage. Courts have also held that it is against public policy to fire an employee for refusing to commit an illegal act or for threatening to report an employer's illegal conduct. And it generally violates public policy to fire a worker for exercising a legal right—to vote or serve on a jury, for example.

Guarding Against Legal Claims

Given the many legal weapons that a disgruntled fired worker can aim at you under the rubric of a wrongful discharge lawsuit, you can understand the danger in blithely relying on your unfettered right to fire any employee. Consider, too, that juries are often sympathetic to fired workers, regarding them as underdogs—sometimes in the face of considerable evidence to the contrary.

Having a Valid Reason

The safest approach any time you fire someone is to be sure you have a legitimate business reason—a reason that you have thought out and documented. If challenged on a particular firing, you should be able to show, for example, that the employee did not adequately perform specific job duties or that the employee violated a clearly stated company policy.

> **EXAMPLE:** The Mail Shoppe employs two men and one woman, Virginia, in its packaging department. One Friday afternoon, the owner fires Virginia. She then files a lawsuit claiming she's been discriminated against because of gender. In court, The Mail Shoppe's owner is able to show that Virginia frequently put too little postage on packages and often neglected to insert the bubble wrap as instructed, causing breakage and numerous customer complaints. The owner also shows that three written warnings were given to Virginia over a six-week period. The judge dismisses the gender discrimination complaint.

In addition to bolstering your legal position, using an open and consistent policy for disciplining and firing employees will usually help improve worker morale. It's reassuring to hardworking, competent employees to know that they won't be fired on a whim. They'll also respect you for knowing who's getting the job done and who isn't—and they'll likely feel relieved when lazy and incompetent workers are let go.

Safely Handling Layoffs

Usually, you're free to lay off or terminate employees because business conditions require a reduction in the workforce. But, if you do cut back, don't leave your business open to claims that the layoffs were really a pretext for getting rid of employees for illegal reasons. If your layoff primarily affects black workers, for example, someone may well question your motives. So if you need to reduce your workforce, be sensitive to how your actions may be perceived. Spread the pain around; don't let the burden of a reduction in force fall on just one group of employees.

If you're a larger employer, you must comply with the Worker Adjustment and Retraining Act, or WARN. (29 U.S.C. §§ 2101 and following.) The law covers your business if either of the following is true:

- You have 100 or more full-time employees.
- You have 100 or more employees whose total work amounts to 4,000 or more hours a week, not counting overtime hours.

To comply with WARN, you must notify employees if you plan to:

- close an employment site, causing 50 or more full-time employees at the site to lose their jobs, or
- lay off at least one-third—but not fewer than 50—of the full-time employees at a site.

In those situations, you must notify each employee—or the employee's union representative—in writing 60 days before you close the site or lay off the employees. You must also send written notice to the state's dislocated worker unit and the chief elected officer of the municipality where the closing or layoff will take place. There are a number of exceptions to WARN. For example, you needn't give a full 60 days' notice if a closing or layoff is caused by unforeseen business circumstances or a natural disaster.

If you fail to give the required notice, your employees can sue you for back pay and benefits. You may also have to pay penalties if you don't give timely notice to the local government.

RESOURCE

Want to know more about WARN? For more information, get the pamphlet *A Guide to Advance Notice of Closings and Layoffs*, prepared by the U.S. Department of Labor. It's available at www.doleta.gov/layoff/pdf/EmployerWARN09_2003.pdf. For detailed information on WARN's requirements and prohibitions—and a complete list of the exceptions to WARN—see *The Essential Guide to Federal Employment Laws*, by Lisa Guerin and Amy DelPo (Nolo).

Guidelines for Firing Employees

Even though your motives for firing someone may be completely honorable and legitimate, you still run a legal risk—the employee may decide to go to court, regardless of your actions. But there are several steps you can take to greatly reduce the chances of a former employee suing your business and being awarded a judgment against you.

Contractual Commitments

Before you fire an employee, check into whether you, or anyone else in the company, made an oral or written contractual commitment that may limit your right to fire. Consider the following:

- Is there a written or oral contract or document (including a hiring letter) that promises the employee a job for a fixed period of time?
- When you hired the employee, did you make any statements about job security?
- Have you assured the employee that you'd fire him or her only for good cause?
- Have you listed causes for termination—in a contract, employee handbook, or elsewhere—in a way that limits you to those specified causes?
- Does your employee handbook or other written policy or memo make any promises about job security?

Your answers to these questions will help you identify whether you've limited your ability to fire the individual. Even if you are positive that you have never given the employee any assurances of job security—either oral or written—you should still proceed with caution, especially when dealing with an employee who has been with your business for a number of years. Some courts have held that a long employment relationship can imply assurances of job security, which in turn can imply an employment contract that limits your ability to fire the employee. If an employee has been working for you only for a few months—or even for a year—you probably don't have to worry about this issue. If the employee has been with your business for, say, ten years, however, you should be careful. If you don't have a really good reason for firing the employee, consider consulting a lawyer before taking action.

Say What You Mean and Mean What You Say

The words you use in hiring someone and in writing an employee handbook can create a contractual commitment unintentionally. To prevent this, your employee handbook and similar documents should reserve your right to terminate employees at your discretion. While you may also wish to list some specific types of conduct that will result in termination, such as dishonesty or excessive absenteeism, those shouldn't be stated in a way that implies they are the *only* reasons to end the relationship. Also, your handbook and other communications with employees should not make any promises about long-term job security. If they do, it's time for a rewrite.

Employment contracts can be a two-way street. While they may limit your right to fire an employee, the flip side is that they usually spell out the employee's obligations to your business. If employees aren't performing well, chances are that they are in breach of the contract, giving you the legal right to terminate the relationship. Because the interpretation of contract terms can involve legal subtleties, consider having a brief conference with a lawyer before firing an employee who has a written contract.

Lawful Reasons for Firing

To head off the possibility that an employee may try to base a wrongful termination action on alleged illegal conduct or motives in your workplace, be prepared to show the real—legitimate—reason for the firing.

Reasons that may support a firing include:
- performing poorly on the job
- refusing to follow instructions
- abusing sick leave
- being absent excessively
- being tardy habitually
- possessing a weapon at work
- violating company rules
- being dishonest
- endangering health and safety
- engaging in criminal activity
- using alcohol or drugs at work
- behaving violently at work
- gambling at work, or
- disclosing company trade secrets to outsiders.

A Firing Is Sometimes Implied

Usually, it's clear when an employee has been fired. That's because the employer typically informs the employee of that fact in no uncertain terms. But sometimes, if an employer's conduct is so extreme that it makes it virtually impossible for the employee to continue on the job, the employer's conduct may be treated as being equal to a formal firing. In legal jargon, this is called a "constructive discharge."

This can occur, for example, where an employer has:

- created an abusive or hostile environment
- insisted that an employee put in excessive overtime
- subjected the employee to intolerable working conditions
- demoted an employee
- offered the employee a "quit or be fired" ultimatum
- substantially changed the employee's job duties, or
- harassed the employee.

The legal consequences of a constructive discharge are exactly the same as an actual discharge: If the employee can show that working conditions really were intolerable, the employee will be able to seek damages for being wrongfully discharged under any of the legal theories discussed above.

Depending on the nature of your business, you may have other legitimate reasons to fire employees as well. Whatever your reasons, it's absolutely essential that you treat your employees evenhandedly. That is, if you regularly let some employees engage in prohibited conduct, you'll be on shaky legal ground if you fire others for the same reason.

EXAMPLE: Andrew, a black attendant, is a half-hour late for work three days in a row. His employer, a medical clinic, fires him. In suing for wrongful discharge based on illegal discrimination, Andrew shows that two white attendants had been similarly tardy in recent weeks but received only a verbal warning to shape up. Even though excessive tardiness is a valid business reason for firing someone, the jury awards damages to Andrew because the employer applied the rules unevenly and unfairly.

Independent Review

Avoid giving an employee's direct supervisor the sole authority to hire and fire. The supervisor may be too close to the situation to make an objective decision. Because firing is such a drastic and traumatic step—and has such potentially serious legal consequences—consider conducting an independent review within your business before anyone is fired. Although this may not be practical in small companies, you should use this procedure if it's feasible.

Any independent review should verify all of the following:

- The firing wouldn't violate antidiscrimination or other statutes.
- The firing wouldn't be a breach of contract, including oral assurances of job security or statements made in an employee handbook.
- Your company has given the employee adequate and documented warnings—except where the misconduct clearly warrants immediate firing.
- You have followed your stated personnel practices.
- You have followed the same procedures in similar situations involving other employees.

Investigating Complaints Against Workers

You may learn of misconduct that requires you to discipline or fire an employee from a complaint by a coworker, a manager, or even a customer or other outsider. This is particularly likely with complaints of sexual harassment or dishonesty.

Investigating the facts can be tricky. The law doesn't require you to learn the truth with absolutely certainty. But, to protect yourself legally, your safest course is to investigate complaints quickly, thoroughly, fairly, and as confidentially as is possible under the circumstances—before you discipline or fire an employee.

Investigations May Help Establish Good Faith

A California case illustrates the value of conducting a fair and thorough investigation. An insurance brokerage firm received complaints that Ralph, a senior vice president, had sexually harassed other employees. Ralph denied the charges, so the company interviewed 21 people who worked with Ralph—including five that he asked be interviewed. The company concluded that it was more likely than not that harassment had occurred, so it fired Ralph.

Ralph sued for wrongful discharge, claiming he had an implied contract requiring good cause for firing him and that there was no good cause because he had not engaged in the alleged misconduct. The jury agreed that the company had not proven that Ralph had sexually harassed anyone—and it returned a verdict of $1.8 million against the company. But, on appeal, the California Supreme Court reversed the verdict.

The court ruled that it wasn't necessary for the company to prove that Ralph had actually committed the sexual harassment. The company had only to show that it had a good faith belief that Ralph had engaged in the misconduct. The results of the company's extensive investigation were sufficient to establish that good faith belief. (*Cotran v. Rollins Hudig Hall Int'l, Inc.*, 948 P.2d 412 (1998).)

RESOURCE

Want more information on investigations? For a detailed discussion of investigating employee complaints, including step-by-step instructions and sample forms, see *The Essential Guide to Workplace Investigations*, by Lisa Guerin (Nolo).

The Investigation

It's usually best to have private interviews with each witness and the accused employee. Listen carefully and take good notes. Don't show any bias for or against the accused. Further investigate any evidence that surfaces, such as a claim that another employee is aware of facts that will shed light on the complaint. Have good reasons for whatever conclusions you reach. If you follow reasonable procedures and reach a reasonable result, you can't be faulted legally, even if another person may have reached a different conclusion.

After an employee files a complaint, it's a good idea to keep the complaining employee informed about the general steps you're taking to investigate. The complaining employee needs to know that you're taking the matter seriously. But that doesn't mean the employee is entitled to know all the details of what you find out. If you give out information too freely, you could easily step on the toes (and violate the privacy rights) of other employees.

Hiring Investigators

If you have qualms about your ability to investigate a complaint, consider hiring an experienced employment consultant or someone else who knows the ropes. Far better to lay out some cash to do it right than risk the consequences of a clumsy investigation. For example, if there's an issue of employee dishonesty or criminal conduct, look into companies that specialize in corporate security.

Similarly, if someone charges sexual harassment because a manager has displayed offensive cartoons or photos in a work area, consider hiring a consultant experienced in sexual harassment issues to review your entire workplace and recommend a course of action. Bringing in an outsider may also help to defuse tensions between workers—especially if anyone involved in the incident doubts the company's ability to be impartial.

CAUTION

If your lawyer investigates, another lawyer should litigate. You may choose to have an experienced employment lawyer conduct a workplace investigation—but be careful if you do. Although the information you share with your attorney is usually confidential and doesn't have to be disclosed in a lawsuit, this may not be true if the attorney acted as the investigator, as opposed to just giving you legal advice. To be safe, if you do decide to have an attorney conduct the investigation, it's probably best not to use someone you want to represent you in a lawsuit—you don't want your confidential communications disclosed in court.

Locating a Good Investigator

When you suspect an employee of dishonesty or criminal conduct, a private investigator may help sort out the facts. The job of interviewing witnesses, analyzing documents, watching for misconduct, and preserving evidence isn't easy. The investigator must follow procedures that respect the accused employee's legal rights. If a court later finds that you trampled an employee's due process rights during an investigation, your business may have to pay for that violation.

It's crucial to find an investigator who's experienced in conducting internal investigations for businesses. There are many people who have recently hung out their shingles as consultants but don't really have training or experience.

This is sensitive work, and the stakes are high. No matter where you find names of possible investigators—from phone book listings, management newsletters, trade associations, or other businesspeople—ask for references. Look for positive feedback from at least two or three other businesses before you hire an investigator.

Alternatives to Firing

Sometimes, firing a troublesome employee is the best course of action. You owe it to your business—and to your diligent, conscientious employees—to get rid of a troublemaker who can't be turned around. But, occasionally, there are good alternatives to firing a worker—alternatives that can help you avoid the risk of a wrongful discharge lawsuit while at the same time providing the spared employee with a chance to improve.

One possibility is to redesign the employee's job to eliminate the problem areas. Or you may assign the employee to another job. For example, an employee who has a tendency to quarrel with customers, but is otherwise organized and efficient, might do an excellent job working alone in the warehouse. Of course, you must be careful not to unload work unfairly on other employees who are already working at peak efficiency.

If yours is a slightly larger business, and there's a personality clash between an employee and a supervisor, you may be able to assign the employee to a different supervisor. Where the conflict is between two employees, neither of whom is a supervisor, you may be able to assign them to separate work areas. If a personal problem is at the root of an otherwise good employee's difficulties, you might offer to pay for at least a limited amount of counseling—or offer the employee a leave of absence to get help with the problem.

Sometimes you and an employee can come to an understanding that the working relationship isn't a good fit for either of you and that the employee is expected to move elsewhere in the near future. Allowing the employee to look for a new job during regular working hours may be one rational way to handle such a situation.

If you decide to pursue an alternative to firing, keep in mind that it doesn't offer full protection against a lawsuit. If the employee can characterize a change of duties as a demotion, for example, the employee may still sue the company. For that reason, it's still important to make sure identified problems, and the solutions, are well documented.

The Firing Process

Where possible, give employees ongoing feedback about job performance, conduct formal job evaluations once or twice a year, and impose progressive discipline. Ideally, a firing shouldn't come suddenly or as a surprise.

RESOURCE

Want more information on improving employee performance through discipline? See *The Progressive Discipline Handbook: Smart Strategies for Coaching Employees,* by Margie Mader-Clark and Lisa Guerin (Nolo).

When you've reached the point where firing an employee is the best or only option, you must mind some legal strictures as you carry out the firing.

TIP

Speedy action is sometimes appropriate. There can be situations in which moving quickly to fire someone—without a warning—may be the best course. For example, if your delivery truck driver is convicted of drunk driving, it makes sense to get rid of the driver. Similarly, you shouldn't feel it necessary to give advance warning to a bookkeeper who has embezzled money from your company. In general, use your judgment and err on the side of giving an employee a chance to correct a problem. But, in extreme circumstances, especially those involving illegal conduct or the risk of harm to others, don't hesitate to act quickly.

Severance Packages

Many employers and employees wrongly believe that every fired employee is legally entitled to severance pay. The truth is that you have to give severance only if you have promised the employee that you would do so—for example, though a contract with the employee, through a written policy in your employee handbook, or through a clearly established pattern of conduct in which you have given severance to other employees in similar circumstances. Even if the law does not require you to pay severance, however, you may wish to offer severance pay and other benefits to help cushion the impact of a firing—and alleviate ill will.

If you're inclined to offer a severance package, it makes sense to be more generous with longtime employees than with those who have been with you just a year or two. For a short-term employee—someone who's worked for you for two years, for example—you might offer one month's pay plus payment of health insurance premiums for 90 days. For an employee who's been on your payroll for 15 years, it might be reasonable to offer six months of salary plus one year's worth of paid health insurance premiums.

You can be creative in putting together a severance package. The benefits you may wish to consider include:

- severance pay
- continuation of employee benefits, such as payment of health insurance premiums for a limited time
- a favorable letter of reference if your normal policy is to give only a former employee's position and term of employment
- releasing the employee from special obligations (such as a covenant not to compete)
- allowing the employee to keep any advance of expense funds or commissions that otherwise would be repayable to your business
- allowing the employee to keep the desk, chair, computer, cellular phone, or tools that you provided
- agreeing not to contest the employee's right to unemployment compensation
- paying for outplacement services, or
- promising to pay an employee's moving expenses, up to a stated limit.

Also, consider paying the employee for unused vacation time that the employee would otherwise lose. Unless state law requires you to pay out unused vacation time, you are free to adopt a policy whereby departing employees forfeit any unused vacation days. (To see the law in your state, check out "State Laws That Control Final Paychecks," in the appendix.

EXAMPLE: Alpine Ski Shop pays its employees for two weeks of vacation time each year but states in its employee's handbook: "You must take your vacation during June, July, or August and while you are on Alpine's payroll. Vacation time not used during that period will be forfeited unless you secure prior approval." Employee Kurt takes one week of his vacation in July and doesn't ask for permission to take the second week later. In October, Alpine fires Kurt because of an attitude problem. As part of a severance package, Alpine pays Kurt for the unused week of vacation time.

CAUTION

Paying for vacation time may be mandatory. In some states, the law doesn't allow an employer to set a policy forcing employees to forfeit unused vacation or sick time once it has accrued. In such states, the accrued vacation or sick time is treated as wages and must be included in an employee's final paycheck. Check with your state department of labor to learn how much latitude you have regarding payment for vacation and sick time. (See the appendix for contact details.)

Preparing the Paperwork

Before you fire an employee, prepare a letter describing the severance package you intend to offer. And, if you want the employee to waive possible legal claims against your business to qualify for the severance benefits, consider preparing a severance agreement as well.

Termination Letter

To soften the shock of a firing, you may wish to present the employee with a letter such as the following during the termination meeting.

Use such a letter if you're not requiring the employee to sign a release waiving possible legal claims against your business to qualify for the severance package.

Release of Claims

You may wish to provide a severance package to a terminating employee only if the employee agrees to waive all potential legal claims—a reasonable condition in many situations. For a release to be enforceable, you must offer the employee something of value—for example, the severance package—in exchange for the employee giving up possible claims against your business.

> ! CAUTION
>
> **If the law already requires you to pay severance** (for example, because you have already promised it to the employee through a written contract), then you must give something to the employee beyond what the severance package

Sample Termination Letter— No Release Required

June 10, 20xx

Dear Joe Jones,

Your employment with XYZ Company is being terminated at 5 p.m. on July 1, 20xx.

You will receive a paycheck that includes earned wages and your accrued vacation time. In addition, you will receive the following severance benefits:

1. Four weeks of additional pay at your regular salary.

2. Payment of your health insurance premiums for six months (or until you begin work at a new job, if that occurs sooner).

3. You will be allowed to keep the $500 advanced to you for job-related expenses.

4. The Company will not contest your right to receive unemployment compensation.

I wish you well in your further endeavors.

Lars Ingram
President, XYZ Company

requires in exchange for the employee signing the release.

Also, give the employee a reasonable time—two or three weeks, for example—to decide whether to accept your severance package and sign the severance agreement containing a release of claims. A coerced release is legally worthless.

Special rules apply if the employee is releasing claims under the Age Discrimination in Employment Act. If you present a release to an individual employee who's 40 years old or older, you must give the employee a fixed period of time in which to decide whether to sign the waiver. That period must be at least 21 days if the waiver has been presented to the employee alone. If you've presented the waiver to a group or class of employees, you must give each worker at least 45 days to decide whether to sign. In either case, a worker has seven days after agreeing to such a waiver to revoke the decision. (See Chapter 8 for details.)

Return of Property

In planning for the termination meeting, make a list of all company property that has been given to the employee. Be prepared to get these items back from the employee either at the meeting or within a reasonable time afterward. Items to think about include:

- automobiles
- computers, cellular phones, and beepers
- confidential manuals and other documents

- keys, credit cards, uniforms, ID badges, and
- parking permits.

Don't overlook any expense account funds you advanced to the employee. You may be entitled to deduct such advances from the employee's final paycheck.

The Termination Meeting

Call the employee into a private office or meeting room and announce your decision. Be honest and direct in stating your reasons for ending the employment. If you've given the employee ongoing feedback, the firing shouldn't come as a complete shock. Make it clear that this is a final decision and that you're not going to change your mind. Go over any severance package the employee will receive—and explain the severance agreement if you require one to be signed.

Then give the employee a reasonable chance to vent about the discharge. Just listen and don't argue. Don't insult or abuse the employee even if the employee expresses anger and disappointment. Typically, this will fade with time. Unless the employee is likely to be a menace in the workplace, allow a day or so—but no longer—to clear out belongings and say goodbye to coworkers.

Heading Off Trouble

As noted, there are many ways to fortify your legal position so that an employee will be less likely to succeed in a claim against you for wrongful discharge. Some additional practical steps can help you keep the good will of an employee who's being terminated, making it less likely that you'll be sued in the first place.

Offering a Chance to Resign

Permitting the employee to resign gives the employee the opportunity to save face—which, in turn, may make the employee less bitter about the termination and less hostile to your business. Be aware, however, that if you give the employee a stark choice between resigning and being fired, it's probably not legally considered a voluntary termination. The employee likely will be eligible for unemployment compensation benefits. (See below for more about this issue.) And a forced resignation may be treated the same as a firing if the employee does decide to sue for wrongful discharge.

Common Sense Can Help Avert Violence

You may have zeroed in on scary newspaper headlines about disgruntled former employees who open fire on former employers. Although the actual incidence of such violence is quite low, it pays to be prudent.

Violence following a firing is most apt to occur in a workplace where there are high levels of stress, autocratic and unpredictable managers, poor communication, and employees who feel powerless.

Be especially careful if you're firing an employee for performing poorly—a charge that may be emotionally loaded. Some workers who are fired without warning can go over the edge because they feel there was nothing they could do to control the situation. In giving feedback before a firing, let the employee know if performance is below par—and focus on the specific ways job performance falls short of the mark. Warn the employee about the possibility of losing the job if you don't see improvement.

At a termination meeting with a potentially volatile employee, confine your discussion to the specific behavior about which the employee was warned. Never attack the employee personally. Remind the employee that you had given fair warning and an ample opportunity to change work habits.

Let the fired employee know that you won't be discussing the reasons for the firing with the rest of the workers. This will help preserve the employee's self-esteem, making violence less likely.

Troubled employees often exhibit behavioral clues that you shouldn't ignore: high absenteeism, known substance abuse, chronic tardiness, fascination with weapons, and harassing and threatening others. If you're about to fire someone who appears to have a potential for violence, consider consulting first with a psychologist who specializes in workplace issues.

Offering a Favorable Reference

If you would be willing to give a former employee a positive reference, say so. Knowing that there will be a favorable recommendation can help temper a worker's ire over a termination. Obviously, such a reference isn't always possible. But, quite often, an employee who wasn't a good fit at your business could do well elsewhere and you won't have a difficult time emphasizing the employee's good qualities.

When prospective employers call, follow through and accentuate the positive. Keep in touch with the former employee by phone and by sending copies of any letters in which you state positive things. (For more on references, see below.)

Help Finding a New Job

You may be able to inform an employee of openings elsewhere that would be better suited to the employee's skills and personality. Or, if it's a longtime employee to whom you feel a lot of loyalty, you may even consider footing the bill to have a personnel agency assist the employee in finding another job. Another possibility is to give an employee paid time off to find a new job—using your phone, if necessary, to call prospects.

Final Paychecks

Most states have a law specifying when you must give a final paycheck to a terminated employee. Most of these laws set different deadlines for employees who have quit and those who have been fired. (See "State Laws That Control Final Paychecks" in the appendix.) If you don't give a final paycheck on time, you may have to pay damages to the employee and perhaps a penalty to the state as well.

Note that, in many states, the law requires that the final paycheck include accrued vacation pay and anything else owed to an employee who's covered by the law. If you have additional questions about final paychecks, contact the wage and hour division of your state's labor department to double-check your state law. (See the appendix for contact details.)

Continuing Health Insurance

If you have 20 or more employees and you offer a group health insurance plan, a federal law called the Consolidated Omnibus Budget Reconciliation Act (COBRA) requires you to offer former employees the option of continuing their coverage for some time after their employment ends. Your state may also have a health insurance continuation law. (See Chapter 4 for more about continuing health care coverage.)

Unemployment Compensation

Employees who are terminated because of cutbacks or because they are not a good fit for a job are generally entitled to unemployment benefits under state unemployment insurance programs. Employees who are fired for serious misconduct—stealing or selling drugs in the workplace, for example—or who voluntarily leave a job without good cause are not entitled to unemployment payments.

Applying these categories to a particular termination isn't always easy. For example, suppose you and an employee get into an argument and the employee leaves shortly afterward. If the employee has quit, benefits are not legally due. If the employee was fired, however, the employee is entitled to unemployment benefits absent truly bad conduct. It's sometimes difficult to discern whether a termination is a quitting or a firing.

The Claims Process

Although the details of unemployment compensation vary in each state, some general principles apply in most cases. As a private employer, you contribute a relatively small amount to an unemployment insurance fund in your state. Your rate is normally based on the size of your payroll and the amount of unemployment benefits paid from your account. Employers with smaller payrolls and low levels of unemployment claims will, over time, pay lower taxes.

An unemployment claim typically proceeds through a number of steps.

Filing the Claim

The former employee files a claim with the state unemployment program. You receive written notice of the claim and can file a written objection—usually within seven to ten days. If you want to file an objection, don't miss this deadline, or you may waive your right to do so.

Eligibility Determined

The state agency makes an initial determination of whether the former employee is eligible to get unemployment benefits. Usually there's no hearing at this stage.

Referee's Hearing

You or the former employee can appeal the initial eligibility decision and request a hearing before a referee—a hearing officer who is on the staff of the state agency. Normally conducted in a private room at the unemployment office, this airing of the situation is the most important step in the process. At the hearing, you and the former employee each have your say. In addition, you're entitled to have a lawyer there and to present witnesses and any relevant written records, such as employee evaluations or warning letters.

Before the hearing, ask to see the agency's complete file on the claim. This will give you a chance to be prepared to refute inaccurate statements. Bring all pertinent employment records to the hearing. Also, line up witnesses who can give firsthand testimony about why the former employee was guilty of misconduct, quit voluntarily, or is otherwise ineligible for benefits.

It may be too expensive to hire a lawyer to handle an unemployment compensation hearing. In some states, you have the alternative of hiring an experienced nonlawyer specialist to oppose claims, at a fraction of what lawyers charge. A clerk in the referee's office may know of someone who performs these services in your area. But since the procedures in the hearing are designed to be simple and nontechnical, you probably won't need any hired help.

Doing Your Own Research

Many states keep records of decisions by the review board. By looking at these records, you can see how cases similar to yours were decided. This can be a helpful resource if you represent your business in an administrative appeal. Your state's unemployment agency can tell you if and where such decisions are kept for public inspection.

Similarly, when an unemployment case is reviewed by a state appeals court, the written decision becomes a public record along with other court decisions. To locate court decisions dealing with unemployment law, start with the annotated version of your state's statutes—often called an annotated code. It should be available at larger public libraries.

Look up the unemployment compensation law, and you'll find short summaries of each case in which an appeals court interpreted the law. If there are cases that sound similar to yours, look up the full decision in the case reports—the books that collect all appeals court decisions in your state. (For more on how to do your own legal research, see Chapter 14.)

> **CAUTION**
>
> **Serious charges may be raised.** The referee's decision sometimes influences what happens in a related civil lawsuit. For example, if the referee rules that the employee quit because of sexual harassment, that ruling may be decisive in a later harassment lawsuit that the employee brings against your business. Consult a lawyer if you anticipate that complicated legal issues—such as sexual harassment, illegal discrimination, or retaliation—may surface at the hearing.

Administrative Appeal

Either side can appeal the referee's decision to an administrative agency, sometimes called a board of review. This appeal usually is based solely on the testimony and documents recorded at the referee's hearing, although some states allow the review board to hear additional evidence. While the review board is free to draw its own conclusions from the evidence and overrule the referee, it usually goes along with the referee's ruling.

Judicial Appeal

Either side can appeal to the state court system, but this is rare. Typically, a court will overturn the agency's decision only if the decision is contrary to law or isn't supported by substantial evidence.

> **RESOURCE**
>
> **Need to know more about unemployment?** For more information, see

Controlling Unemployment Insurance Costs: An Employer's Guide, published by the National Foundation for Unemployment Compensation and Workers Compensation, available online at www.uwcstrategy.org. Although the book recommends taking a more aggressive stance in fighting claims than may be prudent, it also contains lots of useful information.

Saving Money

In theory, you'll save money if you recognize and successfully oppose questionable claims. But this isn't always true, for several reasons. First, lots of claims you think are questionable probably will be allowed under unemployment compensation laws, which are deliberately lenient to give unemployed workers a transitional source of income. Unless there's strong evidence that the employee pilfered from the company or engaged in other fairly extreme conduct, the employee will usually win in a claims contest.

Second, fighting a claim can be time-consuming, emotionally draining, and costly for you—especially when balanced against the fact that a few unemployment claims spread over several years are unlikely to greatly increase your insurance rate. Third, fighting an unemployment claim will guarantee an angry former employee—a person far more likely to file a lawsuit or try to harm you or your business in some other way. Of course, this might happen anyway. But your challenge to the employee's right to receive unemployment

benefits may be the last straw that prompts the former employee to strike back.

Balance the benefits of saving on unemployment taxes against the trouble it takes to fight the claim and the risk of inviting a lawsuit against your business.

In addition to challenging questionable claims, there are other ways you may be able to reduce the costs of unemployment benefits.

Double-check the information your state unemployment agency uses to compute your tax rates and to compute benefits paid to former employees. Make sure the agency's records don't indicate that your business has had more claims filed against it than it really did have. Clerical errors can be costly.

Also, keep in mind that a former employee may be eligible for benefits at first but later become ineligible. For example, three weeks after being fired, a claimant may decide to return to school full time, meaning that the claimant is unavailable to take a new job. Or you may hear that the employee is working for another business but being paid under the table so as to keep getting unemployment benefits. If you learn any such information, notify the state agency promptly.

Protecting Your Business Information

Some employees have access to sensitive business information or trade secrets. When these employees leave—either because they quit or because you've fired them—you may be concerned that they'll use this information to their personal advantages. For example, a former employee may open a business that competes with yours or go to work for a competitor.

Chapter 1 discusses how you may be able to protect yourself by asking certain employees to sign covenants not to compete and agreements not to divulge or use trade secrets. This section explains what to do if a former employee begins to compete unfairly with your business in violation of such a covenant or agreement.

Enforcing Noncompete Agreements

You might assume it would be difficult to learn whether a former employee is competing with you. However, many businesses are fairly public, which makes it difficult for a former employee to hide. Also, there's a good chance that you'll be contacted by your loyal customers if they are approached by the former employee. The lure of a lower price offered by the former employee often isn't enough to win over a customer who suspects the former employee of cheating you.

If the former employee's conduct violates a valid noncompete agreement, you may choose to remind the individual about the terms of the agreement in a letter. You may also be able to contact a competitor if the former employee is using the information on the competitor's behalf.

If that doesn't work, you can seek a court order (called an injunction) to put a legal stop to the unfair activities. You'll probably need to hire a lawyer to help. In some cases, you may want to go straight to court—especially if your company will suffer immediate damage from the employee's conduct, or you don't want to give the employee advance notice that you're going to be bringing a lawsuit.

Fortunately, the procedures for getting a ruling from a judge in this situation are fairly fast and efficient. Your lawyer will likely ask the judge assigned to your case to set an early hearing to decide whether to issue a preliminary injunction—an order that prohibits the former employee from unfairly competing with you while the case is pending. A judge who's convinced that the threat of damage to your business is great may even grant a temporary restraining order forbidding the former employee from taking any action until the initial hearing can be held.

A restraining order or injunction is a powerful legal weapon. An individual who violates such an order can be found in contempt of court. The punishment for contempt is a fine, imprisonment, or both.

Protecting Trade Secrets

A trade secret is information that gives you a competitive advantage because it isn't generally known and can't be readily learned by other people who could benefit from it. It can be a formula, pattern, compilation, program, device, method, technique, or other process that you've made reasonable efforts to keep secret.

Weighing Your Chances of Success

Whether a judge will enforce a covenant not to compete is always an iffy question. The legal system puts a high value on a person's right to earn a living. In California, noncompetes are illegal in all but the most limited circumstances. Elsewhere, covenants not to compete won't be enforced if they're found to be unreasonable. A covenant may be held unreasonable if it covers too wide a geographic area or lasts for too long a time.

EXAMPLE: Walt—a veterinarian who operates three animal hospitals in Anderson County—hires Fred, another veterinarian, to work for him. Fred signs an employment contract that states that, for three years after his employment ends, he won't practice veterinary medicine within 15 miles of any veterinary practice operated by Walt. Together, the three prohibited areas embrace nearly all of Anderson County, plus parts of several adjoining counties. The contract also states that Fred will pay $30,000 in damages if he violates the covenant.

Fred quits his job and begins a mobile veterinary practice in Anderson County, bringing his work within the restricted areas. Walt sues Fred for $30,000, but the court holds the covenant can't be enforced, because it's unreasonably broad. (*Stringer v. Herron*, 424 S.E.2d 547 (1992).)

A covenant may also be held unreasonable if the information revealed to the worker isn't all that sensitive.

EXAMPLE: Image Supplies Inc., a printing supply company in Chicago, hires John as a salesman. John signs a covenant stating that, for one year after his job ends, he won't compete with Image Supplies within 100 miles of Image Supplies' headquarters. John resigns and goes to work for a competitor in the Chicago area.

Image Supplies seeks an injunction—a court order prohibiting John from working for the competitor—because John has the names and locations of its customers and the prices charged to each customer. The court refuses to grant an injunction. It holds that Image Supplies has no protectable business interest in the information that John has. The names of firms in the printing business are easily found in the phone book and trade publications, and anyone can learn about prices by asking the customer. (*Image Supplies Inc. v. Hilmert*, 390 N.E.2d 68 (1979).)

Judges are more likely to enforce restrictive covenants against high-level managers who truly are given inside information. Such former employees are in a position to do real harm.

A judge may order the employee not to use a trade secret even if the employee didn't sign a secrecy agreement—but you must show that what the employee took truly meets the definition. This usually involves establishing two things: that the information was not readily obtainable elsewhere and that you took precautions to keep it secret. For example, if you developed a unique plant fertilizer that you manufacture and distribute, you should be able to establish that you created the fertilizer through extensive trial and error and then made sure that employees learned the formula on a strict need-to-know basis.

Similarly, if you put together a valuable customer list that includes your customers' buying history and buying habits, you should be able to show that you painstakingly built up the list over several years and that you allowed only a limited number of employees to see it.

Handling Postemployment Inquiries

One of your knottiest dilemmas after an employee quits or has been fired is deciding what to tell other businesses that inquire about the former employee. You may be tugged in several directions:

- You want to tell the truth—good, bad, or neutral—about the former worker.
- You may want to help the former worker find another job.

- You may fear that if you do say anything negative, you'll be sued for libel or slander.
- You may feel that the best way to head off possible lawsuits or complaints by angry employees is to help them find new jobs.
- You don't want to overpraise a marginal employee and risk the anger of the new employer.

The law doesn't require you to completely clam up about a former employee. If you follow some basic legal guidelines, you can disclose significant information about the former employee without risking a lawsuit.

Legal Requirements

The key to protecting yourself is to stick to the facts and act in good faith. When you go beyond the facts or are motivated by a desire to harm the former employee or cover up the truth, you can find yourself in deep trouble.

Former employees who feel maligned can sue for defamation—called slander if the statements were spoken or libel if they were written. To win a defamation case, a former employee must prove that you gave out false information and that the information harmed the employee's reputation. If you can prove that the information you gave out was true, the defamation lawsuit will be dismissed.

Employers in most states are entitled to limited protection in defamation cases, even if the information they provide is false. This is based on a legal doctrine called qualified privilege. To receive the benefit of this protection, you must show all of the following:

- You made the statement in good faith.
- You and the person to whom you disclosed the information shared a common interest.
- You limited your statement to this common interest.

The law recognizes that a former employer and a prospective employer share a common interest in the attributes of an employee. To get the protection of the qualified privilege, your main task is to stick to facts that you've reasonably investigated and to lay aside your personal feelings about the former employee.

If you can establish that you're protected by the qualified privilege, the only way a former employee can succeed in a defamation lawsuit is to prove that you knew the information was false but you passed it on anyway, or that you acted recklessly in sorting out the facts.

TIP

Speak candidly. In a trend designed to encourage fuller disclosure in responding to reference checks, some states have laws that allow you to be more candid about former employees. Generally, these laws expand on the common law principles that protect you if you act in good faith. In Kansas, for example, the law presumes that you're acting in good faith when you respond to a reference check. Under that law, to collect damages for a bad reference, the former employee must prove by clear and convincing evidence that you acted in bad faith. If your state has a similar law, you can rest a bit easier when discussing former employees.

Be Careful Within Your Business

Usually, when a former employee sues for defamation, it's because the old employer has gone overboard in giving information to a prospective employer. But you can also get in trouble if you're not discreet in what you say about the former employee within your own company.

To help avoid liability, follow a few commonsense policies.

- Disclose the reasons for a firing strictly on a need-to-know basis—for example, to an employee who handles unemployment compensation claims for your business.
- Avoid discussing firings at meetings and employee gatherings—and never post the details on a bulletin board. Limit announcements to something noncommittal: "Bob has left the company as of last Friday. His position is being filled by Rita."
- Be sure your personnel files reflect fairness, objectivity, and good faith. A former employee who sues you will certainly subpoena employment records. These must be free of unprovable gossip, or your whole case may be jeopardized.

Deciding What to Say

A practical policy—and one that gives you a high degree of legal protection—is simply not to discuss an employee with prospective employers if you can't say something positive. Just tell the person inquiring that it's not your policy to comment on former workers.

Where an employee's record is truly mixed, it's sometimes possible to accent the positive while you try to put negative information into a halfway favorable, or at least less negative, perspective.

> **EXAMPLE:** Madeline, a copywriter for your ad agency, started working for you right out of college. She was a creative writer with lots of clever ideas but never really figured out how to manage the production details for the mail order catalogues that are the bread and butter of your business. After a year, you concluded that this was just not a good fit and you reluctantly gave Madeline 60 days to find a slot elsewhere—hopefully with an agency looking for the dazzling, witty prose that was Madeline's forte.
>
> Possible approach to inquiries: Emphasize that Madeline is so full of creative energy and enthusiasm that she gets bored when it comes to tracking mundane details. Suggest that Madeline would do best in a spot where creative writing and initiative are required, and where new and clever ideas are needed.

Stick to known, provable facts and scrupulously avoid passing along speculation or rumor.

> **EXAMPLE:** Oscar, a salesman for your company, has an explosive temper. You received reports from several customers that Oscar had lost his cool and shouted obscenities at them. In one instance, he was nose to nose with the customer. In another case, he grabbed the customer's shoulder. You were about to discuss these incidents with Oscar when he quit to move to another city. The scuttlebutt around the office was that Oscar would often drink three martinis at lunch.
>
> Possible approach to inquiries: Describe Oscar's strong selling skills and then tell of documented customer complaints, but refrain from repeating gossip you overheard about Oscar's drinking.

It also pays to watch your tongue in informal settings. Don't let down your guard at trade meetings or other places where you're chatting socially with others. If a fired employee was with your business for a while, a supplier or customer may ask, "Where's John these days?" If you reply in a vindictive way, describing all your grievances that led you to fire John, word will likely spread. And John may wind up being blackballed in your field or town. This can lead to legal complications for you and your business.

Employee Privacy

There may be times when you'd like to monitor an employee's activities, look at material on an employee's computer, or even search an employee's belongings or a room or other facility used by the employee. You may, for example, want to see if an employee is conducting personal business on company time, harassing other employees through email messages, stealing from your business, or packing a gun. The problem is that the employee may view your efforts as needlessly intrusive and an invasion of privacy—and, in some cases, the law will support the employee's position.

This is an emerging area of law. No one knows the precise balance between your right to control your workplace and your employees' right to privacy. But, fortunately, legislators and judges recognize an employer's legitimate business interests. Although there are legal pitfalls to be avoided, your hands aren't completely tied. If you're sensitive to the legal nuances, you can take appropriate actions to maintain a safe and productive workplace.

This chapter focuses on several privacy issues that have resulted in litigation, including these:

- Do you have a right to check on the websites employees are visiting?
- How far can you go in monitoring an employee's on-the-job communications—including phone conversations and email?
- What are the legal limits on your use of cameras, recorders, and computer-productivity software?
- When can you safely search an employee's possessions or work area?
- Can you dictate what employees can and cannot do on their own time—such as whom they can and cannot date?

Privacy Issues Discussed Elsewhere in This Book

- For information on respecting the privacy rights of job applicants—including during job interviews; when using job applications, when using aptitude, psychological, and other types of tests; and when investigating an applicant's credit history, employment history, school records, and other background areas—see Chapter 1.
- For information on the requirements of confidentiality when handling employee files, see Chapter 2.
- To learn about the limitations on your right to impose grooming and clothing rules, see Chapter 2.
- To learn about your obligation to keep information about medical leaves and temporary transfers confidential, see Chapter 6.
- To learn about your right to limit smoking in the workplace, see Chapter 7.
- To learn how much you can say about why you fired an employee, see Chapter 10.

As you'll see, you can go a long way toward avoiding worker resentment and legal entanglements by observing two key principles. First, make sure that you do only what's necessary for your business purposes; an employer who tracks employees out of mere curiosity or an obsessive desire to exercise control is skating on thin ice. Second, do your best to reduce employees' expectations of privacy in the workplace. In case after case, judges have ruled that employees have a reasonable expectation of privacy in a wide range of workplace situations. But these same judges also recognize that an employer can remove—or at least diminish—an employee's expectations. The more you're able to do this, the less likely the judge will side with an employee who claims an invasion of privacy, assuming that you have a good business reason for your policies and actions.

Overcoming an employee's privacy expectations may not be all that hard. For starters, you can notify employees of what you plan to do. And it makes sense to tell them why you're taking such actions and what the consequences are. In the case of Internet use, for example, you might inform employees that your computers are for business purposes only and that you may discipline or fire an employee who visits sites unrelated to the business. Many judges say that an employee who receives such notice no longer has a reasonable expectation of privacy in the activities described in the notice. Often, a worker who has received such notice and continues on the job is found to

have given implied consent to the employer's monitoring activities. You can give notice in many ways, such as memos, posters, and an employee handbook.

To build an even stronger defense, you can get each employee's express consent. You can provide a written statement for employees to sign, acknowledging your policies and practices and consenting to your monitoring. Another method is to include your policies and practices in an employee handbook and then require the employee to sign a receipt acknowledging that the employee has received the handbook and consents to the policies and practices described there. With express written consent, you don't have the potential problem of proving in court that the employee did receive notice of your monitoring activities.

Be aware, however, that notice and consent will only go so far. Some states have outlawed specific practices, such as using video cameras in restrooms and changing areas. In these situations—and others where most people would agree that monitoring would be offensive—you won't be able to overcome an employee's reasonable expectation of privacy.

Monitoring Employees at Work

In general, keeping tabs on what employees are doing at work is a legitimate activity for an employer. For one thing, it gives you an objective way to evaluate job performance. For another, it helps you detect theft, thwart disclosure of confidential information, prevent discrimination and harassment, and ensure that employees are using computers and phone lines for business purposes only.

As a result, the law gives you considerable latitude to monitor employees, but not a completely free hand. Employees retain some claim to workplace privacy. The following guidelines will help you avoid legal problems.

Internet Use

If your business provides computers for employees to use in their work, you may worry about whether employees are using the computers as you intend. To put it more bluntly: When employees are quietly tapping away at the keyboard or intently scrutinizing the screen, are they really conducting business? Maybe, maybe not. Especially if the computers can connect to the Internet, the temptations are many. For all you know, employees may be shopping online, viewing pornography, buying or selling stock, checking the latest sports scores, or playing computer games. You may not mind if employees' nonbusiness use of the computer is limited and doesn't interfere with job performance. But you'll understandably be disturbed if employees are whiling away big chunks of time on personal matters.

You can buy inexpensive software that enables you to check on the websites that employees are visiting. If you decide to install Web-tracking software, you'll want to head off potential claims by employees that they reasonably expected privacy in their computer use. Accordingly, it's prudent to take the following precautions:

- Adopt a policy saying that employees are to use your computers for business matters only.
- Inform employees of this policy and also tell them that you're installing software that will show what websites they're visiting.
- Let them know that they can be disciplined or fired for using your computers for personal matters.
- Have employees acknowledge in writing that they've received notice of your policy and of the fact that you use Web-tracking software.

EXAMPLE: Inco Corporation hires Allen and provides a computer for him to use at work. At Inco's request, Allen acknowledges in writing that he's aware of the company's policy that he's to use the computer for business matters only, and that he mustn't use it for "improper, derogatory, defamatory, obscene, or other inappropriate purposes." He also acknowledges that Inco may monitor his computer usage and may discipline or fire him for improper use. Inco fires Allen after discovering that he's used the computer to visit pornographic sites. Allen has no legal basis to complain that Inco has invaded his privacy. His notice of Inco's policy, combined with his written consent to that policy, defeats any claim by Allen that he had a reasonable expectation of privacy concerning his computer use.

Even if you don't install Web-tracking software, you may still want to have a policy prohibiting using the Internet for personal purposes—or at least for inappropriate purposes such as visiting pornographic sites.

In addition to monitoring employee Internet use, you may want to check on how productive employees are in using your business computers. Here again, software can be useful. You can buy a program that monitors an employee's keystrokes. To be on the safe side legally, let employees know what you are doing.

Phone Calls and Email

There are a number of good business reasons for monitoring the phone calls that employees make and the emails they send. For example, you may want to ensure that employees are providing good service to customers and clients. Or you may want to check whether your employees are using your phones and computers for personal purposes. Also, you may want to make sure that employees aren't violating the law or your business policies by engaging in harassment or discrimination. Additionally, monitoring phone calls and email can help you detect the disclosure of trade secrets and other confidential information. If you decide to monitor phone calls and email, you must follow some legal rules.

Under two federal laws—the Omnibus Crime Control and Safe Streets Act of 1968

and the Electronic Communications Privacy Act (ECPA)—you can monitor phones calls and email in either of the following cases:

- Your monitoring is in the ordinary course of your business.
- You have the employee's consent.

 CAUTION

The courts are divided on whether the federal statute applies to email messages stored on your server. The Supreme Court may have to resolve this issue. Rather than get into uncertain legal terrain, it's better to have a clearly stated policy regarding email monitoring and to get employees' express consent.

 CAUTION

Your right to monitor voicemail is unsettled. The federal statute is silent on voicemail messages, and the courts haven't ruled definitively on the matter. The safe course is to deal with voicemail messages, phone calls, and email messages in a single monitoring policy and to obtain employees' written consent to monitor.

This section discusses federal law requirements. Your state's law might also add a twist. Check with your state labor department for more information. (See the appendix for contact details.)

Ordinary Course of Business

Though federal law authorizes you to monitor phone calls and emails in the ordinary course of business, it doesn't say what that is—and the courts have done little to fill in the blanks. That being said, it is clear that this applies if employees use your phones as an inextricable part of your business and if you listen in to make sure the employees are serving your customers well—for example, if you have a telemarketing operation or if a primary component of your business is to sell goods or services by phone.

It will also apply if you want to check up on an employee who you think is giving trade secrets to a competitor or using the phone to make personal calls. In addition, one court has ruled that a burglar and fire alarm company could monitor all calls, based on industry practice and insurance rules.

No matter what, however, ordinary course of business applies only to business calls. If you happen to monitor a personal call, you must stop listening as soon as you determine that it is personal. Similarly, if you come across a personal email, you must stop reading.

Developing a Computer, Telephone, and Email Policy

You can create a computer, telephone, and email policy that not only informs employees that you will monitor their use but also lets them know what constitutes proper and improper use of your computers and phone systems. Here's an example of a policy that you can modify to meet your needs:

- Our computers, phones, and voicemail and email system are intended to facilitate business communications.
- Our management has access at all times to phone calls, voicemail messages, Internet use, and email communications sent or received on our phones, computers, and email system.
- All communications sent or received on our computers are the property of our company.

- Employee privacy doesn't extend to such communications—whether intended for business or personal purposes—or to phone calls or voicemail messages on our equipment and systems.
- Employees must provide management with all passwords and encryption keys.
- Employees must not use our phones, voicemail system, computers, or email system for personal purposes or for commercial purposes unrelated to our company, or for sending offensive, harassing, discriminatory, or defamatory messages.
- Employees who violate these policies may be subject to disciplinary action, up to and including termination.

TIP

Allow employees to use personal devices for private communications. As you know, many employees own cell phones and other electronic devices that let them send and receive messages and use the Internet. It makes sense to let employees use these devices while at work, at least during lunch or breaks. They'll be able to communicate privately—and you'll avoid potential legal problems.

Consent

The second way to monitor phone calls and email messages is to obtain employee consent. An employee's consent can be either implied or express. If you notify employees that you'll be monitoring their phone calls and email messages, they've given their implied consent if they continue to use the phone or send email messages. You can give this notice in an employee handbook or through prominent posters in the work area.

Although implied consent is legally sufficient to permit monitoring under the federal law, you may have trouble later on proving that you actually gave the notice. For that reason, you'll make your life easier by getting each employee's written consent. Have employees acknowledge in writing that they know you'll be monitoring their phone calls and email messages when they use business phones and computers, and that they consent to such monitoring.

Several states impose additional requirements on monitoring phone calls. Primarily, they require the consent of both parties to the call—typically by a beep that both parties can hear or a message notifying both parties of the monitoring. Many states have requirements for monitoring phone calls. To find the rule in your state, you'll need to research your state's statutes and utilities commission rules or check with a lawyer. The extent to which these state requirements apply to email monitoring is unresolved.

RESOURCE

Want more information on monitoring email? For an in-depth discussion of privacy policies—including email and computer policies—check out *Smart Policies for Workplace Technologies*, by Lisa Guerin (Nolo). This excellent resource contains information about legal requirements and practical considerations, and it provides you with policies that you can cut and paste into your own employee handbook.

Monitoring Performance and Workplace Behavior

You may have a legitimate business reason to install video cameras in the workplace. For example, you may want to discourage theft from a cash register, or you may want to assure the safety of employees and customers. You're generally free to use video cameras for such purposes, though it's always a good idea to notify employees that this is your policy. An employee who continues to work for you after getting such a notice has given implied consent to the video monitoring. Some states forbid the use of electronic surveillance in areas such as rest rooms, locker rooms, or lounges, so, to be safe, don't monitor areas where most people would find it highly offensive to be watched.

Monitoring conversations through microphones—either separately or in connection with video cameras—falls under the same rules as apply to phone conversations. You should have employees' consent before you listen in on their conversations. Notifying them in advance will suffice to establish implied consent. Having them sign an express consent is even better, because you don't have to prove that employees received notice.

Searches

Sometimes you may feel a need to search an employee's property or work space. The reasons vary, but the most common is to investigate actual or potential wrongdoing. You may, for example, want to look for evidence of theft or illegal drug use or the presence of a weapon. Although such motives are understandable, they may conflict with an employee's right to privacy.

Most employees would regard their own personal property as private—including their lunch boxes, briefcases, purses, and vehicles. And many employees can reasonably expect that some of the property you provide for their use will be private—for example, a desk, an office, or a locker. If you want to be able to search such property without risking severe legal consequences, you must do your best to eliminate the expectation of privacy.

Consider taking the following precautions:

- Adopt a written policy that lets employees know which of the company's property—and which of their own—may be subject to searches.
- Specifically address workplace facilities—such as desks, lockers, and cabinets—that employees might expect to be private. And, if you anticipate more extensive searches, also address such items as handbags, briefcases, and parcels.
- Make sure that employees are well informed of your policy. (Ideally, you'd like employees to sign an acknowledgment that they've received a copy of the policy and agree to be bound by it.) When you let employees know that you may be searching certain property, it's hard for them to later contend that they reasonably expected privacy.
- If you give an employee a key to a desk or locker but retain a master key, make sure the employee knows. Without that knowledge, the employee may have a very high expectation of privacy that you'll have trouble overcoming.
- Apply your search policy consistently to all employees.
- Limit any searches, if you can, to company-owned property; try not to search the employees' personal property.
- Have a good business reason for any search you conduct—for example, to look for stolen property or controlled substances.

CAUTION

Avoid searching employees themselves. The legal stakes are much higher if you get up close and personal—for example, searching clothing that an employee is wearing or conducting pat downs or strip searches of the employees themselves. If you feel that such searches are needed, call the police and let them handle the problem. Otherwise, the employee may later sue you not only for invasion of privacy but also for a number of other torts, including assault, battery, false arrest, false imprisonment, and intentional infliction of mental distress.

Employee Dating

Some employers decree that managers can't date employees whom they supervise. These employers typically believe that without such a policy, there'd be an increased risk of sexual harassment charges being lodged against the business. The imbalance in power might lead a subordinate employee to claim that he or she was subjected to subtle or direct coercion by a supervisor. On the other hand, other employees might claim that the manager favors an employee he or she is dating. Employers may fear that perception of favoritism (whether justified or not) will affect the morale of other employees, or in the worst case, lead to claims of discrimination or harassment.

Other employers adopt policies that go even further: They prohibit any employee from dating another—supervisor, coworker, subordinate, or otherwise. Their reasoning is that employees who are dating one another can have a negative effect on the workplace atmosphere, especially if the relationship turns sour.

Obviously, policies such as these do intrude into the private lives of employees. Generally, however, it's legally safe to adopt them. But, if you do, make sure that all employees are aware of your stance and that you apply your policies consistently.

CAUTION

Broad statutes may make the outcome uncertain. Statutes in some states, including California, Colorado, New York, and North Dakota, say that an employer can't prohibit employees from participation in a lawful activity off the premises unless the prohibited activity conflicts with the employer's business interests. Dating a coworker is certainly a lawful activity. The unresolved legal issue under these statutes is whether this activity conflicts with an employer's business interests. If you live in a state with a broad privacy statute of this sort and you decide to ban coworker dating, be prepared to articulate a good business reason if an employee challenges your policy.

Other Off-Duty Activities

As a private employer, you have wide latitude to discipline or fire at-will employees for their off-duty activities. You do need to be careful, however, that your actions don't violate anti-discrimination laws—or appear to do so. And, as noted above, some states have laws that forbid you from regulating the lawful off-duty activities of your employees. But these lawful activity laws generally contain broad exceptions that let you discipline or fire a worker for lawful activities that conflict with your business interests.

Consider what happened when Delta Air Lines fired Mike, a baggage handler, for writing a letter to the *Denver Post* criticizing Delta's cost-cutting program. Mike sued Delta, claiming his job was protected by Colorado's off-duty conduct statute. The judge said Mike's right to off-the-job privacy had to be balanced against Delta's business needs. The judge went on to say that the Colorado statute didn't allow employees to strike indiscriminate public blows against the business reputation of their employer. Mike's case was thrown out. (*Marsh v. Delta Air Lines, Inc.*, 952 F.Supp. 1458 (1997).)

The legal activities law in New York specifies four types of off-duty activities that an employer can't act on:

- political activities, such as fundraising or running for office
- legal use of consumable products—which seems intended to cover cigarettes, alcohol, and prescription drugs
- legal recreational activities, or
- union activities.

The New York law does, however, permit an employer to restrict moonlighting and activities that create a conflict of interest. And an employee isn't protected if an off-duty activity—such as drinking alcohol—leads to poor performance on the job. An employer can still fire someone who comes to work intoxicated.

As you can see, even in the handful of states that have lawful activity laws, you have a great deal of discretion in deciding whether to fire or discipline someone for off-duty conduct. And, in the other states, you have virtually a free hand. For example:

- A Kentucky court said it was okay for an employer to fire a worker for attending law school at night.
- A Pennsylvania court said an employer could lawfully fire an employee for looking for work elsewhere.
- A Florida court said a doctor was free to fire an employee who took her daughter to another doctor.

But even though you can use your power as an employer to regulate what an employee does on his or her own time, think long and hard before you do so. If you attempt to restrict employees away from work, you run the risk of employee resentment. This often translates into a reduced work effort.

Although the odds are slim that you'll ever get into legal trouble for firing a worker for off-duty conduct, it's better to be cautious. The following guidelines should protect you from potential liability—and protect you somewhat from worker resentment:

- Let employees know in advance what kinds of off-duty conduct will get them into trouble.

- Apply your rules in an even-handed way to all employees.
- Don't apply your off-duty rules in a way that violates—or appears to violate—the antidiscrimination laws. For example, don't fire someone for conduct that may look like it has a religious, racial, or gender component.
- Don't use off-duty rules as a subterfuge for engaging in illegal discrimination.
- If possible, warn an employee before you resort to discipline or firing for off-duty conduct.

RESOURCE

Want more information on employee privacy? For in-depth research on this subject, consult *Privacy in Employment Law*, by Matthew Finkin (Bureau of National Affairs), and check the website of the Privacy Rights Clearinghouse at www.privacyrights.org. You can also find a lot of free information on privacy in the workplace on Nolo's website at www.nolo.com.

Prohibitions Against Smoking

As explained in Chapter 7, you can—and are sometimes required to—prohibit smoking in the workplace or to otherwise protect nonsmokers from secondhand smoke. Off-duty smoking is another matter. More than half the states have laws that prohibit you from requiring an employee to abstain from smoking away from work. In the states that don't have such laws, you're free to prohibit off-premises smoking. But is it a good idea? Generally not. Trying to impose a smoking ban outside the workplace would be hard to police and would alienate employees who are smokers. True, smokers do increase health care costs and have a higher rate of absenteeism. But you might be better off using a carrot rather than a stick to deal with the problem. As suggested in Chapter 7, you might offer to pay the cost of a smoking cessation program for any employee who succeeds in giving up the habit.

Independent Contractors

Many businesses hire independent contractors rather than employees to perform at least some work. Typically—but not always—independent contractors have special skills that you need to call upon only sporadically. Common examples are a lawyer or accountant, a painter who spruces up your office, or a computer consultant who installs specialized software at your store and teaches your employees how to use it.

There are often advantages to such an arrangement, but there can be a downside, too. If you misclassify a worker as an independent contractor rather than as an employee, you face potentially serious legal problems, particularly when it comes to taxes. The IRS prefers to have a worker classified as an employee rather than as an independent contractor if there's any doubt about the worker's status.

RESOURCE

Get detailed help with contract issues. *Working With Independent Contractors,* by Stephen Fishman (Nolo), provides clear and comprehensive guidance that will help you avoid a collision with the IRS or other government agency over how you classify a worker.

Comparing Employees and Independent Contractors

Sometimes, your company has needs that can be filled equally well by an employee or an independent contractor.

In choosing which route to take, there are several factors worth considering.

Tax Obligations

Employee. You must make the employer's contribution for the worker's Social Security and Medicare taxes. You're also responsible for withholding federal and state income taxes and the worker's share of Social Security and Medicare taxes, and for keeping records and reporting on these items to the federal and state governments. Each year, you must send the employee a Form W-2 showing how much the employee earned and how much you withheld.

Independent contractor. When you hire an independent contractor, you're not required to withhold taxes from the amount you pay the worker, and you don't have to pay any portion of the worker's Social Security and Medicare taxes. Your only tax responsibility is to complete a Form 1099-MISC at the end of the year if you paid the independent contractor $600 or more during the year. You must send copies of this form to both the IRS and the contractor.

Workers' Compensation

Employee. You must carry workers' compensation insurance for an employee. The workers' compensation system provides replacement income and pays medical expenses to employees who are injured or become ill as a result of their jobs.

Independent contractor. Generally, an employer does not pay for workers' compensation for an independent contractor.

Penalties Lurk If You Misclassify a Worker

If you weigh both possibilities and conclude it's in your company's best interests to hire and classify a worker as an independent contractor rather than an employee, fine. But make sure the worker really qualifies for this status under government rules. If you classify a worker as an independent contractor when the worker should have been treated as an employee, you can be required to pay:

- the employer's and employee's share of Social Security and Medicare contributions
- income tax that should have been withheld from the employee's wages, and
- federal unemployment tax.

You may also be liable for the employee's state income taxes that should have been withheld, as well as unemployment compensation taxes. And, if the worker is injured on the job, you may have to pay workers' compensation benefits because you didn't cover the worker under your company's workers' compensation policy.

Unemployment Compensation

Employee. You must contribute to an unemployment insurance fund in your state and pay a federal unemployment tax. An employee who is laid off or fired for a reason other than serious misconduct is entitled to unemployment benefits from the state fund.

Independent contractor. Generally, an employer does not make contributions to a state unemployment fund or pay the federal unemployment tax for an independent contractor.

Job Benefits

Employee. An employer usually provides job benefits for an employee, such as paid vacations, sick leave and holidays, health insurance, and a retirement plan.

Independent contractor. Independent contractors are paid only for time spent working—and are responsible for paying for their own health insurance and retirement savings plan.

Workspace

Employee. An employer provides workspace and equipment for an employee. The employer pays for rent, maintenance, property insurance, and utilities, as well as for tools, computers, furniture, and vehicles, depending on the type of business.

Independent contractor. An independent contractor usually—but not always—pays for workspace and equipment.

Firing the Worker

Employee. If you become unhappy with an employee's work and you don't see improvement, you will likely have to fire the worker—often a traumatic and legally hazardous course of action.

Independent contractor. The emotional and legal bonds with an independent contractor are typically looser. An independent contractor is usually hired for a set assignment to be completed by a fixed deadline. If the independent contractor isn't satisfactory, you can simply turn to another independent contractor for future work. And, if the independent contractor will be doing a series of projects over a long period, a written contract allowing you or the worker to cancel on two weeks' notice can simplify termination.

Cost

Employee. The hourly rate you pay an employee may be relatively low—but the true cost also includes the money you pay for taxes, insurance, job benefits, workspace, and equipment.

Independent contractor. The hourly rate of an independent contractor may be relatively high, because the worker must earn enough to cover business expenses and taxes.

Governmental Regulations

Employee. An employer is subject to a wide range of governmental regulations intended to protect employees—there are, for example, laws dealing with wages and hours (see Chapter 3), employee benefits (see Chapter 4), family and medical leave (see Chapter 6), workplace health and safety (see Chapter 7), and illegal discrimination (see Chapters 8 and 9).

Independent contractor. A company's relationship with an independent contractor— if the worker has been properly classified as such—is subject to fewer legal restrictions. For example, you needn't pay an independent contractor time-and-a-half for overtime hours, and you're not responsible for monitoring health and safety conditions at an independent contractor's own home, shop, or office.

Liability for Worker's Actions

Employee. An employer generally is legally liable for injuries or property damage caused by an employee's negligence. If, for example, an employee carelessly injures a customer while at work or damages someone's property, the employer can be held responsible.

Independent contractor. If you hire an independent contractor, your company generally won't be liable for the negligence of that person. Be aware, however, that in some situations your company may be liable for the actions of an independent contractor— especially if the worker was acting as your agent.

Liability for Injury to Worker

Employee. An employer is responsible for medical treatment if an employee is hurt on the job and for paying money to partially cover the employee's lost wages. This is generally handled through workers' compensation insurance. These payments are required whether or not your company was at fault for the employee's injuries.

Independent contractor. An independent contractor who is injured because of some dangerous situation at your business premises can recover medical bills and lost income from your business, as well as money for pain and suffering. But first, the independent contractor must show that you were negligent. You're not liable for injuries the independent contractor receives elsewhere while working for you unless you had control over those premises.

TIP

Consider leasing workers. If you need extra workers for peak periods, a leasing service may be the answer. Leasing services hire workers as their employees, taking care of all the normal employer responsibilities: payroll, taxes, and insurance. You pay the leasing service to provide qualified workers to you for short-term assignments. Obviously, the leasing service must make a profit, so the cost to you is higher than if you hired the workers directly. The advantage to you is the convenience—and the fact that you're not going to be hassled by government agencies for possibly misclassifying a worker.

Worker's Preferences

Employee. A worker may prefer to be an employee because that status promises a steady, predictable salary, paid vacations, medical care, and other job benefits at the employer's expense, along with freedom from worry about the paperwork and record keeping required of people who are in business for themselves. What's more, an employee usually doesn't have to invest in tools and equipment.

Independent contractor. A worker may prefer to be an independent contractor to have greater control over working hours and conditions and to maintain the freedom to work for several businesses. Some like the fact that there's no withholding of taxes; they feel that they have a better cash flow, even though they're ultimately responsible for paying their taxes. Workers may also see benefits in being treated as independent contractors because they're able to deduct their business expenses from their gross incomes, including money spent on cars, home offices, and even some travel and entertainment.

Employer's Preferences

Employee. An employer may prefer to hire a worker as an employee because the business has that worker's undivided loyalty and the employer can better control the worker's hours and methods of doing the job.

Independent contractor. An employer may prefer to hire a worker as an independent contractor because it allows more flexibility to adjust to fluctuating needs. For example, if an employer anticipates a two-month crunch on a project, farming out the extra work to an independent contractor may involve less workplace disruption than hiring an employee, providing workspace, and then laying off the employee once the project is complete.

The IRS Rules

To determine whether someone is an employee or an independent contractor, the IRS looks at the degree of control you have over the worker. If you control—or can control—not only what is to be done but also how it's done, the worker is an employee.

CAUTION

Other tests may apply. The IRS tests for independent contractor status are emphasized here because the IRS is the agency with which you're most likely to have a problem. Be aware, however, that in dealing with other agencies and laws, slightly different tests may be used. For example, a different test is used to determine if a person is an independent contractor under the Fair Labor Standards Act. And other tests may apply under state laws dealing with workers' compensation insurance and unemployment compensation.

The IRS doesn't care what label you apply to a worker. You can designate someone as a partner, coventurer, agent, or independent contractor. But, if the person legally qualifies as an employee, the IRS insists that you withhold income taxes and the employee's share of Social Security and Medicare contributions—and pay the employer's share of those contributions.

In deciding whether a person is an employee or an independent contractor, the IRS used to rely on a list of 20 factors cobbled together from various court decisions. The IRS, however, didn't spell out what weight it accorded to any one factor, which led to inconsistent rulings and considerable confusion.

Because a worker's status often remained unclear after applying the traditional test, it was easy for the IRS to classify the worker as an employee—an IRS preference grounded in the assumption that the government stands to collect more tax revenue if a worker is classified as an employee rather than as an independent contractor.

Although the IRS hasn't formally repealed the 20-factor test, it decidedly moved away from that test in 1996, when it published the worker classification training materials it now uses for indoctrinating IRS examiners. For employers trying to figure out where they stand on independent contractor issues, the training materials are a vast improvement over the old 20-factor test. The training materials provide welcome guidance on the weight given to various factors.

RESOURCE

Get help from the IRS. For more information on the IRS rule for classifying workers, see IRS Publication 15-A, *Employer's Supplemental Tax Guide.*

To determine whether a worker should be classified as an employee rather than as an independent contractor, IRS examiners are instructed to look primarily at three categories:

- **Behavioral control.** Do you have the right to direct or control how the worker performs specific tasks?
- **Financial control.** Do you have the right to direct or control how the business aspects of the worker's activities are conducted?
- **The relationship.** How do you and the worker perceive your relationship?

The following sections discuss these categories in more detail.

Behavioral Control

The type of instruction or training you give a worker helps show the extent to which you retain the right to control the worker's method of getting the job done. IRS examiners may check on other types of behavioral control as well.

Instruction

The IRS recognizes that you'll probably impose some form of direction on all workers— whether they're independent contractors or employees. For example, you might require that the job be performed within a specified time period. The big question is how far you go in telling the worker how the job should be done, rather than just indicating the end result. Giving a worker autonomy in making decisions is evidence that you're not controlling the worker's behavior.

EXAMPLE: Star Brite Manufacturing Company hires Lou Ann as a management consultant for its sales department. She is to ensure that the department is fully staffed and that sales brochures are stocked and available. She is also to review all sales contracts. Star Brite requires Lou Ann to get prior approval before she hires or fires anyone in the sales department, purchases additional sales materials, or accepts any sales contract.

The IRS views the requirement of prior approval as evidence that Star Brite controls Lou Ann's behavior in the performance of her services. If Star Brite were not to require these prior approvals but were to leave matters to Lou Ann's discretion, this would be evidence of her autonomy in doing the work and therefore consistent with independent contractor status.

The IRS distinguishes between telling a worker what is to be done and how it is to be done. A worker can be an independent contractor even though you indicate what the job entails.

EXAMPLE: Jim is an independent truck driver. Young Industries, Inc., calls him to make a delivery run from the Gulf Coast to the Texas Panhandle. Jim accepts the job and agrees to pick up the cargo the next morning. Upon arriving at the warehouse, Jim is given an address to which to deliver the cargo and is advised that the delivery must be completed within two days. The IRS treats this as a direction of what is be done—not how it is to be done—and therefore consistent with independent contractor status. Jim is still free to choose his route, plan his driving time, and perhaps perform other work along the way.

On the other hand, if you give too much instruction on how the work is to be done, you may have to classify the worker as an employee.

EXAMPLE: Tess, a truck driver, does local deliveries for Zancor. She reports to Zancor's warehouse each morning. The warehouse manager tells Tess what deliveries have to be made, how to load the cargo in the truck, what route to take, and the order in which the cargo is to be delivered. This is instruction on how the work is to be performed—consistent with employee status in the eyes of the IRS.

Training

If you provide periodic or ongoing training to a worker, it's usually strong evidence of an employer-employee relationship. That's not true, however, of training that merely informs a worker about your policies, a new product line, or applicable governmental regulations. Similarly, the IRS won't imply an employer-employee relationship from programs a worker attends voluntarily and without compensation.

Suggestions

Mere suggestions to a worker don't constitute control over the worker's behavior. So, suggesting that a worker avoid Main Street because of traffic congestion is consistent with the worker's status as an independent contractor.

Business Identification

In the past, requiring workers to identify themselves with your business was evidence of employment status. For example, if you required workers to wear a uniform bearing your company's name or to paint your logo on their truck, that would have been an indication that the workers were employees.

Today, the IRS recognizes that safety concerns play into these types or rules: People often want reassurance about who's coming to their homes or workplaces. If there's a valid security reason for requiring a uniform or logo, the requirement is now a neutral factor in analyzing whether an employment relationship exists.

Financial Control

The IRS looks at whether your business has the right to direct or control the economic aspects of the worker's activities.

Significant Investment

Although it's not necessary for a worker to buy or rent costly equipment to be considered an independent contractor, evidence of such an investment does help establish independent contractor status. There are no precise dollar guidelines on what constitutes a significant investment.

There can be a significant investment even if you're selling or leasing the equipment to the worker—but the worker must pay the full market value or full rental value. Otherwise, the evidence may be insufficient to establish a significant investment.

> **EXAMPLE:** Cal operates a backhoe for Yorba Distributing Company. He leases the backhoe from Yorba at less than its fair rental value and can turn it in at any time without liability for further payments. Yorba pays for liability insurance and regular maintenance on the backhoe. Although Cal is paying something to rent the backhoe, the facts here don't establish that he's made a significant investment.

Business Expenses

The extent to which a worker chooses to incur expenses and be responsible for them can affect the worker's potential to make a profit or sustain a loss. A worker's unreimbursed business expenses can be evidence that the worker has the right to control the financial side of business operations—helping to show independent contractor status.

But there are limits to this principle. If the unreimbursed expenses are minor, this isn't evidence of an independent contractor relationship. The same is true of heavier expenses that are customarily borne by an employee in a particular line of business, such as an auto mechanic's tools.

Advertising and Visibility

An independent contractor is generally free to seek out other business opportunities. The fact that a worker advertises or maintains a visible business location to attract new clients is evidence that the worker is an independent contractor. On the other hand, neither advertising nor having a visible business location is a requirement for independent contractor status. A worker with special skills who gets jobs through word of mouth can qualify as an independent contractor.

In addition, the IRS recognizes that a person who has negotiated a long-term contract may find advertising unnecessary and may even be unavailable to work for others for the duration of the contract—and that will not affect the person's status as an independent contractor. Other independent contractors may find that a visible business location doesn't produce enough business to justify the expense.

In short, the IRS treats the absence of advertising or a visible business location as well as the temporary inability to work for others as neutral factors.

> **EXAMPLE 1:** Unicorn Ventures engages Cindy to mow the lawn weekly and trim the hedges yearly at Unicorn's headquarters. Cindy advertises in the yellow pages that she does landscaping. The advertising indicates that Cindy is

available to perform services to the relevant market. This is evidence that she is an independent contractor.

EXAMPLE 2: Cindy negotiates a long-term contract with Unicorn to maintain all of Unicorn's business locations. Cindy decides to drop her yellow pages advertising, although she continues to be available to other businesses. The lack of advertising doesn't automatically change her independent contractor status.

Method of Payment

A worker who's paid hourly, weekly, or by another unit of time is guaranteed a return for labor. This is generally evidence of an employer-employee relationship, even when a commission is also paid. However, in some fields, such as law, it's typical to pay independent contractors on an hourly basis, so the hourly payment can be a neutral factor.

Paying a worker a flat fee for a particular project is generally evidence of an independent contractor relationship, especially if the worker incurs expenses in performing the job. When you pay the worker—daily, weekly, or monthly—isn't relevant.

A person who's paid solely on a commission basis can be either an independent contractor or an employee. The worker's status may depend on the ability to realize a profit or incur a loss in performing services.

Profit or Loss

A worker's ability to earn a profit or incur a loss is probably the strongest evidence that the worker controls the business aspects of the work. The four economic factors discussed above all relate to the worker's potential for profit or loss. A key question is whether the worker can make decisions that affect the worker's bottom line. These might, for example, be decisions involving ordering inventory, investing money, or purchasing or leasing equipment.

A worker's ability to decide whether to work longer hours to earn more money or to work fewer hours and take less money is a neutral factor.

The Relationship

The IRS considers how you and the worker view your relationship. Your perceptions and those of the worker may suggest what the two of you intend regarding the all-important issue of control.

Written Contract

If you have a written contract with a worker, the IRS will focus on its substance—not on labels. Calling the worker an independent contractor isn't enough. The more important clauses are those dealing with the method of compensation, payment of expenses, and, most crucial, the rights and obligations of you and the worker regarding how work is to be performed.

Form W-2

Filing a Form W-2 usually indicates that the worker is an employee—but the IRS may find independent contractor status anyway, depending on the economic realities of the relationship.

Incorporation

If a worker has formed a corporation and you hire the corporation to do the work, the IRS will almost always treat the worker as an employee of the worker's own corporation—not as an employee of your business.

Employee Benefits

Providing a worker with benefits traditionally associated with employee status can be evidence that the worker is an employee. If you give the worker paid vacation days, paid sick days, health insurance, life or disability insurance, or a pension, that's some evidence of employee status. The evidence of employee status is strongest if you provide benefits under a tax-qualified retirement plan, a 403(b) annuity, or a cafeteria plan.

If you exclude a worker from a benefit plan because you don't consider the worker to be an employee, that's relevant but not conclusive evidence that the worker is an independent contractor.

Discharge or Termination

The IRS may look at the conditions under which you or the worker can terminate the working relationship. It's clear, however, that the IRS regards this as a complicated legal question and doesn't usually treat it as a decisive factor in deciding whether a worker has been properly classified.

Sidestep IRS Problems by Contracting With Corporations

If you want to hire someone as an independent contractor but you're not convinced that the worker will pass IRS muster as an independent contractor, the easiest solution is to require the worker to form a corporation.

One-person corporations are simple to create. After the worker incorporates, your business signs a contract with the corporation in which the worker's corporation agrees to provide the needed services. You pay the corporation as specified in the contract. The worker receives a paycheck—and possibly bonuses as well—from the worker's corporation, which is the employer.

The IRS will recognize this arrangement except in cases of clear abuse—and independent contractor status will no longer be an issue.

Permanency

If you and the worker arranged for work to be done with the expectation that the relationship would continue indefinitely rather than for a specific project or period, that's generally evidence that the two of you intended to create an employment relationship. However, this requires more than simply setting up a long-term relationship, which is consistent with either employee or independent contractor status. The IRS recognizes that your relationship with an independent contractor may be long term because that's what your work agreement requires or because you renew the agreement regularly due to superior service, competitive prices, or lack of competition.

For these reasons, if a relationship is long-term but the worker has a clearly defined role (for example, cleaning your windows regularly or providing specialized computer training as needed), the IRS disregards this as a factor in looking at the worker's status. The IRS also treats the temporary nature of a relationship as a neutral factor.

Regular Business Activity

The IRS may look at whether the services performed by a worker are a key aspect of your company's regular business. This can be a bit subtle.

The mere fact that a service is desirable, necessary, or even essential to your business doesn't mean that the service provider is an employee. If you have an appliance store, for example, you need workers to install electricity and plumbing in your building. This work can be done equally well by employees or independent contractors. The IRS examiner focuses on the fact that the work of the electricians and plumbers isn't part of your regular business.

By contrast, the work of an attorney or legal assistant is part of the regular business of a law firm. It's likely that a law firm will direct or control the work of a lawyer or legal assistant it hires, since the firm's name will go on documents the worker produces. In this situation, the IRS will probe for further facts showing the firm's right to direct and control the worker.

Facts of Less Importance

In addition to the three primary categories of evidence listed above, the IRS looks at other facts—but gives them less weight.

Part-Time or Full-Time Work

Whether a worker performs services on a full-time or part-time basis is a neutral fact. The same is true whether a worker performs services for one business or several.

Place of Work

Whether work is performed on your premises or somewhere you select often has no bearing on worker status. Usually it's only relevant as part of the IRS inquiry into your right to control how the work is to be done.

In many cases, services can only be performed at one location. To repair a leaky pipe, for example, a plumber must go to the site where the pipe is located. Similarly, a camera operator must shoot a commercial where the director and actors are located. These requirements aren't evidence of the right to direct and control how the work is to be performed.

Seeking a Safe Harbor

Despite the strict IRS rules, a business that wrongly classifies a worker as an independent contractor may escape the usual harsh consequences in some circumstances.

In theory, at least, you're protected by the safe harbor language of the tax law if you had a reasonable basis for classifying a worker as an independent contractor—for example:

- You relied on court rulings, IRS rulings, or advice given to you by the IRS.
- You were audited by the IRS and weren't assessed employment taxes for workers holding jobs similar to the one held by the misclassified worker.
- You followed a long-standing and recognized practice of your industry.

But theory is one thing and the real world experience of challenging the IRS is another. If you seek the protection of the safe harbor provisions, the IRS won't give up without a fight. Be prepared for a pitched legal battle.

Be aware, too, that in 2010, Congress began considering the Fair Playing Field Act. If adopted, the Act would eliminate this safe harbor. The Act would also require the Secretary of the Treasury to issue new rules clarifying who can and cannot be classified as an independent contractor for employment tax purposes.

Sometimes, work can be performed at many different locations. Off-site work can be consistent with either independent contractor or employee status. If a worker has an office or business location, this can be evidence of an independent contractor relationship—but the IRS gets into this as part of its examination of the worker's investment, unreimbursed expenses, or opportunity for profit or loss.

Hours of Work

The IRS generally considers hours of work when it looks at the extent of the instructions you give the worker. As with work location, some work, by its nature, must be performed at a specific time; the photographer must shoot the commercial at the time scheduled for the director and actors to be present.

Flexible work hours are not given much importance by the IRS, as they can be consistent with either employee or independent contractor status.

Workers Automatically Classified as Employees

In most situations, the status of a worker is determined by the factors already explained. Certain workers, however, fall into special categories, and the usual IRS criteria don't apply to them. For example, the federal tax law says that certain workers are automatically employees—in legal lingo, statutory employees—including the following:

Delivery drivers. Drivers who deliver meat, vegetables, fruit, bakery products, or beverages other than milk, or who pick up and deliver laundry or dry cleaning. These drivers are employees if they're legally agents of a company and are paid on a commission. (An agent is someone who's authorized to act on another's behalf.)

EXAMPLE: Rachel, a bread truck driver, sells on commission to a customer route for Barry's Bakery and no other bakeries; under the federal law, she's a statutory employee of the bakery. But Allen, a restaurant supply distributor who buys bread from Barry's Bakery at wholesale prices and resells it at a profit, is neither an agent nor a statutory employee of Barry's Bakery.

Insurance agents. Insurance sales agents whose main job is selling life insurance, annuity contracts, or both, primarily for one life insurance company.

Home workers. People who work at home according to a company's specifications on materials or goods that are supplied by a company and must be returned to that company or to someone the company designates.

Business-to-business salespeople. People whose main job is to sell for a company and turn in orders to that company from wholesalers, retailers, contractors, hotels, restaurants, or other business establishments. The goods sold must be merchandise for resale or supplies for use in the buyer's business, rather than goods bought for home consumption.

Federal tax law also provides that licensed real estate agents and door-to-door salespeople are generally treated as nonemployees or exempt employees, but they may be treated as employees for the purpose of liability and workers' compensation.

State Laws

The IRS list of factors for differentiating between employees and independent contractors is similar to the standards followed in most states for state taxes and unemployment compensation, but there can be some differences. For example, in deciding whether a worker is an employee for purposes of workers' compensation coverage or unemployment compensation benefits, a state may use a simple economic reality test.

If you plan to hire independent contractors, check first with the labor department in your state to see what rules are in effect. (See the appendix for contact details.)

The Risks of Misclassification

There are at least four ways that the IRS can learn about your hiring and classification practices. First, the IRS may look into the affairs of an independent contractor who hasn't been paying income taxes. Second, disgruntled employees may complain to the IRS if they think independent contractors are getting favored treatment. Third, during tax audits, the IRS routinely checks to see if workers have been misclassified as independent contractors. Fourth, a worker whom you've classified as an independent contractor may file Form 8919, *Uncollected Social Security and Medicare Tax on Wages,* asserting that workers who perform similar services for you under similar control are classified as employees.

The presumption is that the worker is an employee unless proven otherwise. If the IRS questions the status of a worker, it's up to you to prove that the worker is an independent contractor rather than an employee.

If the IRS determines that an employee was misclassified, the cost to your business will be heavy. You'll be responsible for paying the employee's Social Security tax, federal income tax, and federal unemployment insurance for up to three years. In addition, the IRS can add penalties and interest to the tally you must pay.

State government officials are also interested in businesses that misclassify employees as independent contractors. A state employment office may audit your business to see if there's been any misclassification. The audit can be the result of a spot check by the state employment office or a request by an independent contractor for unemployment or workers' compensation benefits. You may wind up owing money to a state unemployment insurance fund.

Hiring Independent Contractors

There are several things you can do to help establish that a worker is properly classified as an independent contractor right from the start of the relationship.

Sign a contract spelling out the worker's responsibilities and how payment is to be determined for each job. (See sample contract, below.) The contract should allow the independent contractor to hire assistants—and should specifically state that the contractor will carry insurance, including workers' compensation. In addition to helping satisfy the federal or state government that a worker is truly an independent contractor, a good written contract will reduce disputes with the independent contractor about the details of the relationship. Your contract should include the following elements:

- Require the independent contractor to supply all or most of the tools, equipment, and material needed to complete the job, and to pay for liability insurance.
- Give the independent contractor the maximum possible freedom to decide how to perform the work.
- Avoid a commitment to reimburse the independent contractor for business expenses; have the independent contractor assume that responsibility.
- Arrange to pay a flat fee for the work rather than an hourly or weekly rate, if that's feasible to do.
- Don't provide employee-type benefits such as paid vacation days, health insurance, or retirement plans.
- Make it clear that the independent contractor is free to offer services to other businesses.

Sample Contract With an Independent Contractor

AGREEMENT

This agreement made on _June 1_ , 20xx, between _Joe Nolo_ , Client, of _555 Parker Street_ and _Lou Moses_ , Contractor, of _41 Willow Lane_ .

1. **Services to Be Performed.** Contractor agrees to perform the following services for Client:

   [Description of services]

2. **Time for Performance.** Contractor agrees to complete the performance of these services on or before _July 1_ , 20xx.

3. **Payment.** In consideration of Contractor's performance of these services, Client agrees to pay Contractor as follows:

   [Description of how payment will be computed]

4. **Invoices.** Contractor will submit invoices for all services performed.

5. **Independent Contractor.** The parties intend Contractor to be an independent contractor in the performance of these services. Contractor shall have the right to control and determine the method and means of performing the above services; Client shall not have the right to control or determine such method or means.

6. **Other Clients.** Contractor retains the right to perform services for other clients.

7. **Assistants.** Contractor, at Contractor's expense, may employ such assistants as Contractor deems appropriate to carry out this agreement. Contractor will be responsible for paying such assistants, as well as any expense attributable to such assistants, including income taxes, unemployment insurance, and Social Security taxes, and will maintain workers' compensation insurance for such employees.

8. **Equipment and Supplies.** Contractor, at Contractor's own expense, will provide all equipment, tools, and supplies necessary to perform the above services and will be responsible for all other expenses required for the performance of those services.

_____

Contractor

_____

Client

Source: _Legal Guide for Starting & Running a Small Business,_ by Fred S. Steingold (Nolo)

- Keep a file containing the independent contractor's business card, stationery samples, ads, and employer identification number. These items can help show that the contractor has an established business.
- Consider asking the independent contractor to incorporate. Then, sign a contract with the corporation instead of the individual.

Also, don't give the independent contractor an employee handbook or a company email address. And don't pay the independent contractor through your normal payroll system, either. These steps help make it clear that the contractor is not an employee, and you're not treating the contractor like one.

 CAUTION

Trade secrets need special protection. In some situations, you may need to disclose trade secrets of your business to an independent contractor. If so, include a clause in the agreement prohibiting the independent contractor from disclosing or making any unauthorized use of the trade secrets.

The IRS Can Be Tough

The IRS has been aggressively cracking down on employers that have misclassified workers as independent contractors. Underlying this crackdown is a belief that tax revenue is slipping through the cracks because independent contractors aren't reporting all of their income.

Also, IRS officials know that potential tax revenue is lost, because even independent contractors who do report their full income can deduct a wide range of business expenses, using deductions that aren't available to employees.

Fighting the IRS can be expensive. Raleigh Air Cargo Express learned that the hard way. For years, the company hired college students and retirees to make occasional freight runs using rented trucks. Because of the sporadic nature of the work, the small North Carolina company paid these workers as independent contractors.

Eventually, Raleigh shifted these workers to employee status—a move that ironically triggered an IRS audit and a demand that Raleigh pay some $47,000 in back taxes, plus interest and penalties. It took Raleigh nearly three years and $27,000 in legal and accounting fees, but the tenacious company eventually got a fair hearing from a sympathetic IRS appeals officer who canceled the IRS claim. And not a moment too soon. Fighting the IRS nearly put Raleigh out of business.

Moral of the story: The fate of your business can hang on something as tenuous as getting the right IRS person to listen to you on the right day.

Unions

Only 7.2% of U.S. workers in the private sector belonged to unions in the year 2009 (about half as many as in 1983)—and most of them worked in larger businesses. Why membership is declining is open to debate. Perhaps unions are less necessary today because of the growing array of laws that protect workers. Perhaps the changing nature of work plays a role.

The effect is clear: If your business isn't unionized now, it's unlikely that it ever will be. Still, workers do have the legal right to form unions and, despite the odds, a union could be formed in your workplace. What's more, even non-union employees have the right to act together to improve working terms and conditions. So you need a basic understanding of workers' rights, as well as your own.

SEE AN EXPERT

This chapter discusses the legal highlights of the relationship between employers and workers who choose to unionize. If your workplace is already unionized or if workers decide to form a union, it's wise to consult a lawyer experienced in labor law. (See "Getting Help From a Lawyer," in Chapter 14, for more on finding and working with a lawyer.)

The National Labor Relations Act

The National Labor Relations Act, or NLRA (29 U.S.C. §§ 151 and following), is the most sweeping law regulating the formation of unions. It establishes the right of most—but not all—workers to organize into unions and, through union representatives, to negotiate an employment contract covering all members of the union.

Private sector employees who are not covered by the NLRA include:

- managers and supervisors
- confidential employees—such as company accountants
- farmworkers
- members of an employer's family
- most domestic workers, and
- workers in certain industries—such as the railroad industry—who are covered by other labor laws.

The National Labor Relations Board (NLRB) administers the law and interprets its provisions. The role of the NLRB in overseeing the unionizing of a workplace is discussed below.

Unionizing a Workplace

Workers who choose to form or join a union usually believe that they'll have more bargaining clout than they would if they dealt with their employer one on one. They feel that the union can get them better pay, benefits, and working conditions than they could obtain individually—and that, through structured grievance procedures, the union can get them a fairer shake in resolving workplace disputes.

And, just as business trade associations may offer attractive services and products to employers, larger unions may provide valuable enticements to workers—for example, low-interest credit cards, home mortgage programs, free or reduced-rate legal services, low-cost prescription plans, and competitive car insurance.

The Bargaining Unit

Employees can form their own union or can choose to affiliate with a national union. Either way, the employees must be part of a proper bargaining unit—a group of employees who perform similar work and logically have similar concerns about issues such as pay rates, work hours, and working conditions.

A workplace may have several bargaining units—each represented by a different union —and some workers in such a workplace may not be represented by any union.

> **EXAMPLE:** Offices Unlimited sells office equipment and supplies. The checkout clerks have formed one bargaining unit and the warehouse workers another. Other workers, such as the sales assistants, are not represented by a union.

If a majority of workers in a bargaining unit authorize a union to represent them, the union becomes the sole representative of all the employees in that unit to bargain over wages, hours, and other working conditions. This is known as collective bargaining.

Voicing Your Opposition

You may have good reasons to refuse to recognize a union. For example, you may object that it includes workers who have managerial duties. Or you may suspect that some signatures indicating a wish to unionize were not truly voluntary but were the result of intimidation.

Employers' most common challenge is to question the union's description of the bargaining unit. One basis for a challenge is that the workers included by the union don't do similar work. You may also be able to exclude from the bargaining unit any employee who has authority to:

- assign work or direct employees
- evaluate work
- grant time off
- schedule work hours
- discipline employees
- hire or fire
- keep time records, or
- adjust grievances.

An employee who can effectively recommend action on any of these tasks can also be excluded.

Authorization Cards

Workers express their wishes to be represented by a union by signing authorization cards. If you receive authorization cards signed by a majority of the workers in a bargaining unit, you can voluntarily recognize the union as the sole representative of the unit—but you don't have to do so. If you don't voluntarily recognize the union, the workers can ask for an election to be conducted by the NLRB.

NLRB Elections

If 30% or more of the workers in a proposed bargaining unit have signed authorization cards, the union can petition the NLRB to hold a secret election to determine whether a majority of the workers support the union. The union's petition will include a description of the group of workers the union would like to have included in the bargaining unit.

Then the NLRB will conduct an election to determine whether the workers in the bargaining unit want to be represented by the union. If a majority of the workers who vote cast their ballots for the union, it's officially certified as the sole bargaining agent for the unit.

TIP

Authorization cards may be enough. Under the proposed Employee Free Choice Act, a union would be granted recognition if a majority of employees sign authorization cards, making the secret ballot unnecessary. If the act is passed, we'll notify you at www.nolo.com.

Negotiating a Contract

After a union is voluntarily recognized as the official representative of the bargaining unit or is certified by the NLRB, the representatives of the union and the employer negotiate a contract—a collective bargaining agreement. A contract typically covers wages, benefits, work breaks, overtime, holidays, vacation and sick time, seniority for promotions, and safety rules. Often, there's a grievance procedure under which workers can bring their complaints to the union, which then takes the problems to the employer. Employees represented by the union pay monthly dues—often through a payroll deduction called a checkoff.

SEE AN EXPERT

Negotiating a labor contract is governed by special rules that don't apply to ordinary business contracts. For that reason, it's wise to consult a labor lawyer who's experienced in labor negotiations. (See "Getting Help From a Lawyer," in Chapter 14, for information about hiring a lawyer.)

Employer Rights and Limitations

If you are an employer facing unionization efforts in your workplace, the law shapes how you may and may not voice any objections.

What Is Permitted

You can try to dissuade employees from forming or joining a union. You can, for example, use letters, posters, brochures, and speeches to tell employees that they currently enjoy many job benefits and that their wages and benefits compare favorably to those of other workers in your industry. Make sure you can document your claims.

You're legally allowed to state that your door is open to hear complaints and that you will attempt to take appropriate action. You can explain that you prefer to settle complaints with employees personally rather than through union agents.

Pointing out potentially negative features of union representation is also permitted. For example, you might emphasize that workers will be paying dues and fees if they unionize and will be subject to union rules and regimentation.

You can explain, too, that those signing authorization cards aren't bound to vote for the union in the secret balloting conducted by the NLRB and that they don't have to stand for undue pressure by the union. Depending on the composition of your workforce, you might mention that the union's emphasis on seniority may put newer workers at a disadvantage.

What Is Not Permitted

Some actions in opposing a union are off limits. Most courts have ruled that under the NLRA you may not:

- ask employees for their thoughts on union matters or how they plan to vote
- attend union meetings or spy on employees
- grant or promise employees promotions, pay raises, desirable work assignments, or other special favors if they oppose unionizing efforts

- close down a worksite or transfer work or reduce benefits to pressure workers not to support unionization
- dismiss, harass, reassign, or otherwise punish or discipline workers—or threaten to—if they support unionization, or
- refuse to bargain collectively with the employees' union representative.

 SEE AN EXPERT

Sometimes the distinctions between what you can and can't do are subtle. Before acting to oppose a union, consult a lawyer who knows the ropes.

Employee Rights and Limitations

Generally, courts have ruled that the NLRA gives workers the right to:

- discuss union membership and distribute union literature during nonwork time in nonwork areas, such as an employee lounge or locker room
- sign a card asking you to recognize the union and bargain with it
- sign petitions and grievances concerning employment terms and conditions
- ask coworkers to sign petitions and grievances, and
- display pro-union sentiments by wearing message-bearing items such as hats, pins, and T-shirts on the job.

However, this does not give workers free reign. In a recent decision by the National

Labor Relations Board, an employer's prohibition on using the company email system to solicit union members was upheld. And of course, workers have no right to threaten or intimidate other workers to gain support for a union.

Union organizers who are not employed by your business have no right to be on your premises. But don't rush to call the police to have outside organizers ejected as trespassers—especially if their activities are not disrupting your business. Such an approach may alienate employees. It's better to emphasize to workers the advantages of staying union-free.

Making Unions Unnecessary

Unions usually gain a foothold because employees are dissatisfied with some aspects of their work life. Contented workers don't generally seek to unionize, as it entails some degree of bureaucracy and workplace politics.

Be sensitive to what's going on in the workplace, and make reasonable changes if required. Encourage employees to come to you with their workplace complaints—and listen carefully to what they're saying. If there's a health or safety problem, fix it. If a workplace procedure is annoying or seems unfair to workers, look into changing it.

Be fair and consistent in enforcing work rules and disciplining employees. They need to know what to expect—and they can become frustrated and angry if you act arbitrarily.

To the extent possible, give employees some control over how they perform their jobs. In almost any job position, it's possible to allow some degree of worker autonomy. Employees who have some freedom to put their imprints on their work tend to be most content on the job. Periodically survey what similar businesses are paying their workers—and make sure that the wages and benefits you provide are competitive. Offer incentives for excellent performance.

Try to keep your workforce steadily employed. Hiring employees for seasonal overloads and laying them off when the work levels off creates feelings of insecurity. Consider hiring temporary workers for seasonal increases in the workflow.

Lawyers and Legal Research

When you own or run a business, you need lots of legal information on employment issues. For example, you may need to learn how an antidiscrimination law is being interpreted by the EEOC or whether an agreement with a departing employee will be enforced by a court. Lawyers, of course, are prime sources of this information. But, if you bought all the needed information at the rates they charge—$200 to $300 or more an hour— you'd quickly empty your bank account. Fortunately, for an intelligent employer, there are a number of other ways to acquire a good working knowledge of the legal principles and procedures necessary to handle employment and other issues.

How frequently you'll need a lawyer's help will depend on the nature of your business, the number of employees you hire, how many locations you have, and the kinds of problems you run into with employees and governmental agencies. Your challenge isn't to avoid lawyers altogether, but to use them cost effectively.

Lawyers aren't the only source for legal help. The U.S. Department of Labor, the Internal Revenue Service, the U.S. Equal Employment Opportunity Commission, the U.S. Department of Justice, and other federal agencies offer publications at little or no cost explaining federal laws and regulations that affect employers. Many are referred to in this book. Similarly, many state agencies have helpful printed materials available. And representatives of federal and state agencies can help explain how the laws they administer are interpreted.

Keep in mind that professionals who charge less than lawyers—for example, accountants and workplace consultants—can also help you within their areas of expertise.

Getting Help From a Lawyer

Ideally, you should find a lawyer who's willing to help you educate yourself. Then you can do the preliminary work on your own, turning to your lawyer from time to time for advice and fine tuning.

In working with a lawyer, remember that you're the boss. A lawyer, of course, has specialized training, knowledge, skill, and experience in dealing with legal matters. But that's no reason for you to abdicate control over legal decision making and how much time and money should be spent on a particular legal problem. You have an intimate knowledge of your business and are in the best position to call the shots—even though a lawyer may be willing or even eager to do it all for you.

You almost surely can't afford all the services a lawyer might offer, so you need to set priorities. When thinking about a legal problem, ask yourself: "Can I do this myself?" "Can I do this myself with some help from a lawyer?" or "Should I simply put this in my lawyer's hands?"

Getting Leads

Of the almost 900,000 lawyers in America today, probably fewer than 50,000 have sufficient training and experience in employment law to be of real help to you. Don't expect to locate a good employment lawyer by simply looking in the phone book or reading an advertisement. There's not enough information in those sources to help you make a valid judgment. Almost as useless are lawyer referral services operated by bar associations. Generally, these services make little attempt to evaluate a lawyer's skill and experience.

A better approach is to talk with people in your community who own or operate excellent businesses. These people are likely to have ferreted out the best lawyers. Ask them who their lawyers are and a little about their experiences. Ask them about other lawyers they've worked with and what led them to make a change. If you talk to half a dozen employers, chances are you'll come away with several leads on good, experienced business lawyers.

Other people who provide services to the business community may also help you identify lawyers you might consider hiring. For example, speak with your banker, accountant, insurance agent, and real estate broker. These people come into frequent contact with lawyers who represent employers and are in a position to make informed judgments. Friends, relatives, and business associates within your own company can also provide names of lawyers. But ask them specifically about lawyers who have had experience working for employers; a good divorce lawyer would likely make a poor employment adviser, for example.

There are several other sources to which you can turn for possible candidates in your search for a lawyer:

- The director of your state or local chamber of commerce may know of several employment lawyers who have the kind of experience that you seek.
- Articles about employment law in trade magazines and newspapers are often written by lawyers. Track down these authors and call them. Most will be flattered to help or provide other referrals.
- The director of your state's continuing legal education (CLE) program—usually run by a bar association, a law school, or both—can identify lawyers who have lectured or written on employment law for other lawyers. Someone who's a "lawyer's lawyer" presumably has the extra depth of knowledge and experience to do a superior job for you—but may charge more, unfortunately.
- The chairperson of a state or county bar committee for business lawyers may be able to point out some well-qualified practitioners in your vicinity.
- Nolo's lawyer directory, at www.nolo.com/lawyers. The Nolo directory offers comprehensive profiles of the lawyers who advertise there, including each attorney's education, background, areas of expertise, fees, and practice philosophy—including

whether the lawyer is willing to review documents or coach clients who are doing their own legal work. Nolo has confirmed that every attorney advertiser has a valid license and is in good standing with the state bar association where the attorney practices.

Once you have the names of several lawyers, a good source for more information about them is the *Martindale-Hubbell Law Directory,* available at most law libraries, at some local public libraries, and on the Internet at www.martindale.com. This resource contains biographical sketches of most practicing lawyers and information about their experience, specialties, education, and the professional organizations to which they belong. Many firms also list their major clients in the directory—an excellent indication of the types of industries and problems with which they've had experience. Be aware, however, that lawyers purchase the space for their biographical sketches, so don't be overly impressed by long entries.

In addition, many lawyers listed in the directory, whether or not the lawyer has purchased space for a biographical sketch, are rated AV, BV, or CV. These ratings come from confidential opinions that Martindale-Hubbell solicits from lawyers and judges.

The first letter is for legal ability, which is rated as follows:

A—Very High to Preeminent
B—High to Very High
C—Fair to High.

The V part of the rating stands for Very High General Recommendation—meaning that the rated lawyer adheres to professional standards of conduct and ethics. But the V part is practically meaningless, because lawyers who don't qualify for it aren't rated at all. Martindale-Hubbell prudently cautions that such absence shouldn't be construed as a reflection on the lawyer, since there could be many reasons for the absence of a rating. Some lawyers, for example, ask that their rating not be published, and others are too new to a community to be known among the local lawyers and judges who are the sources for the information on which the ratings are based.

Don't make the rating system your sole criterion for deciding on a potential lawyer for your business. But you can be reasonably confident that a lawyer who gets high marks from other business clients and an "AV" rating from Martindale-Hubbell will have experience and expertise.

Shopping Around

After you get the names of several good prospects, shop around. Most lawyers will be willing to speak with you for a half hour or so at no charge so that you can size them up and make an informed decision about whether to hire them. Look for experience and for the ability to listen and communicate. These characteristics may be apparent almost immediately but in some cases may take longer to evaluate. So, even after you've hired a lawyer who seems right for you, stay open to the possibility that you may have to make a change later.

Pay particular attention to the rapport between you and your lawyer. No matter how experienced and well recommended a lawyer is, if you feel uncomfortable with that person during your first meeting or two, you may never achieve an ideal lawyer-client relationship. Trust your instincts and seek a lawyer whose personality is compatible with your own.

Your lawyer should be accessible when you need legal services. Unfortunately, the complaint logs of all legal regulatory groups indicate that many lawyers are not. If you consistently face delays of several days before you can talk to your lawyer on the phone or get an appointment, you'll lose precious time, not to mention sleep. And almost nothing is more aggravating to a client than to leave a legal project in a lawyer's hands, then wait weeks or even months while nothing happens.

You want a lawyer who will work hard on your behalf and follow through promptly on all assignments. Unfortunately, it's usually difficult to tell at the outset how attentive the lawyer will be later on. But it can be helpful to ask how the lawyer intends to keep in touch with you. Perhaps you can exact a promise that you'll receive a status report at least monthly.

Paying a Lawyer

When you hire a lawyer, have a clear understanding about how fees will be computed.

And, as new jobs are brought to the lawyer, ask specifically about charges for each. Many lawyers initiate fee discussions, but others forget or are shy about doing so. Bring up the subject yourself. Insist upon a written explanation of how the fees and costs will be paid.

Comparison shopping among lawyers will help you avoid overpaying. But the cheapest hourly rate isn't necessarily the best. A novice who charges only $80 an hour may take three hours to review a consultant's work-for-hire contract. A more experienced lawyer who charges $200 an hour may do the same job in half an hour and make better suggestions. If a lawyer will be delegating some of the work on your case to a less experienced associate, paralegal, or secretary, that work should be billed at a lower hourly rate. Be sure to get this information recorded in your initial written fee agreement.

Types of Fee Arrangements

There are four basic ways lawyers charge fees, usually depending on the type of legal help you require.

Hourly Fees

In most parts of the United States, you can get competent services for your business for $200 to $300 an hour. You will probably have to pay more in large metropolitan areas.

Costs Can Mount Up

In addition to the fees they charge for their time, lawyers often bill for some costs as well—and these costs can add up quickly. When you receive a lawyer's bill, you may be surprised at both the amount of the costs and the variety of the services for which the lawyer expects reimbursement. These can include charges for:

- long distance phone calls
- photocopying
- faxes
- overnight mail
- messenger service
- witness fees
- court filing fees
- process servers
- work by investigators
- work by legal assistants or paralegals
- deposition transcripts
- online legal research, and
- travel.

You'd think that a lawyer would absorb the cost of many of these items as normal office overhead—part of the cost of doing business—but that's not always the case. So, in working out the fee arrangements, discuss the costs you'll be expected to pay. Try to avoid being charged for long distance calls, photocopies, and faxes—and negotiate an overall cap on costs, if possible.

Flat Fees

Sometimes, a lawyer quotes you a flat fee for a specific job. For example, a lawyer may offer to draw up an employment agreement for $300 or to represent you in a labor department dispute for $3,000. You pay the same amount regardless of how much time the lawyer spends.

Contingent Fees

A contingency fee is a percentage (such as 33⅓%) of the amount the lawyer obtains for you in a negotiated settlement or through a trial. If the lawyer recovers nothing for you, there's no fee. However, the lawyer does generally expect reimbursement for out-of-pocket expenses such as filing fees, long distance phone calls, and transcripts of testimony. Contingent fees are common in personal injury cases but relatively unusual in employer's-side employment cases (they are common in plaintiff's-side employment cases), because usually you don't recover anything—a victorious suit means you just don't have to pay the employee. The only time you might expect a contingency fee arrangement is if you are suing an employee for a substantial amount of money—for stealing and using your trade secrets, for example—and the employee has the financial wherewithal to pay up.

Retainer Fees

You may be able to hire a lawyer for a flat annual fee, called a retainer, to handle all of your routine legal business. You'll usually pay in equal monthly installments, and, normally, the lawyer will bill you an additional amount for extraordinary services—such as representing you in a wrongful discharge lawsuit filed by a former employee. Obviously, the key to making this arrangement work is to have a written agreement clearly defining what's routine and what's extraordinary.

Saving on Legal Fees

There are many ways to hold down the cost of legal services.

Be organized. It's important to gather important documents, write a short chronology of events, and concisely explain a problem to your lawyer. Papers can get lost in a lawyer's office, so keep a copy of everything that's important.

Ask the lawyer to be your coach. Make it clear that you're eager to do as much work as possible yourself, with the lawyer coaching you from the sidelines. For example, you can write your own employee handbook, giving your lawyer the relatively inexpensive task of reviewing and polishing the document. In defending a wrongful discharge case, you can assemble needed documents and line up witnesses. But get a clear understanding about who's going to do what. You don't want to do the work and get billed for it because the lawyer duplicated your efforts. And you certainly don't want any crucial elements to fall through cracks because you each thought the other was attending to the work.

Read trade journals in your field. You'll find specific legal developments that your lawyer may have missed. Send pertinent clippings to your lawyer—and encourage your lawyer to do the same for you. This can dramatically reduce legal research time.

Show that you're an important client. The single most important thing you can do to tell your lawyer how much you value the relationship is to pay your bills on time. Beyond that, let your lawyer know about plans for expansion and your company's possible future legal needs. And drop your lawyer a line when you've recommended your lawyer to your business colleagues.

Group your legal matters together. You'll save money if you consult with your lawyer on several matters at one time. For example, in a one-hour conference, you may be able to review with your lawyer the annual updating of your corporate record book, renew your lease, and get final approval of a noncompetition agreement you've drafted for new employees to sign. Of course, you'll want to work with a lawyer who has experience with all your legal matters.

RESOURCE

Get more information on lawyers and lawsuits. For detailed information on finding and working with a lawyer, and an explanation of every step in a lawsuit, from start to finish, see the ebook *The Lawsuit Survival Guide: A Client's Companion to Litigation*, by Joseph Matthews (Nolo), available at www.nolo.com.

A Tax Tip

If you visit your lawyer on a personal legal matter (such as reviewing a contract for the purchase of a house) and you also discuss a business problem (such as a pending OSHA inspection), ask your lawyer to allocate the time spent and send you separate bills. At tax time, you can easily list the business portion as a tax-deductible business expense.

you feel able to talk freely with your lawyer about your degree of participation in any legal matter and your control over how the lawyer carries out a legal assignment. If you can't frankly discuss these sometimes sensitive matters with your lawyer, it's time to hire another one. Otherwise, you'll surely waste money on unnecessary legal fees and risk having legal matters turn out badly. Remember that you're always free to change lawyers and to get all important legal documents back from a lawyer you no longer employ.

Resolving Problems With Your Lawyer

If you see a problem emerging with your lawyer, nip it in the bud. Don't just sit back and fume; call, visit, or write your lawyer. The problem won't get resolved if your lawyer doesn't even know about it. An open exchange is essential for a healthy lawyer-client relationship.

Whatever it is that rankles, have an honest discussion about your feelings. Maybe you're upset because your lawyer hasn't kept you informed about what's going on in your case or has missed a promised deadline. Or maybe last month's bill was shockingly high or lacked any breakdown of how your lawyer's time was spent.

One good test of whether a lawyer-client relationship is a good one is to ask yourself if

Your Rights as a Client

As a client, it's reasonable to expect:
- to be treated courteously by your lawyer and staff members
- to receive an itemized statement of services rendered and a full explanation of billing practices
- to be charged reasonable fees
- to receive a prompt response to phone calls and letters
- to have confidential legal conferences, free from unwarranted interruptions
- to be kept informed of the status of your case
- to have your legal matters handled diligently and competently, and
- to receive clear answers to all questions.

If your lawyer consistently fails to meet these basic expectations, consider taking your business elsewhere.

! **CAUTION**

Out with the old—then, in with the new. Be sure to fire your old lawyer before you hire a new one. Otherwise, you could find yourself being billed by both lawyers at the same time.

If you have a dispute over fees, the local bar association may be able to mediate it for you. And, if a lawyer has violated legal ethics, the bar association can take action to discipline or even disbar the lawyer. Where a major mistake has been made—for example, a lawyer has missed the deadline for filing a case—you may have to sue for malpractice. However, because it's expensive and time-consuming to file a malpractice suit (and requires you to hire another lawyer), you're better off carefully choosing a professional at the outset and working hard to resolve any disputes privately.

Legal Research

Law libraries are chock-full of valuable information—information that you can easily find on your own. All you need is a rudimentary knowledge of how that information is organized. And these days, basic research materials are even available online.

Finding a Law Library

If you want to hold the books in your hands—and want access to secondary materials that aren't available free online—your first step is to find a law library that's open to the public. You may find such a library in your county

courthouse or at your state capitol. Public law schools generally permit the public to use their libraries, and some private law schools grant access to their libraries—sometimes for a modest fee. The reference department of a major public library may have a fairly decent legal research collection. Finally, don't overlook the law library in your own lawyer's office. Most lawyers, on request, will gladly share their books with their clients.

RESOURCE

There are sources that provide good guidance as you plunge into your own legal research:

Legal Research: How to Find & Understand the Law, by Stephen Elias and the editors of Nolo (Nolo). This nontechnical book explains how to use all major legal research tools and helps you frame your research questions.

Nolo's Plain-English Law Dictionary, by the editors of Nolo and Gerald and Kathleen Hill, is a practical guide to legal terms and phrases.

Black's Law Dictionary, edited by Bryan Garner (West Publishing Co.). This dictionary used by lawyers and law students contains more than 43,000 definitions, plus almost 3,000 quotations.

Federal and State Laws

Employment is governed by both federal law and state law. Federal statutes deal with wages and hours, continuation of health insurance coverage when employment ends, withholding employee taxes and Social Security contributions, unpaid family and medical leave, illegal discrimination, and workplace safety. State statutes often touch on many of these same topics, as well as unemployment compensation and workers' compensation. The law of wrongful discharge—except where it involves claims of illegal discrimination—is primarily a matter of state law, most of which comes from judges' decisions rather than from statutes.

Sources of Legal Research

In doing legal research, there are several sources you may find useful, broadly categorized as primary and secondary sources. You use primary sources to find out the current status of the law. They include:

- constitutions (federal and state)
- legislation laws—also called statutes or ordinances—passed by Congress, state legislatures, and local governments
- administrative rules and regulations (issued by the federal and state administrative agencies charged with implementing statutes), and
- case law (decisions of federal and state courts interpreting statutes—and sometimes making law, known as common law, if the subject isn't covered by a statute).

A small or midsized employer rarely gets involved in questions of constitutional law. You're far more likely to be concerned with law created by a federal or state statute or by an administrative rule or regulation. At the federal level, that includes the Internal

Revenue Code and regulations adopted by the Internal Revenue Service; regulations dealing with wages and hours adopted by the U.S. Department of Labor; and antidiscrimination statutes such as Title VII of the Civil Rights Act, administered by the Justice Department and the Equal Employment Opportunity Commission.

At the state level, you'll likely be interested in state statutes dealing with many of the same topics. When employees sue, they often make claims under both state and federal laws, even though those laws cover the same territory. Additionally, you'll want to educate yourself about unemployment compensation and workers' compensation, which are matters of state law only.

You may also need to look into county and city ordinances addressing workplace issues such as tobacco smoke and discrimination.

How to Begin

Obviously, primary sources—statements of the "raw law"—are important. But most legal research begins with secondary sources— books or other resources that comment on, summarize, organize, or describe the law.

It often makes sense to start with one of the two national encyclopedias, *American Jurisprudence 2d* (cited as Am. Jur. 2d) or *Corpus Juris Secundum* (cited as C.J.S.). If your state has its own encyclopedia, check that, too. These encyclopedias organize the case law and some statutes into narrative statements organized alphabetically by subject. Through citation footnotes, you can locate the full text of the cases and statutes on which the entries are based.

It's also helpful if you can find a treatise on the subject you're researching. A treatise is simply a book or series of books that covers a specific area of law. You may want to look at books such as:

- *Labor Law in a Nutshell*, by Douglas L. Leslie
- *Workers' Compensation and Employee Protection Laws in a Nutshell*, by Jack B. Hood, Benjamin A. Hardy, Jr., and Harold S. Lewis, Jr., or
- *Sex Discrimination in a Nutshell*, by Claire Sherman Thomas.

The entire "Nutshell" series is published by West Publishing Company, and covers many other areas of employment law as well.

Nolo publishes a comprehensive guide to employment law, *The Essential Guide to Federal Employment Laws*, by Lisa Guerin and Amy DelPo. This book gives detailed information on the most important federal employment statutes, including whom they cover, what they require and prohibit, record keeping and posting rules, and tips for compliance. It also includes the text of the laws themselves. Nolo has other books relating to specific areas of employment law as well, available at www. nolo.com.

Law reviews (collections of articles on legal topics published by law schools) and other legal periodicals may also contain useful summaries of the law. The *American Bar Association*

Journal as well as the journal published by your state bar association should be available in the law library that you use. In these journals, you'll often find timely articles on legal issues. You can locate law review and bar journal articles through *The Index to Legal Periodicals*. Be forewarned, however, that law school reviews contain articles by law professors and students and are usually of more academic than practical interest.

One good periodical for background information is *The Practical Lawyer*, published by the Joint Committee on Continuing Legal Education of the American Law Institute and American Bar Association (ALI-ABA). Each edition contains half a dozen clear and practical articles—many of which address topics of interest to employers. The checklists and forms are superb. This resource is virtually unknown outside the legal profession. For subscription information, visit www.ali-aba.org/and select "Publications."

Finally, practically every state has an organization that provides continuing legal education to practicing lawyers. Some of these organizations publish excellent books on business law subjects that focus on the law in your state and contain state-specific forms and checklists. You can also find a wealth of relevant information in the course materials prepared for continuing legal education seminars. To locate the organization that provides continuing legal education in your state, call your local or state bar association.

How to Read a Case Citation

There are several places where a case may be reported. If the case was decided by the U.S. Supreme Court, you can find it in either the United States Reports (U.S.) or the Supreme Court Reporter (S.Ct.). If it is a federal case decided by a court other than the U.S. Supreme Court, it will be in either the Federal Reporter, (F, F.2d, or F.3d) or the Federal Supplement (F. Supp.).

Most states publish their own official state reports. All published state court decisions are also included in the West Reporter System. West has divided the country into seven regions—and publishes all the decisions of the supreme and appellate state courts in the region together. These reporters include the following:

A. and A.2d. Atlantic Reporter (First and Second Series), which includes decisions from Connecticut, Delaware, the District of Columbia, Maine, Maryland, New Hampshire, New Jersey, Pennsylvania, Rhode Island, and Vermont.

N.E. and N.E.2d. Northeastern Reporter (First and Second Series), which includes decisions from New York,* Illinois, Indiana, Massachusetts, and Ohio.

N.W. and N.W.2d. Northwestern Reporter (First and Second Series), which includes decisions from Iowa, Michigan, Minnesota, Nebraska, North Dakota, South Dakota, and Wisconsin.

P. and P.2d. Pacific Reporter (First and Second Series), which includes decisions from Alaska, Arizona, California,* Colorado, Hawaii, Idaho, Kansas, Montana, Nevada, New Mexico, Oklahoma, Oregon, Utah, Washington, and Wyoming.

S.E. and S.E.2d. Southeastern Reporter (First and Second Series), which includes decisions from Georgia, North Carolina, South Carolina, Virginia, and West Virginia.

So. and So.2d. Southern Reporter (First and Second Series), which includes decisions from Alabama, Florida, Louisiana, and Mississippi.

S.W. and S.W.2d. Southwestern Reporter (First and Second Series), which includes decisions from Arkansas, Kentucky, Missouri, Tennessee, and Texas.

A case citation gives the names of the parties on each side of a case, the volume of the reporter, the beginning page number, and the year it was decided. For example, the citation *Smith v. Jones Int'l*, 123 N.Y.S.2d 456 (1994), identifies Smith and Jones as the parties having the legal dispute. The case is reported in volume 123 of the New York Supplement, Second Series, beginning on page 456; the court issued the decision in 1994.

---

*All California appellate decisions are published in a separate volume, the California Reporter (Cal. Rptr.), and all decisions from New York appellate courts are published in a separate volume, New York Supplement (N.Y.S.).

How to Read a Case Citation (continued)

Remember, when researching how courts have dealt with particular issues, look to the case law most relevant to that subject. So if you're researching discrimination claims in Delaware, look at both federal case law— how federal courts have interpreted federal discrimination statutes—and state case law— how Delaware state courts have interpreted Delaware discrimination statutes. For more information, see *Legal Research: How to Find & Understand the Law,* by Stephen Elias (Nolo).

Online Research

The logical starting point for online research is Nolo's own website, www.nolo.com, where you'll discover valuable information, including material on employment law and links to statutes and cases. In addition, Nolo's *Legal Research: How to Find & Understand the Law,* by Stephen Elias and the editors of Nolo, contains an entire chapter on online research.

Virtually all of the federal agencies that enforce employment laws and regulations have websites that contain an enormous amount of information about the rights and responsibilities of employers and employees in the workplace. These websites also contain information about resources that can help you both understand the law and abide by it. These websites can be very valuable tools for you:

- U.S. Department of Labor at www.dol.gov
- U.S. Equal Employment Opportunity Commission at www.eeoc.gov
- U.S. Department of Justice at www.justice.gov, and
- Internal Revenue Service at www.irs.gov.

State agencies that enforce state employment and labor laws often have websites as well. Contact your state department of labor for details. (See the appendix for contact information.)

Lawyers who do computer research rely primarily on two systems: Westlaw and Lexis. A small but growing number of public law libraries offer these services. Those that do offer them usually require a sizable advance or a credit card; you pay as you go. Ask a law librarian for details, but be prepared for sticker shock. You can end up paying as much as $300 an hour.

It's more practical to use other online sources that cost you nothing more than the usual charge for online access time.

For an introduction to the vast amount of information that's out there, sample these sites:

- Lawyers Weekly at www.lawyersusaonline.com. Here you'll find up-to-date news on a wide range of legal topics.
- The Thomas Legislative Information site at http://thomas.loc.gov. Named for Thomas Jefferson, this site contains a

wealth of information on bills pending in Congress and laws recently adopted.

- Lectric Law Library at www.lectlaw. com. This is a good place to explore a wide range of business law issues. Many employment law topics are covered in reasonable depth.

- The Commerce Clearinghouse Business Owner's Toolkit at www.toolkit.cch. com. This handy site includes a wealth of information, news, and tools for employers, including sample policies and forms and extensive human resource materials.

Tips for Researching Employment Law

When looking up statutes, use the annotated versions. They typically come in multivolume sets and contain the text of the laws, references to court and administrative decisions interpreting the statutes, and citations to treatises and articles that discuss the law.

Statutes are frequently amended, but these large volumes aren't published quite as often. Instead, the publisher sends updating supplements that are inserted in the back of the books to make sure you have the most recent updates.

Most federal statutes and many state statutes are interpreted in regulations that have the force of law. For example, the U.S. Department of Labor has enacted many regulations concerning the Fair Labor Standards Act. Where regulations exist, they're an essential part of your research.

Using the Shepard citation system, you can look up a case that interests you and find a list of every other case that refers to it. This can expand your research—and also let you know if the law has changed recently. *Legal Research: How to Find & Understand the Law,* by Stephen Elias (Nolo), has a good, easy-to-follow explanation of how to use the Shepard's system.

Appendix

Labor Departments and Agencies

U.S. Department of Labor

Francis Perkins Building
200 Constitution Avenue, N.W.
Washington, DC 20210
866-487-2365
www.dol.gov

You can find a list of regional offices of the Wage and Hour Division at the Department of Labor's website at www.dol.gov/whd/america2.htm.

State Labor Departments

You can find a comprehensive list of state labor resources, including state labor departments, at the website of the U.S. Department of Labor at www.dol.gov/whd/state/state.htm.

State Drug and Alcohol Testing Laws

Note: The states of California, Colorado, Delaware, Kansas, Kentucky, Massachusetts, Michigan, Missouri, Nevada, New Hampshire, New Jersey, New Mexico, New York, Pennsylvania, South Dakota, Texas, Washington, West Virginia, Wisconsin, Wyoming, and the District of Columbia are not included in this chart because they do not have specific drug and alcohol testing laws governing private employers. Additional laws may apply. Check with your state department of labor for more information.

Alabama

Ala. Code §§ 25-5-330 to 25-5-340

Employers affected: Employers who establish a drug-free workplace program to qualify for a workers' compensation rate discount.

Testing applicants: Must test upon conditional offer of employment. Must test all new hires. Job ads must include notice that drug and alcohol testing required.

Testing employees: Random testing permitted. Must test after an accident that results in lost work time. Must also test upon reasonable suspicion; reasons for suspicion must be documented and made available to employee upon request.

Employee rights: Employees have 5 days to contest or explain a positive test result. Employer must have an employee assistance program or maintain a resource file of outside programs.

Notice and policy requirements: All employees must have written notice of drug policy. Must give 60 days' advance notice before implementing testing program. Policy must state consequences of refusing to take test or testing positive.

Drug-free workplace program: Yes.

Alaska

Alaska Stat. §§ 23.10.600 to 23.10.699

Employers affected: Employers with one or more full-time employees.

Testing employees: Employer may test:
- for any job-related purpose
- to maintain productivity or safety
- as part of an accident investigation, or
- upon reasonable suspicion.

Employee rights: Employer must provide written test results within 5 working days. Employee has 10 working days to request opportunity to explain positive test results; employer must grant request within 72 hours or before taking any adverse employment action.

Notice and policy requirements: Before implementing a testing program employer must distribute a written drug policy to all employees and must give 30 days' advance notice. Policy must state consequences of a positive test or refusal to submit to testing.

Arizona

Ariz. Rev. Stat. §§ 23-493 to 23-493.11

Employers affected: Employers with one or more full-time employees.

Testing applicants: Employer must inform prospective hires that they will undergo drug testing as a condition of employment.

Testing employees: Employees are subject to random and scheduled tests:
- for any job-related purpose
- to maintain productivity or safety
- as part of an accident investigation, or
- upon reasonable suspicion.

Employee rights: Policy must inform employees of their right to explain positive results.

Notice and policy requirements: Before conducting tests employer must give employees a copy of the written policy. Policy must state

State Drug and Alcohol Testing Laws (continued)

the consequences of a positive test or refusal to submit to testing.

Drug-free workplace program: Yes.

Arkansas

Ark. Code Ann. §§ 11-14-105 to 11-14-112

Employers affected: Employers who establish a drug-free workplace program to qualify for a workers' compensation rate discount.

Testing applicants: Must test for drug use upon conditional offer of employment, may test for alcohol but not required. Job ads must include notice that testing required.

Testing employees: Employer must test any employee:

- upon reasonable suspicion
- as part of a routine fitness-for-duty medical exam
- after an accident that results in injury, or
- as follow-up to a required rehabilitation program.

Employee rights: Employer may not refuse to hire applicant or take adverse personnel action against an employee on the basis of a single positive test that has not been verified by a confirmation test and a medical review officer. An applicant or employee has 5 days after receiving test results to contest or explain them.

Notice and policy requirements: Employer must give all employees a written statement of drug policy and must give 60 days' advance notice before implementing program.

Drug-free workplace program: Yes.

Connecticut

Conn. Gen. Stat. Ann. §§ 31-51t to 31-51bb

Employers affected: All employers.

Testing applicants: Employer must inform job applicants in writing that drug testing is required as a condition of employment.

Testing employees: Employer may test:

- when there is reasonable suspicion that employee is under the influence of drugs or alcohol and job performance is or could be impaired
- when authorized by federal law
- when employee's position is dangerous or safety-sensitive, or
- as part of a voluntary employee assistance program.

Employee rights: Employer may not take any adverse personnel action on the basis of a single positive test that has not been verified by a confirmation test.

Florida

Fla. Stat. Ann. §§ 440.101 to 440.102

Employers affected: Employers who establish a drug-free workplace program to qualify for a workers' compensation rate discount.

Testing applicants: Must inform job applicants that drug and alcohol testing is required as a condition of employment.

Testing employees: Must test any employee:

- upon reasonable suspicion
- as part of a routine fitness-for-duty medical exam, or
- as part of a required rehabilitation program.

Employee rights: Employees who voluntarily seek treatment for substance abuse cannot be fired, disciplined, or discriminated against, unless they have tested positive or have been in treatment in the past. All employees have the right to explain positive results within 5 days. Employer may not take any adverse personnel action on the basis of an initial positive result that has not been verified

State Drug and Alcohol Testing Laws (continued)

by a confirmation test and a medical review officer.

Notice and policy requirements: Prior to implementing testing, employer must give 60 days' advance notice and must give employees written copy of drug policy. Policy must state consequences of a positive test result or refusal to submit to testing.

Drug-free workplace program: Yes.

Georgia

Ga. Code Ann. §§ 34-9-410 to 34-9-421

Employers affected: Employers who establish a drug-free workplace program to qualify for a workers' compensation rate discount.

Testing applicants: Applicants are required to submit to a substance abuse test after they have been offered employment.

Testing employees: Must test any employee:
- upon reasonable suspicion
- as part of a routine fitness-for-duty medical exam after an accident that results in an injury, or
- as part of a required rehabilitation program.

Employee rights: Employees have 5 days to explain or contest a positive result. Employer must have an employee assistance program or maintain a resource file of outside programs.

Notice and policy requirements: Employer must give applicants and employees notice of testing and must give 60 days' notice before implementing program. All employees must receive a written policy statement; policy must state the consequences of refusing to submit to a drug test or of testing positive.

Drug-free workplace program: Yes.

Hawaii

Haw. Rev. Stat. §§ 329B-1 to 329B-5

Employers affected: All.

Testing applicants: Same conditions as current employees.

Testing employees: Employer may test employees only if these conditions are met:
- employer pays all costs including confirming test
- tests are performed by a licensed laboratory
- employee receives a list of the substances being tested for
- there is a form for disclosing medicines and legal drugs, and
- the results are kept confidential.

Idaho

Idaho Code §§ 72-1701 to 72-1714

Employers affected: Employers who establish a drug-free workplace program to qualify for a workers' program to qualify for a workers' compensation rate discount.

Testing applicants: Employer may test as a condition of hiring.

Testing employees: May test as a condition of continued employment.

An employer who follows drug-free workplace guidelines may fire employees who refuse to submit to testing or who test positive for drugs or alcohol. Employees will be fired for misconduct and denied unemployment benefits.

Employee rights: An employee or applicant who receives notice of a positive test may request a retest within 7 working days. Employer may not take any adverse employment action on the basis of an initial positive result that has not been verified by a confirmation test. If the retest results are negative, the employer must pay for the cost; if they are positive, the employee must pay.

Notice and policy requirements: Employer must have a written policy that includes a statement

State Drug and Alcohol Testing Laws (continued)

that violation of the policy may result in termination due to misconduct, as well as what types of testing employees may be subject to.

Drug-free workplace program: Yes (compliance is optional).

Illinois

775 Ill. Comp. Stat. § 5/2-104(C)(3)

Employers affected: Employers with 15 or more employees.

Testing employees: Statute does not "encourage, prohibit, or authorize" drug testing, but employers may test employees who have been in rehabilitation.

Drug-free workplace: Yes (compliance is optional).

Indiana

Ind. Code Ann. §§ 22-9-5-6(b), 22-9-5-24

Employers affected: Employers with 15 or more employees.

Testing employees: Statute does not "encourage, prohibit, or authorize" drug testing, but employers may test employees who have been in rehabilitation.

Drug-free workplace: Yes (compliance is optional).

Iowa

Iowa Code § 730.5

Employers affected: Employers with one or more full-time employees.

Testing applicants: Employer may test as a condition of hiring.

Testing employees: Statute does not encourage, discourage, restrict, limit, prohibit, or require testing. Employer may test employees: during unannounced testing of employees selected from those at an entire worksite; upon reasonable

suspicion; during and after rehabilitation; or following an accident that caused a reportable injury or more than $1,000 property damage.

Employee rights: Employee has 7 days to request a retest. Employers with 50 or more employees must provide rehabilitation for any employee testing positive for alcohol use who has worked for at least one year and has not previously violated the substance abuse policy. Employer must have an employee assistance program or maintain a resource file of outside programs.

Drug-free workplace program: Yes (compliance is optional).

Louisiana

La. Rev. Stat. Ann. §§ 49:1001 to 49:1012

Employers affected: Employers with one or more full-time employees. (Does not apply to oil drilling, exploration, or production.)

Testing applicants: Employer may require all applicants to submit to drug and alcohol test. Employer does not have to confirm a positive result of a preemployment drug screen but must offer the applicant the opportunity to pay for a confirmation test and a review by a medical review officer.

Employee rights: Employees with confirmed positive results have 7 working days to request access to all records relating to the drug test. Employer may allow employee to undergo rehabilitation without termination of employment.

Maine

Me. Rev. Stat. Ann. tit. 26, §§ 681 to 690

Employers affected: Employers with one or more full-time employees. (Law does not require or encourage employers to conduct substance abuse testing.)

State Drug and Alcohol Testing Laws (continued)

Testing applicants: Employer may require applicant to take a drug test only if offered employment or placed on an eligibility list.

Testing employees: Employer may test based upon probable cause but may not base belief on a single accident; must document the facts and give employee a copy. May test when:

- there could be an unreasonable threat to the health and safety of coworkers or the public, or
- an employee returns to work following a positive test.

Employee rights: Employee who tests positive has 3 days to explain or contest results. Employee must be given an opportunity to participate in a rehabilitation program for up to 6 months; an employer with more than 20 full-time employees must pay for half of any out-of-pocket costs. After successfully completing the program, employee is entitled to return to previous job with full pay and benefits.

Notice and policy requirements: All employers must have a written policy approved by the state department of labor. Policy must be distributed to each employee at least 30 days before it takes effect. Any changes to policy require 60 days' advance notice. An employer with more than 20 full-time employees must have an employee assistance program certified by the state office of substance abuse before implementing a testing program.

Maryland

Md. Code Ann., [Health-Gen.] § 17-214

Employers affected: Law applies to all employers.

Testing applicants: May use preliminary screening to test applicant. If initial result is positive, may make job offer conditional on confirmation of test results.

Testing employees: Employer may require substance abuse testing for legitimate business purposes only.

Employee rights: The sample must be tested by a certified laboratory; at the time of testing employee may request laboratory's name and address. An employee who tests positive must be given:

- a copy of the test results
- a copy of the employer's written drug and alcohol policy
- a written notice of any adverse action employer intends to take, and
- a statement of employee's right to an independent confirmation test at own expense.

Minnesota

Minn. Stat. Ann. §§ 181.950 to 181.957

Employers affected: Employers with one or more full-time employees. (Employers are not required to test.)

Testing applicants: Employers may require applicants to submit to a drug or alcohol test only after they have been given a job offer and have seen a written notice of testing policy. May only test if required of all applicants for same position.

Testing employees: Employers are not required to test. Employers may require drug or alcohol testing only according to a written testing policy. Testing may be done if there is a reasonable suspicion that employee:

- is under the influence of drugs or alcohol
- has violated drug and alcohol policy
- has been involved in an accident, or
- has sustained or caused another employee to sustain a personal injury.

Random tests permitted only for employees in safety-sensitive positions. With 2 weeks'

State Drug and Alcohol Testing Laws (continued)

notice, employers may also test as part of an annual routine physical exam. Employer may test, without notice, an employee referred by the employer for chemical dependency treatment or evaluation or participating in a chemical dependency treatment program under an employee benefit plan. Testing is allowed during and for 2 years following treatment.

Employee rights: If test is positive, employee has 3 days to explain the results; employee must notify employer within 5 days of intention to obtain a retest. Employer may not discharge employee for a first-time positive test without offering counseling or rehabilitation; employee who refuses or does not complete program successfully may be discharged.

Notice and policy requirements: Employees must be given a written notice of testing policy which includes consequences of refusing to take test or having a positive test result. Two weeks' notice required before testing as part of an annual routine physical exam.

Mississippi

Miss. Code Ann. §§ 71-7-1 to 71-7-33, 71-3-205 to 71-3-225

Employers affected: Employers with one or more full-time employees. Employers who establish a drug-free workplace program to qualify for a workers' compensation rate discount must implement testing procedures.

Testing applicants: May test all applicants as part of employment application process. Employer may request a signed statement that applicant has read and understands the drug and alcohol testing policy or notice. (Must test applicants if drug-free workplace.)

Testing employees: May require drug and alcohol testing of all employees:

- upon reasonable suspicion
- as part of a routinely scheduled fitness for duty medical examination
- as a follow-up to a rehabilitation program, or
- if they have tested positive within the previous 12 months.

Employee rights: Employer must inform an employee in writing within 5 working days of receipt of a positive confirmed test result; employee may request and receive a copy of the test result report. Employee has 10 working days after receiving notice to explain the positive test results. Employer may not discharge or take any adverse personnel action on the basis of an initial positive test result that has not been verified by a confirmation test. Private employer who elects to establish a drug-free workplace program must have an employee assistance program or maintain a resource file of outside programs.

Notice and policy requirements: 30 days before implementing testing program employer must give employees written notice of drug and alcohol policy which includes consequences:

- of a positive confirmed result
- of refusing to take test, and
- of other violations of the policy.

Drug-free workplace program: Yes.

Montana

Mont. Code Ann. §§ 39-2-205 to 39-2-211

Employers affected: Employers with one or more employees.

Testing applicants: May test as a condition of hire.

Testing employees: Employees may be tested:

- upon reasonable suspicion
- after involvement in an accident that causes personal injury or more than $1,500 property damage

State Drug and Alcohol Testing Laws (continued)

- as a follow-up to a previous positive test, or
- as a follow-up to treatment or a rehabilitation program.

Employer may conduct random tests as long as there is an established date, all personnel are subject to testing, the employer has signed statements from each employee confirming receipt of a written description of the random selection process, and the random selection process is conducted by a scientifically valid method.

Employer may require an employee who tests positive to undergo treatment as a condition of continued employment.

Employee rights: After a positive result, employee may request additional confirmation by an independent laboratory; if the results are negative, employer must pay the test costs.

Notice and policy requirements: Written policy must be available for review 60 days before testing. Policy must state consequences of a positive test result.

Nebraska

Neb. Rev. Stat. §§ 48-1901 to 48-1910

Employers affected: Employers with 6 or more full-time and part-time employees.

Testing employees: Employer may require employees to submit to drug or alcohol testing and may discipline or discharge any employee who refuses.

Employee rights: Employer may not take adverse action on the basis of an initial positive result unless it is confirmed according to state and federal guidelines.

North Carolina

N.C. Gen. Stat. §§ 95-230 to 95-235

Employers affected: Law applies to all employers.

Testing applicants: May test as a condition of hire. Applicant has right to retest a confirmed positive sample at own expense. If first screening test produces a positive result, applicant may waive a second examination that is intended to confirm the results.

Testing employees: Employers are not required to test. Employer must preserve samples for at least 90 days after confirmed test results are released.

Employee rights: Employee has right to retest a confirmed positive sample at own expense.

North Dakota

N.D. Cent. Code §§ 34-01-15, 65-01-11

Employers affected: Any employer who requires a medical exam as a condition of hire or continued employment may include a drug or alcohol test.

Testing employees: May test following an accident or injury that will result in a workers' compensation claim, if employer has a mandatory policy of testing under these circumstances, or if employer or physician has reasonable grounds to suspect injury was caused by impairment due to alcohol or drug use.

Ohio

Ohio Admin. Code §§ 4123-17-58, 4123-17-58.1

Employers affected: Employers who establish a drug-free workplace program to qualify for a workers' compensation rate discount.

Testing applicants: Must test all applicants and new hires within 90 days of employment.

Testing employees: Must test employees:
- upon reasonable suspicion
- following a return to work after a positive test
- after an accident which results in an injury

State Drug and Alcohol Testing Laws (continued)

requiring offsite medical attention or property damage over limit specified in drug and alcohol policy, and
- at random to meet requirements for greater discounts.

Employee rights: Employer must have an employee assistance plan. Employer must offer health care coverage which includes chemical dependency counseling and treatment. Not required for employers with fewer than 25 employees.

Notice and policy requirements: Policy must state consequences for refusing to submit to testing or for violating guidelines. Policy must include a commitment to rehabilitation.

Drug-free workplace program: Yes.

Oklahoma
Okla. Stat. Ann. tit. 40, §§ 551 to 565

Employers affected: Employers with one or more employees. (Drug or alcohol testing not required or encouraged.)

Testing employees: Before requiring testing, employer must provide an employee assistance program. Random testing is allowed. May test employees:
- upon reasonable suspicion
- after an accident resulting in injury or property damage over $500
- on a random selection basis
- as part of a routine fitness-for-duty examination, or
- as follow-up to a rehabilitation program.

Employee rights: Employee has right to retest a positive result at own expense; if the confirmation test is negative, employer must reimburse costs.

Notice and policy requirements: Before requiring testing employer must:

- adopt a written policy
- give a copy to each employee and to any applicant offered a job, and
- allow 30 days' notice.

Policy must state consequences of a positive test result or refusing to submit to testing.

Oregon
Or. Rev. Stat. §§ 659.840, 659A.300, 438.435

Employers affected: Law applies to all employers.

Testing applicants: Unless there is reasonable suspicion that an applicant is under the influence of alcohol, no employer may require a breathalyzer test as a condition of employment. Employer is not prohibited from conducting a test if applicant consents.

Testing employees: Unless there is reasonable suspicion that an employee is under the influence of alcohol, no employer may require a breathalyzer or blood alcohol test as a condition of continuing employment. Employer is not prohibited from conducting a test if employee consents.

Employee rights: No action may be taken based on the results of an on-site drug test without a confirming test performed according to state health division regulations. Upon written request, test results will be reported to the employee.

Rhode Island
R.I. Gen. Laws §§ 28-6.5-1 to 28-6.5-2

Employers affected: Law applies to all employers.

Testing applicants: May test as a condition of hire.

Testing employees: May require employee to submit to a drug test only if there are reasonable grounds, based on specific observations, to believe employee is using controlled substances that are impairing job performance.

State Drug and Alcohol Testing Laws (continued)

Employee rights: Employee who tests positive may have the sample retested at employer's expense and must be given opportunity to explain or refute results. Employee may not be terminated on the basis of a positive result but must be referred to a licensed substance abuse professional. After referral, employer may require additional testing and may terminate employee if test results are positive.

South Carolina

S.C. Code Ann. §§ 41-1-15, 38-73-500

Employers affected: Employers who establish a drug-free workplace program to qualify for a workers' compensation rate discount.

Testing employees: Must conduct random testing among all employees. Must conduct a follow-up test within 30 minutes of the first test.

Employee rights: Employee must receive positive test results in writing within 24 hours.

Notice and policy requirements: Employer must notify all employees of the drug-free workplace program at the time it is established or at the time of hiring, whichever is earlier. Program must include a policy statement that balances respect for individuals with the need to maintain a safe, drug-free environment.

Drug-free workplace program: Yes.

Tennessee

Tenn. Code Ann. §§ 50-9-101 to 50-9-114

Employers affected: Employers who establish a drug-free workplace program to qualify for a workers' compensation rate discount.

Testing applicants: Must test applicants upon conditional offer of employment. Job ads must include notice that drug and alcohol testing is required.

Testing employees: Employer must test upon reasonable suspicion; must document behavior on which the suspicion is based within 24 hours or before test results are released, whichever is earlier; and must give a copy to the employee upon request. Employer must test employees:
- who are in safety-sensitive positions
- as part of a routine fitness-for-duty medical exam
- after an accident that results in injury, or
- as a follow-up to a required rehabilitation program.

Employee rights: Employee has the right to explain or contest a positive result within 5 days. Employee may not be fired, disciplined, or discriminated against for voluntarily seeking treatment unless employee has previously tested positive or been in a rehabilitation program.

Notice and policy requirements: Before implementing testing program, employer must provide 60 days' notice and must give all employees a written drug and alcohol policy statement. Policy must state consequences of a positive test or refusing to submit to testing.

Drug-free workplace program: Yes.

Utah

Utah Code Ann. §§ 34-38-1 to 34-38-15

Employers affected: Employers with one or more employees.

Testing applicants: Employer may test any applicant for drugs or alcohol as long as management also submits to periodic testing.

Testing employees: Employer may test employee for drugs or alcohol as long as management also submits to periodic testing. Employer may require testing to:
- investigate possible individual employee impairment

State Drug and Alcohol Testing Laws (continued)

- investigate an accident or theft
- maintain employee or public safety, or
- ensure productivity, quality, or security.

Employee rights: Employer may suspend, discipline, discharge, or require treatment on the basis of a confirmed positive test result.

Notice and policy requirements: Testing must be conducted according to a written policy that has been distributed to employees and is available for review by prospective employees.

Vermont

Vt. Stat. Ann. tit. 21, §§ 511 to 520

Employers affected: Employers with one or more employees.

Testing applicants: Employer may not test applicants for drugs or alcohol unless there is a job offer conditional on a negative test result and applicant is given written notice of the testing procedure and a list of the drugs to be tested for.

Testing employees: Random testing not permitted unless required by federal law. Employer may not require testing unless:

- there is probable cause to believe an employee is using or is under the influence
- employer has an employee assistance program which provides rehabilitation, and

- employee who tests positive and agrees to enter employee assistance program is not terminated.

Employee rights: Employer must contract with a medical review officer who will review all test results and keep them confidential. Medical review officer is to contact employee or applicant to explain a positive test result. Employee or applicant has right to an independent retest at own expense. Employee who successfully completes employee assistance program may not be terminated, although employee may be suspended for up to 3 months to complete program. Employee who tests positive after completing treatment may be fired.

Notice and policy requirements: Must provide written policy that states consequences of a positive test.

Virginia

Va. Code Ann. § 65.2-813.2

Employers affected: Employers who establish drug-free workplace programs to qualify for workers' compensation insurance discount.

Drug-free workplace program: State law gives insurers the authority to establish guidelines and criteria for testing.

State Laws on Employee Arrest and Conviction Records

The following chart summarizes state laws and regulations on whether an employer can get access to an employee's or prospective employee's past arrests or convictions. It includes citations to statutes and agency websites, as available.

Many states allow or require private sector employers to run background checks on workers, particularly in fields like child care, elder care, home health care, private schools, private security, and the investment industry. Criminal background checks usually consist of sending the applicant's name (and sometimes fingerprints) to the state police or to the FBI. State law may forbid hiring people with certain kinds of prior convictions, depending on the kind of job or license involved.

Federal law allows the states to establish procedures for requesting a nationwide background check to find out if a person has been "convicted of a crime that bears upon the [person's] fitness to have responsibility for the safety and well-being of children, the elderly, or individuals with disabilities." (42 U.S.C.A. § 5119a(a)(1).)

If your state isn't listed in this chart, then it doesn't have a *general statute* on whether private sector employers can find out about arrests or convictions. There might be a law about your particular industry, though.

It's always a good idea to consult your state's nondiscrimination enforcement agency or labor department to see what kinds of questions you can ask. The agency guidelines are designed to help employers comply with state and federal law. For further information, contact your state's agency.

Alaska

Alaska Stat. 12.62.160, 12.62.180

Agency guidelines for preemployment inquiries: Alaska Department of Labor and Workforce Development, Alaska Employer Handbook, "Preemployment Questioning," at www.labor. state.ak.us/employer/aeh.pdf.

Arizona

Ariz. Rev. Stat. § 13-904(E)

Rights of employees and applicants: Unless the offense has a reasonable relationship to the occupation, an occupational license may not be denied solely on the basis of a felony or misdemeanor conviction.

California

Cal. Lab. Code § 432.7

Rules for employers:
- **Arrest records.** May not ask about an arrest that did not lead to conviction; may not ask about pretrial or posttrial diversion program. May ask about arrest if prospective employee is awaiting trial.
- **Convictions.** May ask about conviction even if no sentence is imposed.

Agency guidelines for preemployment inquiries: Department of Fair Employment and Housing, "Preemployment Inquiry Guidelines," DFEH-161 at www.dfeh.ca.gov/DFEH/Publications/ PublicationDocs/DFEH-161.pdf.

Colorado

Colo. Rev. Stat. §§ 24-72-308(b)(II)(f)(I), 8-3-108(m)

Rules for employers: May not inquire about arrest for civil or military disobedience unless it resulted in conviction.

Rights of employees and applicants: May not be required to disclose any information in a sealed record; may answer questions about arrests or convictions as though they had not occurred.

Agency guidelines for preemployment inquiries: Colorado Civil Rights Division, "Employment

State Laws on Employee Arrest and Conviction Records (continued)

Discrimination," at www.dora.state.co.us/civil-rights/publications_and_services.htm.

Connecticut

Conn. Gen. Stat. Ann. §§ 46a-79, 46a-80, 31-51i

Rules for employers: State policy encourages hiring qualified applicants with criminal records. If an employment application form contains any question concerning criminal history, it must include a notice in clear and conspicuous language that (1) the applicant is not required to disclose the existence of any arrest, criminal charge, or conviction, the records of which have been erased; (2) define what criminal records are subject to erasure; and (3) any person whose criminal records have been erased will be treated as if never arrested and may swear so under oath. Employer may not disclose information about a job applicant s criminal history except to members of the personnel department or, if there is no personnel department, person(s) in charge of hiring or conducting the interview.

Rights of employees and applicants: May not be asked to disclose information about a criminal record that has been erased; may answer any question as though arrest or conviction never took place. May not be discriminated against in hiring or continued employment on the basis of an erased criminal record. If conviction of a crime has been used as a basis to reject an applicant, the rejection must be in writing and specifically state the evidence presented and the reason for rejection.

Special situations: Each consumer reporting agency that issues a consumer report that is used or is expected to be used for employment purposes and that includes in such report criminal matters of public record concerning the consumer shall provide the consumer who is the subject of the consumer report (1) notice that the consumer reporting agency is reporting criminal matters of public record, and (2) the name and address of the person to whom such consumer report is being issued.

Delaware

Del. Code Ann. tit. 11, § 4376

Rights of employees and applicants: Do not have to disclose an arrest or conviction record that has been expunged.

Florida

Fla. Stat. Ann. § 112.011

Rights of employees and applicants: May not be disqualified to practice or pursue any occupation or profession that requires a license, permit, or certificate because of a prior conviction, unless it was for a felony or first-degree misdemeanor and is directly related to the specific line of work.

Georgia

Ga. Code Ann. §§ 35-3-34, 42-8-62, 42-8-63

Rules for employers: In order to obtain a criminal record from the state Crime Information Center, employer must supply the individual's fingerprints or signed consent. If an adverse employment decision is made on the basis of the record, must disclose all information in the record to the employee or applicant and tell how it affected the decision.

Rights of employees and applicants: Probation for a first offense is not a conviction; may not be disqualified for employment once probation is completed.

Hawaii

Haw. Rev. Stat. §§ 378-2, 378-2.5, 831-3.2

Rules for employers:
- **Arrest records.** It is a violation of law for any employer to refuse to hire, to discharge, or to

State Laws on Employee Arrest and Conviction Records (continued)

discriminate in terms of compensation, conditions, or privileges of employment because of a person's arrest or court record.

- **Convictions.** May inquire into a conviction only after making a conditional offer of employment, provided it has a rational relation to job. May not examine any convictions over 10 years old.

Rights of employees and applicants: If an arrest or conviction has been expunged, may state that no record exists and may respond to questions as a person with no record would respond.

Agency guidelines for preemployment inquiries: Hawaii Civil Rights Commission, "What is Employment Discrimination?" at www.hawaii. gov/labor/hcrc/pdf/HCRCemploymdiscrim.pdf.

Idaho

Agency guidelines for preemployment inquiries: Idaho Human Rights Commission, "Pre-Employment Inquiries Guide," in "Conducting a Lawful Employment Interview," at http://labor. idaho.gov/lawintvw3.htm.

Illinois

775 Ill. Comp. Stat. § 5/2-103

Rules for employers: It is a civil rights violation to ask about an arrest or criminal history record that has been expunged or sealed, or to use the fact of an arrest or criminal history record as a basis for refusing to hire or to renew employment. Law does not prohibit employer from using other means to find out if person actually engaged in conduct for which they were arrested.

Kansas

Kan. Stat. Ann. §§ 22-4710

Rules for employers: Cannot require an employee to inspect or challenge a criminal

record in order to obtain a copy of the record, but may require an applicant to sign a release to allow employer to obtain record to determine fitness for employment. Employers can require access to criminal records for specific businesses.

Agency guidelines for preemployment inquiries: Kansas Human Rights Commission, "Guidelines on Equal Employment Practices: Preventing Discrimination in Hiring," at www. khrc.net/hiring.html.

Louisiana

La. Rev. Stat. Ann. § 37:2950

Rights of employees and applicants: Prior conviction cannot be used as a sole basis to deny employment or an occupational or professional license, unless conviction is for a felony and directly relates to the job or license being sought.

Special situations: Protection does not apply to medical, engineering and architecture, or funeral and embalming licenses, among others listed in the statute.

Maine

Me. Rev. Stat. Ann. tit. 5, § 5301

Rights of employees and applicants: A conviction is not an automatic bar to obtaining an occupational or professional license. Only convictions that directly relate to the profession or occupation, that include dishonesty or false statements, that are subject to imprisonment for more than 1 year, or that involve sexual misconduct on the part of a licensee may be considered.

Agency guidelines for preemployment inquiries: The Maine Human Rights Commission, "Pre-Employment Inquiry Guide," at www.maine.gov/ mhrc/guidance/pre-employment_inquiry_guide. html, suggests that asking about arrests is an

State Laws on Employee Arrest and Conviction Records (continued)

improper race-based question, but that it is okay to ask about a conviction if related to the job.

Maryland

Md. Code Ann. [Crim. Proc.], § 10-109; Md. Regs. Code 09.01.10.02

Rules for employers: May not inquire about any criminal charges that have been expunged. May not use a refusal to disclose information as sole basis for not hiring an applicant.

Rights of employees and applicants: Need not refer to or give any information about an expunged charge. A professional or occupational license may not be refused or revoked simply because of a conviction; agency must consider the nature of the crime and its relation to the occupation or profession; the conviction's relevance to the applicant's fitness and qualifications; when conviction occurred and other convictions, if any; and the applicant's behavior before and after conviction.

Agency guidelines for preemployment inquiries: DLLR's Office of Fair Practices, "Guidelines for Pre-Employment Inquiries Technical Assistance Guide," at www.dllr.maryland.gov/oeope/preemp. shtml.

Massachusetts

Mass. Gen. Laws ch. 151B, § 4; ch. 276, § 100A; Mass. Regs. Code tit. 804, § 3.02

Rules for employers: If job application has a question about prior arrests or convictions, it must include a formulated statement (that appears in the statute) that states that an applicant with a sealed record is entitled to answer, "No record."

- **Arrest records.** May not ask about arrests that did not result in conviction.
- **Convictions.** May not ask about first-time convictions for drunkenness, simple assault,

speeding, minor traffic violations, or disturbing the peace; may not ask about misdemeanor convictions 5 or more years old.

Rights of employees and applicants: If criminal record is sealed, may answer, "No record" to any inquiry about past arrests or convictions.

Agency guidelines for preemployment inquiries: Massachusetts Commission Against Discrimination, "Discrimination on the Basis of Criminal Record," at www.mass.gov/mcad/crimrec.html.

Michigan

Mich. Comp. Laws § 37.2205a

Rules for employers: May not request information on any arrests or misdemeanor charges that did not result in conviction.

Rights of employees and applicants: Employees or applicants are not making a false statement if they fail to disclose information they have a civil right to withhold.

Agency guidelines for preemployment inquiries: Michigan Civil Rights Commission, "Preemployment Inquiry Guide," at www. michigan.gov/documents/pre-employment_inquery_guide_13019_7.pdf.

Minnesota

Minn. Stat. Ann. §§ 364.01 to 364.03

Rules for employers: State policy encourages the rehabilitation of criminal offenders; employment opportunity is considered essential to rehabilitation.

Rights of employees and applicants: No one can be disqualified from pursuing or practicing an occupation that requires a license, unless the crime directly relates to the occupation. Agency may consider the nature and seriousness of the

State Laws on Employee Arrest and Conviction Records (continued)

crime and its relation to the applicant's fitness for the occupation. Even if the crime does relate to the occupation, a person who provides evidence of rehabilitation and present fitness cannot be disqualified.

Agency guidelines for preemployment inquiries: Minnesota Department of Human Rights, "Hiring, Job Interviews, and the Minnesota Human Rights Act," at www.humanrights.state. mn.us/employers/hiring.html.

Nebraska

Neb. Rev. Stat. § 29-3523

Rules for employers: After one year from date of arrest, may not obtain access to information regarding arrests if no charges are completed or pending.

Nevada

Nev. Rev. Stat. Ann. §§ 179.301, 179A.100(3)

Rules for employers: May obtain a prospective employee's criminal history record only if it includes convictions or a pending charge, including parole or probation.

Special situations: State Gaming Board may inquire into sealed records to see if conviction relates to gaming.

Agency guidelines for preemployment inquiries: Nevada Equal Rights Commission, "Guide to Pre-Employment," at http://detr.state. nv.us/Nerc_pages/premployment_guide.htm.

New Hampshire

N.H. Rev. Stat. Ann. § 651:5(X)(c)

Rules for employers: May ask about a previous criminal record only if question substantially follows this wording, "Have you ever been arrested for or convicted of a crime that has not been annulled by a court?"

New Jersey

N.J. Stat. Ann. §§ 5:5-34.1, 5:12-89 to 5:12-91, 32:23-86; N.J. Admin. Code tit. 13, §§ 59-1.2, 59-1.6

Rules for employers: May obtain information about convictions and pending arrests or charges to determine the subject's qualifications for employment. Employers must certify that they will provide sufficient time for applicant to challenge, correct, or complete record, and will not presume guilt for any pending charges or court actions.

Rights of employees and applicants: Applicant who is disqualified for employment based on criminal record must be given adequate notice and reasonable time to confirm or deny accuracy of information.

Special situations: There are specific rules for casino employees, longshoremen and related occupations, horse racing, and other gaming industry jobs.

New Mexico

Criminal Offender Employment Act, N.M. Stat. Ann. § 28-2-3

Special situations: For a license, permit, or other authority to engage in any regulated trade, business, or profession, a regulating agency may consider convictions for felonies and for misdemeanors involving moral turpitude. Such convictions cannot be an automatic bar to authority to practice in the regulated field, though.

New York

N.Y. Correct. Law §§ 750 to 754; N.Y. Exec. Law § 296(16)

Rules for employers:
- **Arrest records.** It is unlawful discrimination to ask about any arrests or charges that

State Laws on Employee Arrest and Conviction Records (continued)

did not result in conviction, unless they are currently pending.

- **Convictions.** Employers with 10 or more employees may not deny employment based on a conviction unless it relates directly to the job or would be an "unreasonable" risk to property or to public or individual safety.

Rights of employees and applicants: Upon request, applicant must be given, within 30 days, a written statement of the reasons why employment was denied.

North Dakota

N.D. Cent. Code § 12-60-16.6

Rules for employers: May obtain records of convictions or of criminal charges (adults only) occurring in the past three years, provided the information has not been purged or sealed.

Agency guidelines for preemployment inquiries: North Dakota Department of Labor, "Employment Applications and Interviews," www.nd.gov/labor/publications/docs/employment.pdf.

Ohio

Ohio Rev. Code Ann. §§ 2151.357, 2953.33, 2953.55

Rules for employers: May not inquire into any sealed convictions or sealed bail forfeitures, unless question has a direct and substantial relation to job.

Rights of employees and applicants: May not be asked about arrest records that are sealed; may respond to inquiry as though arrest did not occur.

Oklahoma

Okla. Stat. Ann. tit. 22, § 19(F)

Rules for employers: May not inquire into any criminal record that has been expunged.

Rights of employees and applicants: If record

is expunged, may state that no criminal action ever occurred. May not be denied employment for refusing to disclose sealed criminal record information.

Oregon

Or. Rev. Stat. §§ 181.555–181.557 181.560, 659A.030

Rules for employers: Before requesting information, employer must notify employee or applicant; when submitting request, must tell State Police Department when and how person was notified. May not discriminate against an applicant or current employee on the basis of an expunged juvenile record unless there is a "bona fide occupational qualification."

- **Arrest records.** May request information about arrest records less than 1 year old that have not resulted in acquittal or have not been dismissed.
- **Convictions.** May request information about conviction records.

Rights of employees and applicants: Before State Police Department releases any criminal record information, it must notify employee or applicant and provide a copy of all information that will be sent to employer. Notice must include protections under federal civil rights law and the procedure for challenging information in the record. Record may not be released until 14 days after notice is sent.

Pennsylvania

18 Pa. Cons. Stat. Ann. § 9125

Rules for employers: May consider felony and misdemeanor convictions only if they directly relate to person's suitability for the job.

Rights of employees and applicants: Must be informed in writing if refusal to hire is based on criminal record information.

State Laws on Employee Arrest and Conviction Records (continued)

Agency guidelines for preemployment inquiries: Pennsylvania Human Relations Commission at http://sites.state.pa.us/PA_Exec/ PHRC/publications/literature/Pre-Employ%20 QandA%208x11%20READ.pdf.

Rhode Island

R.I. Gen. Laws §§ 12-1.3-4, 28-5-7(7)

Rules for employers:
- **Arrest records.** It is unlawful to include on an application form or to ask as part of an interview if the applicant has ever been arrested or charged with any crime.
- **Convictions.** May ask if applicant has been convicted of a crime.

Rights of employees and applicants: Do not have to disclose any conviction that has been expunged.

South Dakota

Agency guidelines for preemployment inquiries: South Dakota Division of Human Rights, "Preemployment Inquiry Guide," at www.state.sd.us/dol/boards/hr/preemplo.htm suggests that an employer shouldn't ask or check into arrests or convictions if they are not substantially related to the job.

Utah

Utah Admin. R. 606-2(v).

Rules for employers:
- **Arrest records.** It is not permissible to ask about arrests.
- **Convictions.** Asking about felony convictions is permitted but is not advisable unless related to job.

Agency guidelines for preemployment inquiries: Utah Labor Division Anti-Discrimination Rules, Rule R606-2 "Preemployment Inquiry Guide," at www.rules.utah.gov/publicat/code/r606/r606-002.htm.

Vermont

Vt. Stat. Ann. tit. 20, § 2056c

Rules for employers: Only employers who provide care for children, the elderly, and the disabled or who run postsecondary schools with residential facilities may obtain criminal record information from the state Criminal Information Center. May obtain record only after a conditional offer of employment is made and applicant has given written authorization on a signed, notarized release form.

Rights of employees and applicants: Release form must advise applicant of right to appeal any of the findings in the record.

Virginia

Va. Code Ann. § 19.2-392.4

Rules for employers: May not require an applicant to disclose information about any criminal charge that has been expunged.

Rights of employees and applicants: Need not refer to any expunged charges if asked about criminal record.

Washington

Wash. Rev. Code Ann. §§ 43.43.815, 9.94A.640(3), 9.96.060(3), 9.96A.020; Wash. Admin. Code § 162-12-140

Rules for employers:
- **Arrest records.** Employer who asks about arrests must ask whether the charges are still pending, have been dismissed, or led to conviction that would adversely affect job performance once and the arrest occurred within the last ten years.

State Laws on Employee Arrest and Conviction Records (continued)

- **Convictions.** Employer who obtains a conviction record must notify employee within 30 days of receiving it and must allow the employee to examine it. May make an employment decision based on a conviction only if it is less than 10 years old and the crime involves behavior that would adversely affect job performance.

Rights of employees and applicants: If a conviction record is cleared or vacated, may answer questions as though the conviction never occurred. A person convicted of a felony cannot be refused an occupational license unless the conviction is less than 10 years old and the felony relates specifically to the occupation or business.

Special situations: Employers are entitled to obtain complete criminal record information for positions that require bonding, or that have access to trade secrets, confidential or proprietary business information, money, or items of value.

Agency guidelines for preemployment inquiries: Washington Human Rights Commission, "Pre-employment inquiry guide," at http://apps.leg.wa.gov/WAC/default.aspx?cite=162-12.

West Virginia

Agency guidelines for preemployment inquiries: West Virginia Bureau of Employment Programs, "Pre-employment Inquiries Technical Assistance Guide," at www.wvbep.org/Shared/empinqu.asp. The state's website says that employers can only make inquiries about convictions directly related to the job.

Wisconsin

Wis. Stat. Ann. §§ 111.31 and 111.335

Rules for employers: It is a violation of state civil rights law to discriminate against an employee on the basis of a prior arrest or conviction record.

- **Arrest records.** May not ask about arrests unless there are pending charges.
- **Convictions.** May not ask about convictions unless charges substantially relate to job.

Special situations: Employers are entitled to obtain complete criminal record information for positions that require bonding and for burglar alarm installers.

Agency guidelines for preemployment inquiries: Wisconsin Department of Workforce Development, Equal Rights Division, Civil Rights Bureau, "Fair Hiring & Avoiding Discriminatory Interview Questions," dwd.wisconsin.gov/dwd/publications/erd/pdf/erd_4825_pweb.pdf.

State Laws on Employee Access to Personnel Records

This chart deals with only those states that authorize access to personnel files. Generally, an employee is allowed to see evaluations, performance reviews, and other documents that determine a promotion, bonus, or raise; access usually does not include letters of reference, test results, or records of a criminal or workplace-violation investigation. Under other state laws, employees may have access to their medical records and records of exposure to hazardous substances; these laws are not included in this chart.

Alaska

Alaska Stat. § 23.10.430

Employers affected: All.

Employee access to records: Employee or former employee may view and copy personnel files.

Conditions for viewing records: Employee may view records during regular business hours under reasonable rules.

Copying records: Employee pays (if employer so requests).

California

Cal. Lab. Code §§ 1198.5; 432

Employers affected: All employers subject to wage and hour laws.

Employee access to records: Employee has right to inspect at reasonable intervals any personnel records relating to performance or to a grievance proceeding.

Conditions for viewing records: Employee may view records at reasonable times, during break or nonwork hours. If records are kept offsite or employer does not make them available at the workplace, then employee must be allowed to view them at the storage location without loss of pay.

Copying records: Employee also has a right to a copy of any personnel document employee has signed.

Connecticut

Conn. Gen. Stat. Ann. §§ 31-128a to 31-128h

Employers affected: All.

Employee access to records: Employee has right to inspect personnel files within a reasonable time after making a request, but not more than twice a year. Employer must keep files on former employees for at least one year after termination.

Written request required: Yes.

Conditions for viewing records: Employee may view records during regular business hours in a location at or near worksite. Employer may require that files be viewed on the premises and in the presence of employer's designated official.

Copying records: Employer must provide copies within a reasonable time after receiving employee's written request; request must identify the materials employee wants copied. Employer may charge a fee that is based on the cost of supplying documents.

Employee's right to insert rebuttal: If employee disagrees with information in personnel file and cannot reach an agreement with employer to remove or correct it, employee may submit an explanatory written statement. Rebuttal must be maintained as part of the file.

Delaware

Del. Code Ann. tit. 19, §§ 730 to 735

Employers affected: All.

Employee access to records: Current employee, employee who is laid off with reemployment rights, or employee on leave of absence may inspect personnel record; employee's agent is not

State Laws on Employee Access to Personnel Records (continued)

entitled to have access to records. Unless there is reasonable cause, employer may limit access to once a year.

Written request required: At employer's discretion. Employer may require employee to file a form and indicate either the purpose of the review or what parts of the record employee wants to inspect.

Conditions for viewing records: Records may be viewed during employer's regular business hours. Employer may require that employees view files on their own time and may also require that files be viewed on the premises and in the presence of a designated official.

Copying records: Employer is not required to permit employee to copy records. Employee may take notes.

Employee's right to insert rebuttal: If employee disagrees with information in personnel file and cannot reach an agreement with employer to remove or correct it, employee may submit an explanatory written statement. Rebuttal must be maintained as part of the personnel file.

Illinois

820 Ill. Comp. Stat. §§ 40/1 to 40/12

Employers affected: Employers with 5 or more employees.

Employee access to records: Current employee, or former employee terminated within the past year, is permitted to inspect records twice a year at reasonable intervals, unless a collective bargaining agreement provides otherwise. An employee involved in a current grievance may designate a representative of the union or collective bargaining unit, or other agent, to inspect personnel records that may be relevant to resolving the grievance. Employer must make

records available within 7 working days after employee makes request (if employer cannot meet deadline, may be allowed an additional 7 days).

Written request required: At employer's discretion. Employer may require use of a form.

Conditions for viewing records: Records may be viewed during normal business hours at or near worksite or, at employer's discretion, during nonworking hours at a different location if more convenient for employee.

Copying records: After reviewing records, employee may get a copy. Employer may charge only actual cost of duplication. If employee is unable to view files at worksite, employer, upon receipt of a written request, must mail employee a copy.

Employee's right to insert rebuttal: If employee disagrees with any information in the personnel file and cannot reach an agreement with employer to remove or correct it, employee may submit an explanatory written statement. Rebuttal must remain in file with no additional comment by employer.

Iowa

Iowa Code §§ 91B.1, 91A.2

Employers affected: All employers with salaried employees or commissioned salespeople.

Employee access to records: Employee may have access to personnel file at time agreed upon by employer and employee.

Conditions for viewing records: Employer's representative may be present.

Copying records: Employer may charge copying fee for each page that is equivalent to a commercial copying service fee.

State Laws on Employee Access to Personnel Records (continued)

Maine

Me. Rev. Stat. Ann. tit. 26, § 631

Employers affected: All.

Employee access to records: Within 10 days of submitting request, employee, former employee, or authorized representative may view and copy personnel files.

Written request required: Yes.

Conditions for viewing records: Employee may view records during normal business hours at the location where the files are kept, unless employer, at own discretion, arranges a time and place more convenient for employee. If files are in electronic or any other nonprint format, employer must provide equipment for viewing and copying.

Copying records: Employee entitled to one free copy of personnel file during each calendar year, including any material added to file during that year. Employee must pay for any additional copies.

Massachusetts

Mass. Gen. Laws ch. 149, § 52C

Employers affected: All. (Employers with 20 or more employees must maintain personnel records for 3 years after termination.)

Employee access to records: Employee or former employee must have opportunity to review personnel files within 5 business days of submitting request, but not more than twice a calendar year. (Law does not apply to tenured or tenure-track employees in private colleges and universities.) Employer must notify an employee within 10 days of placing in the employee's personnel record any information to the extent that the information is, has been used or may be used, to negatively affect the employee's qualification for employment,

promotion, transfer, additional compensation or the possibility that the employee will be subject to disciplinary action. (This notification does not count towards employee's two allotted opportunities to view personnel file).

Written request required: Yes.

Conditions for viewing records: Employee may view records at workplace during normal business hours.

Copying records: Employee must be given a copy of record within 5 business days of submitting a written request.

Employee's right to insert rebuttal: If employee disagrees with any information in personnel record and cannot reach an agreement with employer to remove or correct it, employee may submit an explanatory written statement. Rebuttal becomes a part of the personnel file.

Michigan

Mich. Comp. Laws §§ 423.501 to 423.505

Employers affected: Employers with 4 or more employees.

Employee access to records: Current or former employee is entitled to review personnel records at reasonable intervals, generally not more than twice a year, unless a collective bargaining agreement provides otherwise.

Written request required: Yes. Request must describe the record employee wants to review.

Conditions for viewing records: Employee may view records during normal office hours either at or reasonably near the worksite. If these hours would require employee to take time off work, employer must provide another time and place that is more convenient for the employee.

Copying records: After reviewing files, employee may get a copy; employer may charge only actual

State Laws on Employee Access to Personnel Records (continued)

cost of duplication. If employee is unable to view files at the worksite, employer, upon receipt of a written request, must mail employee a copy.

Employee's right to insert rebuttal: If employee disagrees with any information in personnel record and cannot reach an agreement with employer to remove or correct it, employee may submit a written statement explaining his or her position. Statement may be no longer than five 8½" by 11" pages.

Minnesota

Minn. Stat. Ann. §§ 181.960 to 181.966

Employers affected: 20 or more employees.

Employee access to records: Current employee may review files once per 6-month period; former employee may have access to records once only during the first year after termination. Employer must comply with written request within 7 working days (14 working days if personnel records kept out of state). Employer may not retaliate against an employee who asserts rights under these laws.

Written request required: Yes.

Conditions for viewing records: Current employee may view records during employer's normal business hours at worksite or a nearby location; does not have to take place during employee's working hours. Employer or employer's representative may be present.

Copying records: Employer must provide copy free of charge. Current employee must first review record and then submit written request for copies. Former employee must submit written request; providing former employee with a copy fulfills employer's obligation to allow access to records.

Employee's right to insert rebuttal: If employee disputes specific information in the personnel

record, and cannot reach an agreement with employer to remove or revise it, employee may submit a written statement identifying the disputed information and explaining his or her position. Statement may be no longer than 5 pages and must be kept with personnel record as long as it is maintained.

Nevada

Nev. Rev. Stat. Ann. § 613.075

Employers affected: All.

Employee access to records: An employee who has worked at least 60 days and a former employee, within 60 days of termination, must be given a reasonable opportunity to inspect personnel records.

Conditions for viewing records: Employee may view records during employer's normal business hours.

Copying records: Employer may charge only actual cost of providing access and copies.

Employee's right to insert rebuttal: Employee may submit a reasonable written explanation in direct response to any entry in personnel record. Statement must be of reasonable length; employer may specify the format; employer must maintain statement in personnel records.

New Hampshire

N.H. Rev. Stat. Ann. § 275:56

Employers affected: All.

Employee access to records: Employer must provide employees a reasonable opportunity to inspect records.

Copying records: Employer may charge a fee reasonably related to cost of supplying copies.

Employee's right to insert rebuttal: If employee disagrees with any of the information in

State Laws on Employee Access to Personnel Records (continued)

personnel record and cannot reach an agreement with the employer to remove or correct it, employee may submit an explanatory written statement along with supporting evidence. Statement must be maintained as part of personnel file.

Oregon

Or. Rev. Stat. § 652.750

Employers affected: All.

Employee access to records: Within 45 days after receipt of request, employer must provide employee a reasonable opportunity to inspect personnel records used to determine qualifications for employment, promotion, or additional compensation, termination, or other disciplinary action. Employer must keep records for 60 days after termination of employee.

Conditions for viewing records: Employee may view records at worksite or place of work assignment.

Copying records: Within 45 days after receipt of request, employer must provide a certified copy of requested record to current or former employee (if request made within 60 days of termination). If employee makes request after 60 days from termination, employer shall provide a certified copy of requested records if employer has records at time of the request. May charge amount reasonably calculated to recover actual cost of providing copy.

Pennsylvania

43 Pa. Cons. Stat. Ann. §§ 1321 to 1324

Employers affected: All.

Employee access to records: Employer must allow employee to inspect personnel record at reasonable times. (Employee's agent, or employee who is laid off with reemployment rights or on leave of absence, must also be given access.) Unless there is reasonable cause, employer may limit review to once a year by employee and once a year by employee's agent.

Written request required: At employer's discretion. Employer may require the use of a form as well as a written indication of the parts of the record employee wants to inspect or the purpose of the inspection. For employee's agent: Employee must provide signed authorization designating agent; must be for a specific date and indicate the reason for the inspection or the parts of the record the agent is authorized to inspect.

Conditions for viewing records: Employee may view records during normal business hours at the office where records are maintained, when there is enough time for employee to complete the review. Employer may require that employee or agent view records on their own time and may also require that inspection take place on the premises and in the presence of employer's designated official.

Copying records: Employer not obligated to permit copying. Employee may take notes.

Employee's right to insert rebuttal: The Bureau of Labor Standards, after a petition and hearing, may allow employee to place a counterstatement in the personnel file, if employee claims that the file contains an error.

Rhode Island

R.I. Gen. Laws § 28-6.4-1

Employers affected: All.

Employee access to records: Employer must permit employee to inspect personnel files when given at least 7 days' advance notice (excluding weekends and holidays). Employer may limit access to no more than 3 times a year.

State Laws on Employee Access to Personnel Records (continued)

Written request required: Yes.

Conditions for viewing records: Employee may view records at any reasonable time other than employee's work hours. Inspection must take place in presence of employer or employer's representative.

Copying records: Employee may not make copies or remove files from place of inspection. Employer may charge a fee reasonably related to cost of supplying copies.

Washington

Wash. Rev. Code Ann. §§ 49.12.240 to 49.12.260

Employers affected: All.

Employee access to records: Employee may have access to personnel records at least once a year within a reasonable time after making a request.

Employee's right to insert rebuttal: Employee may petition annually that employer review all information in employee's personnel file. If there is any irrelevant or incorrect information in the file, employer must remove it. If employee does not agree with employer's review, employee may request to have a statement of rebuttal or correction placed in file. Former employee has right of rebuttal for two years after termination.

Wisconsin

Wis. Stat. Ann. § 103.13

Employers affected: All employers who maintain personnel records.

Employee access to records: Employee and former employee must be allowed to inspect personnel records within 7 working days of making request. Access is permitted twice per calendar year unless a collective bargaining agreement provides otherwise. Employee involved in a current grievance may designate a representative of the union or collective bargaining unit, or other agent, to inspect records that may be relevant to resolving the grievance.

Written request required: At employer's discretion.

Conditions for viewing records: Employee may view records during normal working hours at a location reasonably near worksite. If this would require employee to take time off work, employer may provide another reasonable time and place for review.

Copying records: Employee's right of inspection includes the right to make or receive copies. If employer provides copies, may charge only actual cost of reproduction.

Employee's right to insert rebuttal: If employee disagrees with any information in the personnel record and cannot come to an agreement with the employer to remove or correct it, employee may submit an explanatory written statement. Employer must attach the statement to the disputed portion of the personnel record.

State Minimum Wage Laws for Tipped and Regular Employees

The chart below gives the basic state minimum wage laws. Depending on the occupation, the size of the employer's business, or the conditions of employment, the minimum wage may vary from the one listed here. Minimum wage rates in a number of states change from year to year; to be sure of your state's current minimum, contact your state department of labor or check its website, where most states have posted the minimum wage requirements. (See the beginning of this appendix for contact information.) Also, some local governments have enacted ordinances that set a higher minimum wage—contact your city or county government for more information. "Maximum Tip Credit" is the highest amount of tips that an employer can subtract from the employee's hourly wage. The employee's total wages minus the tip credit cannot be less than the state minimum wage. If an employee's tips exceed the maximum tip credit, the employee gets to keep the extra amount.

"Minimum Cash Wage" is the lowest hourly wage that an employer can pay a tipped employee.

State and Statute	Notes	Basic Minimum Hourly Rate (*=tied to federal rate)	Maximum Tip Credit	Minimum Cash Wage for Tipped Employee	Minimum Tips to Qualify as a Tipped Employee (monthly unless noted otherwise)
United States 29 U.S.C. § 206 29 U.S.C. § 203	This is the current federal minimum wage	$7.25	$5.12	$2.13	More than $30
Alabama	No minimum wage law				
Alaska Alaska Stat. § 23.10.065		$7.25	No tip credit	$7.25	N/A
Arizona Ariz. Rev. Stat. § 23-363	Adjusts annually for inflation, posted at www.ica.state.az.us; does not apply to small businesses (those with gross revenue of less than $500,000 that are exempt from federal minimum wage laws)	$7.35	$3.00	$4.35	Averaged total of actual tips and cash minimum must equal minimum wage for each pay period
Arkansas Ark. Code Ann. §§ 11-4-210 and 11-4-212	Applies to employers with 4 or more employees	$6.25	$3.63	$2.63	Not specified

State Minimum Wage Laws for Tipped and Regular Employees (continued)

State and Statute	Notes	Basic Minimum Hourly Rate (*=tied to federal rate)	Maximum Tip Credit	Minimum Cash Wage for Tipped Employee	Minimum Tips to Qualify as a Tipped Employee (monthly unless noted otherwise)
California Cal. Lab. Code § 1182.12		$8.00	No tip credit	$8.00	N/A
Colorado Colo. Const. Art. 18, § 15; 7 Colo. Code Regs. § 1103-1	Adjusted annually for inflation, posted at www.coworkforce.com	$7.24	$3.02	$4.22	More than $30
Connecticut Conn. Gen. Stat. Ann. §§ 31-58(j), 31-60, Conn. Admin. Code § 31-62-E2		$8.00 or FLSA + ½%	31% in hotel and restaurant industries; 11% bartenders; 35¢ others	$5.52 in hotel and restaurant industries; $7.12 bartenders; $7.65 others	$10 per week (full-time employees); $2 per day (part-time employees)
Delaware Del. Code Ann. tit. 19, § 902(a)		$7.15 or FLSA rate if higher	$4.92	$2.23	More than $30
Dist. of Columbia D.C. Code Ann. § 32-1003		$7 or FLSA + $1.00 ($8.25) if DC rate is below the federal rate	$5.48	$2.77	Not specified
Florida Fla. Const., Art. X § 24 Fla. Stat. Ann. § 448.110	Adjusted annually, posted at www.floridajobs.org	$7.25	$3.02	$4.23	More than $30
Georgia Ga. Code Ann. § 34-4-3	Applies to employers with 6 or more employees and more than $40,000 per year in sales	$5.15	Minimum wage does not apply to tipped employees	N/A	N/A

State Minimum Wage Laws for Tipped and Regular Employees (continued)

State and Statute	Notes	Basic Minimum Hourly Rate (*=tied to federal rate)	Maximum Tip Credit	Minimum Cash Wage for Tipped Employee	Minimum Tips to Qualify as a Tipped Employee (monthly unless noted otherwise)
Hawaii *Haw. Rev. Stat. §§ 387-1 to 387-2*		$7.25	25¢	$7.00	More than $20; employee's cash wage plus tips must be at least 50¢ higher than the minimum wage
Idaho *Idaho Code § 44-1502*		$7.25	$3.90	$3.35	More than $30
Illinois *820 Ill. Comp. Stat. § 105/4; Ill. Admin. Code tit. 56, § 210.110*	Applies to employers with 4 or more employees	$8.25	40%	$4.95	At least $20
Indiana *Ind. Code Ann. § 22-2-2-4*	Applies to employers with 2 or more employees	$7.25*	$5.12	$2.13	Not specified
Iowa *Iowa Code § 91D.1*	In first 90 calendar days of employment, minimum wage is $6.35	$7.25	40%	$4.35	At least $30
Kansas *Kan. Stat. Ann. § 44-1203*	Applies to employers not covered by the FLSA	$7.25	40%	$2.13	More than $20
Kentucky *Ky. Rev. Stat. Ann. § 337.275*		$7.25*	$5.12	$2.13	More than $30
Louisiana	No minimum wage law				

State Minimum Wage Laws for Tipped and Regular Employees (continued)

State and Statute	Notes	Basic Minimum Hourly Rate (*=tied to federal rate)	Maximum Tip Credit	Minimum Cash Wage for Tipped Employee	Minimum Tips to Qualify as a Tipped Employee (monthly unless noted otherwise)
Maine Me. Rev. Stat. Ann. tit. 26, §§ 663(8), 664		$7.50*	50%	$3.75	More than $30
Maryland Md. Code Ann., [Lab. & Empl.] §§ 3-413, 3-419		$7.25*	50%	$3.63	More than $30
Massachusetts Mass. Gen. Laws ch. 151, § 1; Mass. Regs. Code tit. 455, § 2.02		$8.00 or 10¢ above FLSA rate if it is higher	$5.37	$2.63	More than $20
Michigan Mich. Comp. Laws §§ 408.382 to 408.387a	Applies to employers with 2 or more employees; excludes all employers subject to the FLSA, unless state minimum wage is higher than federal	$7.40	$4.75	$2.65	Not specified
Minnesota Minn. Stat. Ann. § 177.24	$5.25 for small employer (business with annual receipts of less than $625,000)	$6.15	No tip credit	$6.15	N/A
Mississippi	No minimum wage law				
Missouri Mo. Rev. Stat. §§ 290.502, 290.512	Doesn't apply to retail or service business with gross annual sales of less than $500,000	$7.25	Up to 50%	$3.62	Not specified

State Minimum Wage Laws for Tipped and Regular Employees (continued)

State and Statute	Notes	Basic Minimum Hourly Rate (*=tied to federal rate)	Maximum Tip Credit	Minimum Cash Wage for Tipped Employee	Minimum Tips to Qualify as a Tipped Employee (monthly unless noted otherwise)
Montana *Mont. Code Ann. §§ 39-3-404, 39-3-409; Mont. Admin. R. 24.16.1508 & following*	$4.00 for businesses with gross annual sales of $110,000 or less; adjusted annually. http://erd.dli.mt.gov/labor-standards/wage-and-hourwage-payment-act/state-minimum-wage.html	$7.35	No tip credit	$7.35	N/A
Nebraska *Neb. Rev. Stat. § 48-1203*	Applies to employers with 4 or more employees	$7.25	$5.12	$2.13	Not specified
Nevada *Nev. Rev. Stat. Ann. § 608.160; Nev. Admin. Code ch. 608 § 110; Nev. Const. Art. 15 § 16*	Adjusted annually, posted at www.laborcommissioner.com	$6.55 if employer provides health benefits $7.55 if no health benefits provided	No tip credit	$5.85	N/A
New Hampshire *N.H. Rev. Stat. Ann. § 279:21*		$7.25	55%	45%	More than $30
New Jersey *N.J. Stat. Ann. § 34:11-56a4*		$7.25*	$5.12*	$2.13	Not specified
New Mexico *N.M. Stat. Ann. § 50-4-22*		$7.50	$5.37	$2.13	More than $30

State Minimum Wage Laws for Tipped and Regular Employees (continued)

State and Statute	Notes	Basic Minimum Hourly Rate (*=tied to federal rate)	Maximum Tip Credit	Minimum Cash Wage for Tipped Employee	Minimum Tips to Qualify as a Tipped Employee (monthly unless noted otherwise)
New York N.Y. Lab. Law § 652; N.Y. Comp. Codes R. & Regs. tit. 12, §§ 137-1.4, 138-2.1		$7.25*	Depends on occupation	Depends on occupation	Depends on occupation
North Carolina N.C. Gen. Stat. §§ 95-25.2(14), 95-25.3		$7.25	$5.12	$2.13	More than $20
North Dakota N.D. Cent. Code § 34-06-22; N.D. Admin. Code R. 46-02-07-01 to -03		$7.25	33% of minimium wage	67% of minimum wage	More than $30
Ohio Ohio Rev. Code Ann. § 4111.02; Ohio Const. art. II § 34a	Same as federal minimum wage for employers with gross income under $271,000; adjusted annually, posted at www.com.ohio.gov/laws	$7.40	50%	50% of minimum wage	More than $30
Oklahoma Okla. Stat. Ann. tit. 40, §§ 197.2, 197.4, 197.16	Applies to employers with 10 or more full-time employees OR gross annual sales over $100,000 not otherwise subject to FLSA	$7.25	50% of minimum wage for tips, food, and lodging combined	50% of minimum wage	Not specified
Oregon Or. Rev. Stat. §§ 653.025, 653.035(3)	Adjusted annually; posted at www.boli.state.or.us	$8.50	No tip credit	$8.50	N/A

State Minimum Wage Laws for Tipped and Regular Employees (continued)					
State and Statute	Notes	Basic Minimum Hourly Rate (*=tied to federal rate)	Maximum Tip Credit	Minimum Cash Wage for Tipped Employee	Minimum Tips to Qualify as a Tipped Employee (monthly unless noted otherwise)
Pennsylvania 43 Pa. Cons. Stat. Ann. §§ 333.103 and 333.104; 34 Pa. Code §§ 231.1 and 231.103		$7.25*	$4.42	$2.83	More than $30
Rhode Island R.I. Gen. Laws §§ 28-12-3 & 28-12-5		$7.40	$4.31	$2.89	Not specified
South Carolina	No minimum wage law				
South Dakota S.D. Codified Laws Ann. §§ 60-11-3 to -3.1		$7.25	$5.12	$2.13	More than $35
Tennessee	No minimum wage law				
Texas Tex. Lab. Code Ann. §§ 62.051 & 62.052		$7.25	$5.12	$2.13	More than $20
Utah Utah Code Ann. § 34-40-102; Utah Admin. R. 610-1		$7.25	$5.12	$2.13	More than $30
Vermont Vt. Stat. Ann. tit. 21, § 384(a); Vt. Code R. 24 090 003	Applies to employers with 2 or more employees; adjusted annually, posted at www.vtlmi.info	$8.15	$4.25	$3.95 for employees of hotels, motels, restaurants, and tourist places; no tip credit otherwise	More than $120

State Minimum Wage Laws for Tipped and Regular Employees (continued)

State and Statute	Notes	Basic Minimum Hourly Rate (*=tied to federal rate)	Maximum Tip Credit	Minimum Cash Wage for Tipped Employee	Minimum Tips to Qualify as a Tipped Employee (monthly unless noted otherwise)
Virginia *Va. Code Ann.* *§§ 40.1-28.9 and 28.10*	Applies to employees not covered by FLSA	$7.25	Tips actually received	Minimum wage less tips actually received	Not specified
Washington *Wash. Rev. Code Ann. § 49.46.020;* *Wash. Admin. Code § 296-126-022*	Adjusted annually; posted at www.lni. wa.gov	$8.67	No tip credit	$8.55	N/A
West Virginia *W.Va. Code §§ 21-5C-1, 21-5C-2, 21-5C-4*	Applies to employers with 6 or more employees at one location who are not covered by the FLSA	$7.25	20% of minimum wage	80% of minimum wage	Not specified
Wisconsin *Wis. Admin. Code DWD 272.03*		$7.25	$4.92	$2.33	Not specified
Wyoming *Wyo. Stat. § 27-4-202*		$5.15	$3.02	$2.13	More than $30

State Meal and Rest Break Laws

Note: The states of Alabama, Alaska, Arizona, Arkansas, District of Columbia, Florida, Idaho, Iowa, Louisiana, Maryland, Michigan, Mississippi, Missouri, Montana, New Jersey, New Mexico, North Carolina, Ohio, Oklahoma, South Carolina, South Dakota, Texas, Utah, Virginia, and Wyoming are not listed in this chart because they do not have laws or regulations on rest and meal breaks for adults employed in the private sector. Many states also exclude professional, administrative, and executive employees from these rules.

Other exceptions may apply. For example, many states have special break rules for specific occupations or industries, which are beyond the scope of this chart. Check the statute or check with your state department of labor if you need more information. (See beginning of this appendix for contact list.)

California

Cal. Lab. Code §§ 512, 1030; Cal. Code Regs. tit. 8, §§ 11010-11170

Applies to: Employers in most industries

Exceptions: Motion picture and other occupations. See wage orders, *Cal. Code Regs. tit. 8, §§ 11010 to 11160*, for additional exceptions.

Meal Break: 30 minutes, unpaid, after 5 hours, except when workday will be completed in 6 hours or less and employer and employee consent to waive meal break. Employee cannot work more than 10 hours a day without a second 30-minute break, except if workday is no more than 12 hours; second meal break may be waived if first meal break was not waived. On-duty paid meal period permitted when nature of work prevents relief from all duties and parties agree in writing.

Rest Break: Paid 10-minute rest period for each 4 hours worked or major fraction thereof; as practicable, in the middle of the work period; not required for employees whose total daily work time is less than 3½ hours

Breastfeeding: Reasonable time to breastfeed infant or to express breast milk; paid if taken concurrent with other break time; otherwise, unpaid

Colorado

Colo. Code Regs. tit. 7 § 1103-1(7)-(8)

Applies to: Retail and service, food and beverage, commercial support service, and health and medical industries

Exceptions: Numerous exceptions are listed in the regulation.

Meal Break: 30 minutes, unpaid, after 5 hours of work; on-duty paid meal period permitted when nature of work prevents break from all duties.

Rest Break: Paid 10-minute rest period for each 4 hours or major fraction worked; if practical, in the middle of the work period

Connecticut

Conn. Gen. Stat. Ann. §§ 31-51ii, 31-40w

Applies to: All employers, except as noted

Exceptions: Employers who pay for rest breaks as described below, those with a written agreement providing other break rules, and those granted an exemption for reasons listed in statute

Meal Break: 30 minutes, unpaid, after first 2 hours of work and before last 2 hours for employees who work 7½ or more consecutive hours

Rest Break: As alternative to meal break, a total of 30 minutes paid in each 7½-hour work period

Breastfeeding: Employee may use meal or rest break for breastfeeding or expressing breast milk.

State Meal and Rest Break Laws (continued)

Delaware

Del. Code Ann. tit. 19, § 707

Applies to: All employers, except as noted

Exceptions: Employers with alternative written agreement and those granted exemptions specified in statute. Law does not apply to teachers.

Meal Break: 30 minutes, unpaid, after first 2 hours and before the last 2 hours, for employees who work 7½ consecutive hours or more

Georgia

Ga. Code Ann. § 34-1-6

Applies to: All employers

Breastfeeding: Reasonable unpaid break time to breastfeed infant or to express breast milk

Hawaii

Haw. Rev. Stat. § 378-2

Applies to: All employers

Breastfeeding: Allowed during any break required by law or collective bargaining agreement

Illinois

820 Ill. Comp. Stat. §§ 140/3, 260/10

Applies to: All employers

Exceptions: Employees whose meal periods are established by collective bargaining agreement

Employees who monitor individuals with developmental disabilities or mental illness, or both, and who are required to be on call during an entire 8-hour work period; these employees must be allowed to eat a meal while working.

Meal Break: 20 minutes, no later than 5 hours after the beginning of the shift, for employees who work 7½ or more continuous hours

Breastfeeding: Reasonable unpaid break time to breastfeed infant or express breast milk

Indiana

Ind. Code §§ 22-2-14, 5-10-6-2

Applies to: All employers

Breastfeeding: Reasonable unpaid break time to express breast milk

Kansas

Kan. Admin. Reg. 49-30-3

Applies to: Employees not covered under FLSA

Meal Break: Not required, but if less than 30 minutes is given, break must be paid.

Kentucky

Ky. Rev. Stat. Ann. §§ 337.355, 337.365; Ky. Admin. Regs. tit. 803, 1:065 § 4

Applies to: All employers, except as noted

Exceptions: Written agreement providing different meal period; employers subject to Federal Railway Labor Act

Meal Break: Reasonable off-duty period close to the middle of the shift; can't be required to take it before the third or after the fifth hour of work

Rest Break: Paid 10-minute rest period for each 4-hour work period; rest period must be in addition to regularly scheduled meal period.

Maine

Me. Rev. Stat. Ann. tit. 26, § 601

Applies to: Most employers

Exceptions: Small businesses with fewer than 3 employees on duty who are able to take frequent breaks during the workday; collective bargaining or other written agreement between employer and employee may provide for different breaks.

Breastfeeding: Adequate unpaid time to express breast milk, or employee may use rest or meal time.

State Meal and Rest Break Laws (continued)

Meal and Rest Break: 30 minutes, unpaid, after 6 consecutive hours of work, except in cases of emergency

Massachusetts

Mass. Gen. Laws ch. 149, §§ 100, 101

Applies to: All employers, except as noted

Exceptions: Excludes iron works, glass works, paper mills, letterpresses, print works, and bleaching or dyeing works. Attorney general may exempt businesses that require continuous operation if it won't affect worker safety. Collective bargaining agreement may also provide for different breaks.

Meal Break: 30 minutes, if work is for more than 6 hours

Minnesota

Minn. Stat. Ann. §§ 177.253, 177.254, 181.939

Applies to: All employers

Exceptions: Excludes certain agricultural and seasonal employees
   A collective bargaining agreement may provide for different rest and meal breaks.

Meal Break: Sufficient unpaid time for employees who work 8 consecutive hours or more

Rest Break: Paid adequate rest period within each 4 consecutive hours of work to utilize nearest convenient rest room

Breastfeeding: Reasonable unpaid break time to breastfeed infant or express milk

Nebraska

Neb. Rev. Stat. § 48-212

Applies to: Assembly plant, workshop, or mechanical establishment

Exceptions: Other written agreement between employer and employees

Meal Break: 30 minutes off premises for each 8-hour shift

Nevada

Nev. Rev. Stat. Ann. § 608.019

Applies to: Employers with two or more employees

Exceptions: Employees covered by collective bargaining agreement; exemptions for business necessity

Meal Break: 30 minutes for 8 continuous hours of work

Rest Break: Paid 10-minute rest period for each 4 hours or major fraction worked; as practicable, in middle of the work period; not required for employees whose total daily work time is less than 3½ hours

New Hampshire

N.H. Rev. Stat. Ann. § 275:30-a

Applies to: All employers

Meal Break: 30 minutes after 5 consecutive hours, unless the employer allows the employee to eat while working and it is feasible for the employee to do so

New York

N.Y. Lab. Law § 162, 206-c

Applies to: Factories, workshops, manufacturing facilities, mercantile (retail and wholesale) establishments

Meal Break: Factory employees, 60 minutes between 11 a.m. and 2 p.m.; mercantile employees, 30 minutes between 11 a.m. and 2 p.m. If a shift starts before 11 a.m. and ends after 7 p.m., every employee gets an additional 20 minutes between 5 p.m. and 7 p.m. If a shift starts between 1 p.m. and 6 a.m., a factory

State Meal and Rest Break Laws (continued)

employee gets 60 minutes, and a mercantile employee gets 45 minutes, in the middle of the shift. Labor commissioner may permit a shorter meal break; the permit must be in writing and posted conspicuously in the main entrance of the workplace.

Breastfeeding: Reasonable unpaid break time to express breast milk for up to three years after child's birth

North Dakota

N.D. Admin. Code § 46-02-07-02

Applies to: Applicable when two or more employees are on duty

Exceptions: Waiver by employee or other provision in collective bargaining agreement

Meal Break: 30 minutes for each shift over 5 hours; unpaid if employee is completely relieved of duties

Oregon

Or. Admin. R. §§ 839-020-0050, 839-020-0051

Applies to: All employers except as noted

Exceptions: Agricultural workers and employees covered by a collective bargaining agreement

Meal Break: 30 minutes, unpaid if relieved of all duties; paid time to eat if employee cannot be relieved of duty; a 20-minute paid break, if employer can show that it is industry practice or custom. If shift of 7 hours or less, meal break must occur between hours 2 and 5; if shift longer than 7 hours, meal break must be between hours 3 and 6.

Rest Break: Paid 10-minute rest period for each 4 hours or major fraction worked; if practical, in the middle of the work period

Rest period must be in addition to usual meal break and taken separately; can't be added to

meal period or deducted from beginning or end of shift to reduce length of total work period.

Rest period is not required for certain solo adult employees serving the public, although they must be allowed to use rest room.

Breastfeeding: Reasonable unpaid rest period, no greater than 30 minutes for each 4 hours worked, to express milk to child 18 months or younger

Pennsylvania

43 Pa. Cons. Stat. Ann. § 1301.207

Applies to: Employers of seasonal farmworkers

Meal Break: 30 minutes after 5 hours

Rhode Island

R.I. Gen. Laws §§ 28-3-8, 28-3-14, 23-13-2.1

Applies to: Employers with 5 or more employees

Exceptions: Employers of health care facility or employers with fewer than 3 employees on any shift

Meal Break: 20 minutes, unpaid, within a 6-hour shift or 30 minutes, unpaid, within an 8-hour shift

Breastfeeding: Reasonable unpaid break time to breastfeed infant or express breast milk

Tennessee

Tenn. Code Ann. §§ 50-2-103(h), 50-1-305

Applies to: Employers with 5 or more employees

Meal and Rest Break: 30 minutes unpaid for employees scheduled to work 6 consecutive hours or more unless work is such that there is ample time for breaks throughout the day

Breastfeeding: Reasonable unpaid break time to breastfeed infant or express breast milk, and employer shall make reasonable efforts to provide a space (other than a toilet stall) for employee to express breast milk in privacy.

State Meal and Rest Break Laws (continued)

Vermont

Vt. Stat. Ann. tit. 21, § 304

Applies to: All employers

Meal Break: Employees must be given reasonable opportunities to eat and use toilet facilities during work periods.

Washington

Wash. Admin. Code §§ 296-126-092, 296-131-020

Applies to: All employers except as noted

Exceptions: Newspaper vendor or carrier, domestic or casual labor around private residence, sheltered workshop; separate provisions for agricultural labor.

Meal Break: 30-minute break, if work period is more than 5 consecutive hours, not less than 2 hours nor more than 5 hours from beginning of shift. This time is paid if employee is on duty or is required to be at a site for employer's benefit. Employees who work 3 or more hours longer than regular workday are entitled to an additional half hour, before or during overtime.

Agricultural employees: 30 minutes if working more than 5 hours; additional 30 minutes if working 11 or more hours in a day

Rest Break: Paid 10-minute rest break for each 4-hour work period, scheduled as near as possible to midpoint of each work period. Employee cannot be required to work more than 3 hours without a rest break.

Scheduled rest breaks are not required where nature of work allows employee to take intermittent rest breaks equivalent to required standard.

10-minute paid rest break for every 4 hours worked.

West Virginia

W.Va. Code § 21-3-10a; W.Va. Code St. R.§ 42-5-2(2.6)

Applies to: All employers

Meal Break: At least 20-minute break for each 6 consecutive hours worked, unless employees are allowed to take breaks as needed or to eat lunch while working

Rest Break: Rest breaks of 20 minutes or less must be counted as paid work time.

Wisconsin

Wis. Admin. Code § DWD 274.02

Applies to: All employers

Meal Break: Recommended but not required: 30 minutes close to usual meal time or near middle of shift. Shifts of more than 6 hours without a meal break should be avoided. If employee is not free to leave the workplace, meal period is considered paid time.

State Health Insurance Continuation Laws

Alabama

Ala. Code § 27-55-3(4)

Special Situations: 18 months for subjects of domestic abuse who have lost coverage they had under abuser's insurance and who do not qualify for COBRA

Arizona

Ariz. Rev. Stat. §§ 20-1377, 20-1408

Employers affected: All employers who offer group disability insurance

Length of coverage for dependents: Insurer must either continue coverage for dependents or convert to individual policy upon death of covered employee or divorce. Coverage must be the same unless the insured chooses a lesser plan.

Qualifying event: Death of an employee; change in marital status

Time employer has to notify employee of continuation rights: No provisions for employer. Insurance policy must include notice of conversion privilege. Clerk of court must provide notice to anyone filing for divorce that dependent spouse entitled to convert health insurance coverage.

Time employee has to apply: 31 days after termination of existing coverage

Arkansas

Ark. Code Ann. §§ 23-86-114 to 23-86-116

Employers affected: All employers who offer group health insurance

Eligible employees: Continuously insured for previous 3 months

Length of coverage for employee: 120 days

Length of coverage for dependents: 120 days

Qualifying event: Termination of employment; death of insured employee; change in insured's marital status

Time employee has to apply: 10 days

California

Cal. Health & Safety Code §§ 1373.6, 1373.621; Cal. Ins. Code §§ 10128.50 to 10128.59

Employers affected: Employers who offer group health insurance and have 2 to 19 employees

Eligible employees: All covered employees are eligible.

Length of coverage for employee: 36 months

Length of coverage for dependents: 36 months

Qualifying event: Termination of employment; reduction in hours; death of employee; change in marital status

Time employer has to notify employee of continuation rights: 15 days

Time employee has to apply: 31 days after group plan ends; 30 days after COBRA or Cal-COBRA ends (63 days if converting to an individual plan)

Special situations: Employee who is at least 60 years old and has worked for employer for previous 5 years may continue benefits for self and spouse beyond COBRA or Cal-COBRA limits (also applies to COBRA employers). Employee who began receiving COBRA coverage on or after 1/1/03 and whose COBRA coverage is for less than 36 months may use Cal-COBRA to bring total coverage up to 36 months.

Colorado

Colo. Rev. Stat. § 10-16-108

Employers affected: All employers who offer group health insurance

Eligible employees: Employees continuously insured for previous 6 months

Length of coverage for employee: 18 months

Length of coverage for dependents: 18 months

Qualifying event: Termination of employment;

State Health Insurance Continuation Laws (continued)

reduction in hours; death of employee; change in marital status

Time employer has to notify employee of continuation rights: Within 10 days of termination

Time employee has to apply: 30 days after termination; 60 days if employer fails to give notice

Connecticut

Conn. Gen. Stat. Ann. §§ 38a-538, 38a-554; 31-51o

Employers affected: All employers who offer group health insurance

Eligible employees: Full-time employees or employees who have either worked or expect to work twenty hours a week for at least 26 weeks in a 12-month period

Length of coverage for employee: 30 months, or until eligible for Social Security benefits

Length of coverage for dependents: 30 months, or until eligible for Social Security benefits; 36 months in case of employee's death or divorce

Qualifying event: Layoff; reduction in hours; termination of employment; death of employee; change in marital status

Time employer has to notify employee of continuation rights: 14 days

Time employee has to apply: 60 days

Special situations: When facility closes or relocates, employer must pay for insurance for employee and dependents for 120 days or until employee is eligible for other group coverage, whichever comes first (does not affect employee's right to conventional continuation coverage which begins when 120-day period end).

District of Columbia

D.C. Code Ann. §§ 32-731 to 32-732

Employers affected: Employers with fewer than 20 employees

Eligible employees: All covered employees are eligible

Length of coverage for employee: three months or for the period of time during which the employee is eligible for ARRA subsidy

Length of coverage for dependents: three months or for the period of time during which the employee is eligible for ARRA subsidy

Qualifying event: Any reason employee or dependent becomes ineligible for coverage

Time employer has to notify employee of continuation rights: Within 15 days of termination of coverage

Time employee has to apply: 45 days after termination of coverage

Florida

Fla. Stat. Ann. § 627.6692

Employers affected: Employers with fewer than 20 employees

Eligible employees: Full-time (25 or more hours per week) employees covered by employer's health insurance plan

Length of coverage for employee: 18 months

Length of coverage for dependents: 18 months

Qualifying event: Layoff; reduction in hours; termination of employment; death of employee; change in marital status

Time employer has to notify employee of continuation rights: Carrier notifies within 14 days of learning of qualifying event (employer is responsible for notifying carrier).

Time employee has to apply: 30 days from receipt of carrier's notice

Georgia

Ga. Code Ann. §§ 33-24-21.1 to 33-24-21.2

Employers affected: All employers who offer

State Health Insurance Continuation Laws (continued)

group health insurance

Eligible employees: Employees continuously insured for previous 6 months

Length of coverage for employee: three months plus any part of the month remaining at termination; 9 months if eligible for ARRA subsidy

Length of coverage for dependents: three months plus any part of the month remaining at termination; 9 months if eligible for ARRA subsidy

Qualifying event: Termination of employment (except for cause)

Special situations: Employee, spouse, or former spouse, who is 60 years old and who has been covered for previous 6 months may continue coverage until eligible for Medicare. (Applies to companies with more than 20 employees; does not apply when employee quits for reasons other than health.)

Hawaii

Haw. Rev. Stat. §§ 393-11, 393-15

Employers affected: All employers required to offer health insurance (those paying a regular employee a monthly wage at least 86.67 times state hourly minimum—about $542)

Length of coverage for employee: If employee is hospitalized or prevented from working by sickness, employer must pay insurance premiums for 3 months or for as long employer continues to pay wages, whichever is longer.

Qualifying event: Employee is hospitalized or prevented by sickness from working.

Illinois

215 Ill. Comp. Stat. §§ 5/367e, 5/367.2, 5/367.2-5

Employers affected: All employers who offer group health insurance

Eligible employees: Employees continuously insured for previous 3 months

Length of coverage for employee: 12 months for policies issued, delivered, amended, or renewed after 6/18/2009. This requirement doesn't apply to employees eligible for ARRA subsidy.

Length of coverage for dependents: nine months (see "Special situations")

Qualifying event: Termination of employment; reduction in hours; death of employee; divorce

Time employer has to notify employee of continuation rights: 10 days

Time employee has to apply: 30 days after termination or reduction in hours or receiving notice from employer, whichever is later, but not more than 60 days from termination or reduction in hours

Special situations: Upon death or divorce, 2 years' coverage for spouse under 55 and eligible dependents who were on employee's plan; until eligible for Medicare or other group coverage for spouse over 55 and eligible dependents who were on employee's plan. A dependent child who has reached plan age limit or who was not already covered by plan is also entitled to 2 years' continuation coverage.

Iowa

Iowa Code §§ 509B.3, 509B.5

Employers affected: All employers who offer group health insurance

Eligible employees: Employees continuously insured for previous 3 months

Length of coverage for employee: nine months

Length of coverage for dependents: nine months

Qualifying event: Any reason employee or dependent becomes ineligible for coverage

State Health Insurance Continuation Laws (continued)

Time employer has to notify employee of continuation rights: 10 days after termination of coverage

Time employee has to apply: 10 days after termination of coverage or receiving notice from employer, whichever is later, but no more than 31 days from termination of coverage

Kansas

Kan. Stat. Ann. § 40-2209(i)

Employers affected: All employers who offer group health insurance

Eligible employees: Employees continuously insured for previous 3 months

Length of coverage for employee: 18 months

Length of coverage for dependents: 18 months

Qualifying event: Any reason employee or dependent becomes ineligible for coverage

Time employee has to apply: 31 days from termination of coverage

Kentucky

Ky. Rev. Stat. Ann. § 304.18-110

Employers affected: All employers who offer group health insurance

Eligible employees: Employees continuously insured for previous 3 months

Length of coverage for employee: 18 months

Length of coverage for dependents: 18 months

Qualifying event: Any reason employee or dependent becomes ineligible for coverage

Time employer has to notify employee of continuation rights: Employer must notify insurer as soon as employee's coverage ends; insurer then notifies employee

Time employee has to apply: 31 days from receipt of insurer's notice, but no more than 90 days after termination of group coverage

Louisiana

La. Rev. Stat. Ann. §§ 22:1045, 22:1046

Employers affected: All employers who offer group health insurance and have fewer than 20 employees

Eligible employees: Employees continuously insured for previous 3 months

Length of coverage for employee: 12 months

Length of coverage for dependents: 12 months

Qualifying event: Termination of employment

Time employee has to apply: Must apply and submit payment before group coverage ends

Special situations: Surviving spouse who is 50 or older may have coverage until remarriage or eligibility for Medicare or other insurance

Maine

Me. Rev. Stat. Ann. tit. 24-A, § 2809-A

Employers affected: All employers who offer group health insurance

Eligible employees: Employees continuously insured for previous 3 months

Length of coverage for employee: One year (either group or individual coverage at discretion of insurer)

Length of coverage for dependents: One year (either group or individual coverage at discretion of insurer); upon death of insured, continuation only if original plan provided for coverage

Qualifying event: Termination of employment

Time employee has to apply: 90 days from termination of group coverage

Special situations: Temporary layoff or work-related injury or disease: Employee and employee's dependents entitled to one year group or individual continuation coverage; (must have been continuously insured for previous

State Health Insurance Continuation Laws (continued)

6 months; must apply within 31 days from termination of coverage)

Maryland

Md. Code Ann., [Ins.] §§ 15-407 to 15-410

Employers affected: All employers who offer group health insurance

Eligible employees: Employees continuously insured for previous 3 months

Length of coverage for employee: 18 months

Length of coverage for dependents: 18 months upon death of employee; upon change in marital status, 18 months or until spouse remarries or becomes eligible for other coverage

Qualifying event: Involuntary termination of employment; death of employee; change in marital status

Time employer has to notify employee of continuation rights: Must notify insurer within 14 days of receiving employee's continuation request

Time employee has to apply: 45 days from termination of coverage. Employee begins application process by requesting an election of continuation notification form from employer.

Massachusetts

Mass. Gen. Laws ch. 175, §§ 110G, 110I; ch. 176J, § 9

Employers affected: All employers who offer group health insurance and have fewer than 20 employees

Eligible employees: All covered employees are eligible

Length of coverage for employee: 18 months; 29 months if disabled

Length of coverage for dependents: 18 months upon termination or reduction in hours; 29 months if disabled; 36 months on divorce, death

of employee, employee's eligibility for Medicare, or employer's bankruptcy

Qualifying event: Involuntary layoff; death of insured employee

Time employer has to notify employee of continuation rights: When employee becomes eligible for continuation benefits

Time employee has to apply: 60 days

Special situations: Termination due to plant closing: 90 days' coverage for employee and dependents, at the same payment terms as before closing

Minnesota

Minn. Stat. Ann. § 62A.17

Employers affected: All employers who offer group health insurance and have 2 or more employees

Eligible employees: All covered employees are eligible

Length of coverage for employee: 18 months; indefinitely if employee becomes totally disabled while employed

Length of coverage for dependents: 18 months for current spouse; divorced or widowed spouse can continue until eligible for Medicare or other group health insurance. Upon divorce, dependent children can continue until they no longer qualify as dependents under plan. Upon death of employee, spouse and/or dependent children can continue for 36 months.

Qualifying event: Termination of employment; reduction in hours

Time employer has to notify employee of continuation rights: Within 14 days of termination of coverage

Time employee has to apply: 60 days from termination of coverage or receipt of employer's notice, whichever is later

State Health Insurance Continuation Laws (continued)

Special benefits: Additional subsidy available to those eligible for ARRA subsidy, if insured meets income limits

Mississippi

Miss. Code Ann. § 83-9-51

Employers affected: All employers who offer group health insurance and have fewer than 20 employees

Eligible employees: Employees continuously insured for previous 3 months

Length of coverage for employee: 12 months

Length of coverage for dependents: 12 months

Qualifying event: Termination of employment; divorce; employee's death; employee's eligiblity for Medicare; loss of dependent status

Time employer has to notify employee of continuation rights: Insurer must notify former or deceased employee's dependent child or divorced spouse of option to continue insurance within 14 days of their becoming ineligible for coverage on employee's policy.

Time employee has to apply: Employee must apply and submit payment before group coverage ends; dependents or former spouse must elect continuation coverage within 30 days of receiving insurer's notice.

Missouri

Mo. Rev. Stat. § 376.428

Employers affected: All employers who offer group health insurance and are not subject to COBRA

Eligible employees: All employees

Length of coverage for employee: 18 months

Length of coverage for dependents: 18 months if eligible due to termination or reduction in hours; 36 months if eligible due to death or divorce

Qualifying event: Termination of employment; death of employee; divorce; reduction in hours

Time employer has to notify employee of continuation rights: Same rules as COBRA

Time employee has to apply: Same rules as COBRA

Montana

Mont. Code Ann. §§ 33-22-506 to 33-22-507

Employers affected: All employers who offer group disability insurance

Eligible employees: All employees

Length of coverage for employee: One year (with employer's consent)

Qualifying event: Reduction in hours

Special situations: Insurer may not discontinue benefits to child with disabilities after child exceeds age limit for dependent status.

Nebraska

Neb. Rev. Stat. §§ 44-1640 and following, 44-7406

Employers affected: Employers not subject to federal COBRA laws

Eligible employees: All covered employees

Length of coverage for employee: six months

Length of coverage for dependents: One year upon death of insured employee. Subjects of domestic abuse who have lost coverage under abuser's plan and who do not qualify for COBRA may have 18 months' coverage (applies to all employers).

Qualifying event: Involuntary termination of employment (layoff due to labor dispute not considered involuntary)

Time employer has to notify employee of continuation rights: Within 10 days of termination of employment must send notice by certified mail.

State Health Insurance Continuation Laws (continued)

Time employee has to apply: 10 days from receipt of employer's notice.

Nevada

Nev. Rev. Stat. Ann. §§ 689B.245 and following, 689B.0345

Employers affected: Employers with fewer than 20 employees

Eligible employees: Employees continuously insured for previous 12 months

Length of coverage for employee: 18 months

Length of coverage for dependents: 36 months; insurer cannot terminate coverage for disabled dependent child who is too old to qualify as a dependent under the plan.

Qualifying event: Involuntary termination of employment; involuntary reduction in hours; death of employee; divorce or legal separation; loss of dependent status; employee's eligibility for Medicare

Time employer has to notify employee of continuation rights: 14 days after receiving notice of employee's eligibility

Time employee has to apply: Must notify employer within 60 days of becoming eligible for continuation coverage; must apply within 60 days after receiving employer's notice

Special situations: While employee is on leave without pay due to disability, 12 months for employee and dependents (applies to all employers)

New Hampshire

N.H. Rev. Stat. Ann. §§ 415:18(VII)(g), (VII)(a)

Employers affected: Employers with 2 to 19 employees

Eligible employees: All insured employees are eligible.

Length of coverage for employee: 18 months; 29 months if disabled at termination or during first 60 days of continuation coverage

Length of coverage for dependents: 18 months; 29 months if disabled at termination or during first 60 days of continuation coverage; 36 months upon death of employee, divorce or legal separation, loss of dependent status, or employee's eligibility for Medicare

Qualifying event: Any reason employee or dependent becomes ineligible for coverage

Time employer has to notify employee of continuation rights: Within 15 days of termination of coverage

Time employee has to apply: Within 31 days of termination of coverage

Special situations: Layoff or termination due to strike: 6 months' coverage with option to extend for an additional 12 months. Surviving, divorced, or legally separated spouse who is 55 or older may continue benefits available until eligible for Medicare or another employer-based group insurance.

New Jersey

N.J. Stat. Ann. §§ 17B:27-51.12, 17B:27A-27

Employers affected: Employers with 2 to 50 employees

Eligible employees: Employed full time (25 or more hours)

Length of coverage for employee: 18 months; 29 months if disabled at termination or during first 60 days of continuation coverage

Length of coverage for dependents: 18 months; 29 months if disabled at termination or during first 60 days of continuation coverage; 36 months upon

State Health Insurance Continuation Laws (continued)

death of employee, divorce or legal separation, loss of dependent status, or employee's eligibility for Medicare

Qualifying event: Termination of employment; reduction in hours; change in marital status; death

Time employer has to notify employee of continuation rights: At time of qualifying event, employer or carrier notifies employee.

Time employee has to apply: Within 30 days of qualifying event

Special benefits: Coverage must be identical to that offered to current employees.

Special situations: Total disability: employee who has been insured for previous 3 months and employee's dependents, entitled to continuation coverage that includes all benefits offered by group policy (applies to all employers)

New Mexico

N.M. Stat. Ann. § 59A-18-16

Employers affected: All employers who offer group health insurance

Eligible employees: All insured employees are eligible.

Length of coverage for employee: Six months

Length of coverage for dependents: May continue group coverage or convert to individual policies upon death of covered employee or divorce or legal separation

Qualifying event: Termination of employment

Time employer has to notify employee of continuation rights: Insurer or employer gives written notice at time of termination.

Time employee has to apply: 30 days after receiving notice

New York

N.Y. Ins. Law §§ 3221(f), 3221(m)

Employers affected: All employers who offer group health insurance and have fewer than 20 employees

Eligible employees: All covered employees are eligible.

Length of coverage for employee: 36 months

Length of coverage for dependents: 36 months

Qualifying event: Termination of employment; death of employee; divorce or legal separation; loss of dependent status; employee's eligibility for Medicare

Time employee has to apply: 60 days after termination or receipt of notice, whichever is later

North Carolina

N.C. Gen. Stat. §§ 58-53-5 to 58-53-40

Employers affected: All employers who offer group health insurance

Eligible employees: Employees continuously insured for previous 3 months

Length of coverage for employee: 18 months

Length of coverage for dependents: 18 months

Qualifying event: Termination of employment

Time employer has to notify employee of continuation rights: Employer has option of notifying employee as part of the exit process.

Time employee has to apply: 60 days

North Dakota

N.D. Cent. Code §§ 26.1-36-23, 26.1-36-23.1

Employers affected: All employers who offer group health insurance

Eligible employees: Employees continuously insured for previous 3 months

State Health Insurance Continuation Laws (continued)

Length of coverage for employee: 39 weeks

Length of coverage for dependents: 39 weeks; 36 months if required by divorce or annulment decree

Qualifying event: Termination of employment

Time employee has to apply: Within 10 days of termination or of receiving notice of continuation rights, whichever is later, but no more than 31 days from termination

Ohio

Ohio Rev. Code Ann. §§ 3923.38, 1751.53

Employers affected: All employers who offer group health insurance

Eligible employees: Employees continuously insured for previous 3 months who were involuntarily terminated for reasons other than gross misconduct on the part of the employee

Length of coverage for employee: 12 months

Length of coverage for dependents: 12 months

Qualifying event: Involuntary termination of employment

Time employer has to notify employee of continuation rights: At termination of employment

Time employee has to apply: Whichever is earlier: 31 days after coverage terminates; 10 days after coverage terminates if employer notified employee of continuation rights prior to termination; 10 days after employer notified employee of continuation rights, if notice was given after coverage terminated

Oklahoma

Okla. Stat. Ann. tit. 36, § 4509

Employers affected: All employers who offer group health insurance

Eligible employees: Employees insured for at least 6 months; (all other employees and their dependents entitled to 30 days' continuation coverage)

Length of coverage for employee: 63 days for basic coverage; 6 months for major medical at the same premium rate prior to termination of coverage (only for losses or conditions that began while group policy in effect)

Length of coverage for dependents: 63 days for basic coverage; 6 months for major medical at the same premium rate prior to termination of coverage (only for losses or conditions that began while group policy in effect)

Qualifying event: Any reason coverage terminates

Special benefits: Includes maternity care for pregnancy begun while group policy was in effect

Oregon

Or. Rev. Stat. §§ 743.600 to 743.610

Employers affected: Employers not subject to federal COBRA laws

Eligible employees: Employees continuously insured for previous 3 months

Length of coverage for employee: 9 months

Length of coverage for dependents: 9 months

Qualifying event: Termination of employment

Time employee has to apply: 10 days after termination or after receiving notice of continuation rights, whichever is later, but not more than 31 days

Special situations: Surviving, divorced, or legally separated spouse who is 55 or older and dependent children entitled to continuation coverage until spouse remarries or is eligible for other coverage; must include dental, vision, or prescription drug benefits, if they were offered

State Health Insurance Continuation Laws (continued)

in original plan (applies to employers with 20 or more employees)

Pennsylvania

PA Stat. 40 P.S. § 764j

Employers affected: Employers that offer group health insurance and have 2 to 19 employees

Eligible employees: Employees continuously insured for at least 3 months

Length of coverage for employee: 9 months

Length of coverage for dependents: 9 months

Qualifying event: Termination of employment; reduction in hours; death of employee; change in marital status; employer's bankruptcy

Time employer has to notify employee of continuation rights: 30 days after qualifying event

Time employee has to apply: 30 days after receiving notice

Rhode Island

R.I. Gen. Laws §§ 27-19.1-1, 27-20.4-1 to 27-20-4-2

Employers affected: All employers who offer group health insurance

Eligible employees: All insured employees are eligible

Length of coverage for employee: 18 months (but not longer than continuous employment); cannot be required to pay more than one month premium at a time

Length of coverage for dependents: 18 months (but not longer than continuous employment); cannot be required to pay more than one month premium at a time

Qualifying event: Involuntary termination of employment; death of employee; change in marital status; permanent reduction in workforce; employer's going out of business

Time employer has to notify employee of continuation rights: Employers must post a conspicuous notice of employee continuation rights.

Time employee has to apply: 30 days from termination of coverage

Special situations: If right to receiving continuing health insurance is stated in the divorce judgment, divorced spouse has right to continue coverage as long as employee remains covered or until divorced spouse remarries or becomes eligible for other group insurance. If covered employee remarries, divorced spouse must be given right to purchase an individual policy from same insurer.

South Carolina

S.C. Code Ann. § 38-71-770

Employers affected: All employers who offer group health insurance

Eligible employees: Employees continuously insured for previous 6 months

Length of coverage for employee: 6 months (in addition to part of month remaining at termination)

Length of coverage for dependents: Six months (in addition to part of month remaining at termination)

Qualifying event: Any reason employee or dependent becomes ineligible for coverage

Time employer has to notify employee of continuation rights: At time of termination must clearly and meaningfully advise employee of continuation rights

South Dakota

S.D. Codified Laws Ann. §§ 58-18-7.5, 58-18-7.12; 58-18C-1

State Health Insurance Continuation Laws (continued)

Employers affected: All employers who offer group health insurance

Eligible employees: All covered employees

Length of coverage for employee: 18 months; 29 months if disabled at termination or during first 60 days of continuation coverage

Length of coverage for dependents: 18 months; 29 months if disabled at termination or during first 60 days of continuation coverage; 36 months upon death of employee, divorce or legal separation, loss of dependent status, or employee's eligibility for Medicare

Qualifying event: Termination of employment; death of employee; divorce or legal separation; loss of dependent status; employee's eligiblity for Medicare

Special situations: When employer goes out of business: 12 months' continuation coverage available to all employees. Employer must notify employees within 10 days of termination of benefits; employees must apply within 60 days of receipt of employer's notice to or within 90 days of termination of benefits if no notice given.

Tennessee

Tenn. Code Ann. § 56-7-2312

Employers affected: All employers who offer group health insurance

Eligible employees: Employees continuously insured for previous 3 months

Length of coverage for employee: Three months (in addition to part of month remaining at termination)

Length of coverage for dependents: Three months (in addition to part of month remaining at termination); 15 months upon death of employee or divorce

Qualifying event: Termination of employment; death of employee; change in marital status

Special situations: Employee or dependent who is pregnant at time of termination entitled to continuation benefits for 6 months following the end of pregnancy

Texas

Tex. Ins. Code Ann. §§ 1251.252 to 1251.255

Employers affected: All employers who offer group health insurance

Eligible employees: Employees continuously insured for previous 3 months

Length of coverage for employee: Nine months; for employees eligible for COBRA, 6 months after COBRA coverage ends

Length of coverage for dependents: Nine months; for employees eligible for COBRA, 6 months after COBRA coverage ends

Qualifying event: Termination of employment (except for cause); employee leaves for health reasons

Time employee has to apply: 60 days from termination of coverage or receiving notice of continuation rights from employer or insurer, whichever is later

Special situations: Layoff due to a labor dispute: employee entitled to continuation benefits for duration of dispute, but no longer than 6 months

Utah

Utah Code Ann. § 31A-22-722

Employers affected: All employers who offer group health insurance

Eligible employees: Employees continuously insured for previous 3 months

Length of coverage for employee: 12 months

Length of coverage for dependents: 12 months

State Health Insurance Continuation Laws (continued)

Qualifying event: Termination of employment; retirement; death; divorce; reduction in hours; sabbatical; disability

Time employer has to notify employee of continuation rights: In writing within 30 days of termination of coverage

Time employee has to apply: Within 30 days of receiving employer's notice of continuation rights

Vermont

Vt. Stat. Ann. tit. 8, §§ 4090a to 4090c

Employers affected: All employers who offer group health insurance and have fewer than 20 employees

Eligible employees: All covered employees are eligible.

Length of coverage for employee: 18 months

Length of coverage for dependents: 18 months

Qualifying event: Termination of employment; reduction in hours; death of employee; change of marital status; loss of dependent status

Time employer has to notify employee of continuation rights: Within 30 days of qualifying event

Time employee has to apply: Within 60 days of receiving notice following the occurrence of a qualifying event

Virginia

Va. Code Ann. §§ 38.2-3541 to 38.2-3452; 38.2-3416

Employers affected: All employers who offer group health insurance

Eligible employees: Employees continuously insured for previous 3 months

Length of coverage for employee: 90 days; 9 months if involuntarily terminated during any period when ARRA subsidy is available

Length of coverage for dependents: 90 days; 9 months if coverage lost due to involuntary termination of employee during any period when ARRA subsidy is available

Qualifying event: Any reason employee or dependent becomes ineligible for coverage; for 9-month coverage provision: involuntary termination of employment

Time employer has to notify employee of continuation rights: 15 days from termination of coverage; 30 days if eligible for ARRA subsidy

Time employee has to apply: Must apply for continuation and pay entire 90-day premium before termination of coverage; 60 days if eligible for ARRA subsidy

Special situations: Employee may convert to an individual policy instead of applying for continuation coverage (must apply within 31 days of termination of coverage).

Washington

Wash. Rev. Code Ann. § 48.21.075, 48.21.250, 48.21.260

Employers affected: All employers who offer and pay for group health insurance

Eligible employees: Insured employees on strike

Length of coverage for employee: Six months if employee goes on strike

Length of coverage for dependents: Six months if employee goes on strike

Qualifying event: Any reason employee or dependent becomes ineligible for coverage

Time employee has to apply: 31 days after the date the employee's group coverage terminates or 31 days after the date the employee receives notice of termination of coverage, whichever is later

State Health Insurance Continuation Laws (continued)

Special situations: Former employees may continue benefits for a period of time agreed upon with the employer. At the end of that time, the employee may then convert to an individual policy unless terminated for misconduct—in that case, employee's spouse and dependents may convert, but not employee.

West Virginia

W.Va. Code §§ 33-16-2, 33-16-3(e)

Employers affected: Employers providing insurance for at least 2 employees

Eligible employees: All employees are eligible

Length of coverage for employee: 18 months in case of involuntary layoff

Qualifying event: Involuntary layoff

Wisconsin

Wis. Stat. Ann. § 632.897

Employers affected: All employers who offer group health insurance

Eligible employees: Employees continuously insured for previous 3 months

Length of coverage for employee: 18 months (or longer at insurer's option)

Length of coverage for dependents: 18 months (or longer at insurer's option)

Qualifying event: Any reason employee or dependent becomes ineligible for coverage

Time employer has to notify employee of continuation rights: Five days from termination of coverage

Time employee has to apply: 30 days after receiving employer's notice

Wyoming

Wyo. Stat. § 26-19-113

Employers affected: Employers not subject to federal COBRA laws

Eligible employees: Employees continuously insured for previous 3 months

Length of coverage for employee: 12 months

Length of coverage for dependents: 12 months

Time employee has to apply: 31 days from termination of coverage

State Family and Medical Leave Laws

California

Cal. Gov't. Code §§ 12945 and 12945.2; Cal. Lab. Code §§ 230 and following; Cal. Unemp. Ins. §§ 3300 and following

Employers Covered: For pregnancy leave: employers with 5 or more employees; for domestic violence leave and school activity leave: employers with 25 or more employees; for family medical leave: employers with 50 or more employees; for paid family leave: employers whose employees contribute to state temporary disability insurance (SDI) fund

Eligible Employees: For pregnancy, domestic violence, or school activity leave: all employees; for family medical leave: employee with more than 12 months of service with the employer, and who has at least 1,250 hours of service with the employer during the previous 12-month period; for paid family leave benefits program: employees who contribute to SDI fund

Family Medical Leave: Up to 4 months for disability related to pregnancy (in addition to 12 weeks under family leave law); up to 12 weeks of leave per year to care for seriously ill family member. Employees who contribute to SDI fund may receive paid family leave benefits for up to 6 weeks of leave per year to care for a seriously ill family member (including a registered domestic partner) or bond with a new child.

School Activities: 40 hours per year, not more than 8 hours per calendar month

Domestic Violence: Reasonable time for issues dealing with domestic violence or sexual assault, including health, counseling, and safety measures. Family member or domestic partner of a victim of a felony may take leave to attend judicial proceedings related to the crime.

Colorado

Colo. Rev. Stat. §§ 19-5-211; 24-34-402.7

Employers Covered: For adoption leave: all employers who offer leave for birth of a child; for domestic violence leave: employers with 50 or more employees

Eligible Employees: For adoption leave: all employees; for domestic violence leave: employees with one year of service

Family Medical Leave: Employee must be given same leave for adoption as allowed for childbirth (doesn't apply to stepparent adoption).

Domestic Violence: Up to 3 days' leave in any 12-month period to seek restraining order, obtain medical care or counseling, relocate, or seek legal assistance for victim of domestic violence, sexual assault, or stalking

Connecticut

Conn. Gen. Stat. Ann. §§ 31-51kk to 31-51qq; 46a-60

Employers Covered: For pregnancy leave: employers with 3 or more employees; for family medical or serious health leave: employers with 75 or more employees

Eligible Employees: For pregnancy leave: all employees; for family medical or serious health condition leave: any employee with one year and at least 1,000 hours of service in last 12 months

Family Medical Leave: Reasonable amount of pregnancy leave required; 16 weeks per any 24-month period for childbirth, adoption, employee's serious health condition, care for family member with serious health condition, or bone marrow or organ donation; 26 weeks per 12-month period for each family member who is also a current member of the armed forces and is undergoing medical treatment

State Family and Medical Leave Laws (continued)

District of Columbia

D.C. Code Ann. §§ 32-501 and following; 32-1202, and 32-131.01 and following

Employers Covered: Employers with 20 or more employees

Eligible Employees: Employees who have worked at company for at least one year and at least 1,000 hours during the previous 12 months

Family Medical Leave: 16 weeks per any 24-month period for childbirth, adoption, pregnancy/maternity, domestic violence, or care for family member with serious health condition; additional 16 weeks per any 24-month period for employee's serious health condition; paid leave for the employee's or family member's physical or mental illness, injury, or medical condition; for the employee's or family member's medical care, diagnosis, or preventive medical care. Amount of paid leave depends on employer size: Employers with 100 or more employees must provide at least one hour of paid leave for every 37 hours worked, up to seven days of leave per year; employers with 25 to 99 employees must provide at least one hour of paid leave for every 43 hours worked, up to five days of leave per year; employers with fewer than 25 employees must provide at least one hour of paid leave for every 87 hours worked, up to three days of leave per year.

School Activities: Up to 24 hours of unpaid leave per year (all employees, all employers)

Domestic Violence: Paid leave, described under "Family Medical Leave," may also be used for employee or family member who is a victim of stalking, domestic violence, or abuse to get medical attention, get services, seek counseling, relocate, take legal action, or take steps to enhance health and safety.

Florida

Fla. Stat. § 741.313

Employers Covered: All employers

Eligible Employees: All employees

Domestic Violence: Up to 3 working days in any 12-month period if employee or family/household member is victim of domestic violence, with or without pay at discretion of employer; applies to employers with 50 or more employees, and employee must be employed for at least 3 months

Hawaii

Haw. Rev. Stat. §§ 398-1 to 398-11; 378-1, 378-71 to 378-74

Employers Covered: For childbirth, adoption, and serious health condition leave: employers with 100 or more employees; for pregnancy leave and domestic violence leave: all employers

Eligible Employees: For childbirth, adoption, and serious health condition leave: employees with 6 months of service; for pregnancy and maternity leave: all employees

Family Medical Leave: 4 weeks per calendar year for childbirth, adoption, or care for family member with serious health condition; "reasonable period" of pregnancy/maternity leave required by discrimination statute and case law; may include up to 10 days' accrued leave or sick leave

Domestic Violence: Employer with 50 or more employees must allow up to 30 days' unpaid leave per year for employee who is a victim of domestic or sexual violence or if employee's minor child is a victim. Employer with 49 or fewer employees must allow up to 5 days' leave.

Illinois

820 Ill. Comp. Stat. §§ 147/1 and following; 180/1 and following

State Family and Medical Leave Laws (continued)

Employers Covered: Employers with 15 or more employees

Eligible Employees: For school activities leave: employees who have worked at least half-time for 6 months; for domestic violence leave: all employees

School Activities: Eight hours per year (no more than 4 hours per day); required only if employee has no paid leave available

Domestic Violence: If employer has at least 50 employees, up to 12 weeks' unpaid leave per 12-month period for employee who is a victim of domestic violence or sexual assault or for employee with a family or household member who is a victim; if employer has at least 15 but not more than 49 employees, up to 8 weeks' unpaid leave during any 12-month period

Iowa

Iowa Code § 216.6

Employers Covered: Employers with 4 or more employees

Eligible Employees: All employees

Family Medical Leave: Up to 8 weeks for disability due to pregnancy, childbirth, or legal abortion

Kentucky

Ky. Rev. Stat. Ann. § 337.015

Employers Covered: All employers

Eligible Employees: All employees

Family Medical Leave: Up to 6 weeks for adoption of a child under 7 years old

Louisiana

La. Rev. Stat. Ann. §§ 23:341 to 23:342; 23:1015 and following; 40:1299.124

Employers Covered: For pregnancy/maternity leave: employers with 25 or more employees; for leave to donate bone marrow: employers with 20 or more employees; for school activities leave: all employers

Eligible Employees: For pregnancy/maternity or school activities leave: all employees; for leave to donate bone marrow: employees who work 20 or more hours per week

Family Medical Leave: "Reasonable period of time" not to exceed four months for pregnancy/maternity leave, if necessary for pregnancy or related medical condition; up to 40 hours' paid leave per year to donate bone marrow

School Activities: 16 hours per year

Maine

Me. Rev. Stat. Ann. tit. 26, §§ 843 and following

Employers Covered: For domestic violence leave: all employers; for family medical leave: employers with 15 or more employees at one location

Eligible Employees: All employees for domestic violence leave; employees with at least one year of service for family medical leave

Family Medical Leave: 10 weeks in any two-year period for childbirth, adoption (for child 16 or younger), employee's serious health condition, or care for family member with serious health condition

Domestic Violence: "Reasonable and necessary" leave for employee who is victim of domestic violence, sexual assault, or stalking, or whose parent, spouse, or child is a victim, to prepare for and attend court, for medical treatment, and for other necessary services

Maryland

Md. Code Ann., Lab. & Empl. § 3-801, 3-802

Employers Covered: Employers with 15 or more employees

State Family and Medical Leave Laws (continued)

Eligible Employees: All employees

Family Medical Leave: Employee must be given same leave for adoption as allowed for childbirth.

Massachusetts

Mass. Gen. Laws ch. 149, §§ 52D, 105D; ch. 151B, § 1(5)

Employers Covered: For maternity and adoption leave: employers with 6 or more employees; for school activities leave: employers with 50 or more employees

Eligible Employees: For maternity and adoption leave: full-time female employees who have completed probationary period, or 3 months of service if no set probationary period; for all other leave: employees who are eligible under FMLA

Family Medical Leave: Eight weeks total for childbirth/maternity or adoption of child younger than 18 (younger than 23 if disabled); additional 24 hours total per year (combined with school activities leave) to accompany minor child or relative age 60 or older to medical and dental appointments

School Activities: 24 hours per year total (combined with medical care under "other")

Minnesota

Minn. Stat. Ann. §§ 181.940 and following

Employers Covered: For childbirth/maternity and adoption leave: employers with 21 or more employees at one site; for bone marrow donation: employers with 20 or more employees; for school activities: all employers

Eligible Employees: For maternity leave: employees who have worked at least half-time for one year; for bone marrow donation: employees who work at least 20 hours per week; for school activities: employees who have worked at least one year

Family Medical Leave: Six weeks for childbirth/ maternity or adoption; up to 40 hours paid leave per year to donate bone marrow; parent can use accrued sick leave to care for sick or injured child.

School Activities: 16 hours in 12-month period; includes activities related to child care, preschool, or special education

Montana

Mont. Code Ann. §§ 49-2-310, 49-2-311

Employers Covered: All employers

Eligible Employees: All employees

Family Medical Leave: Reasonable leave of absence for pregnancy/maternity and childbirth

Nebraska

Neb. Rev. Stat. § 48-234

Employers Covered: Employers that allow workers to take leave for the birth of a child

Eligible Employees: All employees

Family Medical Leave: Employee must be given same leave as allowed for childbirth to adopt a child, unless child is over 8 (or over 18 for special needs child); does not apply to stepparent or foster parent adoptions.

Nevada

Nev. Rev. Stat. Ann. §§ 392.920, 613.335, 392.4577

Employers Covered: All employers

Eligible Employees: All employees

Family Medical Leave: Same sick or disability leave policies that apply to other medical conditions must be extended to pregnancy, miscarriage, and childbirth.

School Activities: Employers may not fire or threaten to fire a parent, guardian, or custodian for attending a school conference or responding to a child's emergency. Employers with 50 or

State Family and Medical Leave Laws (continued)

more employees must provide parent with a child in private school a leave of 4 hours per school year, which must be taken in increments of at least 1 hour, to attend parent-teacher conferences, attend school-related activities during regular school hours, attend school-sponsored events, or volunteer or be involved at the school.

New Hampshire

N.H. Rev. Stat. Ann. § 354-A:7(VI)

Employers Covered: Employers with 6 or more employees

Eligible Employees: All employees

Family Medical Leave: Temporary disability leave for pregnancy/childbirth or related medical condition

New Jersey

N.J. Stat. Ann. §§ 34:11B-1 and following; 43-21-1 and following

Employers Covered: Employers with 50 or more employees; for paid family leave, employers subject to the New Jersey Unemployment Compensation Law

Eligible Employees: Employees who have worked for at least one year and at least 1,000 hours in previous 12 months; for paid family leave benefits program: employees who worked 20 calendar weeks in covered New Jersey employment; or earned at least 1,000 times New Jersey minimum wage during 52 weeks preceding leave

Family Medical Leave: 12 weeks (or 24 weeks reduced-leave schedule) in any 24-month period for pregnancy/maternity, childbirth, adoption, or care for family member with serious health condition. Employees may receive paid family leave benefits for up to 6 weeks of leave per year to care for a seriously ill family member (including a registered domestic partner) or bond with a new child.

New Mexico

N.M. Stat. Ann. § 50-4A-1 and following

Employers Covered: All employers

Eligible Employees: All employees

Domestic Violence: Employer must provide intermittent paid or unpaid leave time for up to 14 days in any calendar year, taken by an employee for up to eight hours in one day, to obtain or attempt to obtain an order of protection or other judicial relief from domestic abuse or to meet with law enforcement officials, to consult with attorneys or district attorneys' victim advocates or to attend court proceedings related to the domestic abuse of an employee or an employee's family member.

New York

N.Y. Lab. Law §§ 201-c, 202-a

Employers Covered: Employers that allow workers to take leave for the birth of a child must allow adoption leave; employers with 20 or more employees at one site must allow leave to donate bone marrow.

Eligible Employees: All employees are eligible for adoption leave; employees who work at least 20 hours per week are eligible for leave to donate bone marrow.

Family Medical Leave: Employees must be given same leave as allowed for childbirth to adopt a child of preschool age or younger, or no older than 18 if disabled; up to 24 hours' leave to donate bone marrow.

State Family and Medical Leave Laws (continued)

North Carolina

N.C. Gen. Stat. §§ 95-28.3, 50B-5.5

Employers Covered: All employers

Eligible Employees: All employees

School Activities: Parents and guardians of school-aged children must be given up to 4 hours of leave per year.

Domestic Violence: Reasonable time off from work to obtain or attempt to obtain relief from domestic violence and sexual assault

Oregon

Or. Rev. Stat. §§ 659A.029, 659A.150 and following, 659A.312, 659A.270 and following

Employers Covered: For childbirth, adoption, and serious health condition leave: employers with 25 or more employees; for domestic violence leave: employers with 6 or more employees; for leave to donate bone marrow: all employers

Eligible Employees: For childbirth, adoption, serious health condition or domestic violence leave: employees who have worked 25 or more hours per week for at least 180 days; for leave to donate bone marrow: employees who work an average of 20 or more hours per week

Family Medical Leave: 12 weeks per year for pregnancy/maternity, adoption, or childbirth; additional 12 weeks per year for serious health condition, care for family member with serious health condition, or care for child who has an illness, injury, or condition that requires home care; up to 40 hours or amount of accrued paid leave (whichever is less) to donate bone marrow

Domestic Violence: Reasonable leave for employee who is victim of domestic violence, sexual assault, or stalking, or whose minor child is a victim, to seek legal treatment, medical services, counseling, or to relocate/secure existing home

Rhode Island

R.I. Gen. Laws §§ 28-48-1 and following

Employers Covered: Employers with 50 or more employees

Eligible Employees: Employees who have worked an average of 30 or more hours a week for at least 12 consecutive months

Family Medical Leave: 13 weeks in any two calendar years for childbirth, adoption of child up to 16 years old, employee's serious health condition, or care for family member with serious health condition

School Activities: Up to 10 hours a year

South Carolina

S.C. Code Ann. § 44-43-80

Employers Covered: Employers with 20 or more workers at one site in South Carolina

Eligible Employees: Employees who work an average of at least 20 hours per week

Family Medical Leave: Up to 40 hours paid leave per year to donate bone marrow—employers are not required to grant such leave.

Tennessee

Tenn. Code Ann. § 4-21-408

Employers Covered: Employers with 100 or more employees

Eligible Employees: Employees who have worked 12 consecutive months as full-time employees

Family Medical Leave: Up to 4 months of unpaid leave for pregnancy/maternity and childbirth (includes nursing); employee must give 3 months' notice unless a medical emergency requires the leave to begin sooner; these laws must be included in employee handbook.

State Family and Medical Leave Laws (continued)

Vermont

Vt. Stat. Ann. tit. 21, §§ 471 and following

Employers Covered: For childbirth and adoption leave: employers with 10 or more employees; for family medical leave: employers with 15 or more employees

Eligible Employees: Employees who have worked an average of 30 or more hours per week for at least one year

Family Medical Leave: 12 weeks per year for childbirth, adoption of child age 16 or younger, employee's serious health condition, or care for family member with a serious health condition; combined with school activities leave, additional 4 hours of unpaid leave in a 30-day period (up to 24 hours per year) to take a family member to a medical, dental, or professional well-care appointment or respond to a family member's medical emergency

School Activities: Combined with leave described above, 4 hours' total unpaid leave in a 30-day period (but not more than 24 hours per year) to participate in child's school activities

Washington

Wash. Rev. Code Ann. §§ 49.78.010 and following, 49.12.265 and following, 49.12.350 and following, 49.76.010 and following, 49.86.005 and following

Employers Covered: All employers must allow employees to use available paid time off to care for sick family members (including state registered domestic partners); employers with 50 or more employees must provide leave to care for newborn, adopted, or foster child, or family member with serious health condition.

Eligible Employees: All employees who accrue paid sick leave may use it to care for sick family members (including state registered domestic

partners); employees who have worked at least 1,250 hours in the previous year are eligible for parental leave to care for newborn, adopted, or foster child, or leave to care for a family member with serious health condition.

Family Medical Leave: In addition to any leave available under federal FMLA, employee may take leave for the period of time when she is sick or temporarily disabled due to pregnancy or childbirth; employers with 50 or more employees must allow up to 12 weeks during any 12-month period for the birth or placement of a child, employee's serious health condition, or care for a family member with a serious health condition; all employees can use paid sick leave to care for a sick family member.

Domestic Violence: Reasonable leave from work, with or without pay, for employee who is victim of domestic violence, sexual assault, or stalking, or whose family member is a victim, to prepare for and attend court, for medical treatment, and for other necessary services.

Wisconsin

Wis. Stat. Ann. § 103.10

Employers Covered: Employers with 50 or more employees

Eligible Employees: Employees who have worked at least one year and 1,000 hours in the preceding 12 months

Family Medical Leave: 6 weeks per 12-month period for pregnancy/maternity, childbirth, or adoption; additional 2 weeks per 12-month period to care for family member (including domestic partner) with a serious health condition; additional 2 weeks per 12-month period to care for the employee's own serious health condition

Right-to-Know Laws (Hazardous Chemicals)

Alaska	*Alaska Stat. § 18.60.067; Alaska Admin. Code tit. 8, § 61.1110*	**Maine**	*Me. Rev. Stat. Ann. tit. 22, § 1471-M; Code Me. R. § 12-179 ch.2 §1*
California	*Cal. Lab. Code §§ 6360 to 6399.7; 8 CCR §§ 337 to 339*	**Maryland**	*Md. Code Ann., [Lab. & Empl.] §§5-401 to 5-410; Md. Regs Code §§ 09.12.20.01 to 09.12.20.21*
Connecticut	*Conn. Gen. Stat. Ann. §§ 31-369 to 31-385*	**Massachusetts**	*Mass. Gen. Laws ch. 111F, § 454 CMR 21.01 to 21.09*
Delaware	*Del. Code Ann. tit. 16, §§ 2401 to 2417; Code Del. Regs. 16 4000 4456*	**Michigan**	*Mich. Comp. Laws §§ 408.1014a to 408.1014n; Mich. Admin. Code r. 325.70107*
District of Columbia	*D.C. Code Ann. §§ 32-1101 to 32-1124; D.C. Mun. Regs. tit. 7 §§ 2000 to 2009*	**Minnesota**	*Minn. Stat. Ann. §§ 182.653 to 182.655; Minn. R. 5206.0100 to 5206.2000*
Hawaii	*Haw. Rev. Stat. §§ 396-1 to 396-20; Haw. Admin. Rules § 12-74.1-1*	**Missouri**	*Mo. Rev. Stat. § 292.605*
Illinois	*820 Ill. Comp. Stat. §§ 255/1 to 255/20; 56 Ill. Admin. Code 205.200 to 205.310*	**Montana**	*Mont. Code Ann. §§ 50-78-101 to 50-78-402; Mont. Admin. R. 24.30.102 to 24.30.107*
Indiana	*Ind. Code Ann. §§ 22-8-1.1-1 to 22-8-1.1-51; Ind. Admin. Code tit. 610 §§ 9-2-1 to 9-2-9*	**Nevada**	*Nev. Rev. Stat. Ann. § 618.295*
Iowa	*Iowa Code §§ 89B.1 to 89B.17; Iowa Admin. Code 875-110.1(88,89B) to 875-110.7*	**New Hampshire**	*N.H. Rev. Stat. Ann. §§ 277-A:1 to 277-A:9; NH Code Admin. R. Lab. 1403.01*
Louisiana	*La. Rev. Stat. Ann. §§ 30:2361 to 30:2380; La. Admin. Code tit. 33, pt. V, § 10115*	**New Jersey**	*N.J. Stat. Ann. §§ 34:5A-1 to 34:5A-31; N.J. Admin. Code tit. 7, § 1G-1.1 to 1G-2.1; tit 12 § 110-1.1 to 110-4.14*
		New Mexico	*N.M. Stat. Ann. §§ 50-9-1 to 50-9-25; NM Admin. Code tit. 11 § 5.1*

Right-to-Know Laws (Hazardous Chemicals) (continued)

New York	N.Y. Lab. Law §§ 875 to 883	**Texas**	Tex. Admin. Code tit. 4, §§ 8.1 to 8.12, tit. 25, §§ 295.1 to 295.13; Tex. Health & Safety Code Ann. §§ 502.001 to 502.009, 502.017
North Carolina	N.C. Gen. Stat. §§ 95-173 to 95-218		
Oregon	Or. Rev. Stat. §§ 654.750 to 654.780; 654.305 to 654.336; Or. Admin. R. §§ 437-002-0377, 437-004-9800	**Virginia**	16 VAC 25-90-1910
		Washington	Wash. Rev. Code Ann. §§ 49.70.010 to 49.70.119; Wash. Admin. Code 296-307-550 to 296-307-56045, 296-800-170 to 296-800-18020
Pennsylvania	35 Pa. St. §§ 7301 to 7313; 34 Pa. Code §§ 301.1 to 301.4; § 307.11; § 311.2		
		West Virginia	W. Va. Code § 21-3-18; W. Va. Code St. R. § 42-4-1
Rhode Island	R.I. Gen. Laws §§ 28-21-1 to 28-21-21		
		Wisconsin	Wis. Stat. Ann. §§ 101.58 to 101.599
South Carolina	S.C. Code Ann. § 41-15-100		
Tennessee	Tenn. Code Ann. §§ 50-3-2001 to 50-3-2019; Tenn. Comp. R. & Regs. 0800-1-9-.01 to 0800-1-9-.14	**Wyoming**	WY Rules & Regs. EMP GEN Ch. 26, § 1910.1200

State Laws Prohibiting Discrimination in Employment

Alabama

Ala. Code §§ 25-1-20, 25-1-21

Law applies to employers with: 20 or more employees

Private employers may not make employment decisions based on:
- **Age:** 40 and older

Alaska

Alaska Stat. §§ 18.80.220, 47.30.865

Law applies to employers with: One or more employees

Private employers may not make employment decisions based on:
- **Age:** 40 and older
- **Ancestry or national origin**
- **Disability:** physical or mental
- **AIDS/HIV**
- **Gender**
- **Marital status:** includes changes in status
- **Pregnancy, childbirth, and related medical conditions:** includes parenthood
- **Race or color**
- **Religion or creed**
- **Additional protected categories:** mental illness

Arizona

Ariz. Rev. Stat. §§ 41-1461, 41-1463, 41-1465

Law applies to employers with: 15 or more employees

Private employers may not make employment decisions based on:
- **Age:** 40 and older
- **Ancestry or national origin**
- **Disability:** physical or mental
- **AIDS/HIV**
- **Gender**
- **Race or color**

- **Religion or creed**
- **Genetic testing information**

Arkansas

Ark. Code Ann. §§ 16-123-102, 16-123-107, 11-4-601, 11-5-403

Law applies to employers with: Nine or more employees

Private employers may not make employment decisions based on:
- **Ancestry or national origin**
- **Disability:** physical, mental, or sensory
- **Gender**
- **Pregnancy, childbirth, and related medical conditions**
- **Race or color**
- **Religion or creed**
- **Genetic testing information**

California

Cal. Gov't. Code §§ 12920, 12926.1, 12940, 12941, 12945; Cal. Lab. Code § 1101

Law applies to employers with: Five or more employees

Private employers may not make employment decisions based on:
- **Age:** 40 and older
- **Ancestry or national origin**
- **Disability:** physical or mental
- **AIDS/HIV**
- **Gender**
- **Marital status**
- **Pregnancy, childbirth, and related medical conditions**
- **Race or color**
- **Religion or creed**
- **Sexual orientation**
- **Genetic testing information**
- **Additional protected categories:**

State Laws Prohibiting Discrimination in Employment (continued)

- gender identity
- medical condition
- political activities or affiliations

Colorado

Colo. Rev. Stat. §§ 24-34-301, 24-34-401, 24-34-402, 24-34-402.5, 27-65-115

Law applies to employers with: One or more employees

Private employers may not make employment decisions based on:
- **Age:** 40 to 70
- **Ancestry or national origin**
- **Disability:** physical, mental, or learning
- **AIDS/HIV**
- **Gender**
- **Pregnancy, childbirth, and related medical conditions**
- **Race or color**
- **Religion or creed**
- **Sexual orientation:** includes perceived sexual orientation
- **Additional protected categories:**
  - lawful conduct outside of work
  - mental illness

Connecticut

Conn. Gen. Stat. Ann. §§ 46a-51, 46a-60, 46a-81a, 46a-81c

Law applies to employers with: Three or more employees

Private employers may not make employment decisions based on:
- **Age:** 40 and older
- **Ancestry or national origin**
- **Disability:** present or past physical, mental, learning, or mental retardation
- **AIDS/HIV**
- **Gender**

- **Marital status:** includes civil unions
- **Pregnancy, childbirth, and related medical conditions**
- **Race or color**
- **Religion or creed**
- **Sexual orientation:** includes having a history of being identified with a preference
- **Genetic testing information**

Delaware

Del. Code Ann. tit. 19, §§ 710, 711, 724

Law applies to employers with: Four or more employees

Private employers may not make employment decisions based on:
- **Age:** 40 and older
- **Ancestry or national origin**
- **Disability:** physical or mental
- **AIDS/HIV**
- **Gender**
- **Marital status**
- **Pregnancy, childbirth, and related medical conditions**
- **Race or color**
- **Religion or creed**
- **Sexual orientation**
- **Genetic testing information**

District of Columbia

D.C. Code Ann. §§ 2-1401.01, 2-1401.02, 2-1402.82, 7-1703.03, 32-131.08

Law applies to employers with: One or more employees

Private employers may not make employment decisions based on:
- **Age:** 18 and older
- **Ancestry or national origin**
- **Disability:** physical or mental
- **AIDS/HIV**

State Laws Prohibiting Discrimination in Employment (continued)

- **Gender**
- **Marital status:** includes domestic partnership
- **Pregnancy, childbirth, and related medical conditions:** includes parenthood and breastfeeding
- **Race or color**
- **Religion or creed**
- **Sexual orientation**
- **Genetic testing information**
- **Additional protected categories:**
  - enrollment in vocational, professional, or college education
  - family duties
  - source of income;
  - place of residence or business
  - personal appearance
  - political affiliation
  - victim of intrafamily offense
  - gender identity or expression
  - any reason other than individual merit
  - tobacco use

Florida

Fla. Stat. Ann. §§ 760.01, 760.02, 760.10, 760.50, 448.075

Law applies to employers with: 15 or more employees

Private employers may not make employment decisions based on:
- **Age**
- **Ancestry or national origin**
- **Disability:** "handicap"
- **AIDS/HIV**
- **Gender**
- **Marital status**
- **Race or color**
- **Religion or creed**
- **Additional protected categories:** sickle cell trait

Georgia

Ga. Code Ann. §§ 34-1-2, 34-5-1, 34-5-2, 34-6A-1 and following, 45-19-20 and following

Law applies to employers with: 15 or more employees (disability)

10 or more employees (gender)

Private employers may not make employment decisions based on:
- **Age:** 40 to 70
- **Disability:** physical, mental, or learning or mental retardation
- **Gender:** wage discrimination only
- **Additional protected category:** Domestic and agricultural employees are not protected.

Hawaii

Haw. Rev. Stat. §§ 378-1, 378-2, 378-2.5

Law applies to employers with: One or more employees

Private employers may not make employment decisions based on:
- **Age**
- **Ancestry or national origin**
- **Disability:** physical or mental
- **AIDS/HIV**
- **Gender**
- **Marital status**
- **Pregnancy, childbirth, and related medical conditions:** includes breastfeeding
- **Race or color**
- **Religion or creed**
- **Sexual orientation**
- **Genetic testing information**
- **Additional protected categories:**
  - arrest and court record (unless there is a conviction directly related to job)

State Laws Prohibiting Discrimination in Employment (continued)

- credit history or credit report, unless the information in the individual's credit history or credit report directly relates to a bona fide occupational qualification.

Idaho

Idaho Code §§ 39-8303, 67-5902, 67-5909, 67-5910

Law applies to employers with: five or more employees

Private employers may not make employment decisions based on:
- **Age:** 40 and older
- **Ancestry or national origin**
- **Disability:** physical or mental
- **Gender**
- **Pregnancy, childbirth, and related medical conditions**
- **Race or color**
- **Religion or creed**
- **Genetic testing information**

Illinois

410 Ill. Comp. Stat. § 513/25; 775 Ill. Comp. Stat. §§ 5/1-102, 5/1-103, 5/1-105, 5/2-101, 5/2-102, 5/2-103; 820 Ill. Comp. Stat. §§ 105/4, 180/30; Ill. Admin. Code tit. 56, § 5210.110

Law applies to employers with: 15 or more employees; one or more employees (disability)

Private employers may not make employment decisions based on:
- **Age:** 40 and older
- **Ancestry or national origin**
- **Disability:** physical or mental
- **AIDS/HIV**
- **Gender**
- **Marital status**
- **Pregnancy, childbirth, and related medical conditions**
- **Race or color**

- **Religion or creed**
- **Sexual orientation**
- **Genetic testing information**
- **Additional protected categories:**
  - citizenship status
  - military status
  - unfavorable military discharge
  - gender Identity
  - arrest record
  - victims of domestic violence
  - order of protection status

Indiana

Ind. Code Ann. §§ 22-9-1-2, 22-9-2-1, 22-9-2-2, 22-9-5-1 and following

Law applies to employers with: six or more employees

Private employers may not make employment decisions based on:
- **Age:** 40 to 75 (applies to employers with one or more employees)
- **Ancestry or national origin**
- **Disability:** physical or mental (15 or more employees)
- **Gender**
- **Race or color**
- **Religion or creed**
- **Additional protected category:** off-duty tobacco use

Iowa

Iowa Code §§ 216.2, 216.6, 729.6, 216.6A

Law applies to employers with: four or more employees

Private employers may not make employment decisions based on:
- **Age:** 18 or olde
- **Ancestry or national origin**
- **Disability:** physical or mental

State Laws Prohibiting Discrimination in Employment (continued)

- AIDS/HIV
- Gender
- Pregnancy, childbirth, and related medical conditions
- Race or color
- Religion or creed
- Sexual orientation
- Genetic testing information
- Additional protected categories:
  - gender identity
  - wage discrimination

Kansas

Kan. Stat. Ann. §§ 44-1002, 44-1009, 44-1112, 44-1113, 44-1125, 44-1126, 65-6002(e)

Law applies to employers with: four or more employees

Private employers may not make employment decisions based on:
- **Age:** 40 or older
- **Ancestry or national origin**
- **Disability:** physical or mental
- **AIDS/HIV**
- **Gender**
- **Race or color**
- **Religion or creed**
- **Genetic testing information**
- **Additional protected category:** military service or status

Kentucky

Ky. Rev. Stat. Ann. §§ 207.130, 207.135, 207.150, 342.197, 344.010, 344.030, 344.040

Law applies to employers with: eight or more employees

Private employers may not make employment decisions based on:
- **Age:** 40 or older
- **Ancestry or national origin**

- **Disability:** physical or mental
- **AIDS/HIV**
- **Gender**
- **Pregnancy, childbirth, and related medical conditions**
- **Race or color**
- **Religion or creed**
- **Additional protected categories:**
  - occupational pneumoconiosis with no respiratory impairment resulting from exposure to coal dust
  - off-duty tobacco use

Louisiana

La. Rev. Stat. Ann. §§ 23:301 to 23:368

Law applies to employers with: 20 or more employees

Private employers may not make employment decisions based on:
- **Age:** 40 or older
- **Ancestry or national origin**
- **Disability:** physical or mental
- **Gender:**
- **Pregnancy, childbirth, and related medical conditions:** applies to employers with 25 or more employees
- **Race or color**
- **Religion or creed**
- **Genetic testing information**
- **Additional protected category:** sickle cell trait

Maine

Me. Rev. Stat. Ann. tit. 5, §§ 19302, 4552, 4553, 4571 to 4576, 23; tit. 26, § 833; tit. 39-A, § 353

Law applies to employers with: One or more employees

Private employers may not make employment decisions based on:

State Laws Prohibiting Discrimination in Employment (continued)

- Age
- Ancestry or national origin
- Disability: physical or mental
- Gender
- Pregnancy, childbirth, and related medical conditions
- Race or color
- Religion or creed
- Sexual orientation: includes perceived sexual orientation
- Genetic testing information
- Additional protected categories:
  - gender identity or expression
  - past workers' compensation claim
  - past whistle-blowing
  - medical support notice for child

Maryland

Md. Code, State Government, §§ 20-101, 20-601 to 20-608

Law applies to employers with: 15 or more employees

Private employers may not make employment decisions based on:

- Age
- Ancestry or national origin
- Disability: physical or mental
- Gender
- Marital status
- Pregnancy, childbirth, and related medical conditions
- Race or color
- Religion or creed
- Sexual orientation
- Genetic testing information
- Additional protected category: Civil Air Patrol membership

Massachusetts

Mass. Gen. Laws ch. 149, § 24A; 151B, §§ 1, 4

Law applies to employers with: six or more employees

Private employers may not make employment decisions based on:

- Age: 40 or older
- Ancestry or national origin
- Disability: physical or mental
- AIDS/HIV
- Gender
- Marital status
- Race or color
- Religion or creed
- Sexual orientation
- Genetic testing information
- Additional protected categories:
  - military service
  - arrest record

Michigan

Mich. Comp. Laws §§ 37.1103, 37.1201, 37.1202, 37.2201, 37.2202, 37.2205a, 750.556

Law applies to employers with: One or more employees

Private employers may not make employment decisions based on:

- Age
- Ancestry or national origin
- Disability: physical or mental
- AIDS/HIV
- Gender
- Marital status
- Pregnancy, childbirth, and related medical conditions
- Race or color
- Religion or creed
- Genetic testing information
- Additional protected categories:
  - height or weight
  - misdemeanor arrest record

State Laws Prohibiting Discrimination in Employment (continued)

Minnesota

Minn. Stat. Ann. §§ 144.417, 181.81, 181.974, 363A.03, 363A.08

Law applies to employers with: One or more employees

Private employers may not make employment decisions based on:

- **Age:** 18 to 70
- **Ancestry or national origin**
- **Disability:** physical or mental
- **AIDS/HIV**
- **Gender**
- **Marital status**
- **Pregnancy, childbirth, and related medical conditions**
- **Race or color**
- **Religion or creed**
- **Sexual orientation:** includes perceived sexual orientation
- **Genetic testing information**
- **Additional protected categories:**
  - gender identity
  - member of local commission
  - receiving public assistance

Mississippi

Miss. Code Ann. § 33-1-15

Law applies to employers with: One or more employees

- **Protected categories:**
  - military status
  - no other protected categories unless employer receives public funding

Missouri

Mo. Rev. Stat. §§ 191.665, 213.010, 213.055, 375.1306

Law applies to employers with: six or more employees

Private employers may not make employment decisions based on:

- **Age:** 40 to 70
- **Ancestry or national origin**
- **Disability:** physical or mental
- **AIDS/HIV**
- **Gender**
- **Race or color**
- **Religion or creed**
- **Genetic testing information**

Montana

Mont. Code Ann. §§ 49-2-101, 49-2-303, 49-2-310

Law applies to employers with: One or more employees

Private employers may not make employment decisions based on:

- **Age**
- **Ancestry or national origin**
- **Disability:** physical or mental
- **Gender**
- **Marital status**
- **Pregnancy, childbirth, and related medical conditions**
- **Race or color**
- **Religion or creed**

Nebraska

Neb. Rev. Stat. §§ 20-168, 48-236, 48-1001 to 48-1010, 48-1102, 48-1104

Law applies to employers with: 15 or more employees

Private employers may not make employment decisions based on:

State Laws Prohibiting Discrimination in Employment (continued)

- **Age:** 40 or older (applies to employers with 20 or more employees)
- **Ancestry or national origin**
- **Disability:** physical or mental
- **AIDS/HIV**
- **Gender**
- **Marital status**
- **Pregnancy, childbirth, and related medical conditions**
- **Race or color**
- **Religion or creed**
- **Genetic testing information:** applies to all employers

Nevada

Nev. Rev. Stat. Ann. §§ 613.310 and following

Law applies to employers with: 15 or more employees

Private employers may not make employment decisions based on:
- **Age:** 40 or older
- **Ancestry or national origin**
- **Disability:** physical or mental
- **Gender**
- **Pregnancy, childbirth, and related medical conditions**
- **Race or color**
- **Religion or creed**
- **Sexual orientation:** includes perceived sexual orientation
- **Genetic testing information**
- **Additional protected categories:**
  - opposing unlawful employment practices
  - use of service animal

New Hampshire

N.H. Rev. Stat. Ann. §§ 141-H:3, 354-A:2, 354-A:6, 354-A:7

Law applies to employers with: six or more employees

Private employers may not make employment decisions based on:
- **Age**
- **Ancestry or national origin**
- **Disability:** physical or mental
- **Gender**
- **Marital status**
- **Pregnancy, childbirth, and related medical conditions**
- **Race or color**
- **Religion or creed**
- **Sexual orientation**
- **Genetic testing information**

New Jersey

N.J. Stat. Ann. §§ 10:5-1, 10:5-4.1, 10:5-5, 10:5-12, 10:5-29.1, 34:6B-1, 43:21-49

Law applies to employers with: One or more employees

Private employers may not make employment decisions based on:
- **Age:** 18 to 70
- **Ancestry or national origin**
- **Disability:** past or present physical or mental
- **AIDS/HIV**
- **Gender**
- **Marital status**
- **Pregnancy, childbirth, and related medical conditions**
- **Race or color**
- **Religion or creed**
- **Sexual orientation:** includes affectional orientation and perceived sexual orientation
- **Genetic testing information**
- **Additional protected categories:**
  - gender identity
  - atypical heredity cellular or blood trait
  - accompanied by service or guide dog
  - military service

State Laws Prohibiting Discrimination in Employment (continued)

New Mexico

N.M. Stat. Ann. §§ 24-21-4, 28-1-2, 28-1-7, 50-4A-4

Law applies to employers with: four or more employees

Private employers may not make employment decisions based on:

- **Age:** 40 or older
- **Ancestry or national origin**
- **Disability:** physical or mental
- **Gender**
- **Marital status:** applies to employers with 50 or more employees
- **Pregnancy, childbirth, and related medical conditions**
- **Race or color**
- **Religion or creed**
- **Sexual orientation:** includes perceived sexual orientation; applies to employers with 15 or more employees
- **Genetic testing information**
- **Additional protected categories:**
  - gender identity (employers with 15 or more employees)
  - serious medical condition
  - domestic abuse leave

New York

N.Y. Exec. Law §§ 292, 296; N.Y. Lab. Law § 201-d

Law applies to employers with: 4 or more employees

Private employers may not make employment decisions based on:

- **Age:** 18 and over
- **Ancestry or national origin**
- **Disability:** physical or mental
- **AIDS/HIV**
- **Gender**
- **Marital status**

- **Pregnancy, childbirth, and related medical conditions**
- **Race or color**
- **Religion or creed**
- **Sexual orientation:** includes perceived sexual orientation
- **Genetic testing information**
- **Additional protected categories:**
  - lawful recreational activities when not at work
  - military status or service
  - observance of Sabbath
  - political activities
  - use of service dog
  - arrest or criminal accusation
  - domestic violence victim status

North Carolina

N.C. Gen. Stat. §§ 95-28.1, 127B-11, 130A-148, 143-422.2, 168A-5

Law applies to employers with: 15 or more employees

Private employers may not make employment decisions based on:

- **Age**
- **Ancestry or national origin**
- **Disability:** physical or mental
- **AIDS/HIV**
- **Gender**
- **Race or color**
- **Religion or creed**
- **Genetic testing information**
- **Additional protected categories:**
  - military status or service
  - sickle cell or hemoglobin C trait

North Dakota

N.D. Cent. Code §§ 14-02.4-02, 14-02.4-03, 34-01-17

Law applies to employers with: One or more employees

State Laws Prohibiting Discrimination in Employment (continued)

Private employers may not make employment decisions based on:
- **Age:** 40 or older
- **Ancestry or national origin**
- **Disability:** physical or mental
- **Gender**
- **Marital status**
- **Pregnancy, childbirth, and related medical conditions**
- **Race or color**
- **Religion or creed**
- **Additional protected categories:**
  - lawful conduct outside of work
  - receiving public assistance

Ohio

Ohio Rev. Code Ann. §§ 4111.17, 4112.01, 4112.02

Law applies to employers with: four or more employees

Private employers may not make employment decisions based on:
- **Age:** 40 or older
- **Ancestry or national origin**
- **Disability:** physical or mental
- **Gender**
- **Pregnancy, childbirth, and related medical conditions**
- **Race or color**
- **Religion or creed**
- **Additional protected categories:**
  - armed services
  - caring for a sibling, child, parent, or spouse injured while in the armed services

Oklahoma

Okla. Stat. Ann. tit. 25, §§ 1301, 1302; tit. 36, § 3614.2; tit. 40, § 500; tit. 44, § 208

Law applies to employers with: 15 or more employees

Private employers may not make employment decisions based on:
- **Age:** 40 or older
- **Ancestry or national origin**
- **Disability:** physical or mental
- **Gender:**
- **Pregnancy, childbirth, and related medical conditions:** except abortions where the woman is not in "imminent danger of death"
- **Race or color**
- **Religion or creed**
- **Genetic testing information**
- **Additional protected category:** military service

Oregon

Or. Rev. Stat. §§ 25-337, 659A.030, 659A.122 and following, 659A.303

Law applies to employers with: One or more employees

Private employers may not make employment decisions based on:
- **Age:** 18 or older
- **Ancestry or national origin**
- **Disability:** physical or mental (applies to employers with 6 or more employees)
- **Gender**
- **Marital status**
- **Pregnancy, childbirth, and related medical conditions**
- **Race or color**
- **Religion or creed**
- **Sexual orientation**
- **Genetic testing information**
- **Additional protected categories:**
  - parent who has medical support order imposed by court

State Laws Prohibiting Discrimination in Employment (continued)

- domestic violence victim status
- refusal to attend an employer-sponsored meeting with the primary purpose of communicating the employer's opinion on religious or political matters
- credit history

Pennsylvania

43 Pa. Cons. Stat. Ann. §§ 954–955

Law applies to employers with: four or more employees

Private employers may not make employment decisions based on:

- **Age:** 40 to 70
- **Ancestry or national origin**
- **Disability:** physical or mental
- **Gender**
- **Pregnancy, childbirth, and related medical conditions**
- **Race or color**
- **Religion or creed**
- **Additional protected categories:**
  - relationship or association with disabled person
  - GED rather than high school diploma
  - use of service animal

Rhode Island

R.I. Gen. Laws §§ 12-28-10, 23-6.3-11, 28-5-6, 28-5-7, 28-6-18, 28-6.7-1

Law applies to employers with: four or more employees; one or more employees (gender-based wage discrimination)

Private employers may not make employment decisions based on:

- **Age:** 40 or older
- **Ancestry or national origin**
- **Disability:** physical or mental

- **AIDS/HIV**
- **Gender**
- **Pregnancy, childbirth, and related medical conditions**
- **Race or color**
- **Religion or creed**
- **Sexual orientation:** includes perceived sexual orientation
- **Genetic testing information**
- **Additional protected categories:**
  - domestic abuse victim
  - gender identity or expression

South Carolina

S.C. Code §§ 1-13-30, 1-13-80

Law applies to employers with: 15 or more employees

Private employers may not make employment decisions based on:

- **Age:** 40 or older
- **Ancestry or national origin**
- **Disability:** physical or mental
- **Gender**
- **Pregnancy, childbirth, and related medical conditions**
- **Race or color**
- **Religion or creed**

South Dakota

S.D. Codified Laws Ann. §§ 20-13-1, 20-13-10, 60-2-20, 60-12-15, 62-1-17

Law applies to employers with: One or more employees

Private employers may not make employment decisions based on:

- **Ancestry or national origin**
- **Disability:** physical or mental
- **Gender**
- **Race or color**

State Laws Prohibiting Discrimination in Employment (continued)

- **Religion or creed**
- **Genetic testing information**
- **Additional protected category:** preexisting injury

Tennessee

Tenn. Code Ann. §§ 4-21-102, 4-21-401 and following, 8-50-103, 50-2-201, 50-2-202

Law applies to employers with: eight or more employees; one or more employees (gender-based wage discrimination)

Private employers may not make employment decisions based on:

- **Age:** 40 or older
- **Ancestry or national origin**
- **Disability:** physical, mental, or visual
- **Gender**
- **Pregnancy, childbirth, and related medical conditions:** Refer to chart on Family and Medical Leave
- **Race or color**
- **Religion or creed**
- **Additional protected categories:**
  - use of guide dog
  - volunteer rescue squad worker responding to an emergency

Texas

Tex. Lab. Code Ann. §§ 21.002, 21.051, 21.082, 21.101, 21.106, 21.402

Law applies to employers with: 15 or more employees

Private employers may not make employment decisions based on:

- **Age:** 40 or older
- **Ancestry or national origin**
- **Disability:** physical or mental
- **Gender**
- **Pregnancy, childbirth, and related medical conditions**

- **Race or color**
- **Religion or creed**
- **Genetic testing information**

Utah

Utah Code Ann. §§ 26-45-103, 34A-5-102, 34A-5-106

Law applies to employers with: 15 or more employees

Private employers may not make employment decisions based on:

- **Age:** 40 or older
- **Ancestry or national origin**
- **Disability:** physical or mental
- **AIDS/HIV**
- **Gender**
- **Pregnancy, childbirth, and related medical conditions**
- **Race or color**
- **Religion or creed**
- **Genetic testing information**

Vermont

Vt. Stat. Ann. tit. 21, §§ 495, 495d; tit. 18, § 9333

Law applies to employers with: One or more employees

Private employers may not make employment decisions based on:

- **Age:** 18 or older
- **Ancestry or national origin**
- **Disability:** physical, mental, or emotional
- **AIDS/HIV**
- **Gender**
- **Race or color**
- **Religion or creed**
- **Sexual orientation**
- **Genetic testing information**
- **Additional protected category:** Place of birth

State Laws Prohibiting Discrimination in Employment (continued)

Virginia

Va. Code Ann. §§ 2.2-3900, 2.2-3901, 40.1-28.6, 40.1-28.7:1, 51.5-41

Law applies to employers with: One or more employees

Private employers may not make employment decisions based on:

- Age
- Ancestry or national origin
- **Disability:** physical or mental
- Gender
- Marital status
- Pregnancy, childbirth, and related medical conditions
- Race or color
- Religion or creed
- Genetic testing information

Washington

Wash. Rev. Code Ann. §§ 38.40.110, 49.60.040, 49.60.172, 49.60.180, 49.12.175, 49.44.090, 49.76.120, 49.60.030; Wash. Admin. Code § 162-30-020

Law applies to employers with: eight or more employees; one or more employees (gender-based wage discrimination)

Private employers may not make employment decisions based on:

- **Age:** 40 or older
- Ancestry or national origin
- **Disability:** physical, mental, or sensory
- AIDS/HIV
- Gender
- Marital status
- **Pregnancy, childbirth, and related medical conditions:** including breastfeeding
- Race or color
- Religion or creed
- Sexual orientation
- Genetic testing information

- **Additional protected categories:**
  - hepatitis C infection
  - member of state militia
  - use of service animal
  - gender identity
  - domestic violence victim

West Virginia

W.Va. Code §§ 5-11-3, 5-11-9, 16-3C-3, 21-5B-1, 21-5B-3

Law applies to employers with: 12 or more employees; one or more employees (gender-based wage discrimination)

Private employers may not make employment decisions based on:

- **Age:** 40 or older
- Ancestry or national origin
- **Disability:** physical, mental, or blindness
- AIDS/HIV
- Gender
- Race or color
- Religion or creed

Wisconsin

Wis. Stat. Ann. §§ 111.32 and following

Law applies to employers with: One or more employees

Private employers may not make employment decisions based on:

- **Age:** 40 or older
- Ancestry or national origin
- **Disability:** physical or mental
- AIDS/HIV
- Gender
- Marital status
- Pregnancy, childbirth, and related medical conditions
- Race or color
- Religion or creed

State Laws Prohibiting Discrimination in Employment (continued)

- **Sexual orientation:** includes having a history of or being identified with a preference
- **Genetic testing information**
- **Additional protected categories:**
  - arrest or conviction record
  - member of National Guard/state defense force/military reserve
  - declining to attend a meeting or to participate in any communication about religious matters or political matters

Wyoming

Wyo. Stat. §§ 27-9-102, 27-9-105, 19-11-104

Law applies to employers with: two or more employees

Private employers may not make employment decisions based on:
- **Age:** 40 or older
- **Ancestry or national origin**
- **Disability**
- **Gender**
- **Pregnancy, childbirth, and related medical conditions**
- **Race or color**
- **Religion or creed**
- **Additional protected category:** military service or status

Agencies That Enforce Laws Prohibiting Discrimination in Employment

Alabama
EEOC District Office
Birmingham, AL
205-212-2105
800-669-4000
http://eeoc.gov/field/birmingham/index.cfm

Alaska
Commission for Human Rights
Anchorage, AK
907-274-4692
800-478-4692
http://humanrights.alaska.gov/

Arizona
Civil Rights Division
Phoenix, AZ
602-542-5263
877-491-5742
www.azag.gov/civil_rights/index.html

Arkansas
Equal Employment Opportunity Commission
Little Rock, AR
501-324-5060
800-669-4000
www.eeoc.gov/field/littlerock/index.cfm

California
Department of Fair Employment and Housing
Sacramento District Office
Sacramento, CA
916-478-7200
800-884-1684
www.dfeh.ca.gov

Colorado
Civil Rights Division
Denver, CO
303-894-2997
800-262-4845
www.dora.state.co.us/Civil-Rights

Connecticut
Commission on Human Rights and
Opportunities
Hartford, CT
860-541-3400
800-477-5737
www.ct.gov/chro/site

Delaware
Office of Labor Law Enforcement
Division of Industrial Affairs
Wilmington, DE
302-761-8200
www.delawareworks.com/industrialaffairs/
welcome.shtml

District of Columbia
Office of Human Rights
Washington, DC
202-727-4559
http://ohr.dc.gov/ohr/site/default.asp

Florida
Commission on Human Relations
Tallahassee, FL
850-488-7082
800-342-8170
http://fchr.state.fl.us

Georgia
Atlanta District Office
U.S. Equal Employment Opportunity
Commission
Atlanta, GA
404-562-6800
800-669-4000
www.eeoc.gov/field/atlanta/

Agencies That Enforce Laws Prohibiting Discrimination in Employment (continued)

Hawaii

Hawai'i Civil Rights Commission
Honolulu, HI
808-586-8636 (Oahu only)
800-468-4644 ext. 68636 (other islands)
www.hawaii.gov/labor/hcrc

Idaho

Idaho Commission on Human Rights
Boise, ID
208-334-2873
888-269-7025
http://humanrights.idaho.gov/

Illinois

Department of Human Rights
Chicago, IL
312-814-6200
www.state.il.us/dhr

Indiana

Civil Rights Commission
Indianapolis, IN
317-232-2600
800-628-2909
www.in.gov/icrc

Iowa

Iowa Civil Rights Commission
Des Moines, IA
515-281-4121
800-457-4416
www.state.ia.us/government/crc

Kansas

Human Rights Commission
Topeka, KS
785-296-3206
www.khrc.net

Kentucky

Human Rights Commission
Louisville, KY
502-595-4024
800-292-5566
www.kchr.ky.gov

Louisiana

Commission on Human Rights
Baton Rouge, LA
225-342-6969
http://gov.louisiana.gov/HumanRights/
  humanrightshome.htm

Maine

Human Rights Commission
Augusta, ME
207-624-6290
www.maine.gov/mhrc

Maryland

Commission on Human Relations
Baltimore, MD
410-767-8600
800-637-6247 (in-state only)
www.mchr.state.md.us

Massachusetts

Commission Against Discrimination
Boston, MA
617-994-6000
www.mass.gov/mcad

Michigan

Department of Civil Rights
Detroit, MI
313-456-3700
www.michigan.gov/mdcr

Agencies That Enforce Laws Prohibiting Discrimination in Employment (continued)

Minnesota
Department of Human Rights
St. Paul, MN
651-296-5663
800-657-3704
www.humanrights.state.mn.us

Mississippi
Department of Employment Security
Jackson, MS
601-321-6000
www.mdes.ms.gov

Missouri
Commission on Human Rights
Jefferson City, MO
573-751-3325
877-781-4236
www.labor.mo.gov

Montana
Human Rights Bureau
Employment Relations Division
Department of Labor and Industry
Helena, MT
406-444-2884
800-542-0807
http://erd.dli.mt.gov/human-rights-bureau.
  html

Nebraska
Equal Opportunity Commission
Lincoln, NE
402-471-2024
800-642-6112
www.neoc.ne.gov

Nevada
Equal Rights Commission
Reno, NV
775-823-6690
www.detr.state.nv.us/nerc.htm

New Hampshire
Commission for Human Rights
Concord, NH
603-271-2767
www.nh.gov/hrc

New Jersey
Division on Civil Rights
Newark, NJ
609-292-4605
www.nj.gov/oag/dcr/index.html

New Mexico
Human Rights Division
Santa Fe, NM
505-827-6838
800-566-9471
www.dws.state.nm.us/dws-humanrights.html

New York
Division of Human Rights
Bronx, NY
718-741-8400
www.dhr.state.ny.us

North Carolina
Employment Discrimination Bureau
Department of Labor
Raleigh, NC
919-807-2796
800-NC-LABOR
www.nclabor.com/edb/edb.htm

Agencies That Enforce Laws Prohibiting Discrimination in Employment (continued)

North Dakota
Human Rights Division
Department of Labor
Bismarck, ND
701-328-2660
800-582-8032
www.nd.gov/labor/human-rights/index.html

Ohio
Civil Rights Commission
Columbus, OH
614-466-5928
888-278-7101
www.crc.ohio.gov

Oklahoma
Human Rights Commission
Oklahoma City, OK
405-521-2360
888-456-2558
www.ok.gov/ohrc/

Oregon
Civil Rights Division
Bureau of Labor and Industries
Portland, OR
971-673-0764
www.oregon.gov/BOLI/CRD

Pennsylvania
Human Relations Commission
Harrisburg, PA
717-787-4410
717-787-9784
www.phrc.state.pa.us

Rhode Island
Commission for Human Rights
Providence, RI
401-222-2661
www.richr.state.ri.us/frames.html

South Carolina
Human Affairs Commission
Columbia, SC
803-737-7800
800-521-0725
www.state.sc.us/schac

South Dakota
Division of Human Rights
Pierre, SD
605-773-4493
www.state.sd.us/dol/boards/hr

Tennessee
Human Rights Commission
Knoxville, TN
865-594-6500
800-251-3589
www.tennessee.gov/humanrights

Texas
Commission on Human Rights
Austin, TX
512-463-2642
www.twc.state.tx.us/customers/jsemp/
  jsempsubcrd.html

Agencies That Enforce Laws Prohibiting Discrimination in Employment (continued)

Utah

Antidiscrimination and Labor Division
Labor Commission
Salt Lake City, UT
801-530-6801
800-222-1238
www.laborcommission.utah.gov/
  AntidiscriminationandLabor/
  employmentdiscrimination.html

Vermont

Attorney General's Office
Civil Rights Division
Montpelier, VT
802-828-3171
www.atg.state.vt.us

Virginia

Council on Human Rights
Richmond, VA
804-225-2292
http://chr.vipnet.org

Washington

Human Rights Commission
Seattle, WA
206-464-6500
800-233-3247
www.hum.wa.gov

West Virginia

Human Rights Commission
Charleston, WV
304-558-2616
888-676-5546
www.wvf.state.wv.us/wvhrc

Wisconsin

Equal Rights Division
Madison, WI
608-266-6860
http://dwd.wisconsin.gov/er/

Wyoming

Department of Employment
Cheyenne, WY
307-777-7261
http://doe.wyo.gov/Pages/

State Laws That Control Final Paychecks

Note: The states of Alabama, Florida, Georgia, and Mississippi are not included in this chart because they do not have laws specifically controlling final paychecks. Contact your state department of labor for more information. (See the beginning of this appendix for contact list.)

State	Paycheck due when employee is fired	Paycheck due when employee quits	Unused vacation pay due	Special employment situations
Alaska *Alaska Stat. § 23.05.140(b)*	Within 3 working days.	Next regular payday at least 3 days after employee gives notice.	Only if required by company policy.	
Arizona *Ariz. Rev. Stat. §§ 23-350, 23-353*	Next payday or within 3 working days, whichever is sooner.	Next payday.	Yes, if company has policy or practice of making such payments.	
Arkansas *Ark. Code Ann. § 11-4-405*	Within 7 days from discharge date.	No provision.	No provision.	Railroad or railroad construction: day of discharge.
California *Cal. Lab. Code §§ 201 to 202, 227.3*	Immediately.	Immediately if employee has given 72 hours' notice; otherwise, within 72 hours.	Yes.	Motion picture business: next payday. Oil drilling industry: within 24 hours (excluding weekends and holidays) of termination. Seasonal agricultural workers: within 72 hours of termination.
Colorado *Colo. Rev. Stat. § 8-4-109*	Immediately. (Within 6 hours of start of next workday, if payroll unit is closed; 24 hours if unit is offsite.) Employer decides check delivery.	Next payday.	Yes.	
Connecticut *Conn. Gen. Stat. Ann. §§ 31-71c, 31-76k*	Next business day after discharge.	Next payday.	Only if policy or collective bargaining agreement requires payment on termination.	

State Laws That Control Final Paychecks (continued)

State	Paycheck due when employee is fired	Paycheck due when employee quits	Unused vacation pay due	Special employment situations
Delaware *Del. Code Ann. tit. 19, § 1103*	Next payday.	Next payday.	No provision.	
District of Columbia *D.C. Code Ann. § 32-1303*	Next business day.	Next payday or 7 days after quitting, whichever is sooner.	Yes, unless there is an agreement to the contrary.	
Hawaii *Haw. Rev. Stat. § 388-3*	Immediately or next business day, if timing or conditions prevent immediate payment.	Next payday or immediately, if employee gives one pay period's notice.	No.	
Idaho *Idaho Code §§ 45-606, 45-617*	Next payday or within 10 days (excluding weekends and holidays), whichever is sooner. If employee makes written request for earlier payment, within 48 hours of receipt of request (excluding weekends and holidays).	Next payday or within 10 days (excluding weekends and holidays), whichever is sooner. If employee makes written request for earlier payment, within 48 hours of receipt of request (excluding weekends and holidays).	No provision.	
Illinois *820 Ill. Comp. Stat. § 115/5*	At time of separation if possible, but no later than next payday.	At time of separation if possible, but no later than next payday.	Yes.	
Indiana *Ind. Code Ann. §§ 22-2-5-1, 22-2-9-1, 22-2-9-2*	Next payday.	Next payday. (If employee has not left address, (1) 10 business days after employee demands wages or (2) when employee provides address where check may be mailed.)	Yes.	Does not apply to railroad employees.
Iowa *Iowa Code §§ 91A.4, 91A.2(7)(b)*	Next payday.	Next payday.	Yes.	If employee is owed commission, employer has 30 days to pay.

State Laws That Control Final Paychecks (continued)

State	Paycheck due when employee is fired	Paycheck due when employee quits	Unused vacation pay due	Special employment situations
Kansas *Kan. Stat. Ann.* *§ 44-315*	Next payday.	Next payday.	Only if required by employer's policies or practice.	
Kentucky *Ky. Rev. Stat.* *Ann. §§ 337.010,* *337.055*	Next payday or 14 days, whichever is later.	Next payday or 14 days, whichever is later.	Yes.	
Louisiana *La. Rev. Stat. Ann.* *§ 23:631*	Next payday or within 15 days, whichever is earlier.	Next payday or within 15 days, whichever is earlier.	Yes.	
Maine *Me. Rev. Stat.* *Ann. tit. 26, § 626*	Next payday or within 2 weeks of requesting final pay, whichever is sooner.	Next payday or within 2 weeks of requesting final pay, whichever is sooner.	Yes.	
Maryland *Md. Code Ann.,* *[Lab. & Empl.]* *§ 3-505*	Next scheduled payday.	Next scheduled payday.	Yes, unless employer has contrary policy.	
Massachusetts *Mass. Gen. Laws* *ch. 149, § 148*	Day of discharge.	Next payday. If no scheduled payday, then following Saturday.	Yes.	
Michigan *Mich. Comp.* *Laws §§ 408.471* *to 408.475; Mich.* *Admin. Code R.* *408.9007*	Next payday.	Next payday.	Only if required by written policy or contract.	Hand-harvesters of crops: within one working day of termination.
Minnesota *Minn. Stat. Ann.* *§§ 181.13, 181.14,* *181.74*	Immediately.	Next payday. If payday is less than 5 days from last day of work, then following payday or 20 days from last day of work, whichever is earlier.	Only if required by written policy or contract.	Migrant agricultural workers who resign: within 5 days.
Missouri *Mo. Rev. Stat.* *§ 290.110*	Day of discharge.	No provision.	No.	

State Laws That Control Final Paychecks (continued)

State	Paycheck due when employee is fired	Paycheck due when employee quits	Unused vacation pay due	Special employment situations
Montana *Mont. Code Ann. § 39-3-205; Mont. Admin. Code § 24.16.7521*	Immediately if fired for cause or laid off (unless there is a written policy extending time to earlier of next payday or 15 days).	Next payday or within 15 days, whichever comes first.	Yes.	
Nebraska *Neb. Rev. Stat. §§ 48-1229 to 48-1230*	Next payday or within 2 weeks, whichever is earlier.	Next payday or within 2 weeks, whichever is earlier.	Only if required by agreement.	Commissions due on next payday following receipt.
Nevada *Nev. Rev. Stat. Ann. §§ 608.020, 608.030*	Immediately.	Next payday or 7 days, whichever is earlier.	No.	
New Hampshire *N.H. Rev. Stat. Ann. §§ 275:43(V), 275:44*	Within 72 hours. If laid off, next payday.	Next payday, or within 72 hours if employee gives one pay period's notice.	Yes.	
New Jersey *N.J. Stat. Ann. § 34:11-4.3*	Next payday.	Next payday.	Only if required by policy.	
New Mexico *N.M. Stat. Ann. §§ 50-4-4, 50-4-5*	Within 5 days.	Next payday.	No provision.	If paid by task or commission, 10 days after discharge.
New York *N.Y. Lab. Law §§ 191(3), 198-c(2)*	Next payday.	Next payday.	Yes, unless employer has a contrary policy.	
North Carolina *N.C. Gen. Stat. §§ 95-25.7, 95-25.12*	Next payday.	Next payday.	Yes, unless employer has a contrary policy.	If paid by commission or bonus, on next payday after amount calculated.
North Dakota *N.D. Cent. Code § 34-14-03; N.D. Admin. Code R. 46-02-07-02(12)*	Next payday, or 15 days, whichever is earlier.	Next payday.	Yes.	

State Laws That Control Final Paychecks (continued)

State	Paycheck due when employee is fired	Paycheck due when employee quits	Unused vacation pay due	Special employment situations
Ohio *Ohio Rev. Code Ann. § 4113.15*	First of month for wages earned in first half of prior month; 15th of month for wages earned in second half of prior month.	First of month for wages earned in first half of prior month; 15th of month for wages earned in second half of prior month.	Yes, if company has policy or practice of making such payments.	
Oklahoma *Okla. Stat. Ann. tit. 40, §§ 165.1(4), 165.3*	Next payday.	Next payday.	Yes.	
Oregon *Or. Rev. Stat. §§ 652.140, 652.145*	End of first business day after termination (must be within 5 days if employee submits time records to determine wages due).	Immediately, with 48 hours' notice (excluding weekends and holidays); without notice, within 5 business days or next payday, whichever comes first (must be within 5 days if employee submits time records to determine wages due).	Only if required by policy.	Seasonal farm workers: fired or quitting with 48 hours' notice, immediately; quitting without notice, within 48 hours or next payday, whichever comes first.
Pennsylvania *43 Pa. Cons. Stat. Ann. §§ 260.2a, 260.5*	Next payday.	Next payday.	Only if required by policy or contract.	
Rhode Island *R.I. Gen. Laws § 28-14-4*	Next payday.	Next payday.	Yes, if employee has worked for one full year and the company has verbally or in writing awarded vacation.	
South Carolina *S.C. Code Ann. §§ 41-10-10(2), 41-10-50*	Within 48 hours or next payday, but not more than 30 days.	No provision.	Only if required by policy or contract.	
South Dakota *S.D. Codified Laws Ann. §§ 60-11-10, 60-11-11, 60-11-14*	Next payday (or until employee returns employer's property).	Next payday (or until employee returns employer's property).	No.	

State Laws That Control Final Paychecks (continued)

State	Paycheck due when employee is fired	Paycheck due when employee quits	Unused vacation pay due	Special employment situations
Tennessee *Tenn. Code Ann. § 50-2-103*	Next payday or 21 days, whichever is later.	Next payday or 21 days, whichever is later.	Only if required by policy or contract.	Applies to employers with 5 or more employees.
Texas *Tex. Lab. Code Ann. §§ 61.001, 61.014*	Within 6 days.	Next payday.	Only if required by policy or contract.	
Utah *Utah Code Ann. §§ 34-28-5; Utah Admin. Code 610-3*	Within 24 hours.	Next payday.	Only if required by policy or contract.	
Vermont *Vt. Stat. Ann. tit. 21, § 342(c)*	Within 72 hours.	Next regular payday or next Friday, if there is no regular payday.	No provision.	
Virginia *Va. Code Ann. § 40.1-29(A.1)*	Next payday.	Next payday.	Only if agreed to in a written statement.	
Washington *Wash. Rev. Code Ann. § 49.48.010*	End of pay period.	End of pay period.	No provision.	
West Virginia *W.Va. Code §§ 21-5-1, 21-5-4*	Within 72 hours.	Immediately if employee has given one pay period's notice; otherwise, next payday.	Yes.	
Wisconsin *Wis. Stat. Ann. §§ 109.01(3), 109.03*	Next payday or 1 month, whichever is earlier. If termination is due to merger, relocation, or liquidation of business, within 24 hours.	Next payday.	Yes.	Does not apply to managers, executives, or sales agents working on commission basis.
Wyoming *Wyo. Stat. Ann. §§ 27-4-104, 27-4-507(c)*	5 working days.	5 working days.	Yes.	

Index

E

W

Y

⚖️ NOLO *Online Legal Forms*

Nolo offers a large library of legal solutions and forms, created by Nolo's in-house legal staff. These reliable documents can be prepared in minutes.

Create a Document

- **Incorporation.** Incorporate your business in any state.
- **LLC Formations.** Gain asset protection and pass-through tax status in any state.
- **Wills.** Nolo has helped people make over 2 million wills. Is it time to make or revise yours?
- **Living Trust (avoid probate).** Plan now to save your family the cost, delays, and hassle of probate.
- **Trademark.** Protect the name of your business or product.
- **Provisional Patent.** Preserve your rights under patent law and claim "patent pending" status.

Download a Legal Form

Nolo.com has hundreds of top quality legal forms available for download—bills of sale, promissory notes, nondisclosure agreements, LLC operating agreements, corporate minutes, commercial lease and sublease, motor vehicle bill of sale, consignment agreements and many, many more.

Review Your Documents

Many lawyers in Nolo's consumer-friendly lawyer directory will review Nolo documents for a very reasonable fee. Check their detailed profiles at **Nolo.com/lawyers**.